D0040800

THE

SHOW

THE INSIDE STORY OF

THE SPECTACULAR

LOS ANGELES LAKERS

IN THE WORDS OF

THOSE WHO LIVED IT

ROLAND LAZENBY

McGraw-Hill

New York   Chicago   San Francisco   ~~~~   London   ~~~~   Mexico City
Milan   ~~~~   San Juan   ~~~~   ~~~~   Toronto

The McGraw·Hill Companies

Library of Congress Cataloging-in-Publication Data

Lazenby, Roland.
    The show : the inside story of the spectacular Los Angeles Lakers in the words of those who lived it / Roland Lanzenby.—1st ed.
        p.   cm.
    Includes index.
    ISBN 0-07-143034-2 (alk. paper)
    1. Los Angeles Lakers (Basketball team)—History.   2. Los Angeles Lakers (Basketball team)—Biography.   I. Title.

GV885.52.L67L395   2006
796.323'64'0979494—dc22   2005018571

1 2 3 4 5 6 7 8 9 0   FGR/FGR   0 9 8 7 6 5

ISBN 0-07-143034-2

McGraw-Hill books are available at special quantity discounts to use as premiums and sales promotions, or for use in corporate training programs. For more information, please write to the Director of Special Sales, Professional Publishing, McGraw-Hill, Two Penn Plaza, New York, NY 10121-2298. Or contact your local bookstore.

This book is printed on acid-free paper.

Dedicated to the memory of Jean Lowry Bloomfield,
who enriched my life beyond imagination.

CONTENTS

FOREWORD

Tex Winter

The history of the Lakers organization features a lineup of the biggest names in the game. It begins with George Mikan and runs through Shaquille O'Neal. In between it showcases the likes of Elgin Baylor, Jerry West, Wilt Chamberlain, Kareem Abdul-Jabbar, Magic Johnson, Kobe Bryant, and a host of supporting talent.

Mikan, of course, was the game's first dominant center for the old Minneapolis Lakers. He was quite awkward, actually, but his advantage in the league's early years was a lane that was only six feet wide. He used to set up position in close and go to work on opponents that had no idea how to stop him.

I've mused a few times in recent years what Shaq would do with a six-foot lane. Each possession would be a point-blank situation. Game over. Literally. I'm not sure the NBA itself could have survived such an unstoppable force in those early years. As it was, the league barely survived Mikan.

The Lakers are the kind of club that invites such speculation because of this great assemblage of talent. They have been alive and kicking as a franchise for the better part of six decades, briefly first in Detroit, then in Minneapolis, and finally at home in Southern California. It's a period that coincides with my own tenure in the game, a coaching career that has covered most of six decades.

In that time, the game itself has undergone an amazing transformation. In the old days, it was usually entertaining, but as it changed basketball became entertainment. The Lakers, particularly the Los Angeles edition of the franchise, have always been at the vanguard of that movement.

Even before the Lakers moved westward, the NBA was a players' league, a star-driven operation. The individual player in the NBA has always held a value above team play. That's because the early NBA owners found they could survive if they sold fans on the idea of stars. Certainly the Minneapolis Lakers had their share in Mikan and Jim Pollard and Vern Mikkelsen.

From the early sixties, when West and Baylor led the transplanted Lakers in L.A., the connection with Hollywood and its supply of celebrities only served to amp up the equation. Then Jerry Buss bought the team in 1979 and brought with him his ideas about Showtime and fast-break basketball, powered by more stars than ever. To me, that remains the most remarkable facet of the entire Lakers phenomenon. Despite all the Hollywood influences, the egos, and the drama, the franchise has always managed to get and keep great stars. Buss's vision wouldn't have been possible without the unique abilities of Magic Johnson, this six-nine guard with such great vision and passing style.

Not only was he a star, Magic made others stars, too. Suddenly Hollywood embraced Lakers games as sort of a community lovefest. Everyone in town wanted to see the Magic parade, and with good reason. The Showtime Lakers were as fine a running team as has ever been put on a basketball floor. They were so good and won so much that they set the cornerstone for the franchise. The Lakers became about winning, about Showtime basketball, about the fast break, about entertainment, about the Show.

And in some ways, they were all about individual basketball. That wasn't their blatant approach. Instead, it was an offshoot of the demand for star power. It was a league-wide thing, but the Lakers epitomized it.

But with their approach always came the persistent and troubling question: Where will we find the next star?

So the great individual talent is always the focus, the issue. And that makes it more difficult for Lakers coaches to establish a team concept. That basic conflict feeds that drama that the community and the media crave. That was at least part of the factor in the struggles of Shaquille O'Neal and Kobe Bryant. Certainly their conflicts had to do with basic personality differences as much as anything. But there's no question that the atmosphere in Hollywood magnifies the star pressures and every other element, too.

The situation made my coaching tenure in Los Angeles one constantly evolving challenge. When Phil Jackson and I were coaching the Chicago Bulls in the 1990s, we were always aware of the talented young Lakers teams with Shaq and Kobe. Even then, they had that Hollywood star status, that higher profile. But it was based on their potential, not on anything they had accomplished. They were nothing like our Bulls, but they did have their moments.

Then Phil Jackson brought his aura to the team with his reputation for having won six championships in Chicago. I remember when we as a coaching staff arrived in Southern California, we were greeted by a sense of envy. With our six championships, we had something the Lakers wished they had. So the expectations were unbelievably high when we arrived in the fall of 1999.

Winning the championship that very first season was a storybook tale, complete with one of the most inspiring comebacks in the history of the sport in Game 7 of the Western Conference Finals against Portland. To be able to come through and realize those huge expectations in the 2000 playoffs was almost dreamlike. The team was never happier than in the wake of that first title. Then for us to forge our way to two more titles over the next two seasons went beyond even the craziest expectations. Unfortunately, the conflict that ultimately ravaged the team seems to have overshadowed our special accomplishments. Yet it's not hard to understand why I prefer to think of what our Lakers teams accomplished. It's my hope that in the long run, the big wins will outweigh the big drama, that fans will embrace the Shaq/Kobe era for what it achieved.

Part of that, of course, hinges on the next chapter of the Lakers story. Can the franchise reach again for the stars? What will the new plot twists bring? Those are the kinds of questions they love in Hollywood. While we're waiting for the plot to unfold, the pages of this book offer the chance to run back through the trials and tribulations of six decades of Lakers basketball. Quite often, a sense of the future can be found in the past. And I don't have to tell you, the Lakers are a team with a hell of a past.

ACKNOWLEDGMENTS

More than 500 interviews were recorded for this book over an 18-year period. Many subjects were interviewed over the past three years. Many other interviews were recorded during an assortment of history projects over the years. Several interview subjects have since died. It's hard to describe the immense privilege I feel at having been able to interview men such as George Mikan, Jim Pollard, Chick Hearn, Wilt Chamberlain, Jack Kent Cooke, Danny Biasone, and other giants on the pro basketball landscape. All of the interviews have been assembled here as a mosaic of perspectives on the history and evolution of the Lakers. I am deeply indebted to all who gave their time and consented to discuss their perspectives and answer my questions.

I owe a special debt to Jorge Ribeiro for his friendship and wisdom. I would like to thank Bob Schron, who conducted a dozen interviews for me. In addition, my editor and agent, Matthew Carnicelli, put in long hours in helping to prepare the manuscript for publication.

Once again I have pushed the patience of the publishing staff at McGraw-Hill, including Julia Anderson Bauer and Mark Weinstein, and once again I am most grateful for their efforts.

As always, my wife Karen and children Jenna, Henry, and Morgan provide the real joy in my life that makes my work possible. And I must not forget the new addition to the family, my grandson William Lowry "Buster" Jones.

INTRODUCTION

The Lakers Aura

Even as their team won championships, Lakers fans came to tire of the circumstances. There was the game's overwhelmingly dominant center and the game's resplendent, high-flying, ultra-talented wing player, both seemingly caught in a constant snit over who should have the ball. And the newspapers were having a field day reporting their clashes.

Shaq versus Kobe, right?

Hardly.

We're talking about George Mikan, the pro game's first great center, and Jim Pollard, the original jumping jack, playmaking guard/forward. A half century before Shaquille O'Neal and Kobe Bryant chased their curious chemistry as Lakers teammates, Mikan and Pollard spent their careers with the old Minneapolis Lakers alternating between fighting over the ball and winning championships. They won six of them, in fact, including five NBA titles and one in the old National League. And they debated their chemistry every step of the way.

The bad news for O'Neal and Bryant is that four decades after Mikan and Pollard won their last title, they were still jawing over the issue in interviews for history books. It seems that these hoops conflicts run forever, or until the last sports talk radio show signs off.

As Tex Winter, the longtime observer of the game, explained, "That's basketball."

That's also the Lakers, the ultimate team in the history of the game. As the cover of this book declares, this is their story, told in their own words. Not surprisingly, it's a bit complicated.

There's a team plane crash in a snowstorm, at least two near financial failures, more than a few bewildering real estate transactions, a high-profile rape case, a low-profile indecent exposure case, an unsolved murder, the firings of several winning coaches, and enough sexual hijinks to qualify as a soap opera, all of it occasioned in and around the team's 29 championship battles. As with any Hollywood epic, there's a star-driven cast. The manic Jerry West. The ebullient yet insatiable Magic Johnson. The brooding Kareem Abdul-Jabbar. The dandy Chick Hearn. The splendid Elgin Baylor. The arrogant Jack Kent Cooke. The cunning Jerry Buss. The preening Pat Riley. The lonely Wilt Chamberlain. The childlike Shaq. The ambitious Kobe. The manipulative Phil Jackson. The leering Jack Nicholson. They and a phalanx of splendid role players over the decades all populate the mythical panorama that is the Los Angeles Lakers.

Just which of these is the leading man?

That depends on whom you ask.

BILL WALTON, HALL OF FAMER, FORMER UCLA STAR: "It's all Chick Hearn. I started playing basketball when I was eight years old in 1960, and we didn't have a television. I bought a $9.95 transistor radio and listened to Chick Hearn on the radio. Chick Hearn taught me how to play basketball, how to think about basketball. He taught me how to *love* basketball. I lived for Chick Hearn on the radio every day. Jerry and Elgin and all the guys. Rudy LaRusso. The endless list of characters. But it was always Chick. The love affair with basketball in Los Angeles and the Lakers is all about Chick Hearn. He is the guy who convinced so many millions of people that this is the greatest thing in the world. Once we came and saw what he saw we could never leave. While Chick broadcast 3,300 games, or whatever the number is, I'm sure I listened to at least 2,500 of those games. I planned my life around Chick Hearn. I would sit there as a young boy and just be amazed. I would listen to this game, and I could see it all. I would laugh out loud at the things Chick would say. At the end, in his last year I was listening to a game. I still was laughing out loud."

Others say it's got to be the long-tortured Jerry West, who came to the team in 1960 as a rookie out of West Virginia, starred for 14 years through a blur of unfulfilling championship battles, then stayed on as coach, consultant, and general manager for years. It could well be West's story, except that he doesn't want it to be.

MARK HEISLER, LOS ANGELES TIMES COLUMNIST: "The Lakers mystique is Jerry West. He's the one constant. He's the one guy who's been there from the beginning."

Jerry West: "I don't remember anything about my career. I choose not to. I really don't live in the past. I really don't care about the past."

Perhaps the largest of many ironies in West's life is that he is "the logo." His graceful, slashing silhouette is the centerpiece of the NBA's red, white, and blue logo, which means that, as much as he'd like to forget it, he and everyone else associated with the NBA is reminded of his playing career at virtually every turn. Quite simply, the NBA logo is plastered everywhere. And he's revered accordingly.

Mark Heisler: "They had a young PR guy who was just there for a year or so. And West was introducing himself. He said, 'I'm the logo.' And he was kidding. The thing is about West, in one way, he's tremendously humble and doesn't think he's done anything. There also another side of West where he knows he's Jerry Fuckin' West."

Jack McCallum, *Sports Illustrated* senior writer: "I told him, 'Growing up, you were the guy I sort of modeled myself after, like every white kid in America who had half a jump shot.' West, just totally without ego, looks at me and says, 'Yeah, a lot of guys have told me that.'"

J. A. Adande, *Los Angeles Times* columnist: "Before I moved back to L.A., I was working at the *Washington Post* and the *Chicago Sun-Times*. And I'd call him for stories I was working on. I'd get off the phone, and I'd think, 'I was talking to Jerry West.' I was born in 1970, so I don't remember his career. But he was always *Jerry West*. And again, even though I hadn't seen him play, I was somewhat in awe of him. He has that presence, that name. He used to come by my boys club. His son belonged to my boys club in Santa Monica when I was a kid, so when he was playing some of his biddy basketball games, he'd be in the stands. We'd say, 'There's Jerry West! There's Jerry West!'"

For others, the leading man is clearly Earvin "Magic" Johnson, who wept the first time he donned a Lakers uniform in 1979. In many ways, the Lakers franchise would be defined once and for all by Johnson's prodigious emotional gift, a vast store of unbridled enthusiasm that washed over L.A. like a great tide during the '80s and drowned what was long thought to be the city's unconquerable cynicism. Johnson's tenure would soon come to be labeled the

Showtime era. It didn't come until the team was already 30 years old, yet it proved to be the watershed for the franchise. His emotional energy, his performances, would connect the past and the future of the club, fusing the image of the Lakers across the decades. In so doing, he also managed to change the game itself.

JIM HILL, LONGTIME L.A. SPORTSCASTER AND JOHNSON CONFIDANT: "You could tell it was coming. You could see from the no-look passes, and you could see from Magic's enthusiasm. You could see when the Lakers would score and the opposition would call a time-out and the people were going crazy and Magic's hugging Jamaal Wilkes or somebody else. I remember the first time Jamaal did something and he called time-out. People were going crazy. Magic starts hugging and yelling at Jamaal and patting him on the back and giving high fives every place. Jamaal looked at him like he was crazy. Up to that point, if you were a professional, you were cool, calm, and collected. And you didn't show your emotions on the floor. And here was this 19-year-old kid running and laughing, just like he was on the playground."

HERB WILLIAMS, 17-YEAR NBA VETERAN AND FORMER LAKERS OPPONENT: "Magic's thing was to get everybody else involved. And with him having the ball all the time, he would always be in rhythm. So his thing was always to pass the ball, lookin' for the open guy. And if he had to put a little flair behind it to get the crowd excited, he could do that also."

As the Showtime era progressed, it became clear that Los Angeles itself was donning a new image.

JIM HILL: "It was incredible. Going to watch the Lakers play became like going to watch a heavyweight fight 82 times a year. People dressed up. People were excited. People didn't know what was going to happen. Magic knew that when he went to the arena, he was going not only to win the game but to perform so that when people went to work the next day, they would say, 'Did you see what Earvin did last night?' He would always say that was what he wanted to do. He wanted make people talk about what he had done."

J. A. ADANDE: "He could walk into a restaurant and Warren Beatty or any other of the big Hollywood names would be in the restaurant, but all the eyes would turn to Magic. He had that magnetism that L.A. responds to. He also reveled in it. He loved being the center of attention. The reason he was so successful in L.A., L.A. is all about a show, and he provided the show."

JERRY WEST: "He played the game with a joy but still had this enormous sense of competitive drive with him, an absolutely incredible leader even at that early stage of his life. He was just one of these unique players that made people better. You could just see it. No one had to tell you about it. No one had to write about it. You didn't have to wonder about it. He was a damn thoroughbred. When he was born, somebody did sprinkle a little extra dust on him."

J. A. ADANDE: "Magic had a way of making everybody feel they were a part of it. When I was a kid, I used to go to the games, and I met Magic at his basketball camp. I went to his summer camp four years in a row, so he got to know me through that. I'd show up at the games, and he'd break out of the layup line and come over and say hi to me. I was in fourth, fifth, sixth grade. And I felt like the most important guy at the Forum. Magic came over to talk to me in the middle of the layup line and everybody saw it. Then I proceeded to go back up to my seat in the upper colonnade section, but all the way back up I knew that everyone had seen that happen. He recognized what he did. He knew that coming over, that was gonna make my day."

MIKE WISE, LONGTIME NBA WRITER: "All of a sudden Magic shows up, and Showtime happens. And it's real. You went into the Forum on a Friday night, and if you were a visiting team, you didn't come out of that building a winner. Everybody knew that's just how it was. It wasn't just about Magic. It wasn't just about Kareem. It was about Showtime. There was an aura around the team that was somewhat bigger than the franchise itself. It's why the stars came out, it's why the town started singing Randy Newman after every game: 'I Love L.A.' It's a corny song, but if you were in L.A. and you were visiting and that song was playing after the game, you were like, 'Yeah. This is a great town.' And then all of sudden you go through this time in Los Angeles when you got Rodney King and you got O.J. and you have this earthquake and the town is in this big funk [for] five, ten years. And you're like, 'Wow, L.A.'s lost it. It's gone.' And then all of a sudden Jerry West gets Shaq and Kobe. You hate to say that getting two guys to become part of a franchise can resurrect a city, but in a big way it was part of L.A.'s healing process. The Lakers then became part of something alive. You get a rental car at the airport, and the guy driving the Avis is like, 'Ah, the Lakers are playin' tonight.' It's a communal thing. L.A. is like this big car culture where you don't know your neighbors and everybody is driving around. But the Lakers made it a town. A small town. In that way, it's a really connected history."

Central to it all is the setting, Hollywood itself, and the team's succession of playing venues—the L.A. Sports Arena, the Great Western Forum, Staples Center—the stages on which the drama has played out season after season, each building taking on the atmosphere that is a Lakers game.

DARRYL DAWKINS, A.K.A. CHOCOLATE THUNDER, FORMER NBA PLAYER: "It's Showtime. When you come to a Lakers game, it's gonna be star-studded. You get a chance to play harder than you've ever played. It's all about a show. If you ain't got a show, then stay out. That's just the way it is."

KEVIN WILLIS, LONGTIME NBA PLAYER: "It was that Showtime thing. All the stars came out at night. And the opposing team wanted to be a part of that, wanted to be involved in trying to slow that fast break down and watching Magic do his thing out there. It presented a challenge every time you played the Lakers in the Forum. Guys just loved it. It was an unbelievable atmosphere. It was like being on a stage. The only difference was, the stars were sitting and watching the athletes. You just loved that two-plus hours out there, doing your thing in front of everybody. Showcasing in front of everybody."

JOHN SALLEY, HUMORIST AND FORMER LAKER: "When you walk in Staples, you're enamored by the stars. Jack is one of 'em, but to see Gary Shandling and Dustin Hoffman. You see all these people who take these front row seats. There are the people who you watch on TV or on film, or who you listen to musically. You're like in awe of them. And then the Lakers come out, and you find out that the real stars in Los Angeles are the Lakers. Because all the Hollywood stars are standing and clapping and literally setting their schedules around the Lakers. These are people making literally $20 and $30 million setting their schedules around what the Lakers do. The stars in this town are really the Lakers. Magic's got a star in Hollywood, and they had no choice but to give it to him because he's the most famous star in all of Los Angeles. Period."

It's duly noted that the fans of the Boston Celtics might want to raise a point of contention. The Lakers are the ultimate team? What about the Celtics' 16 NBA titles outclassing the 14 won by the Lakers?

That's certainly a consideration, but let's do some math. Over their long history, the Lakers have played in the league championship series a record 28 times. Over the Celtics' even longer history, they've reached the championship round 19 times, trailing the Lakers as a distant second.

Then there's the issue of winning percentages. The Lakers hold the NBA's all-time lead in winning a whopping 62.1 percent of their regular-season games.

And when it comes to the playoffs, the Lakers again hold a large lead, having won 60.4 percent of their postseason contests. In fact, they've won 71 percent of their playoff series, a league-leading 93 playoff series won.

The Celtics? Again a distant second with 66 playoff series won.

As for consistency, the Lakers have won at least one title or made an appearance in the league championship Finals in every decade of the NBA's existence. They won two titles in the '40s (including their National League title); three titles in the '50s while making four championship appearances; six championship appearances in the '60s; a title and three championship appearances in the '70s; five titles and eight championship appearances in the '80s; a championship appearance in 1991; and three titles and four championship appearances in the first five seasons of the 21st century.

Despite this edge in the numbers, the Lakers over the years have taken a back seat to the Celtics in the minds of many NBA fans. That's because it's about much more than mere numbers.

JERRY SICHTING, FORMER CELTIC: "The first year I came to Boston, the Celtics and Lakers played each other four times in the preseason. The second game was in the Forum. During that game, Maurice Lucas and Robert Parish got into it. Both benches emptied. I remember that when they began breaking it up, K. C. Jones was at the bottom of the pile and had Michael Cooper in a headlock. That's the first time I had ever seen an NBA coach in a fight with one of the players. But that was the Celtics and Lakers."

RICK TELANDER, *CHICAGO SUN-TIMES* COLUMNIST: "The Lakers/Celtics—that might have been the rivalry that built the NBA. Russell/Chamberlain, Bird/Magic. The Lakers are also defined by their foes. Certainly that Celtics rivalry was something that put them in everybody's consciousness."

KAREEM ABDUL-JABBAR: "I have a unique perspective on that. I've been going to NBA games since 1960 when I was in the eighth grade. I've seen a few things. The Lakers were always the noble opposition when I started going to see the games. And that was it. They couldn't beat the Celtics. I was a Celtics fan in those days. But the Lakers were always interesting to watch because of Jerry and Elgin. They went from being the loyal opposition to being a dominant team during the Showtime period. They're back being a dominant team now. Their history with George Mikan and Vern Mikkelsen and all those guys—that really gives them a cachet because before the Celtics started to dominate the Lakers were a dominant team."

DR. JACK RAMSAY, BROADCASTER AND FORMER NBA COACH: "I don't think anybody can match the Celtics in terms of mystique. They won eight championships in a row. They won 11 out of 13. But if you go back to the original Lakers in Minnesota, they won five and one in the old National League. That was a great team. That was a team like the Celtics. Then when the Lakers moved to Los Angeles, they were good, but they couldn't win for a long time because they were always playing the Celtics."

The Lakers' failures against the Celtics became the standard for basketball futility, and the spell wasn't broken until 1985, when Pat Riley coached Los Angeles past the Celtics for the league championship.

MARK HEISLER: "Pat Riley was the height of paranoia. When they were playing the Celtics in the '80s, one day he makes Gary Vitti dump the water because he's afraid that Red [Auerbach had] poisoned it. Riles gives the team a talk about what the Celtics really were—this ancient warlike race of subhumans. It was just incredibly demonizing. What it really is, it just goes to show how humiliated the Lakers felt by the Celtics over all those years. The Celtics were beating them every year, and the Lakers just felt terrible about it. It's hard to underestimate the damage done to the Lakers psyche by all those Celtics victories. The Celtics were incredibly good about rubbing it in. Everybody hated the Celtics. Every time you got into a series against the Celtics, nobody turned their noses up the way they did, with their mystique. They were so good and they won so much and they backed it up so much, it just really flipped people out."

MAGIC JOHNSON: "The good thing is, the Celtics did it their way, and we've done it our way. It's in a Hollywood style, showy, flashy, yet with a lot of substance. We wanted to run and put on a show. The Celtics and Larry did it their way to help shape and mold basketball. They did it their way, and it was different between the Lakers and the Celtics. That's why we're who we are and they're who they are."

MICHAEL COOPER, FORMER LAKER: "What we established in the '80s— what we took over from Jerry West and Wilt in '72—is that winning attitude. That's what L.A. is about. I'm pretty sure if you were to ask any Celtic, any former Celtic, that they would tell you it's about winning. You have to do that as a team. You can't come to a Lakers team thinking it's all about me. You can't think, 'I'm gonna score 30, and I'll be happy and get all the glitz.' No, it's about fitting into the system, understanding who the go-to people are, and doing whatever you have to do to help win the championship. That's what people have to understand coming here."

As much as they were frustrated by the Celtics, the Lakers also established a dominance over other Western Conference teams that has become something of a status quo in its own way. Houston, Portland, San Antonio, Utah, Seattle, and Sacramento have all struggled to compete with the Lakers' superior lineups.

STEVE "SNAPPER" JONES, PORTLAND BROADCASTER AND FORMER NBA PLAYER: "As a Western Conference rival, every team in the West hates the Lakers. The Portland setbacks at the hands of the Lakers are almost legendary. Only Los Angeles has won, so it's a lopsided rivalry. But it is a rivalry, nonetheless. Especially in the regular season. This is what gives teams some hope against a team as formidable as L.A. Because in the regular season, Portland at least has been able to win its games at home against the Lakers. Teams often can get a break versus L.A. in terms of scheduling. L.A. plays us a lot on the back end of back-to-back games—it's NBA scheduling. But in the playoffs, it's different. And that's where the heritage of the Lakers team enters into the equation. There's a mystique surrounding the Lakers. The Lakers honestly deep down feel they will win a series and also win a necessary big game. It takes several cracks at them. San Antonio proved it in 2003. Utah defeated them in 1998, convincingly. But there really hasn't been any slippage. The reason is the magic word—talent. In the '80s, the Lakers had Magic Johnson, Kareem Abdul-Jabbar, and James Worthy. In the '90s and 2000, their nucleus has been Shaquille O'Neal and Kobe Bryant. Both sets of superstars could take over games. They do it with offensive and defensive pressure. The Lakers have an arrogance. They force other teams to adjust to them. They don't think they can lose to you. It's, 'We're gonna beat you no matter what you do.' The Celtics used to have that. But the Lakers are a difficult, difficult foe. Nasty."

The story, it seems, belongs to all of them, the Lakers, their stars, and role players and coaches and even their opponents. It's a long, gnarly tale. Sad. Funny. Twisted. Triumphant. Bittersweet. And full of the unexpected. Always the unexpected.

The Times of Their Lives

The man waited quietly in the Detroit airport, a mix of defeat and relief on his face. Maury Winston, owner of the Detroit Gems, was making his exit from pro basketball. It was the summer of 1947, and he had had enough. Enough bad deals. Enough coaching problems. Enough losing.

Winston, the proprietor of a Detroit jewelry store, had founded the team just a year earlier, in 1946, when everything was booming in the aftermath of World War II. The old National Basketball League (NBL), in operation since 1937, had shrunk to just three clubs during the war. But with peacetime, a lot of people suddenly wanted to own a pro team. Which, in retrospect, seemed a little crazy. The sport had been around for 50 years and in that time nobody had figured out how to make any money from it.

The NBL had expanded to 11 teams in 1946. And another pro league, the Basketball Association of America (BAA), formed that same year with another dozen teams. Three painful seasons later they would merge to form the NBA, but in 1946 it was a basketball free-for-all.

And Maury Winston was the big loser. He had paid about $1,500 to join the league and another $5,000 for a performance bond. He had bought uniforms and about a dozen balls and shelled out another $40,000 or so for salaries. (The average pro contract ran about three grand back then.) To coach, he got Joel Mason from nearby Wayne State. At the time, Mason was known mostly for his football background. He had played end for the Green Bay Packers. At Wayne State, he was the backfield assistant, but he also coached a little basketball. So Winston signed him up. Wisely, Mason didn't give up his day job. He kept coaching and teaching phys ed while running the Gems.

PAUL PENTECOST, LONGTIME FRIEND OF GEMS COACH JOEL MASON: "He worked about 36 hours a day, trying to make that team work."

SID GOLDBERG, SPORTS PROMOTER OF THAT ERA: "They were a ragamuffin team. There wasn't much to them. The people running the Gems really didn't understand basketball. Not many people did in those days."

Mason and Winston had signed mostly local college players. The best known of the group was Wayne State's Howie McCarty, a guard with a one-handed shot. As an isolated early attempt to integrate pro basketball, the Gems also signed Willie King, a former Harlem Globetrotter who played 14 games for the club. But it hardly made an impression. The Gems were depressingly bad, the only consolation being that their pain was practically anonymous.

GEORGE MASKIN, NIGHT SPORTS EDITOR FOR THE OLD *DETROIT TIMES*: "I don't think we gave them any attention. We might have run a paragraph or two in the paper and that's about it. Nobody paid them much attention."

Games often drew fewer than one hundred paying fans. One night late in the season, only six people showed up, and Winston issued each a refund. Part of the problem was the venues. The Gems played some of their games at Holy Redeemer High School, but often it was wherever they could find an open court. Once or twice, they even managed an appearance at the Olympia, a Detroit arena, but only as a warm-up game for a better-known pro team.

PAUL PENTECOST (LAUGHING): "They should have been called the Nomads. They didn't know where they were gonna play from one night to the next."

Mason watched his team run out to a 3–13 record and decided he'd had enough. He turned the coaching duties over to guard Fred Campbell, and the Gems coasted from there, winning once in their last 28 games to finish 4–40. Pro basketball had never seen such a terrible team and wouldn't again for many seasons. Usually, when clubs were this bad, they died with barely a whisper. Sometimes teams didn't even have to be bad to disappear. Their names were colorful, but that wouldn't prevent them from littering pro basketball's graveyard: the Anderson Duffy Packers, the Toledo Jeeps, the Cleveland Chase Brass, the St. Louis Bombers, the Chicago Stags, the Indianapolis Olympians, the Youngstown Bears. The list of franchise cadavers could go on.

But the Detroit Gems were different. It was from their seed of misery that the Lakers' great championship tradition would grow. The miracle of survival would come in a phone call that summer of 1947, as Maury Winston was wondering what to do about his disaster. The caller was Sid Hartman, a young newspaper reporter who represented a few Minneapolis businessmen. They wanted to buy Winston's terrible team. Better yet, they'd pay $15,000 for it.

Sɪᴅ Hᴀʀᴛᴍᴀɴ, Mɪɴɴᴇᴀᴘᴏʟɪs sᴘᴏʀᴛsᴡʀɪᴛᴇʀ ᴀɴᴅ ʙᴇʜɪɴᴅ-ᴛʜᴇ-sᴄᴇɴᴇs Lᴀᴋᴇʀs ᴍᴀɴᴀɢᴇʀ: "We were looking for a franchise. A lot of them were available. For $15,000 you could buy about anything in those days."

The Minneapolis investors could have started a new franchise much more cheaply. Or, as Hartman suspected, they could have waited a week or two and gotten Winston's team for almost nothing. But they had plenty of money.

Sɪᴅ Hᴀʀᴛᴍᴀɴ: "I was representing the Minneapolis businesspeople who wanted to buy the Gems. They wanted a team and didn't want to wait. I'd done my research around the league. I found out the Chicago American Gears were headed for trouble. Maurice White [the owner of the Gears] was drinking. White planned to break away from the National League to form his own league. But the Gears had Mikan. We figured that if the Gears folded, then Mikan would be available. The franchise we were buying had the worst record, so I figured we'd get a first shot at Mikan. Even if we didn't get Mikan, the Gems' record meant we'd probably get the first pick in the 1947 draft."

That was incentive enough for the new owners from Minneapolis. They paid Winston $15,000 for the Gems. Not the players. Not the name. Not the equipment.

Sɪᴅ Hᴀʀᴛᴍᴀɴ: "Even the uniforms weren't worth a damn."

Only the franchise and its rotten record. From that Sid Hartman figured he could make a pretty good beginning.

Sid Hartman

When he began running the Lakers in 1947, Sid Hartman was all of 24 and still had a paper route on the side plus his job as a sportswriter for the *Min-*

neapolis Star Tribune. Strange as this combination seemed, Hartman was only a product of the times. First the Great Depression, then World War II had rocked his generation. Hartman had started in the news business at age nine during the depression with his first delivery route and was soon hanging around the newsroom at the old *Minneapolis Times.* There he found an escape from the bad family life that haunted many households in that era. His father drank heavily, which meant that the streets were a good place to be if the old man was in a bad mood. Besides, Hartman loved sports, and in the '30s the newspaper was where you found out all about them.

SID HARTMAN: "I got to know the sports editors. They kind of adopted me."

By the time he was in high school, he had added the chores of a part-time sportswriter to his news route, bringing his paycheck to a grand total of $23 every two weeks. But writing and delivering the news made for a grinding schedule that left little time for academic work. At 17, he dropped out of school, a few months shy of graduation. He would later earn a diploma with night courses at North High School in Minneapolis. But that didn't really matter, for Hartman was already on his way to becoming an established sportswriter.

His obsession in those days was University of Minnesota athletics. He attended virtually every practice of every sport, waiting, watching, listening for bits of information to fill his columns and stories. He developed a gossipy style, and people read his work because he didn't just talk about the games; he talked about the people. Soon he owned a little black book, which he filled with the phone numbers of coaches and sports editors all over the country. When visiting college teams played against the Golden Gophers, Hartman made a point of having a friendly chat with the coaches. Afterward he would send a short note thanking them for taking the time to talk with him. In time, he would own the phone numbers of many great coaches of that era, including Adolph Rupp, Ray Meyer, Hank Iba, John Wooden, and Pete Newell. He would later boast that he had more unpublished numbers than any other reporter in the country. The coaches, in turn, would invite Hartman to attend their clinics, many of them held at summer resorts in Minnesota.

Over the ensuing seasons, Hartman would expand these cordial relationships into a nationwide network.

SID HARTMAN: "At one time, I was sending out 1,600 Christmas cards a year. I knew a lot of coaches."

Among his many acquaintances, Hartman would become particularly good friends with Morris Chalfen, who promoted ice shows and other entertainment around Minneapolis. Chalfen, in turn, introduced Hartman to Ben Berger, a little Polish immigrant who loved to smoke cigars and roll them in his fingers like George Burns. Both Chalfen and Berger, who owned a chain of movie theaters in North Dakota and Minnesota, were quite wealthy. Before long, the young sportswriter had convinced these middle-aged millionaires that they shared his dream of bringing a professional sports team to Minneapolis. Berger wanted one because it would increase his standing in the community. Hartman simply longed to manage a pro club. It was an escape fantasy for him. If he brought a team to Minneapolis, then maybe he could give up the drudgery of his circulation job and instead spend his time wheeling and dealing for athletes. Football and baseball franchises seemed impossible to obtain in 1946. But Hartman saw that basketball was easily within reach. Besides, he loved the game.

Having built his fortune in North Dakota, Berger knew next to nothing about hoops. But the immigrant loved this country (he would later title his self-financed biography *Thank You, America*); he loved a sense of community. He owned a cluster of theaters in Minneapolis and served on a local prison advisory board. But he wanted to do something more for the city. Hartman convinced him that a hoops team would be a perfect gift. Berger wasn't so sure, but he agreed to test the idea. To see how pro basketball would go in the area, Berger and Chalfen promoted a game in Minneapolis at the end of the 1946 season between the Oshkosh All-Stars and the Sheboygan Redskins, two National teams. The event drew about 5,000, a smashing success in that era of cold gyms and lopsided balls. Seeing the crowd, Berger and Chalfen gave Hartman the nod. He had an open checkbook to begin assembling a team. After buying the Gems franchise, Hartman moved quickly to sign players. His coaching contacts paid off handsomely.

MARTY BLAKE, FORMER GENERAL MANAGER OF THE MILWAUKEE/ST. LOUIS/ATLANTA HAWKS AND LONGTIME NBA SCOUT: "Nobody scouted in those days. Nobody had the money to do that. Hartman knew basketball, and he had a lot of coaching contacts from his newspaper business. They told him who the good players were."

Jim Pollard: The Original Kangaroo Kid

Tops on the list was a Coast Guard veteran from California, Jim Pollard, the crown prince of Amateur Athletic Union (AAU) basketball. At six-foot-six (he would always list his official height at six-three), Pollard was a rare bird in 1940s basketball. He could run and jump and dunk and dribble and pass. He could even execute a reverse jam, though not with so much twist and style as modern dunkers. No one envisioned a midair slam dance in 1947. But he could play above the rim. Many of the players in this whites-only era were mechanical, one- and two-dimensional athletes. Not Pollard. He was a prototype for the future. Hartman would later compare him to Michael Jordan, but Pollard actually was more like Scottie Pippen. He was a terror from the wing.

The fans called him "the Kangaroo Kid." Later, Billy Cunningham would earn the nickname, but Pollard was the original.

HORACE "BONES" McKINNEY, FORMER NBA PLAYER AND LONGTIME COLLEGE COACH: "We used to know when Pollard had been in the building, because the tops of the backboards would be clean where he raked them. Pollard was fast, too. You couldn't press him either. He was too good moving with the ball. He'd get by you in a cat lick."

Because of that, Pollard often would serve as the Lakers' primary ball handler.

JOHN KUNDLA, EARLY LAKERS COACH: "If Jim had played in the modern NBA, he would have been a big point guard, like a Magic Johnson."

Pollard had played center during high school in Oakland, California, then graduated in December 1940 and spent the spring playing with Golden State Creamery, a local AAU team, where the veterans showed him the game. It was his lucky break.

JIM POLLARD: "Those old-timers took me and taught me how to play forward, how to shoot outside and play facing the basket. By the time I got to college, I was a pretty well made forward."

Indeed. That fall, he enrolled at Stanford and as a freshman helped lead the Cardinal to the 1942 NCAA championship. But it was wartime and Pollard left Stanford after one year to enter the Coast Guard, where he dominated the California military leagues. After the war, he settled back into AAU ball. On the East Coast, pro basketball was the big game. On the West Coast, there were only the AAU leagues, but they were every bit as good as the Eastern pros. Most teams were sponsored by top corporations that put the players on their company payrolls (20th Century Fox in Hollywood had a club).

JIM POLLARD: "They paid you under the table a little bit. They called it 'expenses.' Some of the guys made pretty good money."

In 1946, Pollard and the Oakland Bittners (sponsored by a grocery chain) tore up the field in the national AAU tournament in Denver, creating frenzied interest among the Eastern pro teams, all of whom wanted Pollard. Robert "Jake" Embry, owner of the Baltimore Bullets, flew to Denver to try to sign him. Les Harrison of the Rochester Royals made an offer, too. But Pollard declined both. He liked playing with the Bittners just fine, he said.

Hartman, though, called him up and turned on the charm. Hartman convinced Pollard that the Minneapolis team (the name Lakers wouldn't be chosen until right before the season) could be very good. Besides, the deal was pretty sweet: $12,000 a year, plus a $3,000 signing bonus, big money in those days. But Pollard struck a tougher bargain. He signed only after Hartman agreed to bring along three of his Bittner teammates.

SID HARTMAN: "The guy we wanted was Pollard, but he insisted we bring in his buddies."

In their second season of competition, the Basketball Association of America and the National League were in the throes of a bidding war over talent. As a truce, the two leagues agreed to meet in Chicago to discuss the situation. Hartman attended the meeting.

SID HARTMAN: "Maurice Podoloff [the BAA commissioner who would go on to become NBA commissioner] started off the proceedings by telling us how tough it would be for any team to sign Jim Pollard. That's when I raised my hand and stood up. 'Mr. Commissioner,' I said, 'I want to let you know that we've already signed him for Minnesota.'"

If other pro teams didn't take notice that these Minneapolis people were serious about winning, Hartman quickly gave them more to think about. Next he paid the Chicago Stags $25,000—very big money in those days—for the rights to two pro veterans, Tony Jaros and Don "Swede" Carlson. Carlson was a six-foot forward and Jaros was a journeyman guard, but they were Minnesota natives, good for building interest in the team.

Help Wanted

Finding a coach was Hartman's biggest chore. He first offered the job to Hamline University's Joe Hutton Sr., but Hutton decided he liked his security at the college rather than risking that a pro team would survive. So Hartman turned to John Kundla, the twenty-something coach at St. Thomas College, a small four-year Catholic school in St. Paul.

SID HARTMAN: "I made several trips over to Kundla's apartment in northeastern Minneapolis to talk him. Kundla played a lot of softball in those days, and I used to hang around the backstop, trying to talk to him between innings. He finally agreed, but he wanted a three-year contract."

VERN MIKKELSEN, LAKERS HALL OF FAMER: "Kundla was young and had nothing to lose, so he took the job."

In those days, however, even young coaches considered the pro game an invitation to ruin. Despite Hartman's quick success in building a team, he couldn't run the club alone because that conflicted with his newspaper job. To serve as general manager Berger hired Max Winter, a Minneapolis saloon owner with a background in sports promotions and marketing. Hartman then moved into the background, working the club's deals behind the scenes for a $75 weekly salary, which meant that he could give up delivering newspapers.

MARTY BLAKE: "Sid was what you call an ambassador without portfolio. Sid was a consultant. Consultants are people who never have to take the blame when things go wrong."

Hartman was so discreet in his workings that years later some of the team's followers would be astounded to learn of his involvement.

JOHN KUNDLA: "Sid kept his name out of everything. He had to. As soon as Max Winter came in, Sid went behind the scenes."

Yet Hartman continued to arrange promotional deals for the Lakers and was always in the team's offices, just as he had once shadowed athletics at the University of Minnesota. Only now, instead of a cub reporter hanging around practice, Hartman was one of the major players. To avoid a conflict of interest, Hartman seldom wrote about the Lakers. When he began putting together the deal to bring the club to Minneapolis, he had approached his editors and asked for permission to be involved. The editors were eager to have a pro team in Minneapolis so readily gave permission.

SID HARTMAN: "The newspaper knew what I was doing. All newspaper reporters had PR jobs on the side in those days. The idea of conflict of interest was much different then."

Yet Kundla wondered how much the editors knew of Hartman's involvement. It wasn't until decades later that Hartman revealed the full extent of his effort, Kundla said, which left some of the team's followers wondering if the newsman wasn't trying to take more credit than he deserved. Yet there is no question that Hartman was the deal maker who built the team.

JIM POLLARD: "Sid ran that club the first year, as much as Max Winter did. It was Sid Hartman who negotiated with me and signed the Bittners. When I got to Minneapolis, I'd never heard of Max Winter."

Even with Hartman's wheeling and dealing, the team needed a sharp business mind to manage its day-to-day affairs. Winter was perfect.

JIM POLLARD: "Max had an excellent promotional mind, and Sid Hartman made the basketball decisions. Max was a good combination with Sid because Sid was very, very impetuous. If you played a bad game, Sid would say, 'We ought to get rid of him; make a trade.' Max was the one who always said, 'Now you gotta sit down and think about this.' Max was a good leveler for Sid."

Winter was older, wiser, and a natural promoter. Shortly after his hiring, he announced a newspaper contest to name the team. Minneapolis was the land of cool clear lakes. Thus, the Lakers. Once that was settled, Winter turned to other chores. He made the Lakers the first team in pro basketball to have its own cheerleaders, the Lakerettes, a group of modestly dressed high school girls from the suburbs. And each year, Winter called in a producer from New York to make a promotional film on the team, which provided steady grist for the newsreels of the era as the Minneapolis Lakers won championship after championship.

At first, even winning wasn't enough to bring out fans in Minneapolis. Most games were played in the Minneapolis Auditorium, which seated about 9,000. In the early years, though, the Lakers drew as few as 2,500 people, leaving Winter looking for ways to make the atmosphere more cordial. He employed an orchestra to play before the games and went so far as to have crews available to jump-start fans' cars in the parking lot on cold Minnesota nights. As the Lakers kept winning, these efforts paid off. Minneapolis became a model of success for pro basketball.

SID HARTMAN: "There were two or three years in a row when we took in more money than Madison Square Garden."

JOHN KUNDLA: "Sid and Max showed they could get things done in a hurry. They could be controversial, too. But they saw the possibility of everything."

And that was essential. To make it in pro basketball in the '40s, you needed vision. It wasn't a sport for people who couldn't smell trouble or see opportunity.

JIM POLLARD: "Our first training camp [in 1947] was held at a community center in northwest Minneapolis. They called it the Nuthouse. I don't remember why they called it that. It was just the Nuthouse."

Regardless of how or why it was named, the building was certainly emblematic of the state of pro basketball in the '40s. You had to be a bit loony to play. The '40s still sported fancy uniforms [the rave was satin], yet the day-to-day life of the players was a bit ragged. Training methods were minimal.

GEORGE SENESKY, PRO PLAYER FROM THE '40s: "When we played at home, we had a guy who was sort of a trainer, but on the road each guy took a roll of tape with him. You knew how to tape your own ankles. The uniforms were another problem. You couldn't wash them; they had to be dry-cleaned. On the jerseys, you could see the salt marks on them after a while. You had to hang it up in your room after the games so it would dry out. There was no equipment manager. You were responsible. But nobody complained about it. We were so glad to have the opportunity, so glad to be there."

Which makes you wonder why. Out of an average $3,000 salary, a player would take home about $2,000. But as Les Harrison, owner/coach of the Rochester Royals, used to say, "This is still better than carrying a lunch bucket every day."

GEORGE SENESKY: "A lot of us always thought it was going to get better the next year. The best ticket was $2.50, and 50 cents of that was tax. The owners weren't making money either."

The shaky finances contributed to pro basketball's goofy image. In short, the whole game was a "nuthouse." You had to love it to play it. And then, as George Senesky pointed out, you often wondered why you did.

Early Times

Renamed the Lakers, basketball's worst franchise immediately set out to change that status in 1947, the only problem being that the key people weren't exactly sure what they were doing. The coach had gotten most of his experience running high school teams, the front office was steered by a 24-year-old sportswriter, and the core of the roster was a group of AAU players.

JIM POLLARD: "We didn't know what it was all about. I'd only seen about two pro games. And Kundla didn't know any more about the league than I did."

Still, hope was high. The owners chartered a DC-3 to fly the Lakers to their first game against the Oshkosh All-Stars and legendary six-foot-four center Leroy "Cowboy" Edwards, an aging star who could hook with either hand.

JIM POLLARD: "I'll always remember him. That's when I knew I wasn't a center. Edwards started out guarding me. He was muscular and slow. So the first time down the floor I gave him a good fake and drove around him for an easy basket. I said, 'Geez, this is easy. This guy is supposed to be good.' The second time down the floor, I faked and went around him and he just put his arm out. Boy, he clotheslined me good and put me about three rows up in the bleachers. 'Hey skinny,' he said, 'that's no way to do in this league.'"

Cowboy made his point, but the Lakers won that first game and arrived home to find their wives, the owners, Hartman, and Winter at the airport waiting to celebrate.

JIM POLLARD: "We loaded up in cars and went down to the Rainbow Cafe for a big meal. I don't remember Sid and Max ever being more excited than that first game. It really was a thrill because we didn't know what to expect."

After three games, they acquired Herm Schaeffer, a six-foot-one guard, from the Indianapolis Kautskys. A wise, experienced ball handler, Schaeffer could run the floor show.

One game later, the last piece of the dynasty, the biggest piece, fell into place as Sid Hartman had hoped it would. Maurice White, owner of the Chicago American Gears, had broken away from the NBL to form his own league, the Professional Basketball League of America, with George Mikan as the drawing card. It was an ambitious plan with 24 franchises across the country, including such new hoops territories as Houston, New Orleans, and Atlanta. But White was drinking heavily and insisted on controlling the payroll for all of the teams out of his Chicago office. Part of his plan was to begin the season earlier, in September.

That plan only hastened his demise. The PBLA folded two weeks into the season, and White lost $600,000. As Hartman had hoped, the six-foot-ten Mikan was suddenly free to negotiate his own deal with another team, and the Lakers had first crack at him. Several other BAA clubs were hot on the big center's trail.

SID HARTMAN: "All these teams wanted him, but George agreed to come to Minneapolis first to talk business. Max and I spent a long day negotiating with Mikan, but his lawyer, Stacy Osgood, advised him to pass on our offer. We kept trying to get him to sign with us. But Osgood said they had to catch the last plane of the day to Chicago. I was getting ready to drive them to the airport, but Max called me aside. He said if they leave town, we'll never sign Mikan. He told me to take a long route to the airport so that George would miss his flight. I drove around and made sure he missed the plane."

Mikan had to stay overnight, and the next day he agreed to a one-year, $15,000 contract. Hartman could hardly contain his glee. Within a matter of months he had assembled the makings of a dynasty, a team that would win six championships over the next seven seasons.

SID HARTMAN: "That was the most fun I ever had in my life."

Big George

The lenses in George Mikan's glasses were a quarter-inch thick. He once said trying to see without them was like driving a car without wipers during a rainstorm. His eyesight had been reason enough to get him cut from the basketball team at Catholic High in Joliet, Illinois. But Mikan was so tall (he had grown six inches while convalescing from a broken leg as an adolescent), people kept telling him he should play the game. Plus, a scholarship could pay for his education. He had wanted to go to Notre Dame, but that was a costly proposition in 1942.

Instead, he enrolled in classes at DePaul, with the idea that he would catch the train down to Notre Dame over Christmas break and try out for the team. The war was on, and just about every college coach was looking for athletes. Mikan was too tall and too blind to go into the service, so he figured that Notre Dame coach George Keogan might be interested. "He's too awkward, and he wears glasses," Keogan supposedly said after watching Big George work out.

GEORGE MIKAN: "Keogan told me to return to DePaul, that I'd make a better scholar than a basketball player."

He took that advice, and went back to DePaul and resumed classes. But that spring he caught the eye of Ray Meyer, the school's new basketball coach. "There's my future," Meyer said to himself.

Mikan underwent a miraculous development at DePaul. The clumsy, unpolished prospect seemingly blossomed overnight into the premier player in college basketball, the big-time gate attraction during World War II. Remarkably, he developed agility while growing from six-foot-eight to six-ten. By the 1944–45 season, Mikan's junior year, he and Oklahoma A&M's Bob Kurland had become prototypes for what future generations would come to know as a "force." When Mikan entered college in 1942, most coaches had little regard for tall players. Basketball was still the domain of the little man. Considered too awkward for the game, the big guys were called goons. Both Mikan and Kurland soon proved that they weren't goons.

BOB KURLAND: "George and I opened the door to the idea that the big man could play the game, which in our day was, by Eastern standards, played by guys five-ten, five-eleven, who were quick, took the set shot, and so forth. We opened the door for what the game is today."

Mikan and DePaul won the 1945 National Invitational Tournament, in those days the college game's prized trophy. In one NIT game, Mikan scored 53 points, an incredible total for the slow pace of 1940s basketball, and he twice won the NCAA scoring crown. All of this from a guy who hadn't been able to make the Notre Dame varsity three years earlier.

RAY MEYER, MIKAN'S COLLEGE COACH: "He was an awkward kid at first, but he just kept improving. I guided him, but he had talent, and he just kept getting better and better. The superstars are like that. They have something inside."

Mikan had something outside, too: wide shoulders and a pair of bruising elbows. But he wasn't just a brute. Meyer, then a young, ambitious coach, sensed that he could develop Mikan. He hired a coed to give the center dancing lessons to improve his agility, and he set up drills with Mikan guarding a five-foot-five teammate one-on-one to teach Mikan to move his feet defensively. Jumping rope and shadowboxing were also part of the regimen, as was alternately playing catch with a tennis ball and a medicine ball. Then Meyer made him work on his shooting and faking. First 250 right-handed hooks each day, then 250 left-handed. That grueling repetition would become a staple of basketball how-to manuals as "the Mikan drill." Soon Meyer's awkward protégé had developed a simple but punishing style around the basket, based on a solid drop step.

JIM POLLARD: "George didn't have a lot of moves. He never fooled you very often. Some of those old centers gave great fakes. Not George."

Mikan would get into position down low, drop his inside foot back, and pivot toward the hoop. As he did, he'd lead his motion with his inside elbow.

JIM POLLARD: "He didn't get called for the offensive foul because he had both hands on the ball. He'd take it up in the air with both hands. If he took a hand off the ball and threw the elbow, he was going to get called for the foul. But George seldom did that. He was smart."

The foul lane was only six feet wide in those days, which allowed him to set up and score.

MIKE BLOOM, DEFENSIVE SPECIALIST IN THE '40s: "If you let Mikan get position, it was over. He would back in to the basket and go to work with those elbows."

HORACE "BONES" McKINNEY, MIKAN OPPONENT: "When he got you in that pivot, you couldn't do anything about it."

PAUL SEYMOUR, WHO PLAYED FOR THE SYRACUSE NATIONALS: "Mikan was great with those elbows. He used to kill our centers. Used to knock 'em down, draw the foul, then help 'em up and pat 'em on the fanny."

The Chicago American Gears signed Mikan to an unprecedented five-year, $62,000 contract in the spring of 1946, after he had completed his college eligibility, and he went right to work for them, even playing in the *Chicago Herald American* tournament that spring, where he was named the MVP. But that fall Mikan claimed that the cash-thin Gears were cutting his paychecks short and held out for 19 of the 44 regular-season games. He and the team worked out their differences still in time for him to lead the Gears to the NBL championship in the spring of 1947.

His size and dominance made Mikan an overnight sensation, and that gave Gears owner Maurice White ideas. Why not start his own league just to showcase the big guy?

Needless to say, if White didn't have enough cash to run one club, he certainly didn't have enough to float a 24-team league. The Lakers, of course, were waiting with a net to catch Big George in the NBL dispersal draft. Mikan joined the Lakers for their fifth game of the 1947–48 season, at Sheboygan.

JIM POLLARD: "I had never seen George. He walked into that locker room at Sheboygan, and I thought that was the biggest-looking dumb character that I'd ever seen for a guy that was barely 23 years old. He had these great big, thick glasses, and he had this homburg hat on. I said to myself, 'What the hell's a guy 23 years old doing wearing a homburg and a great big storm over-coat?' He walked in and said, 'Hi, fellas. I'm your new center.' When we got out on the floor, we threw him the ball and said, 'Show us what you can do.' I played with that big horse for every game for seven years, and that's the only time I ever heard him say, 'Please don't throw me the ball. They're killing me.' The rest of us just threw him the ball and stood there. They ganged up on him and kicked the hell out of George that first night."

The Lakers lost their first five games with Mikan, making it immediately obvi-ous that before they could rush off to harvest championships, they had to learn to play together. It wasn't easy, because Mikan's and Pollard's individual styles were so different. Pollard was a slashing driver, but Mikan clogged the middle, leaving his teammate little room to drive.

PAUL SEYMOUR: "Pollard could really leap. He got hurt playing with Mikan."

CHARLIE ECKMAN, FORMER NBA REFEREE AND COACH: "The Kangaroo Kid could get up in the air."

JIM POLLARD: "George was great if he stayed on his side of the lane. But a lot of times, as soon as I got the ball on the wing, he would come over to my side of the lane. I would tell him, 'Stay over there a minute.' But that wasn't his style of play. When we first started playing together, I couldn't very well go to the middle because he was there. When I started to drive, he'd go to the basket. So he'd bring his man, six-eight, six-ten, down to the basket where they'd kick the hell out of me. At that time, George didn't know what I could do. He'd go to the basket, and I'd flip the ball to him and he'd miss it. I kept telling him, 'You better get your hands up because 9 out of 10 passes are going to hit you right in the face.' After a while, he learned to give me that one count, to give me that step and give me room to drive, and then he could come in. If his man switched off on me, I'd flip him the ball. It made it easier for George, too. But we had to learn that. It took us a while."

From that awkward chemistry, Mikan and Pollard built a deadly pick-and-roll routine, which Kundla called the J&G (Jim and George) play. Needless to say, it was the coach's favorite because most opponents couldn't stop it.

JOHN KUNDLA: "It was a simple little play. But it was very successful."

The Lakers ran it again and again that season on their way to a league-best 43–17 record. In the playoffs, they moved aside Oshkosh, Tri-Cities, and Rochester to claim their first championship.

JIM POLLARD: "After we won, we had to hustle to catch a train out of Rochester. On the way out, we picked up a couple of six-packs. We put 'em in the stainless steel sink in the men's room on the train. Then we sat there and celebrated our first championship with the train rattling all around and the wheels rolling underneath."

In those days, the Lakers did just about all their traveling by train except when management chartered an occasional DC-3. With Minneapolis so far west of the other franchises, the scheduling was brutal. They rode all night to Chicago, then got off the train and grabbed a cab across the city to yet another station, where they caught the 8:00 A.M. train to Minneapolis. The league champions arrived home the next afternoon at 2:30, almost too tired to celebrate with the small group of family and friends waiting at the station.

Still, it was hard not to be elated. In one season, the franchise had changed names, management, rosters, and status, having gone from worst to best.

Battling the Globetrotters

Just before the 1948 playoffs, the Lakers entered the last of the *Chicago Herald American*'s "world" tournaments and played their way to the finals, where they beat the aging Rens, the all-black barnstorming team from New York. The Lakers were all white, but their most widely publicized contests were against all-black teams, particularly their five-year, seven-game series with the Harlem Globetrotters. In 1948, the Globetrotters were the most popular pro team in the country.

GEORGE PUSCAS, BASKETBALL PUBLICIST OF THE ERA: "Most people back then weren't aware of pro basketball beyond the Harlem Globetrotters. That game between the Lakers and the Globetrotters gave the pros some identity. It helped the NBA tremendously as it was emerging."

The games were played in the Chicago Stadium (Chicago was the 'Trotters' hometown) and in Minneapolis.

SID HARTMAN: "We had people waiting in line here at three o'clock in the morning to get tickets. You couldn't get in Chicago Stadium. There were mobs. Everybody thought the Globetrotters were a super team."

The fan interest wasn't particular to basketball. American society remained deeply segregated after World War II, but white spectators were curious and eager to see black athletes in action. In fact, black baseball teams in Philadelphia and Washington, D.C., regularly drew larger crowds than the white clubs.

The Globetrotters had gotten their start in Chicago in the '20s with a portly 23-year-old promoter, Abe Saperstein, from Chicago's north side. He began booking the team as the Savoy Big Five. (They played their home games in Chicago's Savoy Ballroom.) By the '30s, the name would evolve to the Harlem Globetrotters. Saperstein settled on that because Harlem identified the players as black and Globetrotters suggested world travel.

In later years, they would become known for their humor and slick ball-handling routines, often performed to the accompaniment of "Sweet Georgia Brown." But in the early days, the Globetrotters played their basketball straight. They did, however, thrill fans with a warm-up circle that over the years evolved into the world's classiest ballhandling routine. The entertainment and humor were said to be a means of deflecting the ugly racial moods the team sometimes encountered on the road. Plus, if the local teams had fun and the crowd laughed, people didn't mind losing, and the Globetrotters were often invited back.

In the '40s, Saperstein signed two major stars. Reece "Goose" Tatum, a baseball player from Arkansas, had huge hands, long arms, and a wonderful wit. And when Oklahoma's Langston University team beat the 'Trotters one night, Saperstein promptly lured away their star player, Marcus Haynes. Building on Tatum's creativity, the Globetrotters left the straight game to offer fans their hugely entertaining brand of hoops, filled with gimmicks, gags, and top-notch ballhandling.

SID HARTMAN: "They had some great players on that team. Marcus Tatum, Sonny Boswell, Sweetwater Clifton, and Babe Pressley. And they dropped their comedy against us. They wanted to win."

BILL GLEASON, VETERAN CHICAGO SPORTSWRITER: "When the Lakers and Globetrotters played, those were some tremendously competitive basketball games. You had the two great big men of that era, Mikan and Sweetwater Clifton, playing against one another. They're both from the Chicago area. Clifton could do anything on the basketball court. When he would get bored with being underneath, he'd go in the corners and shoot set shots."

The 'Trotters beat Minneapolis in 1948 and again in '49, which left the Lakers grumbling that Abe Saperstein had used his own refs. The victory, though, boosted morale in the black communities across the country. To many African-Americans, the Globetrotters' win was another knock against segregation. The Lakers, though, thought little, if at all, about the social implications. They were eager for revenge.

JIM POLLARD: "We didn't like playing the Globetrotter games in the first place, because we didn't get paid for them. We got paid the same, whether we played them or not. Plus we didn't like the idea of playing a comedy team."

JOHN KUNDLA: "The first two games, Saperstein hired the refs. After that, we said, 'You get one ref, and we'll get a referee.'"

The second game in 1949, played before a crowd of 10,122 at the Minneapolis Auditorium, resulted in a 68–53 Lakers win. In 1950, the teams met twice, with the Lakers winning both, by 16 and 15 points. The first game was played at Chicago Stadium before 21,666 fans, an astounding turnout for that era.

JIM POLLARD: "The third year we played 'em we kicked the hell out of 'em in Minneapolis. It was no contest. They only had 8 or 9 guys on their squad in Minneapolis. Then we played 'em a few days later in Chicago. They must have had 15 or 16 players. Every time we threw the ball to Mikan, they grabbed him. In the first half alone, he hit 10 or 12 free throws."

The Chicago game also marked the Lakers' first televised broadcast. Rollie Johnson, manager of WCCO in Minneapolis, did the play-by-play. Late in the second half with the Lakers leading by 10, he walked over to the bench and asked Kundla to call a time-out so that the station could get in a final advertisement. Moments later, as Pollard pulled down a rebound and raced up-court, apparently headed for an easy basket, Kundla called time-out.

JOHN KUNDLA: "Jim came over to the bench with this look on his face and asked me what was the matter. I told him Rollie needed a timeout. He got so mad at me he wouldn't go back in the game."

The Lakers still coasted to the win and again swept games in 1951 and '52, which brought an end to the series (except for one final Lakers win in 1958).

SID HARTMAN: "Saperstein didn't want to lose, and we kept on beating them. So he finally cut out the series."

The final blow was an 84–60 Lakers win at Chicago Stadium in January 1952.

JOHN KUNDLA: "We beat 'em so bad in Chicago, he wouldn't play us again. After the game, Abe took a walk, he was so upset. They couldn't find him for hours."

Birth of the NBA

Just before the 1948–49 season, Minneapolis and three of the NBL's best teams—Fort Wayne, Rochester, and Indianapolis—crossed over and joined the new league, the BAA, a move that would lead to the formation of the NBA. But it also brought howls of protest from the remaining National owners, who claimed the Lakers and other teams had sold out to the competing league.

DANNY BIASONE, OWNER OF THE SYRACUSE NATIONALS: "We thought they had sold out. The National League gets no modern recognition. The

NBA has all the money today, so they make it all about them. But we were much better than the BAA. After the leagues merged, it was National teams that won the first seven championships."

The BAA, though, had the big money and the big markets. Begun in 1946 by a group of hockey teams and arena owners, the BAA had franchises based in Boston, New York, Washington, Chicago, Baltimore, Philadelphia, and St. Louis. The BAA's best arenas—Boston Garden, Madison Square Garden, and Chicago Stadium—were the sports palaces of that era. The National League, on the other hand, was a decade older and had many of the name players. But its teams were located in smaller markets—Fort Wayne, Syracuse, Rochester, Dayton, and Oshkosh—with small, often dingy buildings. That situation changed overnight with the move of the four NBL teams, which took up residence in the BAA's Western Division with Chicago and St. Louis. The result was a nicely balanced 12-team league.

JIM POLLARD: "We were excited that we were finally getting to play in the big cities and the big arenas, particularly New York and Madison Square Garden."

The new league had a big-time feel to it, and the Lakers quickly showed they belonged. The Royals won the Western Division regular-season crown with a 45–15 record, while Mikan and the Lakers finished just one game back at 44–16. The best Eastern Division team, the Washington Capitols (coached by 29-year-old Red Auerbach), finished 38–22.

Minneapolis closed the schedule with Mikan, the league's leading scorer, ringing up 48 and 51 points against New York, 53 against Baltimore, and 46 against Rochester, incredible totals in that era of 40-minute games.

JIM POLLARD: "When it came to winning, Big George could be very tough and just a little mean. Toward the end of a ball game, if we were ahead by 20, George would come over to the bench and say, 'Let's beat 'em good. Let's kick the hell out of 'em so they don't want to play us ever again.'"

Powered by Mikan, the Lakers steamed into the 1949 playoffs and overwhelmed whoever happened into their path. They swept both Chicago and Rochester 2–0 on their way to dumping Red Auerbach's Capitols, 4–2, for the championship. Mikan had scored 303 points in 10 playoff games.

JIM POLLARD: "George gloried in that 'I am number one' feeling. That's why he was so successful. He wanted that spot, wanted to be number one, wanted you to be a little bit fearful of him on the court."

VERN MIKKELSEN, LAKERS HALL OF FAME FORWARD: "From time to time, there'd be problems between Pollard and Mikan. They were both great athletes, but George did most of our scoring and got most of the recognition. There were little problems, and they could have been trouble, but Kundla handled that situation just beautifully. Our offense was built around George, and it would have been stupid not to use him."

One night the marquee outside Madison Square Garden read: "Tonite: Geo. Mikan vs. the Knicks." More than anything, that incident summed up his stature in those early years of the game. He was the league's draw, just as he had been for college basketball.

GEORGE MIKAN: "Accolades were something that I had no control over."

The real rub, of course, was Pollard. He was a masterful player, a former leading scorer in the AAU leagues, and he admitted that the attention given to Mikan bothered him.

JIM POLLARD: "The thing about Mikan, everything revolved around him, and he got too much publicity and he tried to do too much himself because of it. But he was a hell of a competitor. We'd get through a game and his question was, 'Did we win?' That was the idea of the whole game. That made us all on George's side, because he was a winner. George and I always argued, but when we stepped on the floor, we always played to win, the hell with who got the points."

The biggest irritation was Mikan's refusal to pass the ball when he was double-teamed.

JIM POLLARD: "It wasn't that he was selfish. It was more a matter of pride."

During one season, Mikan suddenly began passing out of the double-teams, and the Lakers went on an eight-game winning streak, with everybody scoring in double figures.

JIM POLLARD: "Then we went to New York, and George always wanted to put the big show on in New York. George had 38 or 39 points that night, and no one else was in double figures. We lost, and afterward we went drinking with friends. Mikan was at one end of the bar drinking. I told the guy I was drinking with to go up there and ask Mikan how we could have an eight-game winning streak with everybody happy and then come here and lose. My friend went over and asked him that, and then George roared, 'I'm gonna kill that goddamn Pollard!' 'You'll never catch me, George!' I yelled back at him. That was our way of picking on George. He was the bellwether of our club, and we all picked on him."

John Kundla

The conflict between Mikan and Pollard always seemed to hang just under the surface, much as the conflict between Shaquille O'Neal and Kobe Bryant would haunt the Lakers decades later. Like their modern counterparts, the Minneapolis Lakers found ways to cope, mostly through the efforts of their coach.

JIM POLLARD: "It was something that could have torn the team apart. But Kundla kept a very even keel and didn't pick on anybody. He seldom made a big deal out of offensive mistakes. But, boy, would he get upset about defense."

Kundla was forced to wait more than 40 years after his Lakers teams won their last championships to be recognized by the Hall of Fame.

GEORGE MIKAN: "Kundla gets no recognition. He did a great job of molding the team, taking care of the players' idiosyncrasies."

CHARLIE ECKMAN: "It is tough to handle a bunch of prima donnas, and they were prima donnas. Pollard was temperamental, and Mikan was temperamental."

PAUL SEYMOUR: "Some of those coaches back then were not nice people. Red Auerbach was hated around the league. He always had the talent and was always shooting his mouth off. If you walked up to him in the old days, he'd tell you to get lost. John Kundla was a gentleman all the way. He did his job, and he did it well. Everybody thought it was easy because he had a talented team. It's not easy to have those guys and win and keep your senses."

Keeping the Lakers' abundant talent controlled and focused took its toll on Kundla, a shy, quiet man who by every January was gulping milk to combat the ulcers left over from his duty on a navy landing craft in the Pacific during the war. It wasn't that he couldn't get angry. He just didn't very often.

VERN MIKKELSEN: "He had a very, very slow fuse, but when it finally erupted, look out."

Kundla was successful both because of and despite his youth. His age allowed him to joke with his players, to engage in the silly fun experienced by adults who are paid to play games. Four decades later, the Lakers still couldn't agree on who rubbed the Limburger cheese in whose hat. Mikkelsen swore that reserves Tony Jaros and Bud Grant (a Lakers reserve for a couple of seasons before going on to coach the NFL's Minnesota Vikings) ruined several of Kundla's hats. Kundla, though, was sure that he was the one who pulled the cheese trick on somebody else. Kundla also recalled the time his players stuffed pornography in his luggage, which his wife found later.

Then there was the infamous train ride early one very cold morning to a game against the Fort Wayne Pistons. Because of the extreme cold, the Lakers' train experienced several delays, and it soon became apparent they weren't going to make the game on time. At Milwaukee, a messenger boarded the train with a telegram from Pistons owner Fred Zollner, telling the Lakers that he would send the Pistons' team plane for them.

VERN MIKKELSEN: "The Pistons were the envy of the league because they flew to all the games."

The Lakers got off the train, but no one realized that Kundla had gone to the dining car to drink milk for his ulcer. As the train pulled out of the station, the players standing on the platform saw the coach looking plaintively out a window two cars back. As planned, the team caught the plane and made the game at North Side High School in Fort Wayne, where the Pistons played their home games. The Lakers, in fact, had a lead at intermission and had returned to the floor just before the start of the second half when they heard a murmur from the crowd. Kundla had walked in the gym door.

VERN MIKKELSEN: "He walked in pretty sheepishly. At the time we were winning, but we wound up losing the game. We gave John plenty of trouble for that."

The Lakers were the kind of team that could laugh about losses because there weren't that many. When tight situations arose, they always seemed to have an answer.

VERN MIKKELSEN: "George Mikan had a tremendous, total confidence that he could get the job done. He would make believers out of us. Late in close games he always wanted the ball. The tremendous competitor that he was, he would say, 'Let me have the ball. I'll get it done.' More often than not, he did."

2

The Minneapolis Lakers

There was no shot clock in pro basketball in the late '40s, which meant games were interminably slow, especially if the Minneapolis Lakers were involved. George Mikan or Jim Pollard would control a defensive rebound; then the league champions would begin their methodical assault on the opponent's goal. At the offensive end, the Lakers would hold the ball and wait for Mikan to lumber up-court and take position near the basket. Only then would they go to work. Even at this pace, Mikan's spectacles would often fog up and play would be stopped while he toweled off and wiped his lenses dry. After he had dominated the league for a couple of years, opponents grew impatient with these pauses to refresh. They complained that if Big George wanted to wipe his glasses, the Lakers should call a time-out. That was only fair, the league decided.

So John Kundla shifted his time-out strategies to make sure his center had a clean windshield. Kundla also kept a spare set of Mikan's specs in his coat pocket. No one would accuse the young Lakers coach of not knowing who punched his meal ticket. The entire offense was built around Mikan, and in two years of competition no one had been able to stop him when the game really mattered.

As big winners, the Lakers played relatively well with crowds in Minnesota. The Twin Cities of Minneapolis and St. Paul sat astride the Mississippi River. The region had established itself as a hotbed for sports, especially University of Minnesota football in the fall. In winter, the area supported a pair of minor league hockey teams. In the spring, it was AAA baseball. The Lakers connected locally by using a dozen University of Minnesota players on their early rosters. One of them was Bud Grant, who had played end for the football Gophers. The earliest acquisitions by the team had included a couple of pro players who had starred in high school in Minneapolis: Tony Jaros and Don "Swede" Carlson. Carlson had played for the Chicago Stags of the

BAA before coming back to Minnesota. As strong as the Lakers seemed after winning two straight championships, they were a machine with a definite need for replacement parts by the spring of 1949.

Knowing that the team needed to upgrade, Max Winter and Sid Hartman found three good picks in the 1949 draft. The top prizes were thought to be six-foot-seven forward Vern Mikkelsen, a power player out of Minnesota's little Hamline College, and Bob "Tiger" Harrison, a guard from the University of Michigan.

Almost as an afterthought, the Lakers drafted five-foot-nine guard Slater "Dugie" Martin out of the University of Texas. Martin had been an All-American in the high-speed offense run by Texas, but his value was held suspect by Kundla, who had little say in the team's personnel moves. Kundla gave Martin scant playing time, and when he did play, the little guard seemed overwhelmed. Muscular Frankie Brian of the Anderson Duffy Packers scored 40 points against him in an early game, a severe blow, because Martin's long suit was supposed to be his defense. On offense, he was caught in a tug-of-war between the coach and the star. Kundla inserted him into a game at St. Louis with the idea that he would pass the ball to Mikan, then cut to the hoop. But the center angrily told the rookie guard not to cut because he was clogging the middle. Martin was intimidated by Mikan and kept quiet when Kundla called him to the bench for not following instructions.

SLATER MARTIN, LAKERS HALL OF FAMER: "Kundla didn't use me much until our next trip to St. Louis when Herm Schaeffer was hurt. Schaeffer, a nice fellow, came up to me in the locker room before the game. 'Don't be afraid to take your shots,' he said. 'You're letting the big guy cramp your style.' I had one of those lucky nights where everything I threw up went in. I hit eight straight shots from the floor. They came just in time to save my job."

Before long, the veteran Herm Schaeffer had stepped aside and was teaching the rookie how to run the team. Martin soon showed that his quickness gave the Lakers another weapon. And his coach came to love the little guard's style. Both Martin and Kundla had served in the navy in the Pacific during the war. Both thought like coaches, and their mutual understanding grew from there. Martin, the high-scoring college player, became a low-scoring, ball-distributing pro guard, running the Lakers' lumbering offense. Later, after helping the Lakers to four championships, Martin would move on to the

St. Louis Hawks and direct them to yet another title, accomplishments that landed him in the Hall of Fame.

JOHN KUNDLA: "He wanted to win. Slater didn't care who made the points."

With Martin in the lineup, Kundla kept the offense moving at a pace that matched Mikan's abilities, but this retooled group could also get up and move, with Martin running the break and Pollard on the wing.

PAUL SEYMOUR OF THE SYRACUSE NATIONALS: "If the fast break was there, they'd go on you. But most of the time they waited for Mikan to come down the floor and then set things up."

JIM POLLARD: "We didn't fast-break that much because Mikan and Mikkelsen were not that quick, and you didn't want either one of them to dribble. But Martin always wanted to go. He was always looking for the fast break."

The rookie adjustment for Mikkelsen, the son of a Lutheran minister, was just as difficult as Martin's, and just as important to the team's development. At six-foot-seven, 235 pounds, he had played center in high school and college, but he was forced to shift to forward in the pros, which meant that he played facing the basket for the first time in his career. The new position suited his skills. He could leap and knew how to get rebounding position. In adjusting, he developed a bit of an outside shot, although he made his living on the offensive glass.

VERN MIKKELSEN: "I didn't see the ball much. I didn't have to. Mikan and Pollard did most of the scoring. When they had an off night, I cleaned up on the boards."

DOLPH SCHAYES, HALL OF FAME FORWARD FOR THE SYRACUSE NATIONALS: "That made them much more effective. We always had a difficult time with them. If you double-teamed George, then Mikkelsen would clean up. And Pollard was able to drive, and he was a great passer."

JOHNNY "RED" KERR, FORMER NBA PLAYER AND COACH: "Pollard was the slick forward, one of the first jump shooters, and Mikkelsen was the workhorse. He was the guy that took the tough defensive player, rebounded well, was a hard body under the basket. He reminded me of what Rodman was to the Bulls, not the same style of play, but what Rodman was to Michael Jordan and Scottie Pippen. The guy who did the work. Not physically similar to Rodman at all, but the guy who did the work, the offensive rebounding."

Before the 1950 season was over, the new rookies would help make the Lakers into a blueprint for modern teams. Building around the 245-pound Mikan, the dominant center, and Pollard, the quick, acrobatic small forward, the Lakers transformed Mikkelsen into the original power forward. And Slater Martin filled the role of ball handler, or what would come to be known as a point guard. Six-foot-four rookie "Tiger" Harrison, meanwhile, found a place in the lineup as the off guard.

JIM POLLARD: "We were the first team to have those types of players filling the roles, and we became the model for all the modern teams that came after us."

MARTY BLAKE, FORMER HAWKS GENERAL MANAGER AND LONGTIME SCOUT: "The Lakers were a great team. Mikan and Mikkelsen and Pollard and Martin— they could have played today. Mikkelsen would be making $2 million a year, for God sakes. These people today don't realize how good they were."

The Lakers were also the first fully athletic team capable of dunking at will, but the ethic of that era didn't allow for such overtly macho statements.

VERN MIKKELSEN: "All of us could dunk except Slater Martin. But we weren't allowed to much, because Kundla wouldn't let us. It was frowned on as hotdogging."

JIM POLLARD: "One time I got a steal and was taking the ball in for a running dunk. But the ball slipped a bit and hit the back of the rim. It went way up in the air and sailed out to half-court. During the next time-out, Kundla went nuts, giving me the business for dunking."

JOHN KUNDLA: "They could all dunk. But usually they just shot the ball. In practice they did a lot of dunking. But otherwise we kept away from that. You didn't want to embarrass another team or player. Wilt Chamberlain was the one who really started the dunking in the late '50s."

Another issue for the Lakers was their "home court." They played some games at an armory in Minneapolis, others at the Minneapolis Auditorium, and still more across the Mississippi River at Hamline College in St. Paul. They also extended their "home" to neutral courts in four different states. Even with the nomadic nature of their home schedule, the Lakers also got a boost during the playoffs. Usually scheduling conflicts meant that they couldn't use the Minneapolis Auditorium during the playoffs, so they switched their games to St. Paul, where the court was narrower by a few feet.

AL CERVI, SYRACUSE NATIONALS COACH: "They used to say that when Mikan, Mikkelsen, and Pollard stretched their arms across that narrow court, nobody could get through."

PAUL SEYMOUR (LAUGHING): "Those three big bastards made every court look narrow. Mikkelsen was a brute."

SID HARTMAN: "Our front line played volleyball with an awful lot of teams."

Minneapolis would need all advantages for the 1950 season, as the six surviving teams of the NBL—Syracuse, the Anderson Duffy Packers, Tri-Cities Blackhawks, Denver Nuggets, Sheboygan Redskins, and Waterloo Hawks—merged with the BAA to form the newly named National Basketball Association, a 17-team league aligned in three cumbersome divisions. The old Western Division became the Central, where Minneapolis and the Rochester Royals battled to a tie with 51–17 records. Both had 33–1 home records, and the division title came down to a single tiebreaker game. With Mikan scoring 35, the Lakers won at Rochester, 78–76, to claim the division. The Royals had led by six with about three minutes left, but Minneapolis closed the gap, then won on a late set shot from Tony Jaros.

From there, the Lakers swept both Fort Wayne and Anderson 2–0 to meet Syracuse for the championship. The Nationals featured veteran guard Paul Seymour, future Hall of Famer Dolph Schayes, and Al Cervi. This group had mixed it up with the Lakers during the regular season.

PAUL SEYMOUR: "I remember going to the basket against the Lakers that season. I ran into one of Big George's elbows. I had a goose egg on my head, I was on my ass on the floor, and the ref was pointing at me. I chased George right up into the stands. I don't know what I would have done if I had caught him."

The Nationals held the home-court advantage, and the series opened at State Fair Coliseum, just outside Syracuse, where the Nats had a 34–1 record. Mikan scored 37 points to drive the Lakers, but the Nats held a late 66–64 lead. Then Lakers reserve Bud Grant hit a hook shot to tie it. With a shot to win it, Syracuse's Cervi tried to attack the basket and Mikan.

PAUL SEYMOUR: "Cervi decided to win it himself. He went inside and threw up an underhanded shot. Mikan just tapped it away."

AL CERVI: "I was fouled and didn't get the call."

Minnesota quickly rushed the other way, and Tiger Harrison hit a 40-footer at the buzzer to give Minneapolis the first game.

JOHN KUNDLA: "He went wild. He jumped up and down. Tiger had played his high school ball with Seymour, so there was a little more to the competition."

GEORGE MIKAN: "We were giddy after Tiger hit that shot. And somebody made a major mistake in the locker room. They told some reporters that I was allergic to all the smoke in the arena. It made the Syracuse papers the next morning. That next night all the fans came out smoking cigars."

JOHN KUNDLA: "You could hardly see across the floor. It was filled with smoke."

Years later, Mikan jokingly alleged that it was Kundla who had slipped up and told reporters about his allergy.

JIM POLLARD: "It was George who told them about the allergy. I distinctly recall him making the comment."

Either way, the smoke screen allowed the Nats to grab the second game despite 32 points from Mikan. In retrospect, however, it was only good for a laugh. The Lakers snuffed Syracuse in six games. Game 6 brought a round of fistfights and the ejection of Nats player/coach Al Cervi. Mikan finished with 40, while Pollard had 16 points and 10 assists.

PAUL SEYMOUR: "We made 'em mad. Then Mikan showed us how to play after that."

If you counted Mikan's two NBL titles, with Chicago and Minneapolis, he had been the center of four straight championship teams, and the competition realized that even making him take a time-out to wipe his glasses wasn't going to slow the juggernaut.

Rivalry with the Rochester Royals

The Lakers ran off the league's best regular-season record in 1951. And, as he had the two previous seasons, Mikan won the scoring crown. But as the schedule came to a close, their luck turned bad. Mikan suffered a hairline fracture of his ankle. Even that didn't sideline him. Doctors placed his foot in a cast and used ethyl chloride to numb his pain.

JOHN KUNDLA: "He played, but he was at half-speed."

Half-speed of slow must have meant that the Lakers were almost motionless. They still moved into the Western Conference Finals again to meet their old rivals, the Rochester Royals.

JOHN KUNDLA: "It seemed we were always neck and neck with Rochester, with every game going down to the wire."

Between 1949 and 1954, the Lakers won 267 games. The Royals won 266. Twice they finished ahead of Minneapolis in the regular-season standings. But in the head-to-head meetings, the Lakers usually won. (Over the four years, the Lakers won 38 and lost 28 against the Royals.) This old rivalry would strangely find a new life in the 21st century. The Rochester Royals would move to Cincinnati, then to Kansas City and Omaha, before settling in as the

Sacramento Kings. Like their counterparts decades earlier, the Kings would battle furiously against the Lakers only to lose the big ones.

SID HARTMAN: "To me, our games with Rochester, that was the greatest basketball ever played. There was some science to it, some finesse to it."

The Royals presented a slick look, with fancy ballhandling, smooth passing, and a lot of quickness. Hall of Famer Bob Davies ran the offense. A former MVP of the NBL, he had once played 90 games for Rochester while coaching his former college team, Seton Hall, to a 24–3 record. (Imagine a modern college coach pulling that off.) Teamed with Davies in the Royals' backcourt was one of his former Seton Hall players, All-American Bobby Wanzer. Red Holzman, who later coached the Knicks, was the backup.

The players for both teams enjoyed a high regard for one another. But the front offices of the two clubs seemed to be engaged in a running blood feud. Rochester owner/coach Les Harrison had hired the first trainer in the league and had helped to break the NBL color line in 1946 when he added Dolly King to the club's roster. When reporters questioned the move, he told them, "If he can play, he can play." Such distinctions aside, Harrison was viewed as a villain in Minneapolis.

SID HARTMAN: "You had to watch Les Harrison. One time he tried to convince Herm Schaeffer [Lakers guard] that we weren't paying him enough. We were always trying to pay him back for that one."

JIM POLLARD: "One time in a regular-season game at Rochester, we managed to tie the score with a late shot that just beat the buzzer. Then we won in overtime. When it was over, we sat in our locker room exhausted. We could hear Les Harrison. Those locker room walls were pretty thin. He was screaming at Chickie Shapiro, their scorekeeper, for not sounding the horn soon enough."

Another time, the Royals were playing in Fort Wayne when Davies hit a long shot. As Davies fired it up, referee Pat Kennedy blew his whistle but somehow inhaled and sucked the ball of the whistle into his windpipe. He passed out and collapsed. Harrison then supposedly ran onto the floor and screamed at Kennedy, "Pat, Pat, quick before you die, did the bucket count?"

Harrison hated that he couldn't beat the Lakers for a championship. In 1947, he had gone so far as to pay $25,000 to acquire six-foot-nine Arnie

Risen from Indianapolis in an effort to battle Mikan. When that didn't do the trick, he added bulky forward Arnie Johnson to the mix.

JIM POLLARD: "Mikan and Risen had great battles at center. Risen couldn't stop George, but George had a heck of a time stopping Risen, too. And Arnie Johnson was a big bull, and he had great battles with Mikkelsen. Our game was all underneath the boards and battle like heck. Their game was all outside set shooting with Wanzer and Davies and Red Holzman."

LES HARRISON, ROCHESTER OWNER/COACH: "Each year we'd be battling it out for the championship. We had a lot of talented basketball players, but they had George Mikan. That was a little bit of difference."

By 1951, the Royals roster had aged, but Harrison figured they could make one more run at the Lakers for a title. That was more than enough to propel them into the playoffs with momentum. With Mikan injured, the Royals finally had their chance in the playoffs. The Lakers quickly won the first game at home. But then Harrison moved Red Holzman into the starting lineup, and the Royals took command. With Mikan slowed, the Lakers collapsed, losing the next three games. From there, Harrison's team went on to beat the Knicks for the title. This left Mikan burning. He couldn't stand the idea that Rochester had taken one of his championships.

The New Game

Mikan returned from his ankle injury in the fall of 1951 and encountered a new game. A year earlier, in November 1950, the Pistons had run a stall against the Lakers. Only 36 shots were taken the whole game, and Fort Wayne won, 19–18, on a last-second bucket by Larry Foust. But the fans had booed loudly throughout; the NBA couldn't afford to lose what little entertainment value it had mustered. Something had to be done to counteract Mikan's nearly unstoppable offense. The league rules committee decided to widen the lane from 6 feet to 12.

As a result, Big George's scoring average fell from 28.4 to 23.8 points per game, and he finished second in scoring behind Philadelphia's young jump shot specialist, Paul Arizin.

GEORGE MIKAN: "The rule change opened up the lane and made it more difficult for them to defense me. Opposing teams couldn't deter our cutters going through the lane. It moved me out and gave me more shot selection instead of just short pivots and hooks. I was able to dribble across the lane and use a lot more freedom setting the shot up."

Beyond that, it meant a few more shots for Pollard and Mikkelsen, both of whom averaged more than 15 points for the first time in their pro careers. Heading into his third season, Mikkelsen was starting to find himself.

VERN MIKKELSEN: "Widening the lane opened the middle and allowed these marvelous one-on-one deals. It helped all of us."

With the lane widened, the Lakers wouldn't be able to depend on Mikan as much. Sid Hartman knew the team needed better outside shooting, and he knew where to find it. Sitting on Rochester's bench was six-foot-two Pep Saul, a two-handed set-shooting artist.

SID HARTMAN: "We had been rotating Pollard outside, but we needed better shooting. We knew that Les Harrison would never agree to trade Saul or sell him to us. He wouldn't give us anything. We had a bitter, bitter rivalry. So I called Clair Bee, who was coaching the Baltimore Bullets. They were struggling. I told him that we would give him $5,000 for Saul. 'Do you think I can get him from Harrison?' he asked me. I told him, 'You can get him for about $1,500 and keep the change.' He did just what I said. He got Pep from Les, and just a few days after getting him, Clair Bee sold his rights to us. Les Harrison was furious when he realized what had happened. He went to the league and protested, but he couldn't do anything. It was a legitimate deal. Saul's outside shooting was just enough to open up our inside game. He helped us win three straight championships."

In those days of meager money, the Lakers always seemed motivated by the players' share of playoff bonus money, a pittance by today's standards. But the $1,500 or so proved a huge bonus at the time.

RED KERR: "The Lakers had Dugie Martin. They had Myer 'Whitey' Skoog. They were good guards. Those two guys would want a raise, and they'd go in, and management would say, 'We can get two ushers to play with these guys. Your money will come during the playoffs, from the bonus.' And that was how it was viewed. Pollard, Mikkelsen, and Mikan. People used to say that you could get two ushers to play with them, and you could still make the playoffs."

JIM POLLARD: "Each year when training camp opened, Slater Martin would stand up and address the team in that Texas drawl of his. He'd ask if we all had signed our contracts. Then he'd explain that the only way we could make more money would be to win the championship, and the only way to win the championship was to feed the ball to number 99, Big George."

Once again, Rochester nosed Minneapolis aside in the regular season, this time by a single game. But the playoffs were different. Gassed by the addition of Pep Saul's perimeter game, the Lakers pushed aside the Royals three games to one. Suddenly, Minneapolis was slated to meet Ned Irish's New York Knicks for the championship.

In a surprise, the young Knicks forced the Lakers to a seventh game. Each year, the Lakers had to stage their playoff games in nearby St. Paul instead of the Minneapolis Auditorium because of a scheduling conflict. But for Game 7, on April 25, the auditorium was open, which spelled doom for the Knicks, who hadn't won in 11 tries there spanning four seasons. The Lakers won in a swirl, 82–65, giving quiet John Kundla his fourth championship.

Foul Trouble

The Knicks and Lakers met again for the championship in 1953. Minneapolis won the Western Division regular season title with a 48–22 record. New York claimed the Eastern Division with a 47–23 finish, one game worse than the Lakers.

The '52–53 season was a rough, foul-infested year for pro basketball, where strategy had moved toward fouling as coaches attempted to play the percentages. Through the maze of flailing arms and the steady shrill of whistles, New York somehow finished off Boston in the Eastern Division, and the Lakers escaped Fort Wayne in the Western.

Mikan's scoring average was down to 20.6 per game, second in the league behind Philadelphia center Neil Johnston. But Slater Martin had crept into double figures at 10.6 points, mostly by taking advantage of the defenses that always packed in around the Lakers' frontcourt. Martin would never take a shot unless it was an absolute necessity. Nevertheless, he hit .410 from the floor that season, eighth best in the league, an indication of just how many long set shots those old-timers took.

In the championship series, the Knicks quickly established that they had a new confidence and were out to accomplish something. They stayed with the Lakers through three-quarters of Game 1 in Minneapolis (played in a local armory, not the auditorium, because of another scheduling conflict). At that point, according to the old script, the Knicks were supposed to wither sometime in the fourth. Instead, they produced a 30-point period that brought a surprise ending: 96–88, New York.

Just like that, the Lakers had lost their home-court advantage. The next night, they evened the series with a 73–71 win. But with a change in the championship format, the next three games were to be played in New York, leaving the Knicks and their fans thinking championship.

VERN MIKKELSEN: "I can still see the clippings. The New York newspapers were all saying that the series wouldn't go back to Minneapolis. They were right. It didn't."

Mikan was an old hand at playing in the Big Apple, dating back to his college days and the doubleheaders in Madison Square Garden.

GEORGE MIKAN: "They sort of liked me in New York. And I liked New York. Even today when I travel, people will come up to me and say, 'I saw you play in the Garden.'"

In what the Lakers viewed as their sweetest championship, they blasted the Knicks three straight in New York's old 69th Regiment Armory. The first half of Game 3 was tight, partly because Mikan was experimenting with a turnaround jump shot. To help handle their center, the Lakers had employed DePaul coach Ray Meyer, an old friend of Hartman's, as a consultant.

SID HARTMAN: "Ray had tremendous control over Mikan. Ray didn't say much during the first half while George was working his jump shot. He just sat there. But in the locker room at halftime, he said, 'George, take that jump shot and stick it up your ass.'"

Properly admonished, Mikan ditched the jump shot and went back to the old drop-step. With that, the Lakers turned on a fourth-quarter blowout that ended 90–75. The Knicks fought back in Game 4, which turned into another foul fest. With 28 seconds left and Minneapolis leading 69–67, the Lakers' Jim Holstein went to the line and missed. But Minneapolis rookie guard Myer "Whitey" Skoog controlled the rebound and scored for a 71–67 lead. Connie Simmons hit two free throws for the Knicks to bring it to 71–69, and New York even got a final shot to tie it. But Harry Gallatin missed with a hook, and suddenly the Knicks were down 3–1.

JIM POLLARD: "After we got the 3–1 lead, Kundla gave us the next day off, so we toured Broadway's clubs that night after the game. Billy Eckstine was the music rage in those days. Me and Mikkelsen and Holstein would sing his songs to each other in the shower. Eckstine was in town that night, and we caught him at a Broadway club. When he finished his act, he came over to our table. He even brought Count Basie along to chat. We didn't get back to our rooms until about 4:30 that morning. Kundla got us on game day, though. He made us sweat it out in a one-hour practice the day of the game."

Game 5 was set for Friday, April 10. The Lakers opened a solid lead in the second, then stretched it to 20 points in the third, only to see it slip away when Mikan developed foul trouble early in the fourth. Perhaps that's where party time caught up with the Lakers. The Knicks pushed back, paring the lead from 12 to 5, then down to 84–82 with less than two minutes left. But all they could do was foul, and the Lakers made enough of their free throws to stay ahead. Plus, with a jump ball after every late foul (as was the rule then), Mikan controlled the outcome. That was enough for a 91–84 win and the Lakers' fifth title. Which meant another trek to Broadway.

VERN MIKKELSEN: "That was an evening to remember. It was high-test stuff, even in those days."

Syracuse Again

The Lakers' sweet memories didn't end with 1953, although they went into the 1954 season with Mikan sporting an array of battle scars. Over his amateur and professional career, he had suffered two broken legs, broken bones in both feet, and fractures of wrist, nose, thumb, and three fingers. He once figured that he had received a total of 166 stitches. Quite simply, opposing teams found the only way they could stop him was to get rough.

JIM POLLARD: "Nobody gave George anything. He earned his baskets."

The beating had begun to take its toll on Mikan's game, as his scoring average dipped to 18.1 points (third in the league behind Neil Johnston and Bob Cousy). The Milwaukee Hawks had a preseason series with the Lakers in 1953.

MARTY BLAKE, FORMER HAWKS GENERAL MANAGER: "We played 'em seven straight games in the preseason and lost all seven. In the seventh game we were leading by 20 points, and Kundla put on a press. We lost, and our owner, Benny Kerner, had me go out and buy a $10 trophy and give it to 'em."

The season opener that year was also against the Hawks, in Milwaukee, but the Lakers lost after Pollard and Mikan got into a shouting match in front of press row.

JIM POLLARD: "George didn't warn me about a pick. I got whacked, and my man went right in for a score. George and I were yelling at each other as we ran back down the court. It was all right in front of press row. So the next night we played in New York and the newspapers were full of stories that the Lakers dynasty was coming to an end because of George and I were feuding. George and I laughed about it over breakfast, then went out and kicked the hell out of the Knicks. George and I were always very critical of each other, very frank. But that helped our relationship, because nothing festered. We always got it off our chests."

This fussing duo first carried the Lakers to the league's best record, a 46–26 finish, which had been boosted by the addition of rookie center Clyde Lovellette out of Kansas. With the added depth, Mikan and company rolled to the team's sixth championship in seven seasons, a spirited seven-game conquest of the Syracuse Nationals. The Lakers claimed Game 1 and thought they were on their way to an easy time until Syracuse's Paul Seymour hit a wild shot from beyond half-court in the closing seconds of Game 2. It was the first home playoff loss for the Lakers in seven seasons.

PAUL SEYMOUR: "I remember Pollard coming up to me after the game and asking, 'How could you take that shot?' I said, 'I was open.' I knew it was good as soon as it left my hand. We were beat up for that series. I had a broken thumb, and Dolph Schayes and Earl Lloyd both had broken hands."

DOLPH SCHAYES: "The press took to calling us the Bandage Brigade in the papers. It seemed like every game we got somebody else hurt."

Somehow the Nats managed to keep it close. They lost Game 3 in Syracuse but ran free in Game 4 with an 80–69 win to even the series. Then the Lakers bullied them inside to claim the pivotal fifth game in Syracuse, 84–73.

Down 3–2, the Nats had to head back to Minnesota where they had just given the Lakers their first home playoff loss in seven years. The odds didn't seem high for a repeat of that feat. But the Nats had the ball with the score tied in the closing seconds when somehow the ball found its way into the hands of rookie Jim Neal, a six-eleven backup center. His shot, a 27-footer from the right side, dropped through with four seconds left to give Syracuse a 65–63 win.

AL CERVI: "It was a missed pass. Neal was at the top of the key when the ball came to him. He didn't know what to do with it so he shoots it."

In Game 7, the Lakers finally vanquished the Nats with Pollard scoring 21 points.

Moving On

It had been a great ride, but Mikan abruptly ended it after the season by announcing his retirement. Each season he had signed only a one-year contract with the team.

SID HARTMAN: "We always sweated signing him at the end of every year. His last year in the league he made $35,000."

But the center and the Lakers couldn't come to terms for the 1954–55 season, so at age 29 he retired. Some observers said it was none too soon. The league adopted a 24-second shot clock for the upcoming season, which didn't suit his style. Without him, Minneapolis finished 42–30, third best in the eight-team league, and still made it to the 1955 Western Finals but lost to Fort Wayne. Afterward, Pollard decided that he, too, should retire.

The team started badly in 1955–56, and Mikan decided to attempt a comeback in December. Frank Ryan, his law partner and agent, was negotiating a new contract with Max Winter and asked for another $35,000.

FRANK RYAN: "Max Winter said, 'I'd rather sell you my interest in the team for that kind of money.'"

SID HARTMAN: "Right after that, Max Winter left for his annual trip to Hawaii without wrapping up the deal. When Ben Berger heard what Winter had said, he offered to lend Mikan the money to buy him out. Ben had always thought that Max got too much credit for the winning. Mikan was strapped for cash at the time. He always needed money. He had a big house. He lived like a king. He had a law office, but he wasn't doing much law practicing. So he took Ben up on the deal. George borrowed the money and bought out Max. That meant George would come back to play."

With the sale of his stock, Winter left the team to play a major role in the development of the Minnesota Vikings as an NFL expansion franchise. Mikan, however, later decided to sign the stock over to Berger and focused instead on playing himself into shape. He averaged about 10 points over 37 games, and it was obvious his best days were past.

RED KERR: "George had retired, but then attendance was down in Minneapolis. They needed a boost. He made a comeback, and I remember the first time I played against him. I was in my first year with Syracuse that year. He was huge. The lane was small, and he was just a huge guy. You'd go on the right side of him, and he'd just hold his left hand out for the ball. So you'd go on the left side, and he'd switch to his right. The lane was so short, when he'd take a hook shot, he would just take sort of a little layup shot. I had a tough experience that first half. I learned a lot about NBA basketball, with those elbows of his and me playing behind him. At halftime, Al Cervi, my coach, said, 'Red, he can't keep up with you. We're gonna give you the ball to start the third quarter. You run. You get out and run.' When I was playing I could run pretty good. So I scored the first 16 points of the third quarter, and he was just huffin' and puffin'. I don't say I caused his retirement, but I know he retired shortly after that."

SID HARTMAN: "It was stupid for him to come back. He had taken a lot of punishment during his career. His knees were shot."

With its faster format, the pro game was racing off to a new level, leaving Mikan and his Lakers to exist in their own special amber. Yes, he had been a four-eyed, wavy-haired goon, but before age 30 he had mastered the pro game of his time, leading his teams to seven championships in eight seasons.

"Mikan ran the whole show," former Laker Larry Foust once observed. "He was an athlete despite what some people say about his bulk, and nobody ever had better offensive moves under the basket. When George played, he owned that lane."

Bob Short, a local businessman, and a group of investors bought the Lakers for $150,000 the next season, and three years later they moved them to Los Angeles, leaving a distinguished but uncertain past in Minneapolis.

SID HARTMAN: "There was some sadness when the Lakers left. There's such a thing as winning too much. Maybe the Lakers won too much. Maybe people took them for granted. Some people got tired of seeing them dominate completely. Until we got the Timberwolves here in Minnesota, lots of people here still followed the Lakers even though they had moved to Los Angeles."

3

Shortcut to Purgatory

Bob Short and Frank Ryan scrambled to buy the Minneapolis Lakers in 1957, only to realize after the deal was done that they had hitched themselves to a wild ride, the kind that could make or break them. Years later, after they had salted away their millions, they could scoff at their folly. But at the time, it was no laughing matter. Rather, it was a gut-twisting spin through a financial house of horrors, complete with lawsuits, judgments, indecent exposure allegations against a star player, a plane crash landing, and countless other tingling moments of drama.

When he first got started in pro basketball, Bob Short only wanted the fame, fortune, and fun associated with owning a team. Little did he know all the extra thrills that came with the territory. But Short was built for rough terrain.

FRANK RYAN, FORMER LAKERS OWNER: "Bob Short would give you the shirt off his back and fight you for a nickel."

Some associates thought you were more likely to get the fight than the shirt, but nobody doubted Short's acumen.

JIM POLLARD: "Bob was a very aggressive, outspoken individual. If you knew what you were talking about, you could challenge him. But if you didn't, he'd shove you in a corner."

The son of a Minneapolis fireman, Short burned with all sorts of ambitions and was willing to work 14 hours a day to reach them. He had served as an assistant U.S. attorney in Minnesota after earning his law degree from Georgetown in the '40s. From there he moved into the murky world of the trucking business. His drive and the money he made there helped him become a force in the Minnesota Democratic party. He would launch an unsuccessful bid to become lieutenant governor in 1966 and would serve as the national treasurer for Lyndon Johnson's presidential campaign. Yet even politics couldn't compare to the strange intrigue Short found in the nascent NBA in 1957.

SID HARTMAN: "Short had wanted a major league sports team in the worst way. He looked at football and baseball, but nothing was available there. Then he and Ryan read that Ben Berger was hoping to sell the Lakers to out-of-town interests. Berger was quoted in a newspaper article as saying that he would wait a week for local buyers to put together an offer. Otherwise, the Lakers were gonna leave."

Within days, Short and Ryan, his friend from their days together at the University of Minnesota, pulled together a group of 30 investors and offered Berger $150,000. That was good enough, and in a blur Bob Short found himself at the controls of a strange machine. The investors quickly named Short team president and formed a 12-member executive board to oversee operations. Their first move was to boot John Kundla upstairs as general manager and hire George Mikan as coach. The big jolt came shortly thereafter.

JOHN KUNDLA: Clyde Lovellette was our scorer and rebounder. He got into trouble. A woman said he exposed himself at a local bar. We had a public relations disaster on our hands. We thought the best thing was to trade him to Cincinnati. It was a pretty good deal. We got the top pick in the draft."

A future Hall of Famer, Lovellette would go into law enforcement after his playing days and become known as a born-again Christian. But without questioning Lovellette about the incident, Kundla quickly shipped him to the Cincinnati Royals. Also included in the deal was veteran Ed Fleming.

The new owners then used the pick to draft Rodney Clark Hundley, better known as "Hot Rod," out of West Virginia University, where he had been a showboat, flipping behind-the-back passes and infuriating opponents with his dribble-king routine. Once, late in a game, he had even flipped up hook shots for free throws.

RED KERR, FORMER NBA PLAYER AND COACH: "When Rod was in college at West Virginia as a freshman, he had the chance to break the school scoring record. He needed two more points, and he was at the free throw line. He threw up hook shots. When they asked him about it, he said, 'You know, if I broke the record as a freshman what would I have to look forward to as a sophomore?'"

JOHN KUNDLA: "They thought Hundley would have fan appeal. They were desperate to make it entertaining."

Few disagreed that the Lakers needed something. The team's attendance had plunged since the twilight of the Mikan glory years. Upon acquiring the Lakers, the new owners threw $50,000 into the team coffers for operating capital. It disappeared in two weeks, creating an immediate need to trim overhead. So Kundla sent seven-foot center Walter Dukes to Detroit. With the frontcourt stripped of Lovellette and Dukes, the Lakers soon headed into a downward spiral, losing games and money.

In his first pro game, rookie forward McCoy Ingram, a six-foot jumping jack, got the ball after a jump ball and promptly shot it into the opponent's goal. That proved to be typical of what would become a season of confusion for the Lakers. On many nights, attendance in the 10,000-seat auditorium totaled no more than 900. As the gate receipts went down, the unpaid bills stacked up. Soon the club faced judgments and court actions totaling $40,000, forcing Short to call an investors' meeting at the club's offices.

SID HARTMAN: "Short walked into that meeting with a cashier's check for $40,000 and offered to purchase a block of the team's stock that had been authorized but unissued. The other owners were asked if they wanted to buy the stock to cover the debts. None of them wanted to throw away any more money."

So Short paid up, pushing his interest in the club to near majority while diluting the other investors' holdings. Three years later, a group of investors would sue Short and Ryan over the move.

SID HARTMAN: "Short paid about a half million to settle the case, but it left him and Ryan as the team's owners."

In 1957, Short's $40,000 was badly needed, and even that wasn't nearly enough.

JIM POLLARD: "As the losses got deeper, the investors began complaining about Mikan's coaching style. It was pretty low-key, which meant the bench seemed pretty quiet during games. One of the investors thought it might be a good idea if the subs did a little cheering. That was good for a laugh."

ROD HUNDLEY: "My rookie year we were in last place. By the end of the season we were 19–53. There was a lot of poker playing. Slick Leonard, Dick Garmaker, Corky Devlin, and me, we were the four ringleaders that played a lot of cards."

Hundley and Leonard had teamed up in training camp as a pair who liked to drink, smoke, and run around all night.

ROD HUNDLEY: "Mikan missed his playing days. He wanted to run around with us, but we wouldn't let him. We told him that having the coach along just wouldn't be fun."

The Lakers' road trips were dominated by partying and marathon late-night poker games.

JOHN KUNDLA: "There was a lot of gambling."

ROD HUNDLEY: "It was Mikan who gave Slick his nickname 'cause he lost so much money to him. We took a lot of George's money."

When the Lakers weren't gambling, they were barhopping. Hundley recalled a local bar in Minneapolis where they'd go to wait for the secretaries and other working women to get off at five. There seemed like an endless supply of fun. On the road, Hundley seemingly knew every hot spot in every city. Leonard often told the story of opening the door of his New York hotel room to see Hundley staggering down the hall with a naked woman slung over his shoulder. Bob Short and Kundla grew weary of the missed flights and buses. In every town, Hundley seemed to run into complications.

ROD HUNDLEY: "Bob Short was a great man. We were in St. Louis on a Friday night and we were going to play the Hawks that Saturday afternoon. I was going out the door, Bobby Leonard and me. Short noticed us. He said, 'Hey, guys, go on back up to your room, I'll send some girls up. You can take care of your business and then go to bed and get a good night's sleep.' We told him thanks anyway, we didn't work that way."

Hundley supposedly draped his arm around the owner's shoulder and told him, "The thrill is in the chase, baby."

ROD HUNDLEY: "One year during the playoffs I asked Short to loan me 10 bucks. He gave me a $50 bill and didn't expect it back. He was that kind of guy, good to his players. He'd have the team over to his house for Christmas parties, things like that."

But even Short's patience had its limits. Finally, after a night of partying, Hundley and Leonard missed a flight from New York to Syracuse. Furious, Short called them both in. Hundley met with the owner first. Short explained that he was fining them $1,000 each in an effort to get them to tone down. Leonard made only $9,000 and Hundley $10,000 yearly. Hundley was sure it was the largest fine ever levied in the NBA to that time. Stunned, the two Lakers got drunk again that night to drown their blues. The owner had said they'd get the money back if they toned things down.

ROD HUNDLEY: "I told him I'd have to think about it. I wasn't sure that it was worth giving up the partying. He put us on probation the rest of the year. And he gave us the money back at the end of the season. He was a good guy."

By midseason, the Lakers' record stood at 9–30, and the executive committee decided it was time to fire Mikan. To bear the bad news, the committee dispatched Kundla to St. Louis, where the team was playing a road game. The move left Big George fuming, but the owners softened the blow by promoting him to general manager as Kundla closed out the season on the bench. The Lakers went 10–23 down the stretch to finish at 19–53, worst in the league.

ROD HUNDLEY: "Kundla was very serious-minded, a quiet guy. He tried to stop the poker, but we'd still play. He didn't like my passing behind the back either, but that was about the only way I knew."

Kundla tried to focus the team on a serious approach. But it was mostly a group of young Lakers, with money in their pockets for the first time in their lives.

ROD HUNDLEY: "Kundla tried to do the right thing. We just weren't ready to listen."

JOHN KUNDLA: "Rod was talented. And hard to coach. He was a showman, always seemed to make simple plays harder than they had to be. He always overdid it. He never became as good as he could have been. He didn't have the discipline. The pro game requires discipline. It wasn't hard to like Rod. He was young then. And he was on a bad team with some older guys who encouraged his bad habits. That team I took over was full of selfish guys who wanted to play cards and raise hell. They didn't care about the team. I tried to change things, but it was very difficult."

The Lakers finished last in the standings, discovering in the process that being at the bottom didn't necessarily mean the view was looking up.

Baylor Time

The draft prize claimed by the Lakers for their descent into purgatory was one Elgin Baylor, who supposedly had gotten his first name at birth when his father glanced at his wristwatch and liked the sound of the name on the face. "Elgin has more moves than a clock," his college coach, John Castellani, once said. Time, it seems, was the reigning motif of his style of play.

Michael Jordan and Julius Erving would later gain notoriety for their "hang time," that mysterious ability to jump and remain in the air, to "hang," while gliding to the hoop. But it was Baylor who possessed the original commodity. Driving to the basket, he would leave the floor, often not quite sure what he wanted to do, simply relying on his hang time to open his options. Because he was an excellent passer, he could usually find someplace to put the ball for a teammate. Failing that, he could resort to a layup (seldom choosing to dunk). The implication here is that Baylor was a gliding featherweight. Not so. He was six-foot-five and 225 pounds, a powerful rebounder with a special gift for following his own shots and correcting the misses.

ROD HUNDLEY: "Elgin was a shorter version of Karl Malone. He had a lot of power."

CHICK HEARN: "He just might be the best player I ever saw. He was doing things that Dr. J. made famous 20 years later, the hang time and so forth. But Elgin didn't have the TV exposure. Nobody did in those days."

Added to Baylor's dynamic mix was the curiosity of his nervous tick, a twitching of his face, leaving defenders confused as Baylor headed around them to the basket.

JOHN KUNDLA: "It wasn't too long after Elgin got to Minnesota that schoolboys across the state were attempting to emulate the twitch when they played ball. One of Elgin's college teammates visited our practice one day and asked him, 'Hey, Elgin, you still shaking the leaves off your head?'"

RED KERR: "We used to kid about it. If he gave the nervous tick to the left, he was going left. If he gave it to the right, he was gonna go to his right. But when he shook both ways, that's when you fell on your ass, and he was gonna go around you."

JOHN KUNDLA: "Elgin saw a doctor about it, and he told him it was simply a nervous reaction, that there was nothing to worry about. The first time I noticed the tick was when Elgin was a rookie when he was late to practice. I asked him why he was late, and he started twitching."

ROD HUNDLEY: "The tick was a part of the package. People sometimes took it for granted. Chick Hearn called it the built-in head fake."

JOHN KUNDLA: "It hurt his poker face, too. If he got a great hand, he twitched and his teammates folded."

Mostly the condition was a factor on the court, where the player with "more moves than a clock" shook defenders with a tick.

JOHN RADCLIFFE, LONGTIME LAKERS STATISTICIAN: "If they stopped to think about it, he was gone."

Elgin became Bob Short's great hope. The Lakers made him the first pick of the '58 draft, and Baylor, a Washington, D.C., native, sent his uncle to negotiate the contract, a $22,000 deal. "If Elgin had turned me down, I'd have gone out of business," Short said later. He almost did anyway. But Baylor was nothing short of sensational in his rookie debut.

ROD HUNDLEY: "The year before we were embarrassed. With Elgin, we weren't embarrassed anymore."

ELGIN BAYLOR: "I personally liked Minnesota very much. It was a great city, great people, with an exuberance for basketball. I played in Minnesota for three different coaches over two seasons. In those days, everybody except Syracuse and the Celtics ran patterned offenses. They were both running teams, but we were a half-court team. We ran the pick-'n'-roll, the give-'n'-go."

The rookie averaged 24.7 points and 15 rebounds for 1958–59. He was second in the league in most minutes played and led the Lakers in assists, scoring, and rebounding. Midway through that rookie season, Baylor scored 55 in a game, the third highest total in NBA history.

ELGIN BAYLOR: "I never thought about how many points I had. You always thought about winning. The actual specifics of some of those big games, I don't remember."

The team clunked along to a 33–39 record, while the veterans learned to play with the rookie. By the playoffs, they had gotten the hang of it, dumping first Detroit, then defending NBA champion St. Louis to meet Boston for the 1959 league title. The Celtics had defeated Syracuse to advance.

PAUL SEYMOUR, FORMER SYRACUSE PLAYER: "I remember that Cousy said they were gonna take Minneapolis in four straight, and they did. That was a pretty big statement at the time, because nobody had ever won four straight in the Finals."

Regardless, Short had reason for elation. His team had shown signs of emerging from its coma.

JIM POLLARD: "Baylor was clearly the most exciting player in the league. Short hustled to sign him to a long-term contract at $50,000 per year."

The situation, though, remained highly volatile. Kundla had grown weary of the NBA travel schedule, of dealing with Hundley and his counterparts, so he happily accepted the head coaching job at the University of Minnesota (where he would recruit a young University of North Dakota center named Phil Jackson). Needing a coach, Short picked John Castellani, who had coached Baylor at Seattle.

JOHN KUNDLA: "They figured he could handle Baylor. He didn't need handling."

If he had, Castellani wasn't the man for the job. His style was pure laissez-faire. Practices amounted to little more than unorganized pickup games. Rookie Rudy LaRusso from Dartmouth recalled Castellani approaching him early in the season and asking if he knew any plays the team could use. Right then LaRusso realized the Lakers were in trouble. To make matters worse, Baylor was inducted in the army right before the season started, meaning he couldn't be in training camp.

ROD HUNDLEY: "He couldn't come to the team, so we took the team to him to practice. That was kind of fun. Down in Texas. Elgin was in basic training at Fort Sam Houston near San Antonio. Elgin would play soldier all day and then he would join us at night for these open gyms. There'd be a couple of thousand people watching us practice. At night after practice, we sampled the South Texas night life. When we got bored with that, we'd go down into Mexico. We stayed in a barracks, which we pretty soon trashed. The army brass got wind of our partying and poker playing and made us clean the place up. That meant we spent even more time down in Mexico sipping Mexican beer and partying with the senoritas."

Despite the disaster of training camp, Baylor opened the season by scoring 52 against Detroit. A few nights later, on November 8, 1959, he rang up 64 points against the Celtics, breaking the league's single-game record set a decade earlier by Jumpin' Joe Fulks.

Rod Hundley: "When Red Auerbach saw that Elg was going to break the record, he told his players to not let him score. But they kept fouling him and sending him to the line. Castellani was playing Elgin every minute of every game. It wasn't long before he had blisters."

Soon fans were lining up to see this phenomenal young scoring machine wherever the Lakers played. They had lost their 25th game against 11 wins by midseason.

Rod Hundley: "Short brought a stack of ballots into the locker room and asked us to vote for a coach. Castellani was on the ballot, but we voted him down, 8–1. That's when they hired Jim Pollard."

Jim Pollard: "One of my first moves was to stop the poker playing. Slick Leonard and Dick Garmaker were winning a lot of money from Elgin. I didn't think it was good for the team's best player to be losing that much. Elgin wasn't that bad of a player, really. But Slick was a great poker player."

Crash

The trip to St. Louis on January 18, 1960, was supposed to be quick and uneventful. There were a few extra seats on the Lakers' team plane, a DC-3, so Frank Ryan decided to take his wife and 2 of his 10 kids along. After all, the team was set to return right after the Sunday afternoon game, which the Lakers lost, 135–119. As if that wasn't enough, a winter snowstorm, laced with sleet, settled across the Midwest that evening. The team arrived at Lambert Field in St. Louis about 5:30 P.M. only to be confronted with a weather delay for their flight home. Then the plane's generator failed, requiring an extra delay for repairs. Finally, they flew out about 8:30 that night, with the pilot keeping the craft low to avoid the planes stacked over St. Louis waiting to land in bad weather.

The DC-3 was off the ground about 10 minutes, just enough time for the Lakers to set up their portable card table, deal a pinochle hand, and light a cigarette, when the generator again blew, taking the lights, heat, navigation devices, and radio with it. The pilot could have turned around, but he had no radio to guide him through the maze of planes already waiting to land in

St. Louis. So he pushed on, heading the prop plane up through the storm with the idea that at 15,000 feet he might be able to steer his way to Minneapolis by the stars.

JIM POLLARD: "It was frightening, really bumpy. Finally we got up in altitude and things leveled out. So Frank Ryan and I got up and went to the cabin and asked the pilots how things were going. I was trying not to sound too scared. They were operating by a flashlight."

"Well, we're flying home by the stars," pilot Vernon Ullman, a marine veteran, told Pollard. "I'm not sure what the wind conditions are, but we don't have much to worry about until we start coming down."

JIM POLLARD: "We tried to act nonchalant when we went back to the cabin, but it was obvious everybody was scared to death."

Under the best circumstances, the Lakers dreaded the vagaries of winter travel. Normally, the prop plane flew through winter storms, not over them, which meant a lot of bumpy rides. The Lakers, though, were a loose bunch, greeting the circumstances with gallows humor, even taking turns steering the plane's controls on clear nights.

JIM POLLARD: "There was always somebody up front screwin' around with the pilots. They'd flip off the lights or sit in the copilot's seat and fly the plane a little bit. As soon as the plane started dipping, you knew they were screwin' around."

But not on this night. A few days earlier, Jimmy Krebs's new Ouija board had warned that the plane would crash, which was something they now remembered. As the engines droned on, the cabin got colder and quieter. The passengers wrapped themselves in blankets and measured their breathing in the unpressurized plane.

The flight to Minneapolis, normally two hours, stretched to three, then three and a half. Ice formed, first on the wings and windows, then in the cabin itself. Worry became fear. Knowing they were about out of fuel and nowhere near Minneapolis, Ullman decided to take the plane down to look for a place to land. As they descended, his copilot opened the cockpit window, reached out, and scraped the ice from the windshield. Fortunately, the terrain was flat. Shining the flashlight out the cockpit window, the pilots spied a hamlet and a water tower, which read "Carroll, Iowa." They would later discover that they had strayed about 150 miles off course, but at the moment that wasn't the issue. Ullman began buzzing the town, hoping to awaken someone who might turn on the lights at a local airstrip. It soon became obvious there was none. Flashlight in hand, copilot Howard Gifford came back to the cabin and explained the situation. We're about out of fuel. We can try someplace else or we might be able to land in a cornfield, he said. Put this SOB down, the players demanded. "Okay," Gifford said, "buckle your seat belts, put your knees up, and say a little prayer. We're going in."

Gifford returned to the cockpit but failed to latch the door, which flapped open and closed as the wind from the open window rushed through the plane, giving the passengers intermittent views of the pilots struggling to land the plane. While Ullman flew, one copilot stretched his arm out the open window to scrape ice from the windshield while another read the altimeter by flashlight.

ROD HUNDLEY: "The wind was blowing back through there, and the cockpit door was going back and forth, and the pilots were yelling above the roar of the engines. That wind blowing back through the cabin was cold. It must have been about 20 below zero, but we were sweating."

About 300 feet up, the plane began following a car on a road, its lights barely visible through the storm. But then the car headed up a hill, and Ullman abruptly pulled the plane up, sending jitters through the passengers. Baylor decided to take his blanket and lie down in the aisle at the back of the plane. If I'm going to die, I might as well die comfortably, he thought as he braced himself against the seat supports on either side. Krebs began making public vows. If the plane landed safely, he'd quit cheating at cards. He'd play hard on the court. And throw away his Ouija board.

ROD HUNDLEY: "We were all making promises. Garmaker sold life insurance in the off-season. We later kidded him that he was writing policies and throwing them out the window."

The plane made several more passes, each one goosing the passengers' anxiety higher. At one point, Ullman pulled up to avoid high-tension wires. On the final try, the pilot cut the engines and the plane floated into a cornfield. The crop had been left uncut, and three feet of snow rested on top of the corn. Touchdown was pillow soft.

JIM POLLARD: "That landing was so smooth you could have held a cup of coffee and not spilled a drop. That pilot went right down a row of corn, just as straight as a string. At first, after we came to a stop, there was nothing but silence. Then there was a knock on the door. The first guy across the field had a fireman's hat on and a big ax. He looked at me and said, 'Hi. How're you doing?'"

The passengers cheered and upon emptying from the plane engaged in a joyful snowball fight. Soon they calmed down to realize they had a mile hike across the cornfield in crotch-deep snow to the road. Nobody seemed to mind.

JIM POLLARD: "When we got to the road, there was a hearse waiting with the rescue vehicles and cars. When I saw that hearse I got the shakes. The guy driving it was the village undertaker. One of the local guys standing there joked that the undertaker wasn't getting any new business."

Safe and sound, the Lakers retreated to an old hotel in town, which housed mostly seniors.

JIM POLLARD: "They brewed some coffee and one of the guys got the idea to raid the liquor cabinet. Then somebody else broke out the cards. I didn't mind at all that they played a little poker. We were very lucky that night."

Westward?

The dangers seemed well defined for the Lakers in 1960. The opportunities, on the other hand, were far more difficult to gauge. Were they real or an illusion? That winter, Bob Short began talking about moving his team west.

SID HARTMAN: "Morris Chalfen [one of the team's minority owners] was the first one who wanted to move them to L.A. He had thought about that after the Dodgers moved out there from Brooklyn. But Berger had wanted to keep the team in Minneapolis, so they stayed put."

For Short, the choice was easier. The team was doing poorly, and the bills were mounting. Finally, Short announced that if he sold 3,000 season tickets for 1960–61, the Lakers would stay in Minneapolis. But privately he began making plans for a move. It was either that or fold.

Within days after their emergency landing, the Lakers were told they'd have to board the plane again, this time for a flight cross-country to play a series of games on the West Coast. When several players balked at the idea, Short told them they either boarded the plane or found a new job. Reluctantly, they headed west. Their big debut came February 1 against Wilt Chamberlain and the Philadelphia Warriors at the new 14,000-seat Los Angeles Sports Arena near the Southern Cal campus. The event drew 10,202 and featured a preliminary game between the Vagabonds, promoted as "an all-Negro basketball team," and Los Alamitos Navy. In the main event, the Warriors prevailed, 103–96. But that didn't matter. Short and Ryan figured the crowd size was a winner. "We don't want to leave Minneapolis," Short told reporters afterward. "It's more than just a dollar-and-cents thing. It's a civic venture. However, if we can't see a way to operate without constantly subsidizing our investment, we'd ask permission to move our franchise." In fact, they'd already made their decision, having gotten a similar response two nights earlier in another game at the Cow Palace in San Francisco.

FRANK RYAN: "California seemed the place to go."

Despite their poor regular-season record, 25–50, the Lakers found their rhythm again in the playoffs and took a 3–2 lead against the St. Louis Hawks in the Western Finals. But they lost the sixth game at home, their last in Minneapolis, and fell in the seventh in St. Louis on March 26.

A month later, on April 27, Short and Ryan went to a league owners' meeting at the Roosevelt Hotel in New York to ask for permission to move to California. For momentum, Short had announced the previous afternoon that he had reached a tentative agreement for the Lakers to play their games the next season in the L.A. Sports Arena. That story made the morning papers, but it did little to sway the vote. In a morning session, the other owners voted down Short's request 7–1. They were worried about the increased travel costs to play in California.

SID HARTMAN: "It was clear that Ned Irish wanted to get Baylor for the Knicks. That's why it got voted down the first time."

Figuring they were doomed, Short and Ryan pulled aside St. Louis Hawks owner Ben Kerner to plead their case as the meeting recessed for lunch. If we stay in Minneapolis, we'll die, they told him. Then you'll have to die in Minneapolis, Kerner replied. The Lakers were finished, they realized.

SID HARTMAN: "Short and Ryan were headed back to the NBA meeting after lunch when they saw a newspaper headline at the hotel's cigar stand announcing that Abe Saperstein [the founder of the Harlem Globetrotters] had formed the American Basketball League. Saperstein had been promised for years that he would get an NBA franchise. The promised franchise was supposed to be in California. Saperstein ran out of patience and realized the NBA was leading him along. He announced that he was starting his own league. The NBA didn't want Saperstein getting a head start out West so they voted again that afternoon."

The Lakers won the second time, 8–0, and were on their way to the City of the Angels. Before they consented, however, the other owners forced Short to agree to pay each team's extra travel costs for going to the West Coast. Short turned to Ryan. "That'll break us," he said.

"We're already broke," his partner replied.

Freeway

The earliest settlers in Southern California discovered a countryside thick with grizzly bears, those powerful creatures with nasty tempers. By the 1840s the sport of grizzly roping had taken hold in the region, and it thrived there until 1912, when the last griz was killed in Los Angeles County. As the indigenous population of noble foes declined, the locals turned to an array of other sports to fill their leisure.

This search helped produce the first Tournament of Roses in 1890. Pasadena's Valley Hunt Club had hatched the idea of the Tournament of Roses to make folks buried in snow back East aware of Southern California's charms. The Hunt Club staged a host of sporting events over the first dozen years—races, jousting tournaments, tug-of-war contests. Nobody paid much attention until the Tournament committee set up a football game in 1902 between Stanford and Michigan. It wasn't the best situation for the region's foray into spectator team sports. New Year's Day 1902 was hot and dusty. The traffic headed toward the Rose Bowl field at Throop Polytechnic Institute (now Caltech) was a mix of wagons and coughing automobiles festooned with blue and gold pennants (the official colors of the Tournament). Sadly, the park had only one gate, which created first a massive traffic jam, then a depressingly long line into the stadium, and finally an angry, frustrated mob of a crowd.

From that uneven beginning, Southern California sporting enthusiasts turned their focus to boxing, horse racing, college football, track and field, and minor-league baseball—all somehow managed to capture the fancy of Los Angelenos over the first four decades of the 20th century.

The competition of big-time professional sports didn't reach L.A. until the Cleveland Rams grew tired of cold weather and sparse crowds and moved there in 1945. There was even a fling with pro basketball in 1946–47 when Maury Winston, owner of the Chicago American Gears, founded his own league and helped launch the Los Angeles Red Devils, a team that featured baseball great Jackie Robinson. The Red Devils posted a 13–3 record that included a win over George Mikan, but the league folded within months and with it the Devils.

Then came the Dodgers from Brooklyn in 1958. When they won the World Series a year later, Los Angelenos suddenly realized that their town, with its sparkling afternoons and balmy nights, made a perfect stop for the big leagues. Both the Rams and Dodgers regularly drew large, enthusiastic crowds to the Los Angeles Coliseum and then Dodger Stadium.

Still, when the Lakers arrived in 1960 basketball was very much an unknown factor in the city's sports psyche. For years the game had existed merely as a sideshow. John Wooden was putting together decent teams at UCLA, but the Bruins played some of their games at Venice High School and others at a little gym on campus. And the hoops program at Southern Cal fared as well as it could at a football factory. Beyond that, the attraction was a mishmash of AAU and junior college teams, none of which could manage more than an occasional back-page paragraph in the local newspapers.

Basketball, it seemed, was an indoor game, and L.A. was a very outdoor city. Yet the groundwork for dramatic change had already been laid, beginning with the building of a new arena and the arrival of a certain broadcaster in town.

CHICK HEARN: "I was working in Peoria, Illinois, and I got a call one day that KNX radio, CBS, was looking for a football announcer to do University of Southern California games. And also to do the basketball. Basketball on the West Coast at that time was not very well received. Anyway, at that time, I came out and joined KNX CBS radio. About a month after I was out here, NBC television locally and nationally hired me, so I was working for both networks. That was 1957. The Dodgers were heading out. The Rams were very good then. We didn't have the Angels, didn't have the Lakers. Obviously didn't have the Clippers."

Hearn's influence had yet to unfold. A more obvious development came with the completion of the 14,000-seat L.A. Sports Arena near the Coliseum in 1959. Funded by public bonds, the facility transported basketball into the modern age, as if a giant flying saucer had landed in the neighborhood near the University of Southern California on a mission to show L.A. the future. Other arenas in the country couldn't compare to this strange oval. With its space-age decor, the Sports Arena featured elevators to lift spectators to the seating levels and fans to keep the flag waving gracefully during the national anthem. Even the turnstiles were electronic, keeping a running tally of the crowd size on a scoreboard as each spectator entered.

Both UCLA and Southern Cal scrambled to play their games there, leaving the Lakers to settle for an unusual number of Sunday and Monday dates. Otherwise, the Lakers had to search for local venues to play on their other game days. That, strangely, would prove to be something of an early boost. Small venues cloaked dismal crowds better than the cavernous new arena.

CHICK HEARN: "They were drawing nothing. They would play one night at a high school gym. They played the Shrine Auditorium on a stage! If you fell off the side you dropped six feet. They played at the University of California, wherever its various locations were. They just couldn't build a following. Wherever they played, the thousand people who lived in that area might go. But the newspaper coverage was very, very slim. It wasn't very easy elsewhere either. In the East, they were playing doubleheader games at neutral sites, trying to find a crowd."

Bob Short and Frank Ryan, though, were just happy to be there, after struggling to survive in the antiquated auditorium in Minneapolis. They negotiated a three-year lease with a series of 17 one-year options to follow, providing security through the 1980 season, what seemed like a distant signpost at the time.

JERRY WEST: "When the Lakers first came to Los Angeles from Minneapolis they were terrible. They didn't have a lot of very good players. But things changed. When they came to Los Angeles it seemed like the team was invigorated."

West, by God, Virginia

Jerry West came to L.A. in 1960 with a flattop haircut, skinny legs, and a high-pitched mountain twang, like he had just fallen off the turnip truck. Bumpkin personified. It was the age of TV's "Beverly Hillbillies," and the shy, serious country boy found a Hollywood eager to lampoon him. Elgin Baylor first called him "Tweetie Bird" because of the high-pitched voice and the skinny legs. West hated that. Then Baylor came up with another name. "Zeke from Cabin Creek." West wasn't even from Cabin Creek. He was from nearby Chelyan. He hated that name, too.

PETE NEWELL: "I've never seen Jerry walk by an autograph yet. He signed because he believed he owed it to the fans. But when people would ask him to sign 'Zeke from Cabin Creek,' he'd refuse."

Catchy as the name was and eager as the team was to build a following in L.A. in the early years, broadcaster Chick Hearn constantly referred to West as Zeke on game broadcasts, until West's first wife, Jane, quietly asked him to quit using it.

PETE NEWELL: "Jerry was never a very secure kind of person. Believe it or not, he has never had a great self-esteem. Everybody thinks more of Jerry than he does of himself. That's the West Virginia in him."

Hot Rod Hundley once remarked that Jerry West accomplished "ten times as much as I did in my career but he's about a tenth as happy as I am." By the time it was over, West would come to view his career as unfortunate, but its beginnings were mostly idyllic: a grade-schooler hoisting shots from a dirt court toward a homemade goal in the West Virginia hills.

JERRY WEST: "We lived in Chelyan [pronounced 'Sheel-yan']. It was a town of about 500 people. I was the next to youngest of six kids. My father worked for a coal company as an electrician. He didn't follow sports much. He enjoyed the political arena, even though he wasn't really involved, he enjoyed that side of it. Politics is serious in the coal industry."

A small, shy child, West found a special magic in the ball and the hoop. He wanted to be perfect at it.

JERRY WEST: "It was something you could do by yourself. I put the goal up myself. Back then, you learned how to do things for yourself. I started shooting the basketball earlier, when I was shooting from between my legs because I couldn't get it up to the basket. Then I remember I got to where I could shoot it two-handed. Those were the days when it was just something to do, something to pass the time. When I look back at it, I wish I had been in an area that was bigger, because I liked it. But everything you learned, you learned by yourself."

The school for his little community south of Charleston was East Bank High.

JERRY WEST: "My junior year, I guess, was when people started to hear of me. I played for my high school team. My high school team was nondescript in the sense that we had a 13–13 record. That was the only thing they knew me by my junior year."

The anonymity disappeared his senior season. West led East Bank High School to a state championship, then listened as more than 70 colleges across the country begged him to play for them. He liked the University of Maryland, and he listened with interest when the University of Kansas coaches tried to talk him into coming to Lawrence to play alongside Wilt Chamberlain. All along his choice was West Virginia, where Hot Rod Hundley reigned as the silver-tongued star. Hundley was a senior when West was a freshman. When Hundley departed as the number one pick in the NBA draft, West moved in as the team's main force.

As a six-foot-four junior forward, West led the Mountaineers to the 1959 NCAA championship game where they lost by a point to Pete Newell's University of California team.

JERRY WEST: "I had my hands on the ball about midcourt with no time left on the clock, and I said, 'If I could have just gotten one more shot . . .' But it wasn't to be. Those are the things, frankly, that stay with you more than the wins. Those are the things that really are wearying. My basketball career has sort of been on the tragic side of everything. It hasn't been on the positive side. It was so close, yet so far away."

PETE NEWELL: "We keyed our entire defense to Jerry. That first time we played him we didn't know as much about him. We knew he was great. He had an MVP performance, which kept them in the game."

That championship loss was the first for West, and it would soon be followed by more frustration as a pro. Six times he would guide his Lakers into the

NBA championship series only to lose each time to the Boston Celtics. A seventh trip to the NBA Finals brought a seventh straight loss, the last time coming to the New York Knicks. The more elusive it proved to be, the more the championship came to have an almost mesmerizing hold on him.

JERRY WEST: "The closer you get to the magic circle, the more enticing it becomes. In some ways it's like a drug. It's seductive because it's always there, and the desire is always there to win one more game. There's no question with me . . . I don't like to think I'm different, but I was obsessed with winning. And losing made it so much more difficult in the off-season, particularly once I got to be a professional. And even the summer of my junior year in college, it was very frustrating to come up short."

West demanded perfection from himself every night and was inconsolable when he failed to deliver.

PETE NEWELL: "As a player, he would get down on himself."

FRED SCHAUS, FORMER WEST VIRGINIA UNIVERSITY COACH AND FORMER LAKERS COACH AND GENERAL MANAGER: "At times, Jerry tended to brood over the flaws in his game. When he was not playing well, he'd kind of go into a shell. He wouldn't talk to anybody, not the coaches or his own teammates. If he wasn't playing well, he was tough to live with."

JERRY WEST: "I was nervous all the time. But then again, I was a nervous player. That's where I got my energy from."

West and Cincinnati's Oscar Robertson comprised the heart of the U.S. Olympic team in 1960, coached by Newell.

PETE NEWELL: "I was coaching the U.S. Olympic team in 1960. We were picking the team and getting ready for the summer games in Rome. In the first session of tryouts, Jerry didn't play well. Afterward, he came to see me and said he didn't think he was playing well enough to help the team. He said, 'Maybe I don't belong here.' I told him, 'Listen, Jerry. If you don't go to Rome, I don't go.' The next day he had a great practice. He was never a person to seek adulation. Even as a general manager he still downplays himself. But he was driven for it, driven for greatness. His drive was greater than his fear of not succeeding. It's just that he's never been one to sing his own praises, to laud himself."

West went on to join Robertson and Walt Bellamy on the team that overwhelmed the competition for the gold medal. West would say that being presented that medal with Robertson was one of the top moments of his basketball life.

After finishing 25–50, the Lakers had held the second pick in the draft that spring of 1960. Sixteen games into the 1959–60 season, they had acquired 6-foot-11 Ray Felix to help Boomer Krebs in the post, but the combination was barely adequate.

JIM POLLARD: "We still needed a center. But all of our informal scouting reports came back the same. They said, 'Jerry West is the best white player available.' I watched him play and said, 'Forget white, outside of Oscar Robertson, West is the best player, period.'"

As expected, the Cincinnati Royals took Robertson with the first pick. So West, a skinny, six-foot-four forward, became the Lakers' choice. The national collegiate player of the year in 1960, he had averaged 29 points and 17 rebounds per game as a senior forward.

JERRY WEST: "I was in Italy during the Olympics when I found out that the Lakers were moving to Los Angeles. That's also when I found out that the Lakers had hired Fred Schaus, my coach at West Virginia. I thought, 'This is going to be interesting.'"

JIM POLLARD: "West was lightning quick and he could score, so we figured he would make the adjustment to pro guard."

JERRY WEST: "Coming into the league, I really had to change positions, even though I was six-four. I played a lot up front, mostly up front, in college, except defensively out front, pressing and stuff like that. When they needed it, I'd bring the ball up the floor, but I really didn't do that a lot. Basically, defensively, the adjustment wasn't a problem for me. But offensively, instead of starting out 19 or 20 feet offensively and taking one dribble to the hoop or one dribble to get a shot, I had to start out 28 feet, which required a lot more finesse in getting where you wanted to go."

Fred Schaus seemed like an odd coaching choice for the Lakers, but he had credentials. He had been a solid pro player for five seasons with the Fort Wayne Pistons, then had coached West Virginia to the 1959 NCAA championship game. Lakers owners and management hoped that Schaus could work the same kind of promotional magic in Southern California. But that wouldn't happen right away.

Hard Times

Bob Short and Frank Ryan planned to stay in Minneapolis while owning a team in Los Angeles, which meant they needed a Moses to lead the Lakers to the promised land.

CHICK HEARN: "When Bob Short bought the Minneapolis Lakers for a nickel on the dollar and brought them out here, he sent a fellow out here with $15,000 to get them set up, to get the franchise started. He was supposed to buy basketballs, suits, stationery, all the equipment to get everything going. But this guy, whom I won't name, spent all the money entertaining people such as myself and the press. And so they still didn't have anything started."

Short's answer to the disaster was to hire an old friend, Lou Mohs.

FRED SCHAUS: "Lou Mohs was tall and broad-shouldered, with a mane of striking white hair. He was in his 60s and had worked for years as a newspaper circulation director. He knew how to work long hours and he loved basketball."

CHICK HEARN: "Lou Mohs was a very tough man. He demanded top efficiency, and he usually got it."

A Minnesota native, Mohs had starred in athletics at St. Thomas College. While in the newspaper business, he persisted in his love of sports, going to games whenever possible, even scouting talent for his coaching friends. Mohs was Sid Hartman's circulation boss when the young reporter began running the Lakers in 1947. Mohs was so interested in the team that Hartman feared his boss was trying to move him out of the way to take over the Lakers himself. Thirteen years later, after his career had taken him across the country working for major newspapers, Mohs was finally getting the opportunity to run a team.

FRED SCHAUS: "Lou was so happy to be involved he didn't care that the franchise was broke. They ran out of money not long after he got to California, so Lou had to call Bob Short for cash to pay some bills. Short told him, 'Call me for anything, but don't call me for money.'"

Somehow Mohs took that directive and made it work.

CHICK HEARN: "That son of a gun came in with literally nothing to work with. He worked out of a desk and did it all. Tickets. Money. Everything else. He saved the franchise, no question about it. Literally threw his heart and soul into it."

FRED SCHAUS: "It was Lou Mohs who talked me into leaving West Virginia to coach the Lakers. They had tried to get me to take over the team when it was in Minneapolis. But I turned them down. I knew they weren't very sound financially. But things changed when they moved out to Los Angeles. The place had a great climate, and the team had just drafted Jerry West. And Lou Mohs offered me $18,500 a year in salary. That was pretty good money in 1960, so I accepted the offer. If I had known how bad their cash flow problems were, I would never have taken the job. Right after I got out there I knew we were in trouble when all the equipment suppliers were sending their packages COD."

Mohs's answer to the cash crisis was a tightness that infuriated his players. He kept track of every paper clip.

ROD HUNDLEY: "We called him the Black Cat. He did an excellent job of watching Bob Short's money. But every time he'd come around the locker room we'd get beat."

One of Mohs's first ideas was a 13-game exhibition schedule between the Lakers and Boston Celtics, played all across California. These exhibitions began with the team's first season in L.A. Although it would take a while for the local crowds to catch on, the rookie Jerry West got an early lesson in the dominance of Russell and company. In turn, the Celtics got a good early look at West.

BOB COUSY, FORMER CELTICS GUARD: "It was obvious from that first year that Jerry was a superstar. He had tremendous speed and quickness and explosiveness."

Likewise, West got a look at the Celtics' unique fast-breaking style, led by Cousy and ignited by ferocious defense. The Celtics were the perfect team to educate and entertain California crowds.

CHICK HEARN: "The things that saved the game of pro basketball were the 24-second clock and Bob Cousy. Cousy introduced to the game the style that the Globetrotters had made famous around the world, the fancy passing and behind the back and so forth. And the crowds loved it."

Then there was the presence of Russell.

JERRY WEST: "By the time I first played against him in 1960, Bill Russell had already demonstrated his greatness very effectively by leading the Celtics to three championships. I'll never forget the circumstances when I played against him as a rookie with the Lakers. We played them in something like 12 to 14 exhibition games that year and then in another 10 regular-season games. I had my fill of seeing Bill Russell at an early age."

By the second year's exhibition, Chick Hearn had joined the proceedings.

CHICK HEARN: "Boston used to come out in the exhibition season, and we'd travel with them for 13 games in the preseason. It was a caravan of rented cars. It was an experience, like the old barnstorming days of basketball. One night we'd play in Santa Barbara, the next in San Luis Obispo. We played everywhere. In high school gymnasiums. This was all Lou Mohs's work. He was a hustler and a good promoter. He got the thing going, and it worked. They had Cous and Russ and Sharman and Heinsohn and Frank Ramsey and the Jones boys, K.C. and Sam. It developed into a good rivalry. Some of the games were very intense. We did that for several years in the preseason. We'd play like 13 exhibition games. That helped expand the NBA to communities that had never seen a game. As I said, basketball on TV wasn't prevalent at the time. And even when basketball got on TV, the league didn't always make wise choices about which teams would be on. They always did what was cheapest."

That first year, the exhibition games helped prime the pump—but just a little. Only 4,008 paying customers turned out on October 24 to see the Lakers lose their first home game to the Knicks 111–100. The next night the teams played again and the Lakers won, with 3,375 watching. At least those were the numbers Mohs reported.

FRED SCHAUS: "Every day Lou would phone Bob Short in Minneapolis to report the ticket sales for each game. After one of the early games, Mohs told Short that 4,000 seats had been sold. Short asked him, 'Can't you double that when you give it to the press?' Lou said, 'Double it again?'"

MITCH CHORTKOFF, VETERAN LOS ANGELES SPORTSWRITER WHO WORKED AS A PUBLIC RELATIONS ASSISTANT TO THE LAKERS IN 1960: "We shared a building with the minor-league hockey team, the Blades, who were next door. There was a crack in the ceiling where you could hear everything that was said in the next room. Jack Geyer, a former sportswriter, was the general manager of the Blades. As a lark, he would listen to Mohs's conversations with Short. Then he would call Jim Healy, a gossip radio guy in Los Angeles. The reports of Lakers ticket sales would be on Healy's show all the time. Mohs could never figure out the leak."

If Los Angelenos didn't yet realize what had landed in their midst, Baylor gave them the first big clue that November 15 when he scored 71 points, a new single-game league record, against the Knicks in Madison Square Garden.

RED KERR: "There was the night that Elgin got 71 points in Madison Square Garden. Hot Rod Hundley got in a cab that night after the game and told the driver, 'Me and Elgin got 78 points tonight.'"

JOHN RADCLIFFE: "Elgin was very strong. He would get bumped all the time, but it never seemed to throw him off stride. Even in the air, he would get bumped a lot, but his concentration was so good that the shot would still go where he wanted it to go. He used the glass a lot. I never saw him dunk. It wasn't the thing to do in those days."

JERRY WEST: "It was an honor to play with him. I never considered Elgin Baylor as someone I competed against. He is without a doubt one of the truly great players to play this game. I hear people talking about great players today, and I don't see many that compare to him, I'll tell you that. He had that wonderful, magical instinct for making plays, for doing things that you just had to watch. I learned from him, from watching him. I was young, wanting to learn. I had an incredible appreciation for other people's talents. It was incredible to watch Elgin play."

Baylor's performances seemed to entrance his less-talented teammates, especially forwards Tommy Hawkins and Rudy LaRusso. Which left little doubt that the Lakers were Baylor's team, on and off the court.

JOHN RADCLIFFE: "Tommy Hawkins was the hardest worker on the team, but he always had trouble getting the ball to go in the hole. He was a tremendous leaper but he had small hands. He and Rudy LaRusso worked so hard for Elgin. They'd battle and battle, setting picks, getting rebounds, whatever it took."

MERV HARRIS, WHO COVERED PRO BASKETBALL FOR THE OLD *LOS ANGELES HERALD EXAMINER*: "It was fascinating to see the domination of his personality over that team. Elgin was the boss. He was the most physically dominating player, and his status began with that. Whenever Elgin wanted to play poker, they played poker. Wherever Elgin wanted to eat, they went to eat. Whatever Elgin wanted to talk about, they talked about."

ROD HUNDLEY: "Our nickname for Elgin was Motormouth. He never stopped talking. He knew everything, or he thought he did."

The team wasn't without problems, though. Fred Schaus opened the 1960–61 season with Hundley and Frank Selvy as starting guards and the perfectionist West on the bench for long stretches.

JERRY WEST: "Schaus was somebody who was familiar with me, who knew me as a player and pretty well as a person. The negative factor was that I almost felt I had to be so much better than the other people I was playing with. No matter how I played in games or in practices, it seemed like my playing time was almost being handed to me in a different manner."

ROD HUNDLEY: "Schaus wasn't a bad coach. He was just mechanical and predictable. He'd take Jerry West out of games with two minutes left. It didn't matter if he was shooting the ball great. It was automatic. Schaus wouldn't ride a hot hand. Most coaches will, but Schaus wouldn't. Hell, Jerry made the All-Star team, and he wasn't even a starter."

RED KERR: "He was old school, no nonsense, no sense of humor. Tolerance for mistakes? None. Guys didn't like Freddie Schaus."

JERRY WEST: "That was a frustrating period, because I could not learn sitting on the bench. The only thing I could learn were bad habits, with the things that I saw. I had to get out there and get over those first-year jitters and the time in my career where I wasn't a real good player, to get to the point where I could be competent enough to compete on a higher level with these other players."

ROD HUNDLEY: "The worst thing was, they charged Jerry for extra tickets. They took money from him. I was standing right there. Jerry wouldn't say a word. He just sat there and turned red."

JERRY WEST: "I felt after 20 games that I had earned more playing time because the team was doing so poorly. The one thing I always felt, if the team is not winning you have to be free to make changes."

Hundley has said many times that it was silly not to start West and play him more.

FRED SCHAUS: "Rod was fun, and he did a lot of funny things. But he was a fine player, too. He was a great dribbler and passer, and he played pretty fair defense. He was a great scorer, but he was not the great shooter that Jerry West was."

Hundley was disappointed that Schaus chose to bench him instead of Selvy, the Lakers' other guard.

JERRY WEST: "All of a sudden things weren't very good, and I had a chance to step in and start, and I never gave it up. It was a struggle, and then things changed. Then it got to the point where I didn't come out very much. That felt good, because I believe basketball players need to play more, particularly if you can play at a higher level. Getting to that level is the hardest thing. You can't do it unless you have ability and you get the opportunity."

The Lakers began a turnaround with West in the lineup, although it was nothing that the rookie guard engineered by himself. Baylor was in his prime, playing the forward spot in spectacular fashion. He led the team offensively and finished second in the league in scoring (behind Wilt Chamberlain) at a 34.8 points per game pace.

MITCH CHORTKOFF: "They were only drawing about 3,000 that first year. But Baylor and West made it into something. Baylor was so spectacular he could sell tickets with the way he played."

The Lakers finished second in the Western Division with a 36–43 record, just enough to make the playoffs. But the Sports Arena wasn't available, so they moved one of their first-round games with Detroit to the local Shrine Auditorium, where they played on a stage. They survived that series, then took on St. Louis in the Western Finals. They beat the Hawks the first game in St. Louis and later claimed another at home. Suddenly the series was knotted at two-all. Bob Short and Lou Mohs were ecstatic. This was the turnaround they'd been looking for. They knew it was time to do some serious promoting. And maybe even spend a little money.

CHICK HEARN: "The Lakers came out in '60, but they couldn't get anyone to carry their games. No radio station would take them, so they didn't have any broadcasts the first year, despite West and Baylor. After they made the playoffs that first year, I got a call from Bob Short asking if I would go to St. Louis the next night to televise the playoff game. I said, 'You can't get a TV station by tomorrow night, Bob.' This was after midnight on Sunday. I'm talking to him lying on my bed. We didn't have satellite trucks in those days. I said, 'You're not gonna get a TV station that can get it together for tomorrow night. Why don't you go on the station I'm working for here, KNX radio? We can go all over the country, particularly at night.' They had a 50,000 watt clear channel. And so he did that."

The Lakers had tied the Hawks in the Western Finals and were set to play the fifth game in St. Louis that Saturday, March 27. Hearn arranged a KNX broadcast of that game, which the Lakers won 121–112.

CHICK HEARN: "They had been averaging about 3,000 fans per game in Los Angeles. The Hawks had the likes of Cliff Hagan and Bob Pettit and Lenny Wilkens—a very outstanding team. The Lakers beat them in overtime. It was a well-received game, and they came home to 15,000 in the Sports Arena. That's when it really took off."

Indeed. The packed house saw the Lakers fall in overtime that Monday, then the Hawks took the seventh game and the series at home, 105–103. But L.A. had discovered the Lakers, and they would never again go begging for a broadcast or a broadcaster. Hearn was hooked for good. And his swift, smart delivery was perfect for selling Southern California fans on Baylor, West, and the Lakers.

  With their success in the '61 playoffs, the Lakers gathered a quick following in L.A. and soon became popular with the Hollywood crowd. Lakers games became a place to be seen. Soon Lou Mohs was fielding regular requests from stars for complimentary tickets.

MITCH CHORTKOFF: "Back then, if a celebrity wanted a ticket, he had to come see Lou personally. I remember he got a call from Peter Falk, and Lou had never heard of him. This was before the 'Columbo' TV series. The secretary explained that he was an actor, and Lou said, 'Well, he must be a bad actor if he can't buy his own tickets.' Then we convinced him that this was someone you should give tickets to."

Once Lakers management understood the value of the Hollywood connection, games at the Sports Arena became a parade of stars.

CHICK HEARN: "The celebrities had tremendous impact. Put a guy like Jack Nicholson in the front row, and people will come to see the game and the star. Doris Day was a real heartthrob and a real star on the screen. She was a regular in those early days."

RED KERR: "Doris Day and Pat Boone were big fans, on the sideline all the time. She liked Rod very much. They all did. Before Pete Maravich, Rod was

Pete Maravich. He did all that stuff behind the back, that razzle-dazzle stuff. Rod was great."

JERRY WEST: "I have never been enamored with that part of Los Angeles. I don't view those people as stars. I view them as people. That never affected me. I was not close with any of them. I was so shy at that time, and almost painfully shy. Even doing an interview was a chore for me. I never felt comfortable with publicity. Was never interested in it. Some people seek it. Some people like it. That was uncomfortable for me. What I did was just something I loved to do. If people liked to watch it, fine."

The entire NBA, however, seemed to enjoy a chance to go to Southern California for a few games and enjoy the sun. Before long the weather, the Hollywood atmosphere, and the beautiful women all added up to a Lakers home-court advantage.

RED KERR: "It was like a vacation for us, coming out of Syracuse, Boston, snow up to your ass and everything. You go out there and you gotta buy some sunglasses. Movie stars. That was their home-court advantage. It was just that you forgot you were there on business. You'd go out and you'd play them twice, maybe on a Tuesday and a Thursday. So you're out there for three, four days, and you'd just forget that you were there on business. We used to stay with a guy named Pidge Burick. He used to take guys out to the clubs. It was absolutely great. We'd always head down to San Pedro, great wine and food. We're out screwin' around and the Lakers were over at their place practicing."

For the Lakers, 1961–62 was one of those golden, fun-loving seasons in which almost everything seemed to go right. Their only real setback during the regular season even had its advantages. After opening the season on another scoring tear, Baylor was called into reserve duty with the army near Fort Lewis, Washington. As a result, he was able to appear in only 48 regular-season games. He made the lineup mostly on weekends or with an occasional pass, and when he did, he was fresh, ready, and virtually unstoppable. His 38.2 scoring average was second only to that of the prodigious Chamberlain.

When Baylor wasn't there, West had to carry the load, which pushed him to do more with his game. Early in his career, West was less secure in his abilities and often deferred to Baylor on offense. Like many great athletes, West was high-strung, sensitive, and somewhat temperamental, Schaus said.

JERRY WEST: "I didn't feel I was competent enough to be consistent. I would have outlandish scoring games, but maybe the rest of my performance would not be what it should. That was when I would defer more to other players on our team, to Elgin, because of his greatness. I didn't view myself as being in that category, even though I had started to make inroads into being a real good player."

But as his confidence grew, West began demanding the ball in the closing seconds with the game on the line.

JERRY WEST: "I always thought that if we needed a basket, I could score. I didn't care who was guarding or what the defense was."

Noticing this late-game trend, Chick Hearn came up with a new name for the second-year guard: "Mr. Clutch." West didn't complain. He scored better than 30 points over the first four games of the season and went on to average 31. Hidden behind those numbers was West's defense.

JOHN RADCLIFFE: "We didn't keep steals in those days. But if we had, Jerry probably would have led the league. He used to take the ball away from everybody. He knew how to time it just perfectly, taking it down low off the floor."

Against the Knicks on January 17, 1962, West hit for 63, his career single-game high, by making 22 of 36 shots from the field.

JERRY WEST: "I had nights where you just couldn't guard me. I was making them from everywhere. If I made it from the outside, it was an impossible task for the defensive player to guard me. Quickness and the ability to draw fouls is an art. There are people who have great quickness who don't know how to draw fouls."

JOHN RADCLIFFE: "It seemed Jerry could always get a shot. All he had to do was have the defender moving. Then he could get his shot off. It was a flat one. That's how he shot the ball back then. Flat. You could hang your clothes on the line."

JERRY WEST: "I wasn't a point counter. One time I scored sixty-some against the Knicks. Either 61 or 62, I'm not sure. I only played 39 minutes in that game. I wasn't even a real solid basketball player at the time. There were things I could not do. But I had that huge night."

The game, though, revealed that the Lakers still weren't an everyday item in L.A. Only 2,766 fans saw the game at the Sports Arena. Still, the team's second star had come into his own. In that regard, the Lakers' looseness made them the perfect team for West, particularly in 1962.

JERRY WEST: "The players then were closer. There was no reason to be jealous of anyone. No one was making any kind of money at all. Nothing like it is today. The money was so minute, and every day you didn't know if you were going to be there. There was no players' association, nothing to protect your rights as a player. You played for what those guys wanted you to play for. Period."

ELGIN BAYLOR: "It was an enjoyable year. Our camaraderie was great. On and off the court, we did things together. As a team, we gave the effort every night."

Even if you were a bit uptight, it was hard not to enjoy time with the likes of the wisecracking Hundley, Tommy Hawkins, veteran guard Dick "Skull" Barnett, and forward Rudy LaRusso.

JOHN RADCLIFFE: "Dick Barnett was 'Fall back, baby!' That's what he said after his shots. He'd shout it out and hold up his follow-through a little extra long. He was the only person in the NBA over six-four who couldn't stuff. Dick had some hang time, but he couldn't dunk."

Known in Boston as "Roughhouse Rudy" (courtesy of Celtics radioman Johnny Most), the six-foot-eight, 220-pound LaRusso had developed into a tough-minded forward, able to rebound in traffic and hit his jumper from the key. He was a Dartmouth graduate, yet nothing about him suggested Ivy League.

RED KERR: "Rudy was good. He was a defensive player. He was the banger on the team. A guy you didn't respect sometimes during the game, a guy who did the dirty work for them. When it was all over, you'd say, 'You know, that guy killed us.' He was a hard worker, very much a background player."

ROD HUNDLEY: "One time in the Detroit airport, Rudy pulled this stuffed tiger off the shelf in the gift shop and started wrestling it. He fell down on the floor and was rolling around. We were crying we laughed so hard. Rudy was a crazy man. When we went back up there on another trip, he figured it was time for a rematch with that tiger."

JERRY WEST: "Back then, you almost felt like you were a traveling freak show. You traveled with five people getting into a cab. Nothing was first class. Some the hotels we stayed in were embarrassing. There were probably more characters associated with basketball because of the way you traveled. You had to do things to keep it lighthearted. It was hard."

Schaus kept this chemistry going by rotating the road rooming schedule without regard to race, which would not even be a consideration in the modern game but was a factor in the '60s.

Even with Baylor's intermittent schedule, they won the Western Division with a 54–26 record, 11 games better than Cincinnati, and whipped Detroit 4–2 in the division Finals series. For the league championship, they faced the Celtics and fire-breathing center Bill Russell, winners of four titles in five years. To match him, the Lakers had their usual solution, six-foot-eight Jimmy Krebs and six-eleven Ray Felix. Krebs could score but didn't like to work in the post. A former rookie of the year, Felix could muscle around and do a little rebounding.

ROD HUNDLEY: "In one game, Ray took four shots and Bill Russell blocked all four. Finally, Ray backed in and tried to surprise Russell by flipping a shot over his shoulder. The ball went up over the backboard. Ray pointed at Bill and said, 'You didn't get that one, baby!' Bill looked at him like, 'You're crazy, Ray.' Ray was a little nutty. He had strange habits. Like he'd eat his dessert first. We called him Baby Ray, because he called everybody Baby."

FRED SCHAUS: "Krebs was effective against the Celtics because he was a perimeter pivot man. When we sent him outside to shoot, he brought Russell away from the basket."

With Russell unable to hang in the lane, the Lakers worked their offense and sometimes got decent shots. Boston defeated Philadelphia and Chamberlain in the Eastern Finals, drawing a sigh of relief in Los Angeles.

FRED SCHAUS: "In all honesty, we had no post game. We couldn't stop Chamberlain on offense. He was too dominant. Russell was dominant on defense. But he didn't present the same problems that Wilt did. We survived on what West and Baylor did. They were fearless. Both West and Baylor had fantastic playoffs."

The Celtics won big to open the series in the Garden, 122–108. But the Lakers broke back the next night with a 129–122 upset. A record crowd of 15,180 packed the Sports Arena for Game 3 on April 10. In the closing seconds, the Lakers were down 115–111 when West scored four points to tie it. Then Boston's Sam Jones tried to inbound the ball to Bob Cousy with four seconds remaining. West stole it and drove 30 feet for the winning layup, 117–115. Boston coach Red Auerbach complained to the refs that it was impossible for West to dribble the distance to score with only four seconds left. The Lakers bench had feared as much. Everyone there shouted for West to pull up and shoot. But he kept digging for the goal and laid the ball in as the buzzer sounded.

JERRY WEST: "I had deflected the ball on the run. I knew I would have enough time. Most things in my life have been instinctive. I played basketball that way. I always knew what the clock was."

The crowd erupted into celebration with the play, but the Celtics promptly killed any thoughts of prolonged jubilation in L.A. by taking Game 4, 115–103. They headed back to Boston with the series tied at two. There, it was all Baylor. Despite fouling out, he scored 61 points (the record for an NBA Finals game) and had 22 rebounds, while the Celtics' defensive specialist, Satch Sanders, contemplated another line of work. "Elgin was just a machine," Sanders said later. Boston attempted to double-team him, but Baylor passed the ball too well for that to work. He carried the Lakers in that crucial fifth game, 126–121.

JERRY WEST: "It was one of those nights where his every effort seemed to guide him to just the right spot on the floor. He had that wonderful, magical instinct for making plays and doing things that you had to just stop and watch. I hear people talking about forwards today. I don't see many that can compare to him. He wasn't unconscious that night. He just could do those things. It's like when everything is perfect. You wake up in the morning and you feel so good. Your day just goes perfect, not an upset along the way. Your instincts to play the game are one thing. But your instincts to be in the right place are greater than the average player."

ELGIN BAYLOR: "All I remember is that we won the game. I never thought about how many points I had."

From the high of that Game 5 win in Boston, the Lakers headed home with a 3–2 lead and a real opportunity to win the title. The Celtics, though, again doused the jubilation in Los Angeles by tying the series with a 119–105 win in the Sports Arena.

On Wednesday night, April 16, they faced each other in Game 7 in Boston. The Celtics took a 53–47 lead at the half, despite the fact that Sam Jones was only 1 of 10 from the floor. The Lakers knew that a prodigious night from Baylor had delivered them earlier, and to win, they would have to have another. He took 18 shots in the first half and made 8.

The Celtics maintained their lead through most of the third and were ahead 73–67 heading into the period's final minute. But West then scored seven in a row to help tie the game at 75, setting up a fourth quarter that would haunt the Lakers for decades.

The Celtics first rushed up by six, then fell back into a tie at 88 with six minutes left. Then Boston went back up by three again. Then the Celtics' Tommy Heinsohn fouled out, joining Satch Sanders and Jim Loscutoff, all of whom had gone down trying to stop Baylor, who already had 38.

But Russell scored on a stickback seconds after that, and Boston breathed a bit at 96–91, which was a mistake. West canned a jumper, and Baylor hit one of two free throws. 96–94. Boston then added two Russell free throws, and West answered with another jumper. 98–96. Then Sam Jones blocked Laker guard Frank Selvy's shot and hit two free throws at the other end. 100–96. LaRusso picked up an offensive foul with a minute to go, and the Lakers seemed doomed.

Selvy, though, saved them momentarily by getting a rebound and driving the length of the floor for a layup. Seconds later, he repeated the act, driving the length of the floor, missing the shot, then getting the rebound and scoring to tie the game at 100.

The Celtics got the ball back with 18 seconds left. Ramsey tried a driving hook shot in traffic and missed. LaRusso clutched the rebound, and the Lakers had a shot to win it. Schaus called time-out with five seconds to go.

ROD HUNDLEY: "Schaus set up Elgin as the first option, and Jerry was the second. If that failed, he said to get it to whoever else was open. I was in the game to handle the ball. In practice the day before, I fantasized that I made the winning bucket, a set shot. Once I got the ball, I moved right where I dreamed I would have the ball. Jerry and Elgin were covered but Selvy was open on the left baseline."

Cousy, who was guarding him, had gambled for a quick double-team on West.

ROD HUNDLEY: "I passed it to Selvy, and Cousy rushed back over to cover him. He got an open shot. It was an eight-footer, the kind that Selvy always made."

It hit the rim and fell away, to be known forever as the shot that could have ended Boston's dynasty and the Lakers' agony before it ever began. "I would trade all my points for that last basket," Selvy told reporters afterward. "It was a fairly tough shot. I was almost on the baseline."

The ball came off the rim, and Russell, who would finish with 30 points and 40 rebounds, wrapped it in his arms for overtime. The Celtics escaped with their fourth straight title in the extra period as they built a five-point lead and won, 110–107. The Lakers could only think of what could have been.

JERRY WEST: "The major lesson was that you have to play every minute of a championship series. That was the first time I ever felt that maybe good fortune was not on our side. Of all the ones we played, even though we didn't deserve to win that one—they were better than we were—good fortune almost let us win that one. It kept us close but it didn't let us win it."

ELGIN BAYLOR: "Selvy thought Bob Cousy fouled him. I thought Cousy fouled him. He took the shot from a spot where he was very proficient. Cousy said he never fouled him. I was in a position to get the offensive rebound. But somebody behind me shoved me out-of-bounds right into the referee. There was no foul call there, either. I looked around and saw Russell and Sam Jones were behind me. Some years later I got a copy of the game film. It was just what I suspected. Sam Jones had shoved me out-of-bounds. He still smiles about that."

JERRY WEST: "There's been a lot of publicity about Selvy missing the shot. But he made a couple of baskets to get us there. I never really talked to Frank about that. Then again there was no tendency to blame people for things. Frank Selvy happened to miss the shot that we could have won a championship with. I think there's been too much said there in a negative way. There should be more positive. We were real fortunate to get there."

ROD HUNDLEY: "It was tough in the locker room. I was wishing I had taken the shot just like I had dreamed. Selvy felt really bad. He was sitting there with his head hanging down. I told him, 'Don't worry. You only cost us about $30,000, you bastard.'"

"That's all right, baby," Ray Felix told them. "We'll get 'em tomorrow." Tomorrow, of course, never quite came for those '60s Lakers. Or for Ray Felix. They released him after the season and employed two 6-foot-10 rookies, Leroy Ellis and Gene Wiley, to share time in the post.

By the 1963 season, Hot Rod Hundley's partying caught up with his basketball. His skills declined to the point that he became an end-of-game show.

MITCH CHORTKOFF: "If they were way ahead or far behind, Schaus would put Hot Rod in to entertain the fans with his clowning and dribbling. When they won, Hot Rod was the sign that the game was over, like Red Auerbach lighting up his victory cigar."

ROD HUNDLEY: "I'd pull up beside Doris Day where she was sitting at courtside. I'd wink at her and tell her, 'This one's for you, baby.' Then I'd shoot a 30-foot hook. She was gorgeous."

And the fans loved it. Opposing teams, however, weren't so amused, particularly if Hundley worked his act on their home floor.

RED KERR: "Rod had more than a little showboat in him. Cousy would go behind his back and make this great pass and do a lot of stuff. But it wasn't showboat. It was innovative, before anyone else had done it. Hot Rod got to the Lakers, and he was Broadway. He was Showtime before they had Showtime. I remember we played against the Lakers one time and he was doing a couple of things like that. My best friend and roommate, Al Bianchi, was guarding Rod, and Rod came by him and went behind his back with the ball. And Al just knocked him on his ass, stood over him and said, 'I fouled him.' Going behind the back in those days was greeted about like a dunk. We dunked some, but if you did, guys asked, 'What are you doing? You're really showing off, aren't you?' Today, the NBA has packaged these things to be part of the high-wire act. But people didn't like it if Rod showed off too much."

St. Louis Hawks coach Harry "the Horse" Gallatin hated the clown game.

ROD HUNDLEY: "One night I told Harry, 'Don't get too far behind tonight or it'll be Showtime.'"

RED KERR: "Rod was the only guy who came into the league making $10,000 and left making $10,000. The Lakers had made a huge trade to get Rod as their number one draft pick. They had traded Clyde Lovellette. It was a blockbuster."

FRED SCHAUS: "There's no question that if Rod had worked harder, he would have had a more productive NBA career. But he grew up under difficult circumstances. Considering that, he accomplished quite a bit."

With his lust for partying, Hundley saw his skills decline to the point that he retired from the NBA at age 27.

Celtics Blues

The Lakers perhaps didn't realize it at the time, but the 1962 playoffs were just one of the early steps in their shared history with the Celtics. They faced a decade of torment from Bill Russell's blocked shots and Red Auerbach's lit cigars.

There was some hope in that Bob Cousy announced that he would retire after the 1962–63 season. The previous spring, Boston had drafted John Havlicek out of Ohio State. Havlicek was just one of several changing faces in the team's evolution. Later Auerbach would get Don Nelson and Bailey Howell and several more key pieces to the puzzle. Plus Cousy's leaving meant the Jones duo of K.C. and Sam would become a larger factor. Most important, though, was Russell.

FRED SCHAUS: "Russell is the most dominant individual who ever played a team sport."

AL CERVI, FORMER SYRACUSE COACH: "Having Bill Russell made Auerbach a coach. He's the biggest phony who ever walked the streets of America."

PAUL SEYMOUR, FORMER NBA PLAYER AND COACH: "Red was hated around the league. He always had the talent. He was always shooting his mouth off. If you walked up to him in the old days, he was more than likely to tell you to get lost."

FRED SCHAUS: "Red was a very astute judge of talent. When you have a lot of stars, you have to keep them happy and playing as a team. Red did that. I didn't like some of the things he did and said when I competed against him. But the guy who wore Number 6 out there bothered us more. You had to change your complete game because of Russell."

JERRY WEST: "Red was outspoken. His sideline antics were funny. I happened to like him very much. When you talk to his ex-players, they all have great respect for him. I don't know how many players would tell you that about their former coaches."

RED AUERBACH: "Anytime you're winning, you get criticism. Nothing instigates jealousy like winning. When you're winning, they look for a thousand reasons for taking potshots. You don't pay attention. You just keep doing what you're doing."

Boston again claimed the Eastern Division with a 58–22 record in 1963, then faced Oscar Robertson and the Cincinnati Royals in a seven-game shakedown in the Eastern Finals. They survived a Game 7 shootout in Boston Garden, 142–131.

The Lakers beat St. Louis in a seven-game Western final. West had been out with an injury for seven weeks at the close of the season, and although he was back in the lineup for the playoffs, the team still hadn't worked out all the kinks by the time it faced Boston for the championship.

Auerbach allowed that his team was tired and ripe for plucking, but Boston still eased by Game 1 in the Garden, 117–114. Game 2 wasn't much different. The Celtics took a 2–0 series lead, 113–106.

Back at their Sports Arena, the Lakers retaliated with a blowout, 119–99, only to see the Celtics take firm command by sneaking away with Game 4, 108–105. Up 3–1, Auerbach was as confident as ever. "We've never lost three games in a row," he told reporters.

The Lakers headed back to Boston and found the stuff to survive. Tommy Heinsohn was ejected, Cousy fouled out with 12 points, and the L.A. duo went wild. Baylor had 43, West 32, as L.A. pulled to 3–2, 126–119.

The loss fueled speculation that the Celtics had run out of gas, and that the younger Lakers were about to surge ahead. In L.A., a throng estimated at more than 5,000 converged on the Sports Arena hoping to buy playoff tickets. When they found there were none, the scene turned angry. The Lakers quickly calmed things by offering closed-circuit TV seats at $2.50 a head. By Game 6, more than 6,000 such theater seats had been taken, to go along with the 15,000 arena sellout. "We were aware we were testing the future of pay television," Lou Mohs told reporters.

The crowd saw Bill Russell dominate Game 6. He made rebounds a scarce commodity. And Havlicek had the hot hand, scoring 11 straight points to put Boston up by 14 at the half. The lead had dipped to nine with 11 minutes left in the fourth period when Cousy tripped and sprained his left ankle. He didn't return until the five-minute mark. By then, the Lakers had cut the Boston lead to one. At 2:48, the Celtics were holding on, 104–102. Then Heinsohn stole a West pass, drove and scored. From there, Cousy worked the clock as he had in the old days. He dribbled out the last seconds of his career and threw the ball high into the rafters of the space-age arena. Then he and Auerbach hugged as the final touch on a 112–109 win.

TOMMY HEINSOHN, FORMER CELTIC: "The Lakers never seemed to be able to muster a center to even come close to matching up with Bill Russell. And of course we had a great team and they had two great, great players. That was the measure of why that rivalry went that way all the time. Because these two guys, Baylor and West, they're still at the top of my all-time list, the starting five. Elgin Baylor as forward beats out Bird, Julius Erving, and everybody else. A lot of people don't remember him, but he had the total game—defense, offense, everything, rebounding, passing the ball. And Jerry West played what you call the 2 guard now, and he was tough. West was what I call a freak. He had these long arms, and if you tried to match up with him and bring size into the situation, he would out-quick that guy. And if you matched up speed against West, West would shoot over that defender."

Looking High

The idea of finding a center to counter Russell drove Lou Mohs to the brink of excess.

Mitch Chortkoff: "I never saw anybody work so hard all day. Then he would fly to Texas or somewhere to scout a game and be back in the morning in Los Angeles to work."

Marty Blake: "He looked like he always slept in his clothes. He was crazy. He used to work until late at night, then get on a plane and go scouting. It eventually killed him."

After searching high and low, Mohs finally found his center, Willis Reed of Grambling, in the spring of 1964. Blake, then the Hawks' general manager, knew that the Lakers were about to take Reed with their first draft pick.

Marty Blake: "I faked Louie Mohs out. Louie was gonna take Willis Reed, so to keep the Lakers from taking him I came out with a story that the Hawks were going to take Walt Hazzard of UCLA. That forced Louie to use his territorial rights to take Hazzard with the first pick. But then we didn't take Willis because at the last minute Harry Gallatin [the St. Louis coach] didn't think he was good enough. Talk about irony for the Lakers, the Knicks took Willis with the first pick of the second round, and Gallatin wound up coaching him in New York. You get even more irony when you consider that after Bill Russell retired it was Reed who led the Knicks over the Lakers for the title in 1970."

Even worse, Bob Short sold the Lakers and never gave Mohs a bonus for working so hard to build the team, Blake said. Blake himself got a $100,000 bonus when Ben Kerner sold the Hawks to Atlanta investors in 1967. Mohs died just months after retiring from the Lakers that same year.

Marty Blake: "All Bob Short did was cash the money. Louie never got a dime of it."

The Lakers fell to 42–38 for 1964 and were eliminated by St. Louis in the first round of the playoffs. With Wiley and Ellis maturing, they came back strong for 1964–65 and reclaimed the Western Division title with a 49–31 record. But Baylor suffered a severe knee injury on April 3 in the first game of the Western Division Finals against the Baltimore Bullets.

Elgin Baylor: "I went up for a shot, and my knee exploded. I could hear a crack and a pop and everything else."

West and LaRusso were left alone to lead L.A. They got help from their teammates, but it was impossible to replace Baylor. Gone were Selvy, Hundley, and Krebs, who was killed in May 1965 in a freak tree-cutting accident. Wiley and Ellis moved into the starting frontcourt together, and the Lakers also got 14 points per game out of guard Dick Barnett. Jim King, a second-year guard out of Tulsa, rounded out the backcourt. Also filling out the roster were Don Nelson, Darrell Imhoff, and Walt Hazzard.

With Baylor out, the load fell on West, who responded by averaging 40.6 points over 10 playoff games. In fact, over the six-game Western Conference playoff series with the Bullets, West averaged 46.3 points per game, a record that has withstood the test of even Michael Jordan's best. In one game against Baltimore, he scored 52 as Bullet guard Kevin Loughery struggled to stop him.

Kevin Loughery, former Baltimore Bullet: "I had to guard him when he averaged about 50 a game in the playoffs. I hated to guard him because of his quickness. I'd rather guard Oscar Robertson, because Oscar just backed you down and beat you with strength. But Jerry embarrassed you. He was just so quick, one of the quickest guys for that size who ever played the game. In the old days, different from today, we didn't have help defense. You were on your own. You were out there on a little island by yourself playing great players. That was a tough assignment because he was one of the first players that had tremendous, tremendous quickness but also could take the ball over the rim. Plus he was a great defensive player."

West's heroics proved good enough to take the Lakers back to the Finals for yet another meeting with the Celtics. But with Baylor out, Boston waltzed through Game 1 in Boston 142–110, as K. C. Jones held West to 26 points.

FRED SCHAUS: "K. C. Jones used to tackle West rather than let him get off a jump shot."

K. C. JONES, FORMER CELTIC GUARD: "You're guarding Jerry West. Here's a guy who can shoot the ball *and* drive to the basket. He's gonna have the ball 15 seconds of any 24-second period. There's pressure in that. So then he hits a couple on me from outside. I say, 'Uh-oh.' So I get up on him and he drives by me. So now I get scared. And every guy playing defense gets scared, but it depends on how long it took you to come out of it. With West, I had to come out of it in a hurry."

JERRY WEST: "K.C. was aggressive, quick. Great lateral quickness, and on top of it he had real quick hands. He fouled a lot. The great thing he did was that he tried to get you to take shots in areas where you were not used to taking them. At that time in my career, I had just started to develop an ability to take the ball to the basket, particularly to my left. And the one thing he would do would sort of funnel you to Bill Russell. As I went along, I had a lot better success against him, because I learned how to handle the ball and go to my left a lot better. It was an adjustment, a growing adjustment in meaningful games. I think that's the one thing I was able to do best. I was able to improve my game in a different phase year after year. And that's what helped me."

K. C. JONES: "West would go up for the jumper, and I'd charge him. Then, he might give a head and shoulders fake—he was amazingly quick—and I'd go after him, from the side. Then another time, I'd be 10 feet away from him. I'd approach slightly differently, and jump straight up in the air. It seems impossible, but the anxiety we had created by our constant pressure made him waver and sometimes I'd block the shot."

West didn't waver in Game 2. He scored 45, but Boston still controlled the outcome, 129–123. Wounded as they were, the Lakers managed a home win in Game 3, 126–105, as West hit for 43 and Ellis 29. The L.A. crowd celebrated by pelting Auerbach with cigars. Game 4, though, was another Celtics win, 112–99, as Sam Jones scored 37. They went back to Boston to end it,

129–96, as the Celtics outscored the Lakers 72–48 in the second half. At the outset of the fourth period, Boston ran off 20 unanswered points, while the Lakers went scoreless for five minutes. At one stretch, West, now thoroughly exhausted, missed 14 out of 15 shots.

Merv Harris: "Jerry just carried that team out of sheer will. By the fifth game of the Finals, he was just a bundle of raw nerves, a wreck."

Cashing In

For Frank Ryan and Bob Short, the championship loss hardly mattered. Now the sole owners, they had hit the jackpot. The team had turned a whopping $500,000 profit for the 1964–65 season. Suddenly they had leverage to strike new deals, the biggest being a proposed merger between the Dodgers and Lakers, with Short and Ryan owning 20 percent of the new sports conglomerate. But that deal was delayed while Dodgers president Walter O'Malley negotiated a broadcast deal for his club, and in the interim Jack Kent Cooke, a Canadian millionaire living in Pebble Beach, inquired about buying the Lakers. Cooke owned a minor-league baseball team in Canada and one-fourth of the Washington Redskins.

Jack Kent Cooke: "I had never heard of the Lakers or even seen a pro basketball game when one of my investment advisers suggested I purchase the team. The more I looked into them, the more I liked them."

At first Short declared the team wasn't for sale, until his financial advisers suggested that he at least hear Cooke's offer. The Boston Celtics had recently sold for $3 million, so Short reached for something excessive.

Jack Kent Cooke: "He said he wanted $5 million for the Lakers. I asked to see a profit and loss statement and told him I'd think about it. The P&L Short gave me was just thrown together. I couldn't make any sense of it. I wanted to own a sports team, so I agreed to his price. That's when he realized he hadn't asked enough. So he came up with the fact that he'd already sold $350,000 in advance tickets for the next season. He told me he wanted half of that amount. I told him he was holding me up, but I wanted the Lakers, so I agreed to it."

Then Frank Ryan came up with one final request. They wanted cash.

FRANK RYAN: "Walter O'Malley had given his blessing to the deal, but he warned me that Cooke was a tough, smart businessman, to be careful. Walter said we should make him pay cash. We made him put the cash on the cart. His lawyer told us it was outrageous, but I insisted on it."

Bank guards rolled the $5.175 million on a cart through a tunnel under New York's streets from one bank to another.

FRANK RYAN: "It took 12 bank vice presidents to count the money. Once they finished, we took a certified check from the second bank and headed on our merry way. When we got out on the street we saw a newspaper headline that said the NFL was challenging Cooke's right to buy the Lakers."

The NFL had a rule forbidding owners from holding other sports franchises. With O'Malley's warning, Ryan and Short suspected that Cooke might use the NFL's rule to force a last-minute cut rate on the deal.

FRANK RYAN: "I figured it would have cost us a million bucks to fight the thing in court."

But now the issue was moot for Short and Ryan. They had taken the money and run.

Fabulous, Absolutely Fabulous

It didn't take Jack Kent Cooke long to put his personal stamp on the Los Angeles Lakers. A brusque, efficient executive, he immediately set out over the summer of 1965 to transform the team from a small, haphazardly run venture into a sound business. While the Watts riots jarred L.A. and the country that August, Cooke charged into the task of transforming the Lakers with a flurry of memos and acerbic reminders to employees. Nothing escaped his view, from an occasional Chick Hearn mispronunciation to a receptionist's tardiness in answering the front office phones. If the memos didn't get the job done, Jack Kent Cooke tended to shout. This approach quickly divided his followers into two camps: those who loathed him and those who liked him. Sort of.

ROD HUNDLEY, FORMER LAKERS PLAYER AND BROADCASTER: "He was the number one asshole that ever lived. He was totally, absolutely, unbelievably wrapped up in himself and had no respect for anyone but himself."

JOHN RADCLIFFE, LONGTIME LAKERS STATISTICIAN: "Mr. Cooke brought immediate change to the atmosphere around the team. Everybody was on eggshells. We were afraid to make a mistake, because we were gonna get yelled at. He yelled at Fred Schaus, too. It was his style. He didn't hold anything back. He always seemed to imply that people weren't bright."

BILL BERTKA, LONGTIME LAKERS SCOUT AND ASSISTANT COACH: "Mr. Cooke shouted and screamed at anyone who didn't give him perfection. He was interested in the bottom line, in success, in winning. That's all he wanted."

JERRY WEST: "He was a different kind of owner. Completely. At first it was tremendous. Jack Cooke was a much more dynamic man in the sense that he wasn't an absentee owner. An absentee owner like Bob Short has a hard time really looking at what he has there, except for what it does financially."

MERV HARRIS, LONGTIME LAKERS BEAT WRITER: "The Lakers had been a mom-and-pop organization until Cooke arrived. Pro basketball was getting bigger in the mid '60s, and Cooke was the kind of guy to help it get bigger. He was a very complex man. He could be extremely charming, extremely unreasonable, extremely cold."

BILL BERTKA: "He made every conversation a chess match. Mr. Cooke invited me over to his house for a breakfast meeting. When I got there, he came to the door in his bathrobe. As we went inside, he asked me, 'Do you want a cup of coffee?' I told him, 'That would be nice.' 'Bill,' he said, 'I didn't ask you if it would be nice. Do you want a cup of coffee?' It didn't matter what discussion you had with him; he was going to put you on the defensive. That was his tactic on everything."

PETE NEWELL, WHO BECAME LAKERS GENERAL MANAGER IN 1972: "I knew he could be demanding, even irritating, but his demands that we have business discipline were quite useful. Jack required Lakers employees to record the time and subject of every phone call. When it came to the work of a general manager, I found that I had a solid record of every conversation, and I used that to remind other GMs when they made promises or trade offers. Jack was a hands-on owner. He was a workaholic. If you worked for him you were like a doctor. You were on call 24 hours a day, because Jack was on call 24 hours a day. He'd be there at his desk promptly at nine every morning. And he'd require the team staff to be there as well, not a minute late. I'm not saying he got a buggy whip, where he was gonna beat you if you were two minutes late. But the precision he demanded was good for a basketball team."

There were exceptions to his exactness. Cooke could let an employee's honest $50,000 mistake go by without comment, then explode over mere pocket change.

PETE NEWELL: "On big issues, he was at his best. He never seemed to panic."

Because he knew business and possessed a flair for marketing and promotions, Cooke concentrated there in his first months with the team. Eventually, however, his voracious appetite for learning turned to the game itself. In time, Cooke would believe that he understood basketball, a misperception that soon rested at the heart of the Lakers' troubles.

JERRY WEST: "He thought he knew. He didn't know."

ROBERT "JAKE" EMBRY, FORMER OWNER OF THE OLD BALTIMORE BULLETS: "Jack Kent Cooke was a salesman. He was a pretty good one."

In his youth, Cooke was a saxophonist and bandleader in Ontario. He also peddled soap and encyclopedias and went to work in 1937 for Lord Thomson of Fleet, the British media magnate who owned numerous properties in Canada. Lord Thomson saw Cooke's sales and management skills and sent him to rescue a struggling radio station. Within six months Cooke had turned the business around, prompting Lord Thomson to reward him with one-third ownership of the station. From that, their relationship grew into Thomson Cooke Publishing and Broadcasting Limited, the media business they operated until 1952, when Lord Thomson left Canada for England and Cooke set up shop in California.

By 1965, Cooke was a magnate himself, engaged in a "retirement" life of buying and selling businesses, with a penchant for sports franchises. Just before purchasing the Lakers, he had attempted to gain the rights to an American League expansion team in Southern California but lost out to Gene Autry.

After acquiring the Lakers, Cooke turned his focus on a National Hockey League franchise for L.A. To get that, he had to have a place to play. But the commission for the city-owned Sports Arena turned back his attempts to secure an agreement there. The Blades, a minor-league hockey team, already played in the building, and Dan Reeves, their owner, hoped to secure the NHL franchise ahead of Cooke. The commission debate went back and forth until Cooke grew frustrated.

JACK KENT COOKE: "Ernest Debs was the chairman of the commission. I told him, 'Look, if you keep this up you're going to force me to build my own building.' Debs smirked and said, 'Har, har, har.' He didn't laugh. He said the words 'Har, har, har.' I told my lawyers, 'Let's depart from this den of iniquity.'"

They did, and proceeded directly to an architect's office. Never mind that it had been three decades since a privately funded arena had been built in America. Cooke was determined to build his own, a structure worthy of the ancient Romans.

JACK KENT COOKE: "I retained Charles Luckman Associates, who had recently designed the new Madison Square Garden. Within weeks, Luckman presented me with a variety of drawings. I told him I didn't like any of them. 'Well, what do you like?' he asked me. I said, 'Something about 2,000 years ago and 6,000 miles east of here.' Luckman asked what I meant, and I looked over to where Richard Niblack, Luckman's designer, was drawing a column. I wasn't even sure what kind of column it was. I just knew I wanted them to ring the building."

He wanted the place built to last. And he never ever wanted it referred to as an arena. He wanted to call it the Forum. Chick Hearn thought that was a fabulous name.

The Celtics Again

The doctors told Elgin Baylor that his knee injury had ended his playing career, and for a time he believed them.

ELGIN BAYLOR: "The main ligament in my knee had been damaged, and my kneecap was split, almost in half. When it first happened, I was worried that I'd even walk again."

CHICK HEARN: "It ended his career basically. It happened in the first game of a playoff against Baltimore. They had a team at that time [and typical of that era, Baltimore played in the Western Conference]. Elg went up, just leaped for a ball. Snapped the kneecap, the patella, I think they call it. It was never the same after that."

After a time, the pain subsided, and Baylor found he had some mobility.

ELGIN BAYLOR: "The more I thought about it, the more determined I became to prove the doctors wrong."

JERRY WEST: "Afterward to watch the slow, painful process of him getting better and improving and never really getting back to where he was, that was the thing that was difficult for the rest of us to accept. We wanted him back having all his greatness. He came back and played, and played incredibly well. But he wasn't the Elgin Baylor of old."

By training camp that next fall, Baylor was able to see limited action. Before, Baylor had dazzled opponents with a fearless approach to driving and rebounding. After the injury, that part of his game diminished.

ELGIN BAYLOR: "It was very, very difficult. I would try to do a lot of things that I just couldn't do. It was frustrating. But it made me more determined, too. Before I was injured, I loved to penetrate and create, to pass off or take the shot. At times after I returned, I just couldn't do it. My knee wouldn't respond. I couldn't rebound as well. It just wasn't there. I just couldn't run the same. I had to rely more on perimeter shooting and posting up occasionally."

He played in 65 games the following season, 1965–66, and averaged 16.6 points. West scored at a 31.3 clip and became the top option in the Lakers' offense. But Baylor's mere presence made them stronger. And he and West remained very much the ultimate superstar duo.

For 1965–66, the Lakers had also picked up excellent guards from John Wooden's first national championship teams at UCLA. Walt Hazzard came in the 1964 draft and Gail Goodrich arrived a year later.

JERRY WEST: "Great college guards, both of them. Gail went on to have a better pro career than Walt. In Walt's case, getting drafted by the Lakers did him a disservice in some respects. At another place, he would have gotten the opportunity to play."

With the young guards on the payroll, the Lakers opted to ship veteran Dick Barnett to New York for forward Bill Bridges, who would be lost to the Chicago Bulls in the expansion draft less than a year later. The net of those moves left the Lakers short on experienced guards.

JERRY WEST: "I always thought Dick Barnett was a very underrated player. Defensively, he never got his just due. He had a reputation for scorer, for being a character, but he was a very good defensive player. He got traded in a move that was not very popular among the players."

Even with the changes, the Lakers won the Western with a 45–35 record and eliminated the Hawks in a seven-game conference final series. Once again, the issue fell to contending with the Celtics for a championship. For 1966, they not only faced a deficit in the post but in the backcourt as well.

JERRY WEST: "I love to have great centers. But the most frustrating thing in the world is not to have someone competent playing alongside you as a guard."

MERV HARRIS, FORMER LAKERS BEAT WRITER: "When he first came to the Lakers, West was very quiet, not articulate at all. As he came on as a player, he became more at ease, more articulate. But he still had that West Virginia twang. He was always disgusted with many players in the league who weren't dedicated to the game."

The 1966 championship quickly turned into another Celtics/Lakers scrap. The Celtics had a 38–20 lead in Game 1 in the Garden, but the Lakers fought back to a 133–129 win in overtime. Baylor had scored 36, West 41. But instead of the glory and the psychological edge falling to the Lakers, the attention abruptly shifted to Boston. Auerbach picked the postgame to announce that Russell would be his replacement as head coach. Working as a player/coach, Boston's center would become the first black head coach in a major American sport.

The announcement made headlines the next morning, while the Lakers' upset became a secondary story. Observers would claim it was Red Auerbach's mind game effort to diminish the importance of a big Lakers win in Game 1.

With the future of the team settled, the Celtics bore down on the Lakers, winning the second game in the Garden 129–109, then adding two more victories in L.A. for a 3–1 lead. The major problem for the Lakers was

Boston's John Havlicek, who could swing between guard and forward. Schaus had tried to play LaRusso, a forward, on Havlicek, but it hadn't worked. "No one in the league his size is even close to Havlicek in quickness," Schaus told reporters.

So the Lakers coach used the rookie Goodrich on Havlicek. West moved to forward, and this three-guard lineup left L.A. weak on the boards. But it worked. West, Baylor, and Goodrich lashed back and won Games 5 and 6 to tie the series at three apiece.

Once again, the championship had come to a seventh game in Boston Garden. The Celtics took a big lead as Baylor and West were a combined 3 for 18 from the floor in the first half. As usual, the Lakers cut it close at the end, paring the Boston lead to six with 20 seconds left. Massachusetts governor John Volpe figured it was time to light Auerbach's victory cigar. The Lakers took fire with that, cutting the lead to two, 95–93, with four seconds left.

The fans always rushed the floor to celebrate Boston's championships and chose to do so with time remaining in 1966. Russell was knocked down. Orange juice containers on the Boston bench spilled across the floor, and Boston's Satch Sanders lost his shirt to the crowd. Somehow, K. C. Jones got the inbound pass to Havlicek, who dribbled out the clock for Boston's ninth championship. No one was more angered by the early cigar than Schaus.

FRED SCHAUS: "I would have loved to shove that victory cigar down Red Auerbach's throat. We came awfully close to putting that damn thing out."

Close, of course, but no cigar, as the saying goes. And the following season they weren't even that, finishing 36–45, then capping the season by getting swept by the Warriors, 3–0, in the first round of the playoffs. It was enough to convince Schaus that he needed a break from coaching.

FRED SCHAUS: "It was a good time to let someone else try their hand at it. I moved to the front office."

JERRY WEST: "Most of our players responded very positively to Schaus early on. Obviously, later in their careers, when a coach has been around a few years, they've heard all of his stories. Frankly, it wears out. He did a very competent job with our team. We played hard all the time, and I think that's a tribute to the coach."

Schaus replaced Lou Mohs as general manager and began fielding questions from Cooke about a coaching replacement.

JACK KENT COOKE: "At that time I didn't know a lot of coaches, so I asked Fred Schaus for a list of five suggestions."

FRED SCHAUS: "Mr. Cooke read in *Sports Illustrated* that Butch van Breda Kolff had coached Bill Bradley at Princeton. So he was on the list. Butch interviewed extremely well. Mr. Cooke liked his decisive style."

BILL BERTKA: "Butch was a strong personality. They called him the Dutchman. They also called him bullheaded and stubborn."

Van Breda Kolff brought a major change in style to the Lakers. He stressed conditioning and wanted to get the rest of the team involved in the offense along with West and Baylor. For years, the Lakers had complained that Schaus wanted only West and Baylor taking shots, which meant that no one else had confidence in the clutch.

BILL BERTKA: "When van Breda Kolff came in, he brought an eastern style of play, with all five men moving and everybody sharing the ball."

JERRY WEST: "O Lord, was there ever changes. Not only in style but also in the attitude surrounding the team. There was a volatile person who pretty much said what he thought. He felt that was the way to do it. You cannot do that at the professional level. He was a purist. But on the professional level it won't work."

Schaus, who had been a college coach, had blended his pro experience with the midwestern running game to fashion a pro style for his team. But van Breda Kolff's approach was a profound departure from that, and it took the players half a season to adjust.

Beyond style, he treated his pros like college boys, going so far as to institute a bed check. The only problem was, van Breda Kolff would make the check but wind up visiting with his players, sipping beer in their rooms and talking basketball for hours until they begged him to let them get some sleep.

JERRY WEST: "Some coaches want to win every game. In the NBA, you can't do that. It was difficult for him because it's no fun to lose. As a college coach, he might have lost five games in a season. On the pro level, he might lose five in a row over a two-week period. It's more difficult, because coaches have to be able to handle losses."

Some observers would argue that van Breda Kolff got the Lakers close to success, the only problem being that they already knew that territory far better than they cared to.

The New Digs, the Forum

In December 1968, just 18 months after groundbreaking, Jack Kent Cooke's Forum opened for business. Throughout construction, it had been referred to as "Cooke's Folly," which only steeled the owner's determination to make it a structure that would stick in the Sports Arena Commission's craw for a long, long time. He had looked across L.A. and the San Fernando Valley before settling on a 29-acre site in Inglewood, at the intersections of Manchester Boulevard and Prairie Avenue, next to Hollywood Park. Built about the same time, the Spectrum in Philadelphia cost about $5 million, but Cooke plowed $16 million into his Forum. No expense was spared. Each of the 80 columns supporting the roof stood 57 feet high and weighed 55 tons, so large that they had to be formed on the work site.

On New Year's Eve of 1967, the Lakers played their first game there, blasting the San Diego Rockets, who had a young sub named Pat Riley, 147–118.

JACK KENT COOKE: "I was just so proud. It was a special night."

A press release boasted that his Forum would "be in essence a modern version of the greater Coliseum of ancient Rome." The Roman motif set Cooke's creative juices to flowing. A former bandleader, he wrote fight songs and cheers for both his hockey and basketball teams and authored nicknames for his hockey players, then instructed his broadcasters to use them on air. And he designed uniforms for both hockey and basketball. No longer did the Lakers wear their traditional blue and white. Cooke outfitted them in purple and gold, only he hated the word *purple* and insisted that the team call it Forum blue, which left Chick Hearn advising television viewers not to adjust the color on their sets. In the Forum, the Lakers wore gold, the first time in league history that the home team didn't wear white.

JOHN RADCLIFFE, LAKERS STATISTICIAN: "Mr. Cooke dressed the ushers in togas, with slacks for the men and short pants for the women. The ladies did not like 'em, to say the least. The male staff were issued purple blazers with gold patches, to be worn with white dress shirts and black ties. One night I wore a gold turtleneck with my blazer and the next day I got a memo from Cooke reminding me of proper dress. Rod Hundley looked at my blazer one night and said, 'John, you ought to have that thing cleaned and burned.'"

The new building meant a realignment of celebrity seating. When Doris Day and her husband asked to have their seats moved, Cooke learned that they weren't paying for them. So he informed Day's husband that they would have to start paying, leading Day to decide that she wouldn't be attending any more Lakers games. Cooke didn't care. All of L.A. seemed to want seats, including Walter Matthau and Jack Nicholson, who gladly paid.

Now that he had a new building that drew new fans, all Cooke had to do was make sure he had the kind of team that kept them coming. Van Breda Kolff's Lakers struggled along until January, when they acquired Irwin Mueller and Fred Crawford, who gave them quickness off the bench. They then rolled through a 38–9 run, good enough for a 52–30 finish, second place in the Western behind the Hawks.

BILL BERTKA: "That second half of the season, the team realized van Breda Kolff's vision. They were really a happy bunch. They shared the ball and moved it around."

Guard Archie Clark, from Minnesota, proved to be an incredible find, with quickness, strong defense, and an ability to score. He was one of the few players who could carry the team offensively as West had. And Gail Goodrich, now in his third season, had come into his own.

JOHN RADCLIFFE: "They called Goodrich 'Stumpy.' He was only about six feet, but he had the longest arms in the NBA. He was left-handed and fearless going to the basket. He would disappear into a crowd of big men; then suddenly the ball would kiss off the glass and fall in."

At center was Darrell Imhoff, short on talent but long on willingness to sacrifice. He set scores of picks for Baylor, West, and Clark. From the bench, van Breda Kolff urged this group along with an animation rarely seen in Los Angeles.

JOHN RADCLIFFE: "Butch was just all over the place. It was amazing how he would just throw himself down on the seats. The body language alone was enough to get him technicals."

The "Dutchman" drove his Lakers through the playoffs. They nailed the new Chicago Bulls, 4–1, then swept the Warriors in the Western Finals, which left them eight days of watching the Celtics and 76ers battle in the Eastern Finals. They worked to stay fresh, but practice couldn't approximate the intensity of games. As van Breda Kolff feared, they grew stale with the wait.

The Celtics had finished second in the divisional standings at 54–28, eight games behind the 76ers, who won 62 games. Philly took a 3–1 lead in their playoff series, only to watch the Celtics come back. The Lakers followed the games on television and pulled for Boston, figuring player/coach Russell would be easier to beat than Chamberlain.

Boston did come back to whip Philadelphia, advancing to the championship round for the 11th time in 12 years. Jack Kent Cooke was immensely pleased to have the Finals in his new Forum. The Lakers liked their chances going in. "If we can rebound, we can win," West told the writers. "We're little, but we match up well with Boston. We're quick, and we shoot well, and that can be enough in a seven-game series."

They alternated Mel Counts and Darrell Imhoff in the post, and Mueller's quickness helped out on the boards. Archie Clark joined West in the backcourt, with Goodrich and Crawford coming off the bench. Baylor was still the man in the corner, but Tommy Hawkins had returned to the team to provide depth at forward.

The Lakers had returned to the championship series for the fifth time in seven years with little satisfaction to show for their effort.

JERRY WEST: "I never looked at it as pressure. During the season you didn't worry about things like that. But when the playoffs start you always have your goals and aspirations of winning a championship. We were pretty consistent in getting there."

And always consistent in creating early trouble. The Lakers opened the series with a not-too-surprising split in Boston Garden. They lost the first when West shot 7 for 24 and Baylor 11 for 31. But they pulled their usual surprise and won the second. The Celtics returned the favor when the series switched to L.A., winning Game 3, 127–119. Then West scored 38 points, and Baylor added another 30 as L.A. evened the series with a 118–105 win in Game 4, after van Breda Kolff had been ejected.

West, however, sprained his ankle in the closing minutes, dampening the victory. It appeared serious enough to keep him out of Game 5 back in Boston. He played anyway and scored 35, but it wasn't enough to counter the Celtics, who jumped to a 19-point first quarter lead. By the third quarter, the lead was still 18, but L.A. came back after that, tying the score at 108 in the fourth. The Lakers were down four with less than a minute to play when West stole the ball and found Baylor downcourt for a layup. The Lakers then tied it when Clark got another steal and West scored. In overtime, Russell blocked a Baylor shot and Nelson hit a late free throw to give Boston a 3–2 series lead, 120–117.

Then, just as the series returned to L.A. for Game 6 and the tension turned high, things went terribly awry for the Lakers. It began with the national anthem. Johnny Mathis, the featured vocalist, launched into "God Bless America," then realized his mistake and switched to "The Star-Spangled Banner." The best switch of the day, though, was made by Coach Russell, who moved Sam Jones to forward, where he scored over Goodrich, forcing van Breda Kolff to go with a taller, slower lineup. The Lakers never could get it together defensively. Havlicek scored 40, Bailey Howell 30. The Lakers trailed by 20 at the half and Boston danced to its 10th title. "He is an unbelievable man," West said of Russell afterward. "To be frank, we gave them the championship. We gave them the first game, and we gave them the fifth. But I take nothing from them. There is something there, something special. For instance, twice tonight the ball went on the floor and Siegfried dove for it. He didn't just go for it hard, he dove for it. And they're all that way on the Celtics, and you can't teach it."

BILL SHARMAN: "It got to the point where Jerry hated anything green. Jerry told me, 'I couldn't even wear a green sportcoat or a green shirt for a lot of years.' Green really rubbed him the wrong way."

BAILEY HOWELL, FORMER CELTIC: "We weren't a dominant team. Unless everyone was playing well and together, we couldn't win. We wouldn't have won without every guy on that team."

JERRY WEST: "We never really seemingly had the right mix. I believe in chemistry very, very much. Without chemistry, talented teams can fail. We always were close, but we always were a body or a body with chemistry short. It's not easy to find the right people in this league."

JACK KENT COOKE: "That May, Philadelphia 76ers owner Irving Kosloff phoned me in my Forum office and asked if we would be interested in Wilt Chamberlain. Struggling to speak in measured tones, I said that we certainly would be."

Big Norman

His close friends called him "Big Norman." But to the basketball public, he was "Wilt the Stilt." He disliked that name, of course. He was a person, not a stilt. The name, as much as anything, defined his tenuous relationship with the fans and the writers. After all, he was a giant, and they expected giant things of him. That certainly was no more than he expected of himself. Unfortunately, the task was never up to him alone. Basketball is a five-man game. And that seemed to be the crux of the problem for Wilton Norman Chamberlain.

WILT CHAMBERLAIN: "I felt that I was gifted enough to do some things on the basketball floor. I couldn't do everything I wanted to do, because if that was the case, I'd have won every game."

As big and talented as he was, Chamberlain's career progress had often been frustrated by the presence of Boston's Bill Russell. Where Chamberlain struggled most of his career out of context, Russell always seemed to have the right coach, the right teammates, and they got the right results. On the other hand, Chamberlain's career was a profound contradiction. For him, things were wonderfully easy and terribly difficult, all at the same time. "The world is made up of Davids," he once explained, "and I am Goliath."

BILL RUSSELL: "Wilt was my greatest opponent. It's not even close."

WILT CHAMBERLAIN: "Basketball is a team game, played by positions, played in different times. I was fortunate to come along at time that was great basketball, a different kind of a game, played a little bit more technically. I was a different breed of athlete at that particular time."

JERRY WEST: "The ironic thing about Wilt was that he never seemed to be relaxed and fun. I think after he got out of basketball, he became much more relaxed. Much of it had to do with the fact he was Wilt Chamberlain, and no one pulled for him. I think those things really bothered him all his life. There's no question it was tough to be a giant."

As a 6-foot-11 ninth-grader in Philadelphia, he led his undefeated Overbrook High team against West Catholic High in the finals of the city championship, where a scenario developed that would become miserably familiar to Chamberlain over the years. West Catholic packed four players around him inside, but his teammates couldn't make the open shots. Overbrook lost its only game of the season.

Over the next three years, his teams won 58 games and lost just 3, while Chamberlain averaged 36.9 points (he scored 90 in one game). His junior and senior years provided a study in dominance, with Overbrook claiming consecutive city titles.

The pro scouts knew Chamberlain was ready then, but NBA rules forbade the drafting of a high schooler. So he chose the University of Kansas, where the Jayhawks' offense focused on his towering presence. Which meant that opposing defenses did the same.

DICK HARP, FORMER KANSAS COACH: "That was always the problem when Wilt was playing. The defense was always going to concentrate on him. Teams would rig zone defenses around him with three and four men, making it impossible for him to move, particularly around the basket."

And defenders became quite physical with him.

DICK HARP: "It was difficult for the officials to be objective about Wilt. There were many opportunities for officials to call defensive fouls. Most of the time they didn't. Wilt, though, always managed to keep his composure and managed to power through our opponents."

But, as Chamberlain himself noted, his frustrations led to errors in his method. When he rebounded, he liked to take the ball in one hand and slam it against the other, making a gunshot of a sound that startled the smaller players around him. What he should have been doing was whipping a quick outlet pass downcourt. When he blocked shots, he liked to smack the ball loudly and violently and usually out of play. As a result, opponents retained the ball and had another chance to score. This habit would later hurt him when he faced Russell, who always brush-blocked the ball, often creating a Celtics fast break.

DICK HARP: "Wilt understood the game of basketball. He had an opinion about the game and was bright about it. He wanted to use his size in close proximity to the basket. But he didn't develop his skills beyond that. If he wanted to, he could have been a significant playmaker. Wilt had demonstrated he could have shot the ball and been an effective passer."

JERRY WEST: "One thing about him, he always thought he was the best at everything he did. That simply was not the case. If that was the case, he would have been an 80 percent free throw shooter."

Over his sophomore season, Chamberlain averaged 30 points, 19 rebounds, and 9 blocked shots. And Kansas was clearly the best team in college basketball. But in the finals of the NCAA tournament the Jayhawks lost in triple overtime to UNC, an outcome that set the cornerstone of Chamberlain's frustrations. He returned to Kansas the next season, but the Jayhawks lost in postseason play to rival Kansas State, a team coached by Tex Winter.

Disgusted, Chamberlain decided to leave the University of Kansas. Because his class had not graduated, he was still ineligible for the NBA draft. So he played a barnstorming season with the Harlem Globetrotters, made a good sum of money, and waited his turn. That arrived the following season, 1959–60, when he made a heralded return to Philadelphia to play for the Warriors. His presence had an immediate impact on the league's statistical races. He led the NBA in scoring (37.6 points per game) and rebounding (27 per game). The next season, he became the first player in league history to shoot better than 50 percent from the floor. For the 1961–62 season, Chamberlain maximized man's potential for 48 minutes of basketball by averaging 50.4 points per game.

BILL RUSSELL: "For accumulating numbers, there's not anybody to even come close to that. I'll just say that he played 49 minutes a game or something like that. I think that's absolutely incredible. And we won the Eastern Conference by eight games that season."

The next season, Chamberlain scored a mere 44.8 points per game and won the league rebounding title for the fourth straight season. He made each season his statistical fiefdom, and yet they all ended in bitter disappointment. The reason, of course, was the Boston Celtics. Quite often Chamberlain would dominate Russell statistically, but he could never vanquish the Boston center and his teammates in the big games. Chamberlain was actually taller than his listed height of seven-foot-one and towered over the six-foot-nine Russell, which caused the public to marvel at the smaller man's success.

BILL RUSSELL: "Most people couldn't relate to what an imposing physical thing Wilt was. The first time you see him, it's like you're standing in his shadow. He's so big. Then he was really smart and a great athlete. The only saving thing is that he was not me. He was not me."

BOB COUSY: "A lot of people over the years have said that Bill Russell had more heart and desire than Wilt. That wasn't it. Russ was simply quicker than Wilt, and he knew how to use that quickness. That was obvious from the first time I ever saw the two of them on the court together. This is a tremendous advantage Russell had on Wilt. He didn't give him the offensive position he wanted. Russell kept him from overpowering him and going to the basket. Russell had better speed and quickness, so he could always beat Wilt to the spot. He pushed Chamberlain out a little further from the basket, forcing him to put the ball on the floor once or twice. We always felt Russell could handle him one-on-one."

As a result, Chamberlain was forced to develop and shoot a fallaway jumper that was far less effective than his dunks and short bank shot. His critics, meanwhile, saw Chamberlain as a giant fascinated by his own statistics.

JERRY WEST: "I've always felt that that part of him people misinterpreted. They would say, 'He's a selfish guy, he doesn't care, he's not a team player.' That's simply not the truth. It bothered him all the negative publicity he received, which frankly was not justified. It was really pretty ugly. He's like all of us. No athlete wants to fail. Chamberlain certainly didn't want to."

The Warriors moved to San Francisco for 1963–64, and Chamberlain again led the league in scoring. He also broadened the scope of his game by finishing fifth in assists. It didn't matter. The Warriors lost in the NBA Finals that year to Russell and the Celtics.

San Francisco traded Chamberlain to the Philadelphia 76ers in the middle of the next season. "Chamberlain is not an easy man to love," Warriors owner Franklin Mieuli later said of the trade. "I don't mean that I personally dislike him. He's a good friend of mine. But the fans in San Francisco never learned to love him. I guess most fans are for the little man and the underdog, and Wilt is neither. He's easy to hate, and we were the best draw in the NBA on the road, when people came to see him lose."

Chamberlain quickly made the 76ers into a title contender, but that spring they lost a seven-game series to the Celtics again. The following year, Philadelphia actually beat out Boston for the Eastern Division's regular-season crown but got caught flat-footed in the Eastern playoffs and lost to the Celtics 4–1.

Chamberlain's frustrations were no deeper than those felt by West, Baylor, and the Lakers. Bill Russell had simply built a wall around the NBA title. He had made it his personal property, or so it seemed until 1967, when Chamberlain finally led the 76ers to a 68–13 record and the league title, leading many observers to call them the greatest team of all time.

JACK RAMSAY, FORMER 76ER GENERAL MANAGER: "I think Wilt's best season was in '67 when the Sixers won it and Alex Hannum was his coach. He became more of a team player that year than ever before. Wilt was very stats conscious. He wanted to lead the league in scoring, rebounding; lead the league in everything. And he was capable of doing that."

But Boston's comeback victory over the Warriors in the 1968 Eastern Finals soon quieted all the "greatest team ever" talk, and Wilt decided he wanted out of Philadelphia. Jack Kent Cooke was only happy to help him find a ticket.

JACK RAMSAY: "Wilt demanded a trade and we gave in to him, which is how he got to the Lakers. A powerhouse guy. Could do everything. Shoot, rebound, block shots, passes. He led the league in assists one year. That's the incredible stat. No center's ever done that."

JACK KENT COOKE: "We held our talks in June in the library of my Bel Air mansion. Things got off to a very good start. We talked about the fact that we each owned a 1962 Bentley Continental. We talked about antique furniture, art, even the English language."

Finally they talked about money, a five-year deal at $250,000 per season, making Chamberlain what was believed to be the highest paid athlete in any pro sport. The Lakers shipped Archie Clark, Darrell Imhoff, and Jerry Chambers to Philadelphia for Chamberlain. The deal was announced in early July, setting off immediate speculation about Chamberlain, West, and Baylor on the same team. Could they share one ball? "We'll simply have the best team in basketball history," Chamberlain replied.

Seeing an opportunity to tweak the Lakers, Red Auerbach told reporters, "I wonder if Jerry West and Elgin Baylor are going to be willing to be underlings to Wilt Chamberlain?"

Cooke and Chamberlain were infuriated. "A statement like that is typical of Mr. Genius," Cooke shot back. "It's preposterous."

BILL BERTKA: "Butch van Breda Kolff was at a party at my house in Santa Barbara when he heard that Chamberlain was being traded. He was upset. Butch didn't have anything against Chamberlain or his effectiveness. But you had to have Chamberlain in the post, and that dictated a style of offense that Butch didn't particularly like. He'd rather have all five men moving, all five men interchangeable and sharing the ball. Van Breda Kolff had had the great Princeton team. Schaus coached fast-break basketball. When van Breda Kolff came in, he had a great first year, the second year was even better, and then they acquired Wilt. He wasn't an admirer of Wilt's game and how he could fit in."

Within hours, the trouble started. First Chamberlain read in news accounts that van Breda Kolff said he "could handle" his new center, who'd make a great rebounder for the Lakers. Who needs "handling"? Chamberlain wondered.

Then at the Maurice Stokes Game that summer at Kutsher's Club, van Breda Kolff asked Chamberlain to don a Lakers T-shirt and pose with him for a photo. When Chamberlain refused, the coach fumed.

In training camp, the tension increased a notch. Van Breda Kolff thought the center gave him one good day's practice, then began slacking off. Chamberlain thought the coach was trying to run a pro team with college rules.

Then came a season-opening loss to the 76ers where Chamberlain concentrated on defense and rebounding. The next game, Chamberlain scored big points and they beat New York. "Tell the coach," Wilt told the writers afterward when they asked about the difference in the two games.

A few games later, van Breda Kolff angrily benched Chamberlain when rookie Wes Unseld of the Washington Bullets out-rebounded him, 27 to 21. The newspapers enjoyed the proceedings immensely, questioning Chamberlain's $250,000 salary and his sinking scoring average (20.5 points per game). "There are certain deficiencies with every club," Chamberlain replied. "Here with the Lakers I've tried to blend in, lend myself to the deficiencies, try to help overcome them. Here with the likes of Jerry and Elgin we have people who can score. So I've simply tried to get the rebounds, get the ball to one of them so we can score."

The questions about Chamberlain's salary were pointless, Hawks general manager Marty Blake told reporters. "There's no athlete in the world worth $250,000, or even $200,000, unless you can take it in at the gate. In L.A., they take it in at the gate."

Amid the turmoil, Chamberlain still managed to impress.

BILL WALTON: "The first time I met Wilt I was in high school, and Wilt had just come to the Lakers. Our high school team played the preliminary game to a Lakers/San Diego Rocket game in the San Diego Sports Arena. I'm 16 years old and stuttered so badly that I was painfully shy. I'm walking off the court with my head down, and the Lakers are standing there ready to go onto the court. As I walk by, Wilt reaches out his arm and stops me. He steps out of their line and stands in front of me and puts his hand out and says, 'Hey, Bill, I'm Wilt. You're doing really well. Keep it up.' I was like blown away."

BILL BERTKA: "Wilt was always the villain. Wherever Wilt went in those days he was always booed and unappreciated. But, in tribute to the Lakers fans, from the day he stepped on the Forum floor he was never booed, never shown disrespect. He was only appreciated. But it took him about a year here to realize that."

Some observers, however, questioned whether Chamberlain's presence hadn't weakened the team. He often set up on the left low post, dead smack in the way of Baylor's drives.

BILL BERTKA: "Wilt was in the post, so it shut the lane down. That somewhat affected West's game, too, although West was one of the greatest pull-up shooters to ever play the game. Elgin liked to take it all the way to the basket, so it affected Baylor more than West or Goodrich. It certainly didn't affect their scoring. If Wilt was never acquired, the Lakers wouldn't have won that '72 world championship."

Van Breda Kolff sought to move the center to a high post, but Chamberlain figured that only took him away from rebounding. Privately, Chamberlain told friends that the coach favored West and Baylor and blamed him for the losses.

FRED SCHAUS: "I finally had to call the two of them in for a peacemaking session, and I tried to lay down some new rules. No more bashing each other in the press. Van Breda Kolff is the boss. I like both of them, but those two guys just couldn't agree on anything. Six weeks later, I had to fly to Atlanta for another meeting. After that meeting, I told the players to have their own meeting. Baylor was the captain, so he ran it. Wilt was told to stop frowning at his teammates on the court when things went wrong. The players told him to stop being so aloof, that he needed to socialize more."

That helped, but after a February 3 loss to Seattle, van Breda Kolff and Chamberlain screamed at each other for 20 minutes and would have come to blows in the locker room if Baylor hadn't stepped in. "It was embarrassing for everyone to hear them screaming like animals," one Laker confided to a writer. "It was ridiculous. The guys wanted to hide."

BILL BERTKA: "Wilt being the dominant personality that he was and Bill being the dominant personality that he was, there were sparks. Wilt had definite opinions about how the game should be played and how he should be used. So did Butch. Yet they both wanted to win in the worst possible way."

FRED SCHAUS: "After that Seattle blowup, we had yet another meeting and another truce. Wilt asked Butch, 'What do you want me to do?' Butch told him, 'Play defense and rebound.'"

Chamberlain complied, and the Lakers won the conference title.

JACK RAMSAY: "Wilt's skills had diminished by the time he got to L.A. They were on the downside. By that time, I don't think he was capable of scoring at the same level that he once did."

By the 1969 playoffs, the Lakers were a picture of team defense, giving up just 94.7 points a game. Baylor, Chamberlain, and West were the heart of the lineup. But there was more. There was Keith Erickson out of UCLA, recently acquired from Chicago, as sixth man. There were John Egan, the veteran guard, to boost the backcourt, and Mel Counts, the seven-footer and former Celtic, to do the same up front. With Counts playing alongside Chamberlain, Los Angeles could close the lane and make opponents live off of jump shots.

On the strength of their defense, the Lakers advanced to the most disappointing of their Finals meetings with the Celtics. L.A. had taken the top seed in the Western with a 55–27 record and thus had home-court advantage for the Finals with the Celtics, who had finished fourth in the Eastern.

JERRY WEST: "Most of the years we played they were better than we were. But in '69 they were not better. Period. I don't care how many times we played it; they weren't better. We were better. Period. And we didn't win. And that was the toughest one."

In particular, the 1968–69 season found Boston's Bill Russell, now 35, struggling with leg injuries that forced his hospitalization briefly. With Sam Jones also hurting, Boston came to rely on John Havlicek and Bailey Howell again. The playoffs translated into an urgency for the Celtics, particularly Russ who had private thoughts about ending his career.

The Lakers were favored, but they didn't have many young legs either lor, in particular, had begun to show his age. "I don't have to take h as I always did before," Boston's Bailey Howell told the writers. "And as quick on the drive or following the shot."

West, though, was determined not to face another championship loss. He scored 53 with 10 assists in the first game, which Russell called "the greatest clutch performance ever against the Celtics." It was just enough for a 120–118 Lakers win. Afterward, West was so tired he iced down his arms. Boston had opened with Em Bryant covering West, but Bryant was too short to stop West's outside shot. When the Celtics tried to play West close on the perimeter, he drove right past them for a variety of layups. In years past, Russell had always dropped off his man to stop those drives, but Wilt's presence meant the Celtics center couldn't get away with it anymore, West said. "I know he scares a lot of people, but if you're looking for Russell, you're not playing your game."

West cooled down to 41 points in Game 2, while Havlicek upped his total to 43. Very quickly the series became a shoot-out between these two. Chamberlain scored only 4, but he countered Russell on the boards. Even better, Baylor, who had been sluggish, came alive to score the Lakers' last 12 points for another Los Angeles win, 118–112.

Up 2–0, the Lakers had private thoughts of a sweep as the series headed to Boston. In Game 3, the Celtics took a big early lead but lost it after Keith Erickson poked a finger in Havlicek's left eye. The Lakers tied the game heading into the fourth and seemed poised to break the Boston curse and go up 3–0. But Havlicek, with his left eye shut, hit several late free throws to keep Boston alive, 111–105.

Game 4 provided yet another opportunity for the Lakers to strike the deathblow. The two teams combined for 50 turnovers and enough bad shots and passes to last them a month. The Celtics slowed the Lakers' scoring by double-teaming West, forcing him to make the pass rather than take the shot. Over the final four minutes, the two teams had one basket between them. But with 15 seconds left, the Lakers had an 88–87 lead and the ball. All they had to do was get the pass in safely and run out the clock. Instead, Bryant stripped the ball from Egan and the Celtics raced the other way. Sam Jones missed the jumper, but Boston controlled the rebound and called time at 0:07. On the inbounds, Bryant threw the ball to Havlicek, then set a pick to his left. Boston's Don Nelson and Bailey Howell followed in line to make it a triple screen. At the last instant, Havlicek passed to Jones, cutting to his right. Jones stumbled to a halt behind Howell, who cut off West. There, at the 0:03 mark, Jones lofted an 18-footer. He slipped as he took the off-balance shot, and it just cleared Chamberlain's outstretched hand. Jones knew it was going to miss and even tried to pull it back, he explained afterward. The ball went up anyway, hit on the rim, rose up, hit the back of the rim, and fell in. Chamberlain leaped up and lorded over the basket, his face a picture of anguish as the ball came through the net. Boston had tied the series, 89–88, and a dagger in West's heart wouldn't have felt any worse. "The Lord's will," he said later.

"I thought to shoot it with a high arc and plenty of backspin," Jones told the writers. "So if it didn't go in, Russell would have a chance for the rebound." Russell wasn't even in the game, a writer pointed out. "What the hell," Boston's Larry Siegfried said. "You hit a shot like that, you're entitled to blow a little smoke about arc and backspin and things like that."

The Lakers regrouped and headed home for Game 5. In L.A. the Celtics just didn't have it. Russell scored two points with 13 rebounds. Chamberlain owned the inside, with 31 rebounds and 13 points, while West and Egan struck from the perimeter with 39 and 23 points respectively. Boston fell, 117–104, and trailed 3–2.

West clearly was hobbled by the hamstring. He played in Game 6 and scored 26. But the Lakers needed more from him. And certainly more from Chamberlain, who made a measly two points. Boston won 99–90 and tied the series.

Once again a Celtics/Lakers championship had come down to a seventh game. Only this time Game 7 was in L.A.; this time there wouldn't be a Garden jinx. Or would there? West's hamstring had worsened. It was wrapped, and he declared himself ready to go. But everyone wondered. Everyone except Cooke, who began planning his victory celebration. He visualized the perfect finale for a championship season. He ordered thousands of balloons suspended in the Forum rafters. (Team employees spent hours blowing them up.) According to Cooke's plan, they would be released as the Lakers claimed the title. With the balloons raining down on the jubilant Lakers and their fans, the band would strike up "Happy Days Are Here Again." Cooke could see it clearly.

And so could Bill Russell. "Those things are going to stay up there a hell of a long time," he supposedly said.

No one was more infuriated by the balloons than West. The thought of them made him sick with anger. The Celtics, always looking for that extra little boost of emotion, found it in the Forum rafters and in a Lakers memo outlining plans for the celebration, which was passed around the Celtics' locker room before the game. They hit 8 of their first 10 shots on the way to a quick 24–12 lead. The Lakers charged back to pull within 28–25 at the end of the first. At the half, it was 59–56 Celtics.

The Lakers tied the score in the third before going strangely cold for five minutes. West, playing brilliantly despite his heavily bandaged leg, finally hit a shot to slow down the Celtics, who led 71–62 with about five minutes to go in the third. Then, with 3:39 left, Russell took the ball inside against Wilt, scored, and drew Chamberlain's fifth foul to round out a three-point play; 79–66, Boston. Chamberlain had played his entire NBA career, 885 games, and never fouled out. Van Breda Kolff decided to leave him in. With Chamberlain playing tentatively, Boston moved inside and took a 91–76 lead into the fourth, and the balloons upstairs weighed heavily on Cooke's team.

The lead went to 17 early in the fourth, but both Russell and Jones picked up their fifth fouls. In the void, West went to work. A bucket. A free throw. Another bucket. The lead dropped to 12. They traded free throws. Then Havlicek got his fifth, and moments later, Sam Jones closed his career with a sixth foul. He had scored 24 on the day. After a Baylor bucket, and three more points by West, the Celtics answered only with a Havlicek jumper and the lead dropped to nine, 103–94.

At the 5:45 mark, Chamberlain went up for a defensive rebound and came down wincing. His knee. He asked to be taken out. Van Breda Kolff sent in Counts. West hit two free throws, and the lead was seven. Russell and his boys were out of gas, hoping to coast. Another West jumper. And moments later, two more free throws from West. The lead was three, 103–100.

Three minutes to go, and Counts, who shot 4 for 13 on the afternoon, surprised everyone by popping a jumper, 103–102. Chamberlain was ready to come back in. "We're doing well enough without you," the coach told his center.

JERRY WEST: "I just thought he was hurt. Not till afterwards did I know that he should have been back in the ball game, that he asked to go back in the ball game. But if people thought we were better off with Wilt Chamberlain sitting on the bench, that's a bunch of bull."

Boston and L.A. traded missed free throws. With a little more than a minute left, West knocked the ball loose on defense. Nelson picked it up at the free throw line and threw it up. It hit the rim, rose several feet, and dropped back through.

JERRY WEST: "People don't realize there's so much luck involved. If games are close, luck plays a factor. They say luck is an element of design. Bull. It's luck involved. You might shoot a ball from the right side of the basket that 100 percent of the time if shot from that angle [it] will bounce back left. And then one time it will someway somehow bounce back right, and there will be no one but the other team in position to get the thing."

The balloons were all but popped. The Lakers missed twice and the Celtics committed an offensive foul, all of which an angry Chamberlain watched from the bench. After a few meaningless buckets it ended. The Celtics had hung on to win their 11th title 108–106. The debate began immediately afterward. Chamberlain versus van Breda Kolff.

DOUG KRIKORIAN: "West's hamstring injury was the key, to me, not van Breda Kolff benching Wilt in the seventh game. Wilt deserved it in that seventh game. He was playing horribly. Russell completely outplayed him that game. Wilt was like he was in a fog in the first half when the Celtics built an 18-point lead. Russell was dominant in that first half, in that last game. People said that Wilt tended to choke, well he did. This is not revisionist history, this is reality. People never want to bring that up about Wilt, just like the year before Wilt had a 3–1 lead with the 76ers against the Celtics and blew that one, too. So there was something to the saying that Wilt chokes in the big ones. I saw it in that seventh game. His teammates talked about it later. They couldn't believe it. It was like his feet were encased in cement. Russell was scurrying around the court in his final game, and Wilt was doing nothing."

Although they had been friendly through their careers, Russell criticized Chamberlain for leaving the game. Perhaps a broken leg should have taken Chamberlain out, Russell said, but nothing else. The comments caused a rift between the superstars and strained their friendship. Some observers later commented that perhaps Russell had only feigned friendship during their playing days to prevent Chamberlain from becoming angry and playing well against the Celtics.

BILL RUSSELL: "For people to say that, they had no concept of integrity. To say that I was friends with Wilt because I was playing against him was very shallow thinking by people who obviously had no depth in their own personalities. I always felt they were assigning their own motivations to me."

All of this mattered little to Jerry West. He was merely disgusted with another loss. He had finished with 42 points, 13 rebounds, and 12 assists. The Celtics went to the L.A. locker room immediately after the game. Russell took West's hand and held it silently.

"Jerry," Havlicek professed, "I love you."

"He is the master," Boston's Larry Siegfried said of West. "They can talk about the others, build them up, but he is the one. He is the only guard." West was named the MVP, the first and only time in NBA Finals history that the award went to a member of a losing team. The gestures were nice, West said, but they didn't address his agony.

JERRY WEST: "We all have our own little particular feelings when we lose. There's no gratification. When other people come in and express their condolences—and basically that's what it was—it's nice from people that you really respect. They paid their gratitude, I guess. It became personal in the sense that I didn't think I was doing enough. I was searching everything that I'd ever done in my life for the reason, looking for an answer why. Why can't we get a bounce of the ball? And that's what it came to personally. It almost controlled my life. It was a controlling factor in my play. When we played against those guys, I didn't care what it was, I wanted to play my very best. I didn't want any friends on the other team."

Doug Krikorian began covering the Lakers in 1968 and watched up close as West struggled through the loss of three straight championship series.

DOUG KRIKORIAN: "Jerry was never relaxed. He was always nervous. He would take losses hard. I remember him crying, literally tears in his eyes, after the Celtics beat them in that seventh game in '69. But he always talked to the reporters."

Yet there was a final insult. The car awarded with the MVP trophy was green.

JERRY WEST: "I really have blocked [that series] out of my mind. The only games that have any clarity to me are the first one and the last one.

The first one because of the excitement, how the game ended, what the locker room was like. The last one with the ugly feelings I had. I didn't want to ever play basketball again. I was furious with our owner for putting those balloons up there. It made me mad. I didn't like it. That wasn't my style."

Merv Harris: "In a lot of ways, Wilt was actually better off than West. They both had pride and ego. When the game was over, Wilt could leave basketball behind. He had a much broader range of friends and interests than Jerry. His personal prowess was so important to Wilt. Jerry was such a purist, to the point of a mania about the game."

Cooke, in the aftermath, was left with the task of figuring out what to do with all those balloons. He finally decided to send them to a children's hospital. For years they would hang metaphorically over the Lakers' heads, the victory balloons that never rained down. The championships, it seemed, only belonged to Boston.

Elgin Baylor: "It was a challenge to play against Russell and the Celtics. It was fun. It was disappointing to lose. But it was the ultimate challenge. They were a proud team, and they had reason to be."

Bill Russell: "Playing the same guys over and over was a challenge. Any of those guys that were good, you couldn't play them the same way every night. You couldn't play them the same way two games in a row. There were always constant adjustments."

Jerry West: "I didn't think it was fair that you could give so much and maybe play until there was nothing left in your body to give, and you couldn't win. I don't think people really understand the trauma associated with losing. I don't think people realize how miserable you can be, and me in particular. I was terrible. It got to the point with me that I wanted to quit basketball. It was like a slap in the face, like, 'We're not gonna let you win. We don't care how well you play.' I always thought it was personal."

Sam Jones, former Celtic: "[The Lakers] had a great team, but I still felt we were better. We had a lot of injuries, but we found our way again in the playoffs. We didn't feel we had to have home-court advantage. Bill Russell was our advantage. I think he's the greatest player ever to put on a uniform. He wanted to win."

Now the Knicks

Two weeks after the 1969 season closed, Butch van Breda Kolff resigned to become the head coach of the Detroit Pistons and was replaced by Joe Mullaney, the veteran coach from Providence College. Mullaney was another practitioner of Eastern basketball, but where van Breda Kolff was brash, he was mild. "Wilt is special and must be treated special," the new coach said with a smile.

"Mullaney is all right," Wilt observed. "He don't act like he wants to be boss."

Mullaney asked Chamberlain to help trap the ball in the corners. The big center was willing to cooperate, and this defense quickly showed that it would be effective. Alas, the 33-year-old Chamberlain suffered a knee injury nine games into the new '69–'70 season. He had missed just 12 games in 11 seasons. Although the doctors said he would be out for the season, Chamberlain promised, "I will be back."

BILL BERTKA: "The thing I'll remember about Wilt, and I got to know him pretty good, was when he went down with that knee injury. Frank O'Neill, our trainer, almost lived with Wilt in helping him get over that injury. He came back from that injury about as quickly as any human has ever done. Wilt told me, 'I'd never had that feeling before. For the first time in my life, I wasn't needed. I was on the sideline with a knee injury. I couldn't give anybody anything.' He said that was a revelation to him, because he couldn't perform, but he said, 'People encouraged me, people wrote me, they applauded me.' He told me, 'That was an experience I'd never had before. And it motivated me to get back quick to try to help the team.' He said, 'Bill, that's the first time in my life that I sensed compassion. I felt love.'"

DOUG KRIKORIAN: "In '69–70, Jerry should have been MVP of the league. That's when Wilt went out, and Jerry, to me, was the best player in basketball that season."

In Chamberlain's absence, Baylor also found a spark. With Wilt in the post, Baylor had given up his drives and taken up jump shots the previous season, which sent his scoring average and effectiveness plummeting.

MERV HARRIS: "It was a sad thing. The less effective Elgin was as a player, the more he felt troubled by it, the more the power of his personality over the team waned. The team developed its factions. There was one with Elgin and one with Wilt. You could almost see Elgin fade before your very eyes."

Chamberlain, meanwhile, worked diligently at rehabilitation and, as the 1970 playoffs neared, announced his intention to return, surprising even his doctors. "There's been so much unhappiness connected to my basketball—disappointing defeats, unfair criticism, and such—that I really hadn't realized how much the game meant to me," he said. "I've been surprised at the nice fan mail I've gotten since I've been hurt. I guess getting hurt has made me seem human and has made people sympathize with me for the first time. Usually, I've been regarded as some kind of animal."

He played the final three games of the regular season and was force enough to help the Lakers thrive in the Western playoffs. They had finished second in the regular season behind the Atlanta Hawks and Lou Hudson, but with Chamberlain the Lakers swept Atlanta in the divisional Finals.

With Russell now retired, another Eastern center stepped in the path of West and his Lakers. At six-foot-nine and 235 pounds, Willis Reed seemed no threat to overpower Wilt. Reed was a leader, not an overwhelming individual talent, although he could be overwhelming enough at times. Like Russell before him, Reed was quick and intelligent. Unlike Russell, Reed had a smooth shot with some range. Beyond all that, Reed had a presence that began with his overwhelming physical power. He wasn't a great leaper, but he was strong and determined that no one would out-hustle him.

WALT FRAZIER, FORMER KNICKS GUARD: "As a player and a man, he was always on fire."

As the story goes, Reed took on the entire Lakers team in a brawl during the first game of the 1966–67 season and whipped 'em all. By himself.

SAM GOLDAPER, FORMER *NEW YORK TIMES* BASKETBALL WRITER: "He just took over. The most unbelievable fight I ever saw in basketball."

WILLIS REED: "Rudy LaRusso threw a punch at me going up the floor, and the fight was on. I ended up hitting some people but I never did get a shot at Rudy. It was a wild fight."

Reed took on one Laker after another. As the melee elevated and the fans grew rowdier, it drew players, officials, and even police. The Knicks coaching staff happened to catch the whole thing on film.

WILLIS REED: "I remember having this picture of Darrell Imhoff holding me like this and Rudy LaRusso getting ready to put a haymaker on me. And there was this picture in the *New York Times*. And I remember Dolph Schayes for some reason was the head of officials. And they were talking about putting me out of the league. Luckily they had the 16-inch reels of film. That showed it really wasn't something that I started, I wasn't the guy who had initiated the fight. It showed Rudy LaRusso getting ready to punch me. That was how the fight went. But I mean, that was scary, though."

Reed and his Knicks were now ready to challenge for the championship after the collapse of the Celtics in the East in 1970. Coached by Red Holzman and led by Dave DeBusschere, Bill Bradley, and Walt Frazier, the Knicks had defeated Baltimore in the first round in a seven-game series.

In the Eastern Finals, New York defeated Milwaukee with rookie Lew Alcindor, 4–1. By the 1970 championship series, Holzman's team had transformed the Madison Square Garden crowd into a loud, silly horde. The upper deck screamed "dee-fense," and the city-hardened fans seemed to lose a little of their gaming edge and actually softened into something resembling cheerleaders.

Despite the Lakers' overwhelming edge in playoff experience, the Knicks were favored by the oddsmakers. Game 1 showed why. Although Reed had been worn down by battling first Unseld, then Alcindor, and now Chamberlain, he quickly ran circles around Wilt. Dick Barnett also was eager to match up with West, who had gotten the ball and the publicity when the two played together in L.A. New York opened a quick lead, pumped it up to 50–30, lost it, then blew by L.A. rather easily over the last eight minutes to win, 124–112. Reed finished with 37 points, 16 rebounds, and 5 assists. Asked why he had left Reed open outside, Chamberlain replied, "I just didn't come out after him. Next time I will."

As promised, Chamberlain was much more active on defense in Game 2. He hounded Reed into missing 17 shots and blocked the Knicks center's shot at the buzzer to preserve a 105–103 Lakers win. Wilt had only scored 19 to Reed's 29, but his defense had made the difference.

Back home for Game 3 on April 29, the Lakers rolled out to a 56–42 half-time lead. Long-haired forward Keith Erickson, a local kid raised on beach and volleyball in El Segundo and UCLA, helped West push the Lakers' offense along, while Chamberlain and Baylor ruled the inside. The Knicks couldn't seem to find a rebound. Erickson presaged a wild ending by hitting a 40-foot shot to close the first half. But the Knicks abruptly reversed that momentum in the third period. New York forward Dave DeBusschere and former Laker Dick Barnett started dropping shots in from the perimeter, setting off a run that allowed the Knicks to tie it at 100 with 13 seconds to go. The Lakers defense forced New York out of a set play, but Dave DeBusschere took a pass from Frazier, gave a head fake, and dropped in a neat little jumper for a 102–100 Knicks lead with three seconds left. The Lakers were out of time-outs. Chamberlain halfheartedly tossed the ball to West, who dribbled three times as Reed dogged him. Two feet beyond the key, just to the left of the lane, West let fly from 63 feet. Good. DeBusschere, underneath the basket, threw out his arms in disgust and collapsed.

Dr. Robert Kerlan, the Lakers' team physician, was excited enough to momentarily forget his arthritis. He jumped up from his courtside seat and began to celebrate. "I had my cane and I jumped out to the middle of the floor and started to dance," he told writer Scott Ostler. "I looked around and saw I was alone and I wondered where everyone was. Mendy Rudolph was the ref, and he signaled me to get back to my seat. I felt like a perfect ass."

Wilt was fooled, too. He laughed and ran off to the locker room, think-ing the shot had won it. But only the ABA had a three-point rule back then. The officials brought Wilt back out for overtime, 102–102.

In overtime, West missed all five of his shots. Barnett, the former Laker, clinched it for the Knicks with a bucket at the 0:04 mark. West and Erickson had no more miracles. It ended 111–108. Reed had run up MVP numbers, 38 points and 17 rebounds, while DeBusschere had 21 and 15, respectively. Most important, though, the Knicks had the big stat, a 2–1 lead in games.

A flow had been established to the series. Each side had an advantage, the Lakers their inside strength, the Knicks their running and quickness. One side would use its advantage to get a lead, the other would then come back. Injuries became a factor as well. West had jammed his thumb, and both Chamberlain and Reed had aching knees.

Game 4 was another nail-biter. Barnett hit six of seven from the field in the first quarter as the Knicks opened up hot. West was the answer for the

Lakers. Despite a badly sprained thumb, he played 52 minutes and scored 37, with 18 assists and 5 rebounds. Still the game would come to overtime and the hands of Laker reserve forward John Tresvant, who would lead L.A. to a 121–115 win and a 2–2 tie in the series. Baylor did his part, too, with 30 points.

Wilt came out strong for the fifth game in New York and was determined to cover Reed all over the floor. With a little more than eight minutes gone in the first quarter, L.A. had raced to a 25–15 lead. Then Reed caught a pass at the foul line, and Chamberlain was there to meet him. Reed went to his left but tripped over Wilt's foot and fell forward, tearing a muscle in his thigh.

With Reed out, the Garden crowd grew quiet. Holzman tried to prop up his players' spirits during the time-out. He inserted Nate Bowman to play Chamberlain, and that worked for a time. Then Holzman went with reserve forward Bill Hoskett, all of six-foot-seven, who hadn't seen a minute of playing time in the entire playoffs. Hoskett hounded Chamberlain effectively enough, but it really wasn't getting the Knicks anywhere. By the half the Lakers led by 13. In the locker room, Bill Bradley suggested the Knicks go to a 3–2 zone offense, which would either force Chamberlain to come out from the basket or give them open shots.

The Lakers seemed almost possessed by the notion of taking advantage of the mismatch in the post. Time after time, they attempted to force the ball in to Chamberlain, and the Knicks got bunches of steals and turnovers. The fourth period opened with the Lakers holding an 82–75 lead and a troubled hand. They were in obvious disarray. And the Knicks were surging, cheered on by the awakened Garden crowd. "Let's go, Knicks! Let's go, Knicks!" the throng chanted. At just under eight minutes, Bradley hit a jumper to tie it at 87. Then at 5:19, Bradley dropped in another jumper to give the Knicks the lead, 93–91. That prompted a flurry of New York baskets to extend the lead to eight. After a brief flurry, the Knicks took the 3–2 edge, 107–100. L.A. had been forced into 30 turnovers for the game. In the second half, West didn't have a field goal, and Chamberlain scored only four points.

DAVE DEBUSSCHERE: "The fifth game was one of the greatest basketball games ever played."

The Lakers returned home and corrected their mistakes in Game 6. With Reed out, Wilt scored 45 with 27 rebounds. The Lakers rolled, 135–113, to tie the series at three each. The stage was set in New York for the seventh game drama. Would Reed play?

WILLIS REED: "In the training room, they were gonna give me injections of carbocaine and cortisone through a large needle. But the skin on my thighs was so thick the doctor had trouble getting the needle in. It was a big needle. I saw that needle and said, 'Holy shit.'"

The Knicks watched him hobble out, and each of them soaked in the emotion from the noise. The Lakers watched, too, and made no attempt at furtive glances. Reed took a few awkward warm-up shots. Then he stepped into the circle against Chamberlain for the tip-off but made no effort to go for the ball. Once play began Reed scored New York's first points, a semi-jumper from the key, and he played incredibly active defense. Seventeen times the Lakers jammed the ball in to Chamberlain in the post. Reed harassed him into shooting two for nine. And Reed hit another shot (he would finish two for five with four fouls and three rebounds).

It was enough. The emotional charge sent the rest of the Knicks zipping through their paces. They simply ran away from the Lakers. New York led 9–2, then 15–6, then 30–17. When Reed left the game in the third quarter, New York led 61–37. From there they rolled on to the title, 113–99.

"The Lakers dressing room later was a morgue, in which living humans were interred," wrote Bill Libby for the *Los Angeles Times*.

DOUG KRIKORIAN: "What's strange about that '70 series, Wilt goes down with a knee, comes back and everything. They're down 3–1 against Phoenix and make a great comeback and beat the Suns in seven games. Then in the fifth game against the New York Knicks, people always forget they had an 18-point lead at the Garden. That was another game Wilt choked. They blew the 18-point lead. Basically I look at that game as where they blew the series."

Yet another championship loss brought new depths to their emptiness. West and Baylor missed much of the 1971 season with injuries, leaving Chamberlain as the focal point of the offense. Gail Goodrich, who had been lost to Phoenix in the 1968 expansion draft, returned to the Lakers and averaged 25 points per game. That wasn't enough as Kareem Abdul-Jabbar, Oscar Robertson, and the Milwaukee Bucks swept the Lakers aside in the playoffs 4–1 in a series that showcased Kareem versus Wilt.

JERRY WEST: "You had a young player and an aging player in that series. The reigning monarch was paving the way for the arriving monarch. It was just a changing of eras."

In the aftermath, Cooke wanted Joe Mullaney's job.

FRED SCHAUS: "I hated to see it happen to someone as nice as Joe. But when you're dealing with a guy like Jack Kent Cooke, when they've made up their mind, there's nothing you're going to say to change it."

6

Victory

With their failure in the 1971 playoffs, it became clear that time was running out for Jack Kent Cooke's collection of talented Lakers. Bill Russell had been out of basketball for two years, and they still hadn't won a championship. Heading into the 1971–72 season, Elgin Baylor was struggling to come back from yet another injury. Chamberlain had turned 35; West was 33. If this wasn't their last shot, it was close.

The answer, in Cooke's mind, was to try yet another coach. Having worked his way through Fred Schaus, Butch van Breda Kolff, and Joe Mullaney, he made overtures to UCLA coach John Wooden.

JACK KENT COOKE: "We discussed the job over a cup of tea in the library of my Bel Air mansion. John turned it down. He had had his time. He said he was too old to start into professional basketball."

Fred Schaus then asked Cooke to consider 45-year-old Bill Sharman, the former Celtic guard who had just coached the Utah Stars to the 1971 ABA title. Sharman's 1967 San Francisco Warriors had lost the NBA championship series to Wilt's 76ers. Before that, Sharman had made a winner of the miserable program at Cal State Los Angeles. He'd even coached the Cleveland Pipers to the old American Basketball League title in 1962. (The Pipers were owned by a young shipping magnate named George Steinbrenner, so it was established that he could get along in difficult circumstances.)

JACK KENT COOKE: "I was intrigued by Sharman. He had that inner intensity. I later saw the same quality in Joe Gibbs [who coached Cooke's Washington Redskins to three Super Bowl championships]. They were both seemingly quiet, almost shy. I saw this quality after I talked to them 5 or 10 minutes."

Sharman's friends said he was crazy to consider the offer.

BILL SHARMAN: "Everybody told me, 'You don't want that job.' They said the Lakers had not won a championship with Wilt, Jerry West, and Baylor for a number of years. And now Wilt was 36 and Jerry was 32 or 33 and Baylor was 37. They said, 'You've got to go down for two or three years and rebuild and come back up.' So they said it was not an ideal job. An ideal job is when you go to a team that's down and can come up. Don't take a team that's up and getting older. So in that respect I was advised not to take it. On the other hand, I wanted to live in Los Angeles. I thought it was a challenge. I was familiar with the Lakers, and I had known Jerry West. I had played against him, played golf with him. And I had coached college in Los Angeles, and in the ABA, so I was familiar with a lot of the players. I had played against Wilt, too. I knew them."

Sharman took the job, which left his Celtics buddies shaking their heads. The Lakers announced his hiring in July 1971, after working out the legal details with the Utah Stars, who claimed they still had Sharman under contract. Asked his goal, Sharman declared, "The world championship." That plot line, of course, was all too familiar to the reporters covering the team. They wondered what made Sharman think he could write a different ending this time.

The Cult of Personality

The 1971–72 Lakers roster presented a mishmash of gnarly egos.

JACK KENT COOKE: "Egads, they were prima donnas."

The owner, of course, was the granddaddy of them all. His demanding style set the tone for what was a substantial cult of personality. Chamberlain had his giant pride, West was sullen with frustration, and Baylor struggled with his declining skills and influence. To go with them were forward Happy Hairston, an irascible locker-room lawyer who chattered incessantly; Gail Goodrich, a determined scorer who liked to control the ball; and Jim McMillian, a chunky Ivy Leaguer pushing for a starting role. Among the bit players were

Pat Riley, Keith Erickson, and Flynn Robinson, all of whom sported healthy self-concepts.

Bill Bertka, Lakers scout: "On that one team you probably had more diverse, strong personalities than you had on any championship team in the history of the game."

Jerry West: "We had a lot of players who'd had personal success but hadn't enjoyed team success, a lot of very frustrated people. It had been frustrating to lose each year. It was terrible."

Somewhere between their injuries and circumstance, the Lakers had traveled the harrowing path of seven straight championship losses. The mental barriers, the frustration, the sense of confusion encased the team, and breaking them would require a strong coach with a different approach.

Bill Bertka: "You had the strongest personality in Bill Sharman. He was on fire right at that time. He was at the peak of his career with his personal intensity as a coach. He was a great communicator. No frills. No bullshit. With Bill, it was all down to productivity."

Intensity had always been Sharman's trademark as a player.

Bob Cousy, Sharman's longtime Boston Celtics roommate: "I thought I had the strongest killer instinct in basketball until I met Bill. Bill matched mine."

Off the court, Sharman was a sweetheart. On it, he was a demon, a transformation that amazed and amused his teammates. He wasn't known for excessive fighting. But when he did square off, whether the opponent was a seven-footer or just another guard, the bouts were usually one-punch affairs. "Willie didn't talk," former Celtic teammate Ed Macauley recalled. "When he'd had enough, you knew it."

His one-punch victims included six-foot-nine, 230-pound Nobel Jorgensen of the Syracuse Nationals and Hall of Famer Andy Phillip.

DOUG KRIKORIAN: "A brutal fighter. I saw him beat the shit out of Earl Lloyd, a big six-foot-six tough guy. Sharman was like a boxer."

BILL RUSSELL: "Bill Sharman is a dear friend of mine. I remember when I first met him. The first thing he said to me was, 'You know you're gonna have to fight.' I said, 'What are you talking about?' He said, 'They won't let you play in this league unless you fight.'"

BILL SHARMAN: "I was always kind of aggressive. When we played in the '50s, pro basketball was still growing. It was kind of like hockey. The owners didn't say go out and fight. But they didn't discourage it. They didn't throw you out of games for fighting. They kind of let it go. If you backed off and didn't hold your own, other players took advantage of you. I always feel I never started a fight but never backed away from one. If you did, they just kept pushing and grabbing at you. I saw a lot of good basketball players in those days get pushed right out of the league because they wouldn't push back."

Beneath this tough exterior was a neat freak who always folded and put away his clothes on road trips, even for a 12-hour stay in a hotel room. On a Celtics roster bristling with partiers, he was the guy who filled three-by-five-inch note cards with reminders on shooting technique and opponents' defensive tendencies and studied them in the locker room before games. He was the diet and exercise nerd, eating and working out at exact times during the day. Forget the usual beer and steak; Sharman wanted honey, toast, and tea as his pregame meal. Then, in the locker room, he would stretch and do warm-ups. Nobody did that stuff in the '50s. They didn't jog either. But Sharman did. Strangest of all, he went to the gym each morning before a game for shooting exercise, running through exactly the shots he planned to take that night.

BILL SHARMAN: "When I was with the Celtics, we lived pretty close to a high school gym. I'd wake up in the morning and be pretty nervous around the house. So I'd go over a few blocks just to shoot a few baskets. I noticed that I'd go over and think about how many and which shots I'd use in the game. And I'd kind of simulate them on the floor and go through the motions with them. Then I'd shoot some free throws, like I liked to do. Then I'd stretch. After that I'd go home and take a little nap before the game. And I found out by shooting around in the morning it gave me extra confidence that night. I said, 'I know damn good and well it helps me, so if I ever coach, I'm gonna try it.'"

As a coach, he would insist that his players go through these same routines.

BILL SHARMAN: "Jerry West was very eager. He said he thought it would help. Gail Goodrich and the others all said they would try it. Then I got to Wilt Chamberlain. I knew this might be a problem, so I called Wilt about a month before the season started and said, 'Wilt, I'd like to go to lunch with you.' I wanted to talk to him about a lot of things, but in the back of my mind, I wanted to try to ease him into that morning shootaround. I knew Wilt, and I knew that he had always been a late-night person who slept late in the morning. He said, 'Coach, I don't like to get up in the morning. It's gonna be hard on me. But I want us to get along. I kind of have the reputation where people say I don't get along with coaches. We've always been friends. I'll tell you what, let's try it. If it works, I'll go along with it. If it doesn't, I want to talk to you later about it.'"

JOHNNY "RED" KERR, FORMER NBA PLAYER AND COACH: "I loved Bill Sharman, great person, great shooter. [But] we all hated Bill 'cause he innovated the shootaround. Damn, we couldn't sleep, we couldn't lay in the hotel anymore."

Players often grumbled, but Sharman's game-day shootaround soon became a staple of NBA preparation. So would his notions on diet and exercise. Beyond that, he required his players to become students of the game. His Lakers were the first NBA team to break down game film and study it as football coaches did.

BILL SHARMAN: "We didn't have videotapes, but I was strong on visual help. So I had the team take a lot of moving pictures, which back then was all film. It was very expensive, very difficult, because you couldn't scroll the whole thing. Bill Bertka was in charge of putting our film together. He'd call up to San Francisco and arrange for film of a team we were going to play in a couple of days. He'd have the film brought down, and he'd splice it. He'd have maybe seven or eight of the offensive plays of the people we were going to play, five or six of their defensive plays they would use against us, and some of the individual moves. We'd get the players together and turn out the lights. You know players. They might be tired, and they weren't watching it too much. I asked Bill, 'How can we get them to pay attention?' He says, 'I got an idea.' So he went home, and somehow he splices in these Playboy girls. He puts them in there about every three or four minutes. I don't know how he put them in there or how he got them. There'd be a good-looking girl up there on the screen, and then, in another two or three minutes, another real good-looking girl. Everybody laughed, and they enjoyed watching it. So we got their attention."

The son of a newspaper circulation supervisor, Sharman had lettered in five sports (football, basketball, baseball, tennis, and track) in high school in Porterville, California. After a stint in the navy during World War II, he played basketball and baseball at Southern Cal. From there he joined the NBA's old Washington Caps, then moved to baseball with the Brooklyn Dodgers organization and even earned a brief spot on their roster in 1951. But that fall Red Auerbach coaxed him back to basketball. Sharman had been a six-foot-two forward in a control offense at Southern Cal. He couldn't handle the ball too well, but he could shoot, and Auerbach's freelance system required scorers.

For four seasons, 1956–59, Sharman led the Celtics in scoring and had the league's top free throw percentage for eight. An eight-time All-Star, Sharman would later author an instructional book on shooting. As a coach, he used his understanding of the mechanics to improve his players' touch. In L.A., however, Chamberlain's foul shooting presented an unconquerable mountain. After years of trying everything, Wilt admitted he was befuddled at the line. Crowds at the Forum took to cheering wildly when he made one. Dolph Schayes and previous coaches had become obsessed with improving Chamberlain's free throws, thinking that practice would make perfect. Chamberlain did, in fact, become a good practice shooter, only to resume his impotence during games.

WILT CHAMBERLAIN: "My embarrassing moment in basketball was perpetual, which I'm famous for. That's my lack of ability to make foul shots. That was something I could have done and did almost all the time. I was a good foul shooter. So my mental approach to foul shooting was my most embarrassing thing, not being able to conquer something that was never a major problem for me throughout my career, except when I stepped to the line in the NBA."

BILL SHARMAN: "I never could figure out how to help him with free throws."

At first, the Lakers found him to be a strange mix of fight and quiet innovation. He was a Southern California boy, but he was also a Celtic.

PAT RILEY, FORMER LAKER: "It was difficult for us to relate to him in the beginning, because he was covered with Boston green. But in time we came around. He was a low-key guy, but very competitive, very feisty."

It didn't help that Sharman gave them another dose of green when he added K. C. Jones, his Boston teammate, as the first assistant coach in Lakers history. The two former Celtic guards had seen Red Auerbach's running game work wonders with Bill Russell snatching rebounds and firing outlet passes on the fast break. They understandably wanted to perpetuate Red's revolution in L.A.

BILL SHARMAN: "Auerbach was not an Xs and Os man. But he had a great competitive spirit. He knew how to substitute. He knew how to get a team in shape. He knew how to motivate 'em. Put all that together, he was a great professional basketball coach. I got from him how he installed and encouraged the running game and the fast break. The first year in Los Angeles I encouraged the running and the fast break because I felt we had the strong rebounding with Wilt and Happy Hairston. So I really pushed it to run at the other teams."

Sharman's announcement that he planned to make the Lakers a running team brought a lot of laughs around the league. Use Chamberlain, the NBA's resident dinosaur, in a running game? Loony.

Sharman knew he would have to sell the key players on the idea. He invited Wilt to a pricey L.A. restaurant for lunch. They discussed the need for Wilt, the greatest scorer in the history of the game, to focus on defense and rebounding. The big center had heard this line from other coaches. But Sharman was different. He listened to Chamberlain's opinions on the issue. Sharman had played the running game; he knew exactly what it took. Chamberlain had his doubts but said he would cooperate fully.

Next, Sharman asked Happy Hairston to shelve his funky offensive game to focus on rebounding. Dominating the defensive boards was a two-man job. Every great center needs a tough power forward to help out. Hairston's sacrifice would be a key to winning the title, Sharman said. A muscular six-foot-seven 225-pounder, Hairston agreed. He would average 15 boards over the last half of the season and become the first forward to pull down 1,000 rebounds while playing alongside Chamberlain.

BILL WALTON: "Happy was perfectly named. He was always upbeat and he worked so hard and he tried desperately. Chick used to ride Happy all the time. Wilt was so great and Jerry was flawless. Gail was getting 30 a game. And Happy would be struggling and fumbling the ball away. One time the other team scored, and Happy got the ball and took it out-of-bounds and threw the ball inbounds right to the other team. And Chick Hearn said, 'I can't believe it. Jack Kent Cooke should fork up the money to go test Happy Hairston for color blindness.'"

With Hairston and Wilt controlling the defensive boards, the Lakers had West and Gail Goodrich to run the fast break. But Goodrich, who had started his career in L.A., then gone to Phoenix, liked to control the ball.

BILL BERTKA: "When Gail was acquired, people said, 'You're gonna need two basketballs now. One for West and one for Goodrich. You don't have enough basketballs on that team.' That wasn't quite true. Bill Sharman in his discussions with Gail said, 'I want you to play without the ball.' Gail just snapped. When he was at Phoenix, he was a point guard, a high scorer. Gail took great pride in being able to play without the ball and moving without the ball. Gail was a master at it. He and West became one of the highest scoring backcourts in league history that year."

KEVIN LOUGHERY, FORMER BALTIMORE BULLET: "Gail Goodrich was a great player. One thing about him that people don't realize, I guess he was about six-two, six-three, but he had arms down to his toes. He had that seven-foot wingspan. He could go to the basket because of that and take it over the rim. He was a very good post-up player, and very cocky. He believed in himself. He and I had a fight one time. In Baltimore. Neither one of us could fight and Wilt came over and picked us up, each one in one hand, and basically said, 'You guys can't fight. What are you wasting time for?'"

Goodrich and West would both average 25 points per game over the season as they hauled in pass after pass from Chamberlain. West, working his way back from knee surgery, would run the break from the center, with Goodrich finishing from the wing.

GAIL GOODRICH: "Jerry was a great player, and I think we complemented each other. We blended and didn't hurt each other's games."

BILL SHARMAN: "Jerry led the league in assists and still averaged 25 points a game and played great defense. Jerry West is probably the greatest defensive guard who ever played. People don't realize this. They know of him scoring points and everything. He was so good on defense. Had quick hands and stole the ball. He stole more than anybody, although they didn't keep records on it then. And he'd come around behind shooters and block their shots from behind."

JERRY WEST: "It was chemistry. We had the right kind of chemistry. Sharman treated us like we wanted to be treated. He let you play. We weren't encumbered by a hundred plays. We weren't encumbered by things that you see modern teams encumbered by. We weren't overcoached. Bill just had the right approach, said the right things."

Pat Riley figured into the mix as a seldom-used backup guard. His largest Lakers role would come later, as the Showtime's slick-haired coach.

BILL BERKTA: "As a player, [Pat] played behind Jerry West. Jerry played big minutes, so Pat didn't get a lot of minutes. Pat accepted that because he was a true professional. Conditioning was always such a factor then because of the limited practice opportunity. Pat always had himself in tiptop condition. Day and night. The guy had a washboard stomach. He played hard. He was a tenacious defender, and always ready. One of the reasons that West was the player he was is that he had a guy guarding him in practice who was going harder than most games. I remember that so vividly how hard they played against each other in practice. Riley would be playing maniacally out of frustration of not playing in games."

West, Riley, and their teammates may have been the Lakers, but their circumstances were far from elite. They shared the same headaches with a variety of teams in the '70s.

BILL BERTKA: "Practice facilities were an absolute nightmare. You just accepted that because that's the way it was. One day you'd practice at Inglewood High School, one day you'd practice at Loyola University, one day you'd practice at a recreational facility. Teams today have their own facilities for practice. Back then it was almost humorous."

Sharman's last remaining problem was the other forward, where Baylor was a painful question mark. The team's captain, he had been the Lakers' dominant figure for most of his 13-year career. But he had missed all but two games the previous season due to injury. In the off-season, he had worked hard to come back and was now able to play again, only Sharman's new running system required a very active small forward. Baylor just didn't have the mobility. At first, Sharman wasn't sure exactly how to handle it.

Bill Bertka had been ill the first time he scouted Jim McMillian at a college holiday tournament. So he climbed to the nosebleed section, lay on his side, and watched McMillian, a senior at Columbia. Ill as he was, Bertka liked what he saw. Columbia was playing Villanova with Howard Porter. With Bertka's recommendation, the Lakers made McMillian the 13th pick of the first round of the 1970 draft. Soon afterward, Fred Schaus endured a tongue-lashing from Cooke.

BILL BERTKA: "So we drafted [McMillian], and after the draft was over Fred calls me in the office and said, 'Bill, Mr. Cooke was on the intercom with me and he said Ned Irish of the Knicks said he couldn't believe we drafted that little fat guy from Columbia University.'"

McMillian did have a tendency to gain weight. Baylor thought he looked like a chubby Floyd Patterson and dubbed him "Floyd Butterball," or "Butter" for short. But he slimmed down on a grapefruit diet and steadily improved over his rookie season.

BILL BERTKA: "He came to epitomize what you wanted in a small forward. He could run the floor. He could post up. He could pass the ball. He had a nice medium-range jumper, a quick release on his shot. And he was smart."

By the opening of the 1971–72 season, McMillian was pushing Baylor for the starting role as small forward. The Lakers broke out to a 6–3 record that first month. But Sharman wasn't happy with the results. "Elgin started every game," he said, "but Jim McMillian was coming on strong." Just as Sharman wanted, McMillian hustled and ran the floor, putting him in position to run the break with West and Goodrich. After those first nine games, Sharman decided McMillian should start.

The coach knew he had to approach Baylor carefully about a reserve role. One morning before practice at Loyola, Sharman informed his captain that McMillian would start.

BILL SHARMAN: "He just wasn't the Elgin Baylor of old. I knew he felt bad, and I wanted him to keep playing. But he said if he couldn't play up to his standards, he would retire."

The Big Streak

Baylor announced his retirement the next day, and their 33-game win streak began that night. The 1971–72 Lakers would win more games than any other team in NBA history—with a 69–13 record that wouldn't be bested for a quarter of a century.

BILL SHARMAN: "That year was one of those years you dream about. We got off to that wonderful start. All of a sudden we're 39–3. So naturally everybody's gonna be happy and kind of loose."

BILL WALTON: "At UCLA, I went to all the Lakers games. Don't tell the NCAA this, though. I would get front-row Lakers seats at the Forum, and it was great. I used to have breakfast on a regular basis with Jerry West at Hollis Johnson's Westwood Drug Store. We'd go in the back door, and Hollis would bring out gigantic omelets and stacks of pancakes. I'd be wolfing down this food and Jerry would be there eating. On his way to practice, he'd tell me all about the NBA. It was the greatest time. I would go to the games and watch Wilt and Jerry and Gail and Jim McMillian and Elgin, at the end of his career. I was there from '70 through '74, and those were great Lakers years. We were winning 88 straight games at UCLA, and they were winning 33 straight games for the Lakers. It was phenomenal."

JACK KENT COOKE: "One of the happiest times of my life was when the Lakers were on that 33-game winning streak, a record I dare say will never be broken in the history of professional sports. It's as good as my Washington Redskins winning three Super Bowls. Each time they'd play, we'd wait for the win with bated breath."

BILL SHARMAN: "All the pieces just fit."

Especially the big one, the Big Dipper. With Baylor's retirement, Sharman had asked West and Chamberlain to become team captains. West declined, but Wilt relished the leadership role. In the past, he had infuriated Lakers coaches, sometimes snacking on hot dogs or fried chicken on the bench before a game. Now he was all business. He had 25 rebounds, 6 assists, and a dozen points in the first victory of the streak, at home over Baltimore. Next came Oakland and a 19-rebound effort, followed by 22 rebounds and 7 assists against New York in the Forum. In Chicago two nights later, it was 20 rebounds and 8 assists. Most of the assists came from his pulling defensive rebounds and hitting the streaking Goodrich, West, and McMillian for fast-break buckets. Yet even those statistics said little about the blocks and changed shots he forced on defense. Instead of smacking the ball out of bounds as he had in years past, he began brush-blocking shots and starting a fast break the other way. Their 25th straight came in Wilt's hometown of Philadelphia, where he celebrated with 32 points, 34 rebounds, and 12 blocks.

"Sharman has Wilt playing like Russell," Joe Mullaney said.

"Wilt should be the MVP in the league this season," Baylor told one writer, a sentiment echoed by Philadelphia's Billy Cunningham. Many observers rushed to credit Sharman for the "new" Wilt. "I don't think I should get the credit," the coach quickly pointed out. "He's always had a bad rap. Whatever they ask of him, he's done. He's just doing more things better now that he is not mainly a scorer. He must block a zillion shots a game. And he scares guys out of other shots or makes them take bad shots." The secret to the entire running game, Sharman added, "has been Wilt's rebounding and fast passes."

"I really like the man," Wilt said. "I've never had a coach as conscientious as Bill."

Still, Chamberlain, always a stat freak, admitted feeling a twinge every time he looked at his drooping scoring average, down to 14.8 for the season. "I'm happy about it," he said of the streak, "but here I am the greatest scorer in the game of basketball and I've been asked by many coaches not to score. Now where else in a sport can you ask a guy to stop something he's the best in the world doing? It's like telling Babe Ruth not to hit home runs."

BILL WALTON: "I'm sitting courtside at the Forum, and Wilt is just dominating, just killing everybody. This is in the days when he wasn't shooting anymore—just blocking shots and rebounding. I loved to watch Wilt play. The battles between Wilt and Kareem—there was nothing like that. One time Wilt was playing—I think it was against Portland; it didn't really matter—he was blocking every shot and starting fast breaks while just standing down at the defensive end. One time he just reached out and caught the ball. Just took it out of the guy's hand like it was a grapefruit and threw it out to West, who kicked it ahead. The fast break was on, McMillian finishing the break with a little baseline jumper. While the play was on, I followed the ball watching and out of the corner of my eye this huge guy lumbers over to me. Wilt runs over to me, reaches down, sticks his big hand down and says, 'Hey, Billy, how ya doin'? Say hi to Johnny Wooden over there at UCLA for me.' Then he went over and blocked another shot. It was unbelievable."

Each win brought more notoriety for Sharman's shootaround. Soon just about every coach in the league had instituted a game-day practice. Which was bad news for Wilt. "I'm still not for those 11:00 practices," he said as the streak rolled on. "I don't think they've done anything personally for Wilt Chamberlain except to make him lose some sleep. But we're winning and I'm not going to do anything to knock the winning way."

BILL SHARMAN: "After we started out 6 and 3, Wilt started to vacillate on the shootaround. But after we won 33 straight, it was hard for him to say anything. Wilt only missed two morning practices all season, and he called ahead both times."

The streak ran through January 9, 1972, when they lost a road game to rival Milwaukee and Kareem, 120–114. Bucks coach Larry Costello had scouted the Lakers' 23rd consecutive win, a road victory over Atlanta, and quickly devised a defense to cut off their fast break.

BILL SHARMAN: "We knew it had to end sometime."

Through each game, Sharman had been a fiend on the bench, shouting incessantly.

BILL SHARMAN: "I was always a yeller. When I got back from Milwaukee, my throat was sore that whole week. It got to where I couldn't even be heard. The doctor told me not to talk for a week or 10 days. I couldn't do that. We were in the middle of a championship season. I tried using one of those battery-operated megaphones, but in a game I just couldn't use it. I kept hollering. The doctors said I shouldn't, but I thought after the season it would come back. But the damage had been done. My voice never came back."

The voice damage suffered during the streak was permanent, eventually forcing Sharman from coaching. The Lakers went 30–10 the last half of the season; each win brought them closer to that unreachable goal. But as the playoffs neared, the team sensed that old Lakers jinx hovering somewhere nearby.

PAT RILEY: "We had been so snakebit in the '60s. We could never, ever win. Always got beat by Boston in the Finals. We won 33 games in a row. It was incredible, a storybook year. But even as we were winning the world championship, we were waiting for something bad to happen again."

By the end of the season, McMillian was averaging 18.8 points and 6.5 rebounds and had become a Forum favorite, with the crowd erupting over his long jumpers from the corner. "I really can't tell you how I fit into this team," he told reporters. "I'm just the fat little dude wearing Number 5."

BILL SHARMAN: "That year in the playoffs, we played Chicago first. We just overpowered them in four straight. Then we played Milwaukee. They had Kareem and Oscar Robertson and had swept Baltimore in the Finals the year before. A lot of people were calling them the greatest team of all time. They were a major obstacle. We lost our first home game to them in the playoffs, which might have helped us. We had that wonderful record, and we were on a roll. Losing our first game woke everybody up and got us going."

They did manage a win in the second game, 135–134, but were obviously shaky. West had shot 10 for 30 from the field. "I know what I'm doing wrong," he said afterward. "I'm turning my hand too much. But I can't get it stopped. It's got to go away by itself." Somehow they overcame 61 percent shooting from the Bucks in Game 3 in Milwaukee. They drove frequently, drawing fouls and shooting free throws. On defense, Wilt overplayed Kareem to stop his skyhook, forcing him instead into short jumpers and layups. At one point, Chamberlain blocked five shots. In the critical fourth period, Wilt held Kareem scoreless for the last 11 minutes. Kareem still finished with 33, but Chamberlain had done the job. The Lakers won, 108–105, and regained the home-court advantage. Goodrich had scored 30 and McMillian 27 to lead L.A.

The Bucks lashed back in the fourth game, taking a 75–43 rebounding advantage and tying the series at two-all with a 114–88 blowout. Kareem celebrated his 25th birthday with 31 points. West, on the other hand, was only 9 of 23 from the field, and afterward he complained that Sharman was requiring him to play too many minutes.

JERRY WEST: "It was particularly frustrating because I was playing so poorly that my team overcame me to win. Maybe that's what a team is all about. Maybe that's what I was missing all those years. I'm not sure."

PAT RILEY: "Jerry hadn't shot the ball as well as in the past, but we were more of a team. We had a lot more pieces at that time, and we got the job done. We blew through the playoffs that year. That year we weren't going to lose unless somebody got hurt."

The Lakers headed back to the Forum, where they ran away with the fifth game, 115–90, despite West's continued slump. They returned to Milwaukee for the sixth game, and in practice West kicked over a press table after missing an open jumper. In the past, he told the writers, nobody seemed to notice when he had great scoring games because the Lakers always lost in the Finals. Now that they were winning, he said, all people seemed interested in was his slump. As usual, Sharman said, people had failed to notice that West could virtually rule the floor with his defense alone.

BILL SHARMAN: "Jerry wasn't 100 percent, but he was still fantastic. He might have felt it wasn't one of his better years, but I thought he was sensational. He was so cooperative from a coach's standpoint. Anything you wanted to do, he'd go along with it or make suggestions. You couldn't ask for a better player, especially being a superstar. There are so many so-called superstars who have an ego problem or are hard to get along with. He was never, ever a problem."

The cure for these frustrations was another win. They vanquished the Bucks in Milwaukee, 104–100, to take the series, 4–2. Their opponent in the 1972 Finals would be the New York Knicks, who had beaten a resurgent Boston club in the Eastern Finals, 4–1.

The Knicks, however, were not the team of old. Willis Reed was out of action with his nagging knee injuries; his absence changed the entire nature of the team. "We operate on such a small margin of error," Bill Bradley told reporters. "We don't have Willis there to take care of our mistakes."

But the Knicks made no mistakes in Game 1 in the Forum. Lucas scored 26 points, and Bradley hit 11 of 12 shots from the field as New York shot 53 percent from the floor. They used a nearly perfect first half to jump to a good lead and won much too easily, 114–92. Early in the second half, the Forum crowd began filing out dejectedly. It looked like another L.A. fold in the Finals. The Lakers had lost their home-court advantage yet again.

But in Game 2, Dave DeBusschere hurt his side and didn't play after intermission. With no one to hold him down, Happy Hairston scored 12 points in the second half, and L.A. evened the series, 106–92. Luck had always been such a big factor for the Lakers, West said. Each of the previous Finals, they were overcome with a sense that fortune had turned against them. But that all changed after Game 2 in 1972. That night, West lay awake wondering how he would act if they actually had a championship to celebrate. What would he do?

At Madison Square Garden for Game 3, DeBusschere tried to play but missed all six of his field-goal attempts. The Lakers dominated the frontcourt and danced out to a 107–96 win.

Their momentum was holding, although they felt a tremor in the first quarter of Game 4, when Chamberlain fell and sprained his wrist. Obviously in pain, he decided to stay in. It was a crucial decision. The game went to overtime, but at the end of regulation the Lakers center picked up his fifth foul. In 13 NBA seasons, he had never fouled out of a game, a statistic of which he was immensely proud. Immediately speculation started along press row that he would play soft in the overtime. Instead, he came out in a shot-blocking fury that propelled the Lakers to a 116–111 victory. At 3–1, their lead now seemed insurmountable. Here at last were the Lakers, on the cusp of a title.

"The patient is critical and about to die," Walt Frazier observed.

BILL SHARMAN: "Somebody said, 'Are you putting balloons up this time?' We said, 'Nope, no balloons. You don't win till it's over.' They figured that was a jinx."

The early word on Chamberlain was that he would be unable to play Game 5 at the Forum. But as game time neared, he received a shot of an anti-inflammatory drug and took the floor. To assure the title, he scored 24 points and pulled down 29 rebounds as L.A. finally broke the jinx, 114–100. The effort earned Chamberlain his second Finals MVP award.

JERRY WEST: "What's so ironic about '72 is that I played terrible in the Finals. It didn't seem to be justice for me personally. I had contributed so much in years when we lost. And now when we win, I was just another piece of this machinery, so to speak. It's not that I felt so terrible. It's just that I had played so poorly. Even though we'd won, four games to one, I felt I hadn't been able to contribute what I normally did. In other years, I'd laid everything out there on the table. Then all of a sudden that year, I didn't play my best. I felt I hurt the team in certain ways."

Afterward, the Lakers sipped champagne and toasted each other quietly. There was no shaking and spewing. No riotous behavior. And certainly no rain of balloons from the Forum rafters. "Wilt," West said, raising his glass, "was simply the one who got us here."

MARK HEISLER, *LOS ANGELES TIMES* COLUMNIST: "You could see what made Jerry great and what drove him. It was this nagging fear that he hadn't ever done anything. And then when he did do something, when they finally broke through in 1972 and won a title, he didn't know what to do. Pat Riley talks about how Jerry walked in and took a sip of champagne and just walked out. Didn't know what to do with victory. He was very comfortable with defeat, although he hated it and it made him miserable."

BILL SHARMAN: "I remember Mr. Cooke walking in the locker room with the biggest smile on his face. He was so happy, and he went around the room, talking to the players. Then all of sudden in came the writers and the whole room was jammed, just jammed. It doesn't seem like they kept the writers or anybody out more than a minute. We didn't even have a chance to say, 'Okay, gang, we did what we wanted to do.'"

JACK KENT COOKE: "I was very, very, very happy. In sports, it's the winning that counts."

7

The Valley of the Seventies

The joy the Lakers felt finally attaining the 1972 NBA championship title didn't last very long. Something that had taken so many years to wrench from the circumstances evaporated within hours. As a postseason bonus, Jack Kent Cooke gave each player $1,500, the only problem being that the previous season, when they hadn't even reached the Finals, the bonus had been $5,000. The players were miffed and suggested that rather than take the money, everybody should just give it to Sharman.

JERRY WEST: "At least that would have meant a $15,000 gift for the coach. We figured that would be greater than the $12,500 share of playoff money."

What the players wanted was for Cooke to pay the coach's playoff share. Cooke disagreed, saying that Sharman's money should come from the players' allotment. The morning of the team championship dinner, the *Herald Examiner* published a story saying that the players were trying to cut Sharman out of his playoff share.

JERRY WEST: "Cooke got [columnist] Melvin Durslag to write that story. Whenever he wanted something derogatory written about me or Wilt, he got Durslag to do it."

PETE NEWELL, FORMER LAKERS GENERAL MANAGER: "The story broke the morning of the team banquet. The players were furious with Cooke. They felt he was using the circumstances to picture them as selfish. The night of the team party was a tremendous brouhaha. It was worse than an Irish wake. The players refused to speak to Mr. Cooke. Wilt Chamberlain walked in and Cooke rose to greet him. Mr. Cooke had Jim Murray, the great *Los Angeles*

Times columnist, at his table. He was trying to introduce Wilt to Murray but Wilt walked past as if Cooke wasn't there."

JACK KENT COOKE: "I was just appalled by their behavior and very hurt. It was just an air of sullenness. It was Jerry West again. He went up and down the hall sulking."

JERRY WEST: "That's not true. It's too bad that it got blown out of proportion. Everyone there that night felt bad for Bill Sharman. All the players loved him."

PETE NEWELL: "The whole atmosphere of dislike had pushed Freddie Schaus to take the job as head coach at Purdue. I replaced him as general manager. I know when I got in there nobody was speaking to anybody. That was one reason Schaus wanted to get out. All the players were mad at him, too."

Once Again, Then Decline

There was one final, unsatisfying peak before the Lakers descended into the great valley of the '70s. They put their differences with Cooke aside long enough to make a run at one more championship.

Considering the age of the 1972–73 roster, just reaching the Finals was an achievement. Chamberlain was 36; West 34 and philosophical about it. "There's no question that there are a lot of things I can't do that I once could, particularly on offense," he said. He was no longer among the scoring and assist leaders in the league. Neither was Wilt. Although Chamberlain led the league in rebounding and shot an incredible .727 from the floor, critics complained that Chamberlain seemed increasingly lethargic. Goodrich still led the team from the backcourt, and Keith Erickson and Jim McMillian worked from the corners. But Happy Hairston spent much of the season injured. To bolster the frontcourt the team picked up veteran forward Bill Bridges.

This group won the Pacific Division with a 60–22 record and prospered in the playoffs, defeating Chicago in a seven-game series, then brushing aside the surprising Golden State Warriors, who had upset Kareem and Milwaukee. For the fourth time in five seasons, the West and Chamberlain-led Lakers advanced to the championship round. And for the third time, they faced the Knicks, who had won 57 games. New York had finished 11 back of Boston, who had topped the league at 68–14, but the Knicks had upset the Celtics in the seventh game of the Eastern Finals on Sunday, April 29, 1973. They then had to scramble to L.A. for a Tuesday-night Game 1 with the Lakers. New York phoned to ask if the Lakers would consider delaying the series until Wednesday. No way, the Lakers said.

Regardless, both teams looked forward to this rubber match. New York and L.A. had won a championship apiece in their series. Now they had an opportunity to settle the issue. "It will be nice to see Jerry," Walt Frazier said. "Between us it will be a battle of pride."

Not to mention age. The Knicks were just as long in the tooth as the Lakers. Exhausted, they arrived that first Tuesday of May and promptly met a rested monster. Chamberlain blocked seven shots and intimidated five others. Mel Counts, the Lakers' other seven-footer, had nine rebounds. L.A. owned the interior, while the Knicks shot from the perimeter and rebounded poorly. The Lakers jumped out to a 20-point lead with 26 fast-break points. The Knicks did make a good run in the second half, cutting it to 115–112 in the closing seconds. But Erickson got a defensive rebound at the end and whipped the ball out to Bridges to preserve the win.

That, unfortunately, would conclude the highlights for the Lakers. The momentum abruptly shifted to the Knicks once they had rested. "After that," said former Knick Willis Reed, "we took names on them and won the next four games in a row."

DOUG KRIKORIAN: "They were beaten in five games by the Knicks, but again, Jerry was hurt with a hamstring, Happy Hairston was out, Jim McMillian was hurt in that series."

Afterward, Chamberlain peeled off his soaked Lakers jersey for the last time. Never close, this cluster of personalities had run out of things to say to one another, and Sharman didn't have the voice to keep them together another year.

Limbo

What followed is a time Jerry West describes as "the worst period in my life." It is no coincidence that the same could be said about the entire organization.

In early March 1973, Jack Kent Cooke was having dinner while watching a Kings hockey game when he got a call from his doctor, reporting on the results of a life insurance physical.

JACK KENT COOKE: "He told me I had the constitution of a 25-year-old man and the heart of an ox. I was elated. I hung up the phone and immediately had a heart attack. My lower jaw went numb, and my chest tightened. Fortunately, I was having dinner with Dr. Bob Kerlan."

Kerlan, the longtime Lakers team physician, helped Cooke to an office couch, where the doctor administered mouth-to-mouth resuscitation until Cooke could be rushed to a nearby hospital.

PETE NEWELL: "Jack's first visitor during his recuperation was his mother. She was just a beautiful lady. She would go to all the Forum games. Jack just loved her and was so proud of her. He was also very proud of his vocabulary. He was a walking dictionary, and when she came to visit he described in great detail what he'd been through, the catheterization and everything. He used the exact medical terminology. 'Mother,' he said, 'believe it or not, for 30 seconds I was dead. But Dr. Kerlan revived me.' His mother smiled and said, 'Tell me, Jack, which way were you going? Heaven or hell?'"

As it turned out, neither would have him. Just one month after his heart attack, Cooke suffered a second blow. The stock of Teleprompter, his cable television company, plunged because of huge losses. Against doctor's orders, Cooke went to New York, fired most of the management, and started running the company himself. "I spent exactly a year in New York," he said. "I was not about to preside over a bankrupt company."

PETE NEWELL: "That's the way he did things. In six months, he had the stock going in the right direction again, all the fat cut out."

JACK KENT COOKE: "I later sold that company for a major profit. An ungodly amount."

Other endings weren't so happy. That same year, Sharman's wife, Dorothy, was diagnosed with cancer. She spent much of the 1973–74 season hospitalized in New York.

PETE NEWELL: "It was a tough period. Jack Kent Cooke lost his health; Sharman lost his voice; then his wife, Dorothy, died of cancer."

BILL SHARMAN: "We had to take her back to Sloan-Kettering Hospital in New York, where they had better treatment. Mr. Cooke liked her. He called her every day, talked to her from wherever he was. She was there three or four months. I bet he didn't miss three or four days the whole time. After they diagnosed it, she lived a little more than a year. It was very difficult. The doctor said it was terminal. They didn't tell her. I didn't tell her. I wanted to be with her all the time. But if I did, she would have thought, 'I must be dying.' So I'd go with the team for a few days, then I'd fly to New York. Then I'd go with the team, then fly back to New York. My assistant coach, John Barnhill, took care of things. That was a tough decision, a tough situation."

PETE NEWELL: "Bill spent more time back in New York than he did with the team. Mr. Cooke loved Bill. He took care of all those expenses with his wife's illness."

The season became a study in chaos as Newell hastily put together a lineup. Since Chamberlain was gone, the Lakers were without a center. The Buffalo Braves had 23-year-old Elmore Smith, a seven-foot 250-pounder known for blocking shots. "To get him, we had to give up Jim McMillian," said Newell. McMillian was popular with his teammates. Word of the trade stunned the team.

The Lakers also shipped Keith Erickson to Phoenix for the legendary Connie Hawkins and drafted a bruising but unpolished rookie, Kermit Washington. Sharman and Barnhill worked at getting the new faces introduced, but their efforts were further complicated by injuries that caused West to miss 51 games. Despite all the setbacks, the Lakers trailed Golden State by just three games with seven left on the regular schedule. From there they found a last burst of emotion and fought their way to the Pacific Division championship with a 47–35 record. But the effort left them spent, and they fell to the Bucks in the first round of the playoffs, 4–1.

Bitter, Not Sweet

West had played just 14 minutes in the series and scored four points, which led to speculation that he would retire. But he came to training camp in the fall of 1974 in good shape. His mental state, however, had deteriorated from constant bickering with Cooke over money. West believed Cooke had promised him that he and Chamberlain would make the same salary, but when Chamberlain departed in 1973, West learned otherwise, leaving him stewing. In West's eyes, Cooke devalued the game, making it and the people employed by the team simply a part of the business process. For West, basketball was the end, not just the means.

"I thought they were both getting $250,000 a year," said Newell, but in September 1973 when Chamberlain abruptly "retired" to become a player/coach in the rival American Basketball Association, West learned that Cooke had been paying Chamberlain $400,000. The owner justified this by arranging a side deal with the center for other services.

PETE NEWELL: "It wasn't the money. It was the fact that he was told one thing, and another happened. Jerry is not petty, but he believed that he had not been given what was rightfully his. After all, Jerry had been with the team long before Wilt got there. Jerry was a superstar in his own right and a big draw. A lot of people had come to the Forum over the years to see him play."

JERRY WEST: "I always have viewed trust as an important factor, trust in a coach, trust in the people you've got around you. And I lost that trust with Jack Cooke."

Angered, West told his agent to attempt to have his contract renegotiated. But Cooke rebuffed him.

JERRY WEST: "He basically told my agent to go to hell. I felt I was deceived. When you feel that you're deceived you don't want any part of the organization that deceived you. I could've played another very good year. Every athlete says that. But I could've, and I knew I could've. But I could never have played for the Lakers again, and I wasn't going to play for anybody else."

PETE NEWELL: "I begged him to change his mind. It just crushed me when Jerry phoned and said, 'Pete, I'm going to retire.'"

CHICK HEARN: "There's no question about it; Jerry West should have played another two years."

West, though, was as steadfast as the West Virginia hills. He retired at 36, walked away the day after a dazzling performance against Portland in a pre-season game. Newell recalled that Portland's Geoff Petrie was then touted as the league's next young superstar guard, and the Lakers were eager to see how West played against him.

PETE NEWELL: "Jerry had something like 34 points that night. It was just like Jerry to make a statement like that."

The official excuse was a torn stomach muscle, but that was a public relations smoke screen.

JERRY WEST: "It started over money, but then it became personal."

JACK KENT COOKE: "Jerry West was a brilliant young man in many areas. But he was very naive back then in the ways of the world. Jerry was obsessed with money. He's a very rich man now. He's been very careful in the handling of his money. From the moment I purchased the Lakers in 1965, it was a continuing battle every year between Jerry West and me as to whether Elgin Baylor got a penny more than Jerry. Jerry felt the amount of money he got should be greater than Elgin because he did so much more. As far as Wilt Chamberlain was concerned, I never made such a commitment to Jerry. I did, however, make a commitment to him concerning Elgin Baylor. But Wilt Chamberlain was an entirely different story. I should point out that I did not dislike this constant clamoring for equal financial treatment with Elgin Baylor. That revealed Jerry's spirit. It was part of the man."

West said his rounds with Cooke had very little to do with other players' salaries and a lot to do with the owner's manipulation.

JERRY WEST: "Jack Cooke used players' salaries to play mind games. No one ever had to pay me to play basketball. But Mr. Cooke's manipulation made me not want to play for him. My relationship with Mr. Cooke was acrimonious because the negotiations were a game to him. I knew that."

DOUG KRIKORIAN: "Jerry did not like Cooke. Let's face it. He was a cheap guy. Poor Chick Hearn. Chick never made what he should have made. Of course, Jerry [Buss] didn't give him that either. Cooke had his polysyllabic words. He'd try to impress you with his language. I used to be a guest of his. He did this for all the writers in Los Angeles. He'd invite you to be a guest of his at the Kings' games. You'd come and have dinner and then sit in his box. I'd do it with Melvin Durslag or Jim Murray. There'd always be Lorne Greene there and always some famous celebrity. It was always like Jack Kent Cooke would be talking down to you in a nice way. You would know. He would be nice to you, because we could always rip him in the paper."

After West retired in October 1974, he filed suit against the Lakers, claiming Cooke owed him back wages, which set in motion an estrangement between West and the team that would last over the next two seasons. West's departure was a setback, further complicated by the knee injury of newly acquired free agent Cazzie Russell. The Lakers finished 30–52 and for the first time in 14 seasons did not make the playoffs.

BILL SHARMAN: "I kept thinking, 'It's got to get better.' But it never did."

Enter Kareem

Having gone through one season without a superstar, Cooke knew he didn't want to go through another. The Lakers roster had always featured an exceptional talent. So Newell and Cooke set out to find another one. Fortunately, they didn't have to look too far.

In Milwaukee, Kareem Abdul-Jabbar had grown weary of life with the Bucks in a small, cold city and no longer wanted to play for coach Larry Costello. With a year to go on his contract, he informed the team that he wanted to move to New York or L.A.

PETE NEWELL: "Milwaukee had to make a tough decision. Kareem was going to leave the Bucks anyway. They could trade him or end up in a year with nothing."

The choice then fell to the Knicks and Lakers. The Bucks decided they wanted a center and draft choices to replace Kareem.

PETE NEWELL: "The Knicks were trying hard to get Kareem, too. They had a lot of money and no center and no draft choices. We had a center, Elmore Smith, and draft choices."

The Lakers held the second and seventh first-round picks in the 1975 draft, which they used on David Meyers of UCLA and Junior Bridgeman of Louis-ville. They packaged those rookies with Smith and second-year guard Brian Winters for Abdul-Jabbar, a deal that left Knicks executive Alan Cohen fuming. He complained that the Bucks had never given New York a real chance. Jack Kent Cooke merely smiled. The crafty dealmaker had landed another big one.

KAREEM ABDUL-JABBAR: "Mr. Cooke was a very—I won't call him flam-boyant because he was not flamboyant—but he was quite an individual. He was a hands-on owner, and he understood what he was doing. I had a lot of respect for him as a management person. He wasn't just somebody with some money that owned a team. Entertaining, offensive—he could be all of those things. But he understood. He really appreciated what I could do for the team. He set everything up."

Kareem had wanted to go home again, to New York's own special noise. To Amsterdam Avenue and the playgrounds. To jazz, Harlem, and the Lower East Side. To Madison Square Garden and lost love. Ah, the Garden. He was 14 and already seven feet tall when he first played there. Promoters had decided that one of his high school games at Power Memorial Academy should be moved to the Garden to accommodate the crowd.

KAREEM ABDUL-JABBAR: "It was like stars in my eyes that night in 1961. I couldn't understand, when I was a rookie and came back there eight years later, why all those fans were now booing me with so much enthusiasm."

He didn't see that it was he who had jilted them first, when he decided to attend college in L.A. It didn't matter. He was bigger than New York anyway. He was Egypt and Africa and Islam and Westwood and Malibu and Man-hattan and the West Indies—all rolled into one.

So the trade took him back to L.A. They knew him there. Still, it wasn't home. Not then. He knew that the love, like the hate, would have come much easier in New York. California was a place where the emotions seemed to run more tepid, which wasn't exactly conducive to finding the one thing he really wanted. Eventually he would come to understand that they loved him in L.A. Yet even then, after all those years, he could really never be sure.

Born Ferdinand Lewis Alcindor on April 16, 1947, he grew up in Manhattan, the only child of Al and Cora Alcindor. His mother was a singer, and his father studied the trombone at the Juilliard School of Music while working at a variety of jobs to support the family.

Young Lewis was 13, already six-foot-eight and the darling of New York's considerable hoops cult, when he conducted his first newspaper interview. Quiet and bookish, he had decided he wanted to be an engineer. "I know I can't play basketball forever," he explained to a reporter.

He was wrong, of course. But how could he know then that he was built for the long run? The evidence only grew with each succeeding season. His years at Power Memorial produced two national high school titles and a 71-game winning streak. By the spring of his senior year, college coaches all over the country wanted him, and they weren't alone. "I'll trade two first-round draft picks for him right now," quipped Gene Shue, coach of the Baltimore Bullets. But it was UCLA's John Wooden who got him, and together they formed the linchpin of the Bruins' college basketball dynasty.

KAREEM ABDUL-JABBAR: "I always related to [Wooden]. He was about what you had to do to win games."

They did plenty of that, claiming three straight NCAA championships and forcing the college rules committee to adopt the "Alcindor Rule" outlawing dunking his final two seasons. As Wooden often pointed out, Alcindor was the most valuable player ever. The coach emphasized that most valuable didn't necessarily mean most talented. It simply meant that Alcindor was the kind of gifted, versatile center who could take a team beyond the sum of its players. From UCLA, he catapulted to the year-old Milwaukee Bucks. Even to the wise old tough guys of the league he presented a mystery. "How tall is he really?" they asked. The answer in college had been seven-foot-one. The official word from the Bucks was seven-two, but nobody believed it. "You could start the guessing at seven-four," said Nate Bowman of the New York Knicks, "but his arms seem to be eight feet long."

Whatever his size, it was big enough to take the Bucks to the Eastern Conference Finals his rookie season. They lost to New York, but for 1970–71 Milwaukee added Oscar Robertson, and the two of them led their teammates on a businesslike march to the title in just the team's third season of NBA operations. That championship season also marked the completion of Alcindor's conversion to Islam, which he had pursued since 1968. Just before the 1971 All-Star Game, he quietly changed names and married a woman named Habiba. "The game means so much to him that he postponed his honeymoon to play," Robertson told reporters.

The new name, Kareem Abdul-Jabbar, meant "noble, generous, powerful servant of God," yet the task of living up to it seemed quite a test. In October 1972, he was jailed briefly in Denver for suspicion of marijuana possession, only to be released after teammate Lucius Allen was charged. Three months later, in January 1973, seven people, including five children, were murdered in Abdul-Jabbar's Washington, D.C., townhouse. The victims, who belonged to the orthodox Hanafi Muslim sect, were the family of his close friend and adviser Hamaas. The repercussions from that incident left Kareem stunned and doubtful about his own marriage. Before the year was out, he had separated from his wife and retreated within the cocoon of his Milwaukee apartment.

The Bucks, meanwhile, had traded or released key members from the 1971 championship team, moves that led to playoff losses in 1972 and '73. They had mustered the effort to challenge the Celtics for the 1974 championship but lost in an intense seven-game series. The next season, his last in Milwaukee, he broke his hand, smashing it against a basket in anger. With him on the injured list for long stretches, the Bucks sank to 38–44 in 1974–75, and afterward they consummated the deal he had requested.

His years in Milwaukee had produced three league MVP awards and yet another name, when Bucks play-by-play man Eddie Doucette tagged his bread-and-butter shot the "skyhook," certainly a worthy weapon for a noble, generous, powerful servant of God.

Blow

The California drug culture was in full bloom when Kareem arrived in 1975. Since Lou Mohs ran the team in the '60s, Lakers management had employed off-duty L.A. police to identify hookers hanging around the team's locker room. As drugs became more prevalent, team officials asked their security consultants to keep track of that, too. At first the concern was marijuana. Then, as the '70s progressed, freebasing cocaine became the Hollywood party rage.

PETE NEWELL: "You worried like hell. Marijuana and drugs always seemed to break out at parties. The players were celebrities, so they were always invited. And they were anxious to meet the people they saw in the movies. A lot of Hollywood power people liked to showcase the athletes."

When David Stern stepped in as commissioner in 1982, he quickly instituted a drug policy. But the '70s offered no such protection.

DOUG KRIKORIAN: "There was a lot of coke going on. Everyone did coke in those days. Late '70s, early '80s, it was everywhere. Anyone that's ever done cocaine, and I have, it makes one feel . . . If you've done it you know how it makes one feel. Anyone who says he doesn't like it is a liar. There are some people I guess that didn't try it. But it was a problem on some Lakers teams. The late '70s. I won't name names. They were heavily involved."

JOE MCDONNELL, LONGTIME L.A. SPORTS RADIO PERSONALITY: "I remember hearing stories on the road about one player going to another player's room and giving him an envelope full of drugs. It was just commonplace in those days. I had a member of the team in '76–77, which was the best record in the league that year. They were 53–29 under Jerry West. This member of the team told me that 90 percent of the guys were doing some kind of drugs. Ninety percent! And that was before Spencer Haywood showed up."

PETE NEWELL: "We really didn't test the players for drugs because cocaine was not something that was feared that much back then."

Having experimented with cocaine and heroin in college, Kareem had little interest in the coke crowd that sought him out, although there were Lakers who did. After all, powder could be had at every stop on the road. Hotels around the league were transformed into party palaces that drew regular crowds eager to greet the players as the teams came and went.

PETE NEWELL: "The marijuana smell, if you stayed one place in Oakland, it would keep you awake it was so pungent. The place was wall-to-wall hookers. And the lounge was a nonstop party."

JERRY WEST: "I think we were in an awkward era for the league itself. It was floundering, and we didn't have any direction."

With the league front office unprepared or unwilling to take on the drug issue, the Lakers protected their interests the best they could.

PETE NEWELL: "We had two detectives that worked the Hollywood beat in terms of drugs and gambling. We were mainly looking if a player kept the wrong company. Then we'd try to intervene."

Enter West

Pro basketball survived in an atmosphere of decline in 1975. The ABA was on its last legs, and the NBA lagged behind the NFL and pro baseball as a second-rate sport. It was often portrayed as a black game struggling to find support in white America. To make matters worse, the league's television contract was measly, which suggested limited potential. These conditions weren't as bad as they appeared, but that hardly mattered. Basketball's future lay in its development as an entertainment medium, and in the entertainment business appearances were everything.

Critics charged that the sport was boring, that an overly long season resulted in games that seemed meaningless. Kareem was the NBA's top star, and his brooding image did little to help the situation. His last season in Milwaukee had been his first ever as a loser, and many sportswriters read his unemotional response as a lack of interest. Lakers fans, however, mostly remembered Big Lew of UCLA fame, the Dominator. They welcomed him and expected great things. The troubles, of course, began almost immediately, and the vast majority were not of his making.

PETE NEWELL: "We had given up most of our young talent and draft picks to get Kareem."

STU LANTZ, FORMER LAKER: "Elmore Smith was our center. He was traded to Milwaukee in that deal for Kareem, along with about six other players. I remember thinking, 'We're gonna get to the playoffs now for sure.' But that wasn't to be."

Kareem arrived to find a mishmash of a roster to greet him. The real complications, however, began on the bench, where the personal tragedies had finally caught up with Sharman.

BILL SHARMAN: "I was not a good coach my last two years."

Kareem won the rebounding title with a 16.9 average and scored 27.7 points per game, good enough for his fourth league MVP award. But the 1975–76 Lakers could not win on the road and finished 40–42, out of the playoffs for the second consecutive season. Sharman's coaching days were over.

BILL SHARMAN: "My contract ran out, and Mr. Cooke didn't renew it. He said, 'Bill, blah, blah, blah, I'd like for you to be the general manager.' So I knew I realized that I wasn't doing the job I did when my voice was good."

With Newell retiring, Sharman moved up, and Cooke set out in hot pursuit of UNLV's Jerry Tarkanian as the Lakers' next coach. Cooke recalled that he ultimately decided to pass on Tarkanian. But Tarkanian remembered it very differently. He said he was offered the job and accepted it, only to change his mind. At the time, the UNLV coach was just beginning his lengthy court battle with the NCAA.

JERRY TARKANIAN: "I was afraid that if I took the Lakers job the case would be dropped and my name would never be cleared. I backed out at the last minute. The press conference had already been scheduled. So they went ahead and called Jerry West."

BILL SHARMAN: "[Cooke] didn't want Jerry West right away. He mentioned different people. I thought Jerry West would do a good job, so I was pushing Jerry West. Jerry was kind of apprehensive. He didn't sound real eager. But at that time he wasn't involved in anything else. And he wanted to get back into basketball."

Finally Cooke agreed on West, only to find that West wouldn't return his calls. Actually, West dreamed of coaching the Lakers but still couldn't bring himself to talk to Cooke. Adjusting to retirement had been a dream-turned-nightmare for West, who was on his way to becoming divorced from Jane, his first wife. He indulged himself in golf, travel, and what the writers called his "penchant for stewardesses." "I found out it wasn't a very good way to live," he once said. "I won't go into detail, but that period played hell with my marriage."

Finally, desperate to get ahold of West one morning in July 1976, Cooke ordered Chick Hearn to find him. The broadcaster tracked him down at a local golf course and instructed the pro to have West phone between rounds. Still, West refused to budge. When Cooke ordered Hearn to try yet again, he angrily resigned as the voice of the Lakers, only to take the job back moments later when Cooke phoned to patch things up.

West eventually relented after Cooke agreed to bring in more talent. Sportswriter Mitch Chortkoff said West's hiring was part of a settlement of his suit against the team. Cooke, however, denied it, saying it was merely a "coincidence" that the suit was settled at the same time West was hired. West refused to discuss the suit in his interviews.

JERRY WEST: "I needed something to do with my life besides play golf."

West promptly hired two assistants, Stan Albeck for offense and Jack McCloskey for defense, when most NBA teams only had one. "I wanted to coach the Lakers one day," West explained a few months later. "I mean, I love the Lakers. I always felt that loyalty was a tremendously important part in the life of an athlete. But I had this lawsuit going against Cooke, and I figured that would do it for me as coach of the Lakers. Then Cooke asked me if I wanted to coach the team. It was a tremendous adjustment. I guess I'd seen one Lakers game in two years. I called all of the players and told them I would be honest with them and that we were going to have fun. I went out and hired Stan and Jack, because I hated organizational work and I needed a crutch to help me through that part. I'm still nervous. Sometimes I don't know what to say to players after a game. I'm still learning."

Before long, it would become apparent that the coach was the best guard on the roster. Every time the team would go into overtime, Albeck would turn to West and say, "Suit up, Jerry. Just five minutes. Then you can retire again."

Doc Hollywood?

West's frustration began almost immediately after agreeing to coach.

JERRY WEST: "Frankly, I've tried to block those years out of my life because they weren't real pleasant for me."

The ABA folded operations after the 1976 playoffs, with the NBA greedily gobbling up the rosters of its dying teams. The New York Nets would survive to join the NBA, but they were willing to peddle their star player, Julius Erving, to any team with the cash. The Philadelphia 76ers stepped up and offered a $6 million package—three to the team, three to Erving—for Dr. J's rights. West said he asked Cooke to go after Erving.

JERRY WEST: "Obviously, we weren't going to do anything to spend a little bit of money to make us better. We could have gotten Julius Erving. That's the only time I ever got involved. I told Mr. Cooke, 'You should take this guy. He's very exciting. Plus he's a terrific player.' He told me it wasn't my money; it was his money. So be it. I never talked to him about those things anymore. The only time I knew about personnel changes, I'd show up at practice; we'd have a different face there. Cooke would tell me how great the guy was, and we'd have picked him up off of waivers. We picked up a lot of people that were retreads. It was like an open-door policy. We had a lot of guys running in and out of there. It wasn't a very comforting thing. When you're letting people who don't know a damn thing about basketball make your decisions, you're going to have a problem eventually."

It was Abdul-Jabbar who bore much of the hardship from the failures of Lakers teams in the late '70s. Years later, he was stunned to learn that he could have played with Erving.

KAREEM ABDUL-JABBAR: "That blows my mind, knowing that they turned down Dr. J. Mr. Cooke screwed up royally on that one. You do what you can to improve your team."

JACK KENT COOKE: "Jerry was excusing himself for the dreadful job he did as coach. That is sheer balderdash. My record speaks for itself. My God, we acquired the giants of basketball, Wilt Chamberlain, Kareem Abdul-Jabbar. There is no truth whatsoever to it."

BILL SHARMAN: "When I was general manager, [Cooke] said, 'Bill, I don't want you to talk to the coaches about players. Any time you talk to a coach they want the best players in the league and it kind of gets out of hand.'"

Three months after taking over as coach, West figured the Lakers were spending $1.4 million on their payroll, while the Philadelphia 76ers were spending twice that. "Shit," he said. "We've got the bodies of a YMCA pickup team . . . The only thing going for us is that we have fun, and we have Kareem. Cooke promised me some help. He promised. Then these players come up, and he doesn't move."

The first thing West did after agreeing to coach the Lakers was phone Kareem and set up a meeting. You don't know me, and I don't know you, the coach said. But you need to know what I believe in. I don't know much about offense, because I never had to have plays run for me. West thought he could help the team by building a defensive mentality.

KAREEM ABDUL-JABBAR: "I was one always to believe in chain of command. I agreed with Jerry. Who's going to doubt one of the best players of all time?"

Soon opponents noticed a new life in Kareem and the team.

KAREEM ABDUL-JABBAR: "With Jerry, there was something in the atmosphere that became infectious. Everybody wanted to feel about the team the way Jerry did. He was never arrogant. He had great intuition. He wanted to see what each of us could do. When you get that kind of atmosphere going, it does something to bring you near the top of your skills. Maybe something like that happened with me."

Those 1976–77 Lakers started slowly, winning four and losing six, but they found some chemistry on an early eastern trip and ran off a 28–10 streak from there. By March they were challenging for the best record in the league, which they achieved in a win over Denver. But that same night, power forward Kermit Washington was lost for the season to a knee injury. Then Lucius Allen went next.

KAREEM ABDUL-JABBAR: "In 1977, we could have won the world championship had we not had Kermit Washington and Lucius Allen get hurt in the last month of the season. Prior to their getting hurt, we had beaten Portland every time. After they got hurt, we never beat Portland again. We had a chance to win the world championship, and it got away."

Lost with the opportunity was the special atmosphere West had created. Four times in 11 playoff games Kareem scored better than 40 points. But Bill Walton and the Blazers swept L.A. in the second round, leading to media criticism that Kareem had been outplayed. "I'm a target," he responded. "Always have been. Too big to miss."

BILL WALTON: "I lived to play against Kareem Abdul-Jabbar. He was the greatest player I ever played against by far. Not even close. Better than Jordan. Better than Magic. Better than Bird. Better than Dr. J. Better than the best of the best that I played against. Better than Rick Barry. Nobody who ever played against Kareem Abdul-Jabbar will ever forget it. I lived my life to play against this guy. He was my source of motivation for everything I ever did. All the physical rehab from 32 operations, all the weight training, all the conditioning drills. Every day in practice it was always Jabbar, Jabbar, Jabbar."

Over the next two seasons, this criticism of Kareem would gain momentum, leaving West furious at two reporters, Ted Green of the *Los Angeles Times* and Rich Levin of the *Herald Examiner*.

JERRY WEST: "We had two writers that were killing him in the newspaper that should have been fired. It was unfounded bias. People expected more than what he was doing. It was never good enough."

KAREEM ABDUL-JABBAR: "I recall being the scapegoat. I was the best player on the team. I got a lot of things done, so they just used me as the focus for why the Lakers weren't successful. That was very frustrating. It was one of the worst times in my basketball life because I couldn't win. I was the dominant player in the league. I won three MVP awards in that span. It wasn't good enough. But I wasn't the problem. The problem that people had with me was that I wasn't into giving interviews or spending a lot of time with the press.

And they didn't like that. I got into a test of wills with Rich Levin and other people who were writing."

Doug Krikorian: "Kareem Abdul-Jabbar, that first year Jerry West coached him, was as good a player as this league has ever had. You talk about a dominant center. People forget. He single-handedly beat the Golden State Warriors in a series that went seven games. People could not stop Kareem."

Yet West himself contributed to this atmosphere, at one point calling Kareem a dog after a bad game, then losing his temper when the quote made the morning papers.

Jerry West: "I should never have coached. My personal life was in turmoil. It just wasn't a good time for me. That spilled over into it and made me do and say things I should never have said."

Among their many differences, this was one subject upon which Cooke and West agreed.

Jack Kent Cooke: "It was a terrible mistake on my part to make him coach. Like other great athletes, Jerry West couldn't understand why the players he coached couldn't duplicate his feats."

As a coach, West seemed to eat himself alive in silence.

Stu Lantz: "He didn't try to put the handcuffs on players. But a lot of the players then did not have the mental capacity to make quick decisions, or to be intuitively decisive in their decision making, and that would drive Jerry crazy. Especially a flashy player like a John Neuman. There were nights at halftime where Jerry would be upset because Johnny had tried a wraparound pass that went up in the stands."

Kareem Abdul-Jabbar: "Our guards never could seem to get the job done to his satisfaction. But you wouldn't hear a lot about it. Jerry usually was not vocal at all, especially if you were doing a good job. He would just say supportive things. He wouldn't get into any critiques."

For all its trauma, the 1976–77 season closed with Kareem being named MVP for a fifth time.

JERRY WEST: "Those teams in the late 1970s would have been lucky to win 20 games without him. Yet we were always in the playoffs. We just didn't have enough pieces."

JACK RAMSAY, FORMER PORTLAND COACH: "I had great admiration for Jerry as a player. It's very hard for a great player to then coach. The only player that comes to my mind is Lenny Wilkens. Lenny was a Hall of Fame player and became an outstanding coach. Most of your great coaches are not guys who were great players. They're guys who worked hard at their own game and learned it, learned how to teach it. Examined it carefully. Guys who had to figure it out how to get a shot. Conversely, your great players—Jerry West, Bob Cousy, Willis Reed, Bill Russell—they did not have the success they had as players when they turned to coaching."

Kermit

The heartbreak that followed came in a blur. Lost in a strange turn of violent events were the hopes of a promising 1977–78 season. The trouble started just hours into the campaign when Kareem exploded in anger at Milwaukee rookie Kent Benson for shooting a forearm into his solar plexus. He knocked Benson unconscious with a punch. Even worse, the blow broke Kareem's hand, forcing him to miss 20 games.

The incident derailed plans for an imposing Lakers frontcourt. Power forward Kermit Washington had returned from his knee injury but was suddenly left to man the boards alone. Like Sharman before him, Washington was a sweet, gentle family man off the floor. On it, he was a tense, muscular intimidator.

PETE NEWELL: "Kermit came to the Lakers as a rookie in 1973. He had led the nation in rebounding at American University. I was hoping he would make the conversion from being a college center to a pro power forward. He was only six-foot-seven, but he was catlike with his quickness. He hadn't played much organized ball until he reached American. Even then he was playing center in the middle of a zone, so he had little understanding of man-to-man defensive concepts. He had never played facing the basket on offense. Once we got him into camp, we wondered if he had enough skills to make it in the NBA. But he had incredible desire and a strong work ethic."

That was enough to impress Newell, who decided to tutor Washington in all the nuances of post play over the summer of 1975. Their sessions working together formed the basis of an NBA institution: Pete Newell's "Big Man Camp." Over the ensuing summers, undeveloped players from across the league would come to California to work with Newell, a Hall of Fame coach, on developing frontcourt skills. Each year these informal sessions would grow in scope, and nearly a decade later, when the retired Newell decided he could no longer run the camps, he would turn their operation over to Washington and former Laker Stu Lantz.

The work Washington did with Newell in 1975 expanded his game, and he willed himself to become the power forward the Lakers needed. He played the position with the toughness of a stevedore. In the terms of the trade, Washington became an enforcer.

PETE NEWELL: "When Kermit was there nobody messed with Kareem."

Washington's reputation soon spread around the league. One night Boston center Dave Cowens punched him in the jaw.

PETE NEWELL: "That didn't faze Kermit. He backhanded Cowens, and Kevin Stacom came running out from the Celtics bench. Kermit just smacked him in the nose."

Boston's Don Nelson rushed to help his teammates but saw how Washington had handled them and thought better of it. Such brouhahas were standard fare in the NBA of the '70s, and Washington was one of the regular participants. The league issued fines on occasion but generally responded as if it considered these flare-ups were part of the business. (Kareem had been fined $5,000 by new commissioner Larry O'Brien but received no suspension.) A few games after Kareem punched out Benson, Washington took on the Buffalo Braves in a wild melee.

STU LANTZ: "Kermit was hit from behind and beside in Buffalo, which left him gun-shy."

PETE NEWELL: "After that, Kermit told me that he had a great fear of people attacking him from behind, stemming from his days growing up in the inner city. He told me that in the ghetto you always made sure there was a wall at your back when you got into hassles."

The tragedy that these circumstances set up came in a December game in the Forum. Kevin Kunnert of the Houston Rockets was headed upcourt when Washington grabbed his shorts to hold him back. Kunnert turned and threw a couple of punches. When both players squared off, their teammates rushed in to help. Kareem, who had returned to action, grabbed Kunnert and swung him around away from Washington to break up the fight. At the same time, Houston's Rudy Tomjanovich ran up to help his teammate. Washington abruptly whirled and struck Tomjanovich.

JOHN RADCLIFFE: "I was sitting at the scorer's table a few feet away. The blow sounded like a melon striking concrete."

Tomjanovich's face collapsed in a shower of blood.

PETE NEWELL: "It was the most physical blow I've ever seen anybody throw or receive. When he saw this uniform coming at him, from then on it was a blur. He responded almost instinctively."

LOU HUDSON, FORMER LAKER: "Kermit was into karate and happened to throw the right punch at the right time."

STU LANTZ: "All Kermit did was turn and throw, just as Rudy was coming in. With those forces colliding, that's what made the damage as severe as it was. It wasn't like Kermit was this big man-eater waiting to destroy someone's career and face."

Videotape of the gruesome incident was replayed regularly on television, creating further furor. "I know it had a tremendous effect on his life, his family life," said Lantz. "Kermit got hate mail for a long time." His face shattered, Tomjanovich missed the rest of the season while undergoing a series of reconstructive operations. A former All-Star, he resumed his career the next season, yet he never achieved his previous level of play.

Washington was fined and suspended without pay for 60 days, bringing an additional $50,000 in salary losses. Shortly after the incident, the Lakers traded Washington and Don Chaney to the Boston Celtics for Charlie Scott. Tomjanovich later filed a civil suit against the Lakers and won. The league's handling of the incident and its aftermath cast a pall over the Lakers.

Lou Hudson: "All of a sudden we were the negative people. We knew that if Kermit had hit another black player, nothing would have happened. But since he hit a white player and broke his face, he was thrown out of the league."

Kareem Abdul-Jabbar: "Kermit didn't fight it the right way. I don't know about his legal representation, but he should have fought it. He could have made it difficult for them to do that to him. But the Lakers weren't supportive either. They knuckled under. I don't know if Mr. Cooke made a deal or whatever. We had to trade Kermit because they didn't want me and Kermit on the same team."

Pete Newell: "I had to testify at the civil trial in Texas. The club never stood behind him, and that's the thing that bothered me."

With Washington gone, the Lakers had only small forwards Don Ford and Jamaal Wilkes to play the power position and subsequently lost to Seattle in the '78–79 playoffs.

Kareem Abdul-Jabbar: "You know how far we went with them. It was unbelievable how all of that turned around. We couldn't rebuild it."

The turn of events served to drive Abdul-Jabbar even farther into the shell he inhabited the following season, 1978–79.

RON CARTER, FORMER LAKER: "Kareem was always very aloof. I had to go back and do a little research on him. After seeing him every day, I couldn't understand him. Why he was the way he was. He was moody. There were a couple of different personalities. There was a New York guy who was a joke-ster. And I liked him. When he came to practice and screwed around with people. I liked that guy, cracking jokes and just a prankster. But then there was this other introverted, concealed, consumed person who was mean. Those were the commercial airlines days when we weren't doing the jets yet. We'd be in the airports. Kareem would stand in the corner with two walls so no one could come up behind him, the meanest scowl he could muster on his face so that no one would come up to him. He would be standing there at seven-foot-four like a mean sonofabitch. 'Don't ask me anydamnthing!' Of course a kid would miss all of that and walk up to him. Kareem would get so mad that they weren't intimidated. But underneath it all, he was cool. He was not mean-spirited as a person."

With former Bulls general manager Jerry Krause as a scout, the Lakers had begun upgrading their roster through the draft. Among the three first-round picks he found for the Lakers that year was a quick young guard out of Duquesne named Norm Nixon. In short time he would become "Mr. Big" to the Lakers and a favorite target of coach Jerry West.

JOE MCDONNELL: "That's the year they had three number one picks. Norm, Kenny Carr, and Brad Davis. In Norm, they got one of the quicker point guards in the league to match up with the Johnny Davises and Maurice Cheeks, the guys of that time who were really fast. Norm and Jerry West just didn't like each other. Norm always felt that West was using him as his whip-ping boy."

RON CARTER: "[West] exacerbated the problem by being a poor communi-cator. It wasn't that he didn't have the skills—he couldn't articulate what he was seeing and feeling in a non-attacking, aggressive way. Jerry would just blow up and go on a diatribe. At the end of it, he hadn't said anything, other than 'I'm mad as hell.' It would be like, 'Coach, are we gonna run something? Now that you've cursed us out for the entire time-out.' When he would do that, you could look at the body posture of the players and see this was not right. It was no good. Kareem was the first one. He would always be at the end, as far away from Jerry as he could be, with his head down. You didn't know if he was listening or not. I'm sure that helped to infuriate Jerry. Because guys weren't giving the eye contact and the 'yes, we're in this together.' That wasn't happening. My very first game, we're at the Spectrum in Philadelphia, and Jerry punches a blackboard he's so damn mad. It was over some simple thing. We had made four or five transitions up the floor, and we didn't get Kareem the ball. Norm had told me, 'Ron, if we don't get Kareem the ball on this next series, he's gonna stop playing for us tonight.' Because we had made six or seven trips, and he hadn't touched the ball. Norm was good at reading Kareem's posture. So we called fist out, that was to get in the low post. Because Kareem was upset, he didn't do what he usually did 99.9 percent of the time. We threw it to him in the low post. The first thing he does, he looks at the shot clock at the other end to see how much time he has. The second thing he does is look where the defender is. If he's too far to his left, he's gonna make a fake to his right to get him to move, then he's gonna throw the hook. Right? We all know this. But he was so angry that he hadn't touched the ball, he turned and shot. Missed. Julius gets it and dunks on us at the other end. We got into halftime down a point, and Jerry West is so mad he punches the blackboard and breaks his finger. I'm not sure if he breaks it, but he ends up putting it in ice. He's ranting and raving. He finally comes in the locker room and he goes, 'Who took that shot?' And Kareem is shocked because *nobody*, and I mean *nobody*, yells at Kareem. Never once, ever. The only guy that even came close was Norm Nixon. That's the only guy I ever saw question Kareem. Norm would say shit like, 'Oh, you ain't playin' today, big fella?' But Norm was the only one who could get away with that. He was Mr. Big. Everybody else was, 'Kareem, we really need you to get up and down the court for us tonight.'"

STU LANTZ: "I know Jerry was miserable. He was such a perfectionist. Losses were harder on Jerry than winning was good for him. Winning was great, but losing was that much worse for Jerry."

Cashing Out

When he met Jerry West to offer him the Lakers' coaching job in July 1976, Jack Kent Cooke sported a broken arm, which he had sustained just days earlier trying to stop Jeannie, his wife of 42 years, from leaving their vacation home in the Sierra Nevadas. Jeannie, though, made a clean getaway from the marriage she had tried to escape for the previous decade. Weary of life with Cooke and his endless schedule of sporting events, she'd tried suicide four times. "I can't measure up to your competitive nature," she explained in one note.

Bereft of companionship, Cooke packed up his life and moved to Las Vegas, becoming in the process an absentee owner, ruling the Lakers with daily phone calls. For urgent matters, general manager Bill Sharman would jump a flight to Vegas to confer with Cooke in person.

BILL SHARMAN: "It was difficult having an absentee owner. He wanted to be active in the club. He wanted to know what was going on and make decisions like he always did. So you'd have to fly over there and have meetings or talk on the phone. I'd call him after every home game and give him a rundown on who did what, the box scores and everything."

The Lakers owner became even more of a tyrant after the separation. For years the rule around Forum offices had been that if the phone on your desk rang three times, you were fired. And when you answered, you had better know the starting times for all major Forum events. If you didn't, that would get you a pink slip, too. The tales of his insensitivity grew with each passing season. Supposedly there was an occasion when Cooke stood on the Kings' hockey ice, holding his dog Coco and talking to a Forum employee. "I need your coat," Cooke told the employee, who quickly surrendered it only to watch him wrap the dog. Cooke has denied these and many other stories of his brash style, but along with the Fabulous Forum, the Kings, and the Lakers, they remain part of his legacy in L.A.

Forum employees saw the first indication that this reign was coming to an end in 1979, when Jeannie Cooke finally collected the payback for her decades of misery. Judge Joseph Wapner, who would go on to television fame on the syndicated "People's Court," hit Cooke with a $41 million divorce settlement. At the time, the *Guinness Book of World Records* decreed it the largest in history. To pay up, Cooke would have to sell his Forum sports empire, and when it happened, that too would go down as another record deal.

BILL SHARMAN: "It didn't take me by surprise that Mr. Cooke wanted to sell the team. I had heard rumors for four or five years that he might sell. He was involved in so many businesses. You always heard stories about Mr. Cooke buying and selling."

No one could have been more pleased by this news than Jerry West. It wasn't exactly clear who would be running the team, but things had to get better.

JERRY WEST: "It was time for a change. It was a positive divorce, that's what it was."

Ignition

To borrow Pat Riley's phrase, Showtime was the game's "defining moment," and the Lakers were happily caught up in it. Yet even as they lived it, the period was addressed in the past tense, leaving the marketing minds behind the scenes to wonder if they would survive it. From the outset, it was clear that Showtime was a hoops fairy tale, pro basketball's Age of Camelot, when Magic Johnson and Larry Bird were the boy wonders who pulled the proverbial sword from the stone. Until they came along, the game had struggled to find an identity among American professional sports. It had a reputation for selfish athletes and boring, meaningless games. But Bird and Johnson changed all that. They first took their college teams to the 1979 NCAA Finals, where Johnson and Michigan State ended the hopes of Bird and his little team that could, the Indiana State Sycamores. Born overnight, their rivalry drew a massive television audience for that NCAA title game, and just six months later many of those fans followed them into the NBA. For decades pro basketball had attempted to appropriate the excitement of college hoops. At last Bird and Johnson delivered the goods, transforming the NBA into a new kingdom, ruled by the wondrous pass and the unforeseen assist. Ah, Camelot. It was pure storybook, or so it seemed.

MICHAEL COOPER, FORMER LAKER: "Magic meant so much to the game. The key with Magic, and what makes a star turn into a superstar, a star is gonna shine by himself. A superstar is gonna make other people shine. That's what Larry Bird and Magic always did. They made the league what it is today."

MAGIC JOHNSON: "It was a beautiful time. We had graceful, beautiful players. Kareem with his skyhook. James Worthy with the beautiful floaters and finger rolls. Byron Scott with his beautiful jump shot. Michael Cooper with the way he played defense and the alley-oop for the Coop-a-loop. Those are the type of things that we did that made Showtime. And they also changed basketball."

JERRY WEST: "Magic Johnson could make the simple plays look like they were the hardest in the world. And he'd do them in a simple manner. He really wasn't flashy. Magic Johnson very rarely threw a pass behind his back. He just made the right pass at the right time. He was like Willie Mays. Willie Mays could catch a routine fly ball and make it look like an amazing play. His hat would fall off, everything blowing. It looked incredible."

DOUG KRIKORIAN, LONGTIME L.A. SPORTSWRITER: "Magic put on performances you can't believe. Jordan was dominant in the '90s when ESPN and cable were big. *USA Today* was big, when cable hit. People forget that cable wasn't that big in the '80s. Magic was phenomenal. Every game he played, he played great. He didn't give a damn about stats. He played in the NBA 12 seasons, and they were in the NBA Finals nine times. Does that tell you something about Magic?"

JIMMY GOLDSTEIN, LONGTIME L.A. BASKETBALL AFICIONADO: "For me, Showtime was not as fun. I'm a basketball purist, and there were so many blowouts in those days. I like to see a competitive game that goes down to the buzzer. And the Lakers were up in the fourth quarter consistently in those days by 20 or more points, and they put on a show that I felt was sort of rubbing it in the faces of the other teams. Of course the Lakers fans loved it."

ANDREW BERNSTEIN, PHOTOGRAPHER FOR THE NBA: "I never knew which place to look. I never knew what Magic was gonna do every time he came down the court. The excitement in the Forum was incredible. Every game. Constantly."

LOU ADLER, RECORD PRODUCER AND LONGTIME LAKERS FAN: "The moment Magic smiled, I guess L.A. started smiling. The city before had not really gotten into the team, even though they had won that championship. But these were younger guys, they were more outgoing, they were out around the town. They brought the town into the game."

DOUG KRIKORIAN: "When Magic got here, Hollywood descended on the Lakers. And they became the new *in* thing in L.A. My gosh, in that Forum press lounge, you'd see Sean Penn, Rob Lowe, Francis Ford Coppola, Robert Towne, the screenwriter for *Chinatown*—you saw all of these stars there. It was compelling and it crossed over. Sports crossed really over then. The explosion of basketball as entertainment happened during Showtime."

The script for the era seemed nearly perfect. Leave it to Hollywood to crowd the opening with a giant business deal and a murder mystery, neither of which has ever been completely resolved.

Buss

First the deal, actually a classic American rags-to-riches story, of which the protagonist is Jerry Buss, who grows up disadvantaged, first in Southern California, then in Wyoming. The plot includes a harsh stepfather, poverty, icy walks to school, rebellion, and a record of remarkable and persistent academic achievement. Buss becomes frustrated, drops out of high school, works at manual labor, returns to school, and graduates. From this background, he goes to college, earns a degree, gathers momentum, and picks up a Ph.D. in chemistry. Thus credentialed, he goes to work in the aerospace industry, with occasional stints teaching chemistry at Southern Cal. The money is decent, but the job is boring. Besides, his real genius is numbers, and his real love is sports. Buss and college buddy Hampton Mears will go anywhere to see a Southern Cal football game. On the side, Buss and a friend from his work in the aerospace industry, Frank Mariani, buy an old apartment building and become landlords. Here the plot drags, as it often does in critical financial junctures. Scenes of late nights with Buss and Mariani painting and doing maintenance on their building. Then the purchase of another building, followed by shots of Buss hovering over a calculator for long hours, figuring out how to finance even more properties, interspersed by frames of Buss gleefully rolling the dice playing Monopoly, with a French subtitle suggesting that life imitates leisure. From there yet another plot twist, as Buss, the father of four, gets a divorce and emerges as a budding real estate tycoon and blue-jeans-wearing playboy who dates attractive young women as often as they will say yes and dances till his knees ache. Then still shots of business-page headlines about the Southern California real estate boom, followed by more scenes of Buss rapidly working his calculator to acquire more property. Other leisure moments include Buss playing high-stakes poker with stacks of chips in front of him, or spending time with his growing stamp and coin collections. Ultimately, however, stamps and coins prove too tame. With success comes angst that the protagonist is merely a landlord. He wants to play in the great sandbox of American professional sports, so in 1972 he and partners buy the LA Strings of World Team Tennis, and promptly lose a bundle trying to promote tennis at the Sports Arena, sending Buss looking for a better deal at the Forum. There in 1975 he gets to know Jack Kent Cooke, setting in motion the chemistry that makes it all happen. Tennis losses run heavy, but Buss is determined to move beyond real estate into pro sports ownership. He searches for baseball, football, and basketball options, all the time not daring to hope that the answer to his desires is very close.

Cooke and Buss made for a fascinating pair of business adversaries. One, soft-spoken and intense, given to wearing dirty blue jeans and open-collar shirts. The other a loud, overbearing sort, always eager to get the best of every situation. Together they would hatch what was billed at the time as the "largest sports deal in history."

Since 1975, Cooke had watched Buss battle to build the Strings' woeful tennis attendance from 2,000 to 7,000 and complimented him on the effort. Buss, in turn, overlooked Cooke's personal shortcomings to view him as a mentor, a rare resource who could teach him much about sports ownership. They even became friends. Sort of.

JERRY BUSS: "One day, in the middle of one of our many talks, Cooke mentioned that he might like to sell the Forum. I jumped. It was just the opportunity I wanted, but he was coy. I'd fly up to Vegas every six weeks or so, and we'd talk about it."

Mostly, he listened as Cooke told tales of running his two teams. Little actual business was discussed, but the inside details of the two franchises fascinated Buss. He would hop a plane every time Cooke called just so he could get the current scoop. But, outside of that, his hopes of getting the Forum seemed mired in Cooke's parlor games.

JERRY BUSS: "It was a very frustrating time. I guess I always believed that it would happen, although it seemed like forever. I would alternate being down and depressed. Then I'd think it was going to work and I'd be elated. As his divorce proceedings moved along, the sale talks warmed up."

Their meetings picked up pace, and afterward Buss sifted through what had been said, trying to figure Cooke out.

JERRY BUSS: "There were times when I felt I'd gotten in a little over my head. Jack Kent Cooke was remarkably charming when he wanted to be, and he was a very, very tough-willed man. He may have had the toughest will I've ever seen. It was like iron. And he was very quick to take advantage of turns in the negotiations."

To make things happen, Buss had to arrange a trade on seven of his properties for the Forum, which allowed Cooke to avoid the taxes of a cash transaction. Then in late 1978, Cooke mentioned that he might like to include the Lakers and Kings in the package.

JERRY BUSS: "He asked me, 'How would you like to buy the whole thing?' My heart jumped again. The size of the deal doubled. I told him I'd love to purchase the teams, but I said I'd need time to see if it was possible. I started thinking, and I went to L.A. and started rummaging through my holdings. I had no idea what I could get on the open market for them."

JACK KENT COOKE: "That deal was going to work regardless. He was so eager to get it. It was just a matter of the price."

Fortunately, the real estate market was strong in 1979, and Buss soon realized he was in a position to move. But then Cooke decided that he wanted the Chrysler Building in New York instead of Buss's properties. Buss laughed, shook his head, then hustled to find buyers for his buildings. That done, he worked out a trade: his high-rises, complete with buyers to soften the tax blow, for the Chrysler Building.

JERRY BUSS: "Then Cooke decided he wanted to include his 13,000-acre Raljon Ranch in the Sierras in the deal. I drove up to the ranch, saw it, came back, and made an offer. I don't think he knew for sure he wanted to sell, but once he made up his mind, things went smoothly."

Well, almost. With everything in place in early May 1979, Cooke phoned and said, "Jerry, we're going to make the deal." Buss would pay what amounted to $67.5 million for the Forum, Lakers, Kings, and Cooke's ranch. Cooke would get the Chrysler Building and properties in three states. The high-rises would go to the owners of the Chrysler Building.

But on midnight May 17, Buss learned that one of the high-rise buyers in the Chrysler deal had backed out, creating a $2.7 million shortage. Buss scrambled to get the cash together, calling in favors from Mariani and other associates, and just made it by the 12:30 closing time the next day.

RON CARTER, FORMER LAKER AND BUSS EMPLOYEE: "We were sitting in the law firm of Buss's attorneys, a big law firm over on Wilshire Boulevard near UCLA. I remember Cooke calling us. They put him on a speakerphone. What I'll never forget is how these guys—I thought they were great men— but I'll never forget how their posture changed just from hearing Cooke's voice. They sat up in their chairs. Just as if Cooke was in the room. He called Jerry Buss 'son.' 'Hello, Mr. Cooke, how are you? It's Dr. Buss.' 'Son? Are we gonna close this thing?' 'Yessir, Mr. Cooke, we're gonna do it.' It was a mad scramble to get the deal done."

Afterward, Buss was too exhausted to celebrate, other than a few private moments in the Forum, sitting at courtside in the empty building, then walking upstairs to gaze at photographs of Lakers and Kings. "My players," he thought proudly. No longer was he just another landlord.

JERRY BUSS: "It announced the ending of my real estate career and the beginning of my sports career."

Not completely, not yet. In the aftermath, *Sports Illustrated* turned loose one of its investigators trying to isolate all the elements of the deal. After a good effort, the investigator phoned his editors and said it would take six weeks or more just to track the deeds involved. So *SI* hired an accounting firm to cut the time to a week. Three weeks later, the accountants were still trying to figure it all out.

Apparently, Buss had sold 15 to 20 limited partnerships in the acreage on which the Forum sat, with plans to buy out those partnerships over the next 15 to 20 years. It was estimated that Buss actually had only $125,000 cash invested in the entire transaction, not including the costs of the deal itself.

JERRY BUSS: "We had a lot of people working on it. A conservative estimate of the lawyer and accountant hours would be $500,000."

JACK KENT COOKE: "The deal was not complicated at all to me."

Now the murder mystery: Buss knew he had learned much from Cooke about managing an arena, but he figured the former Lakers owner really didn't know how to market the team. Buss, on the other hand, had exact ideas about what he wanted. His notions about entertainment dated to a seminal experience in the early '60s when he was a regular at The Horn, a small nightclub on Wilshire Boulevard in Santa Monica. The club's nightly opener captured his fascination, no matter how often he saw it. The lights would dim, the spotlights would come up, and from one of the tables a singer would rise to croon, "It's showtime." Then a second and a third would stand to join the harmony. Buss would sip his rum and Coke, draw on his lighted cigarette, and let himself drift away in the moment.

He wanted that same atmosphere for his new arena. It would be a place where fans could settle into their courtside seats with a mixed drink and a cigarette and enjoy the show. There would be dancers and celebrities and a hot band to replace the Forum's dead-zone organ music. And there would be no more waitresses running around in cheesy togas. Instead of $15 for those courtside seats, fans would immediately pay $60, and soon the cost would soar into the hundreds and eventually the thousands.

RUSS GRANIK, NBA VICE PRESIDENT: "One of Jerry's first contributions to the league is that he's one of the first owners to really understand how to price a building. I remember him talking to David and me and other owners and saying, 'Look, it's like real estate. The best real estate you can sell at almost any price.' He saw that the seats that are on courtside, or closer to the court, between the baselines, that they really had been underpriced in the NBA for its entire history. But then when you get to the top of the building, Jerry was one of the first to control it, to make sure that those prices didn't go up the same way other prices did. I think virtually everybody has followed that in the last 20 years."

To pump up the prices, Buss's biggest change would have to come with the team itself. Buss thought pro basketball was more than a little boring in 1979. He needed an exciting running team to take center stage for this new "Showtime" atmosphere. Otherwise it wouldn't work. To run, the Lakers had to have the right players and the right coach.

In early May 1979, after Buss and Cooke agreed to the deal but before they closed it, they sat down to discuss coaches. First on the list was Jerry Tarkanian, the coach of UNLV's Runnin' Rebels. "Jerry asked me what I thought of Jerry Tarkanian," said Cooke. "I told him, 'He's a first-class coach.'" At Buss's request, Cooke phoned for Tarkanian in a flash.

JERRY TARKANIAN, FORMER UNLV COACH: "I was in New York recruiting Sidney Green when I got the call. We set up a meeting and promised to keep it quiet."

In 1976, the deal to make Tarkanian the Lakers' coach had been queered when UNLV boosters found out about it and pressured him into staying in Vegas.

JERRY TARKANIAN: "This time we kept it a total secret. This time I wanted the job."

Their first meeting in California went well, so Tarkanian called in his agent and friend of many years, Vic Weiss, to work out the details the next day with Buss and Cooke. (Buss didn't recall Weiss's involvement in hiring Tarkanian, although Cooke and Tarkanian did.) Weiss, a 51-year-old San Fernando Valley auto dealer, boxing manager, and sports aficionado, drove a white Rolls-Royce to the meeting that morning.

JACK KENT COOKE: "We hadn't been talking long when Vic Weiss pulled out a roll of bills that would have choked an ox. He rather casually informed me that he always carried $5,000 to $10,000. I was distracted by this, and he calmly put it back in his pocket. I am sure he did it to show us how well off he was."

The distraction aside, the parties agreed to a five-year, $1 million contract for Tarkanian to coach the Lakers, but there remained small issues—season tickets and autos for Tarkanian's family—to be settled. So Weiss agreed to return the next day with Tarkanian for a final meeting to close the deal. Weiss, however, failed to show the next morning, prompting Cooke to phone Tarkanian at his Newport Beach hotel room. He didn't show here either, Tark replied. Then Weiss's wife phoned Tarkanian because her husband hadn't been home the night before.

Almost a week later, a parking garage attendant at the Universal Sheraton noticed a terrible odor. Weiss was there, stuffed in the trunk of his Rolls. He reportedly was still carrying the rough draft of Tarkanian's agreement with the Lakers.

JERRY TARKANIAN: "I didn't know it at the time, but Vic was apparently involved in shady deals with Rams owner Carroll Rosenbloom [who had long generated suspicion of high-stakes gambling and underworld connections]. I heard he was transporting money for Rosenbloom."

Rosenbloom himself had drowned in Florida under mysterious circumstances just a few weeks earlier. Federal authorities had for some time been investigating Weiss's role in transporting cash to Las Vegas, ostensibly to place bets for Rosenbloom. Reportedly, investigators had even surveilled Weiss during a briefcase exchange in a Las Vegas airport rest room, but no connection could be proved.

And although the LAPD spent years working on the Weiss murder, the case was never solved, although authorities indicated that it appeared to be an organized crime hit. News reports of the murder tipped UNLV backers that their coach was planning to leave.

JERRY TARKANIAN: "A bunch of Vegas boosters got to me and put the guilt trip on me. It got to me, really got to me, so I turned it down. I told Jerry Buss it was gonna be a big mistake for me to turn it down. Going in with Magic would have been something."

Simultaneously, the incident cooled the Lakers on Tarkanian. Instead, Buss first attempted to get West to stay on as coach. When West declined, the Lakers turned to Jack McKinney, a protégé of Portland coach Jack Ramsay.

Although he had never been a pro head coach, McKinney loved an up-tempo offense. Buss wasn't sure about McKinney's credentials, but he came highly recommended. And he knew the running game, which was all the new owner needed to hear.

The Seminal Selection: Magic Johnson

In the final days, as he waited to close the sale, Cooke turned his interest to the team's number one pick in the 1979 draft. His Forum empire was the jewel of his collection, and while his divorce may have forced its sale, the owner wanted to add one last bauble before he turned it loose.

In 1976, 33-year-old Gail Goodrich had played out his option with the Lakers and signed a contract with the New Orleans Jazz. Under the league rules in force at the time, the Jazz owed the Lakers compensation for luring Goodrich away, so Cooke ordered his lawyer to strike a tough bargain with New Orleans general manager Barry Mendelsohn. The Lakers demanded New Orleans' number one picks in 1977 and 1979 and a second-round pick in 1980. It was a blatantly unreasonable asking price for the graybeard Goodrich, who would only play part of three injury-plagued seasons for the Jazz. But Cooke knew he had an edge. If the two teams failed to agree on compensation, Commissioner Larry O'Brien would settle it for them. The Jazz feared that O'Brien, who didn't like one team signing away another's players, would come down hard on them. So they agreed, only to have the Lakers then offer the three picks back to them for veteran power forward Sidney Wicks.

As fortune would have it, the Jazz refused that Wicks deal, and then helped the Lakers cause tremendously by finishing last in the league in 1979, thus ensuring L.A. a coin flip with Chicago, the worst team in the East, for the top pick in that spring's draft. Commissioner O'Brien made the flip at the NBA's New York offices while the Lakers and Bulls listened over the phone in a conference call. Cooke was so nervous, he couldn't go in Hearn's office, where Chick was taking O'Brien's call.

BILL SHARMAN: "Rod Thorn was the general manager in Chicago. He said they had a big promotion where they had a lot of people in their auditorium when they made the flip. He asked, 'Would it be all right with you if I make the call, because we got all these people here?' I said it's either heads or tails; it doesn't make that much difference."

Heads, Thorn said. Tails it was.

JACK KENT COOKE: "Chick let up a yell that could have been heard in downtown Los Angeles."

JIM HILL, VETERAN L.A. SPORTSCASTER AND LAKERS INSIDER: "I remember being there the day the Lakers won the coin toss for the rights to draft Magic. It was Chick Hearn, Bill Sharman, and myself. We were standing by a speakerphone, and the cameras were rolling and the coin was being tossed back in New York. A lot of people were leery as to how this coin was going to land. I jokingly said to Chick, 'What happens if it lands on its edge?' He started laughing. The coin was tossed by Larry O'Brien. The week prior to the coin toss the Lakers were in a horrible slump. I think they had lost something like six of seven games. They won the coin toss. Chick and Bill Sharman started screaming, and the first thing out of Chick's mouth was, 'That's the first thing we've won in a week.'"

Exciting as it was, the victory set up an immediate dilemma. Should they draft Magic Johnson or Sidney Moncrief out of the University of Arkansas?

JACK KENT COOKE: "There was no question in my mind that we should draft Magic Johnson."

Perhaps, but the rest of the Lakers staff seemed to have questions. Johnson had decent athletic skills, but what would you do with a six-foot-nine point guard? Moncrief, on the other hand, was a big, strong off guard with court sense, leadership skills, and smarts.

The team had faced a similar choice in 1975, when the Lakers had the option of acquiring Kareem or Bill Walton. All of the inner sanctum except Chick Hearn favored Kareem, and the trade for him was made with little anguish. But Magic was a tough call. The Bulls offered to trade their top pick, plus Reggie Theus, for the rights to Johnson. Buss, though, wanted Magic, and with owners future and present weighing in, the choice was obvious. Little did they realize then that Showtime had just found its master of ceremonies.

JIM HILL: "They brought Magic out after the draft, and we did interviews with him. He and I sat in the stands in the Forum. I remember him saying, 'I can just see myself now, running up and down this floor, diving into the stands for loose balls, hollering and screaming.' The enthusiasm in his eyes right then told me that this was going to be special."

First, though, he had to come to terms with Cooke, the notorious deal maker.

JIM HILL: "Before they started negotiating, Mr. Cooke ordered sand dabs. Magic said, 'I didn't know what a sand dab was.' He turned to his father and said, 'I don't want a sand dab. I don't know what that is.' Mr. Cooke said, 'Do you know how much a sand dab costs?' He said, 'I don't care how much it costs. I just want a burger and some fries.' So they laughed about that, and then Mr. Cooke made him an offer, about $400,000 or so. Magic said, 'I don't know about that offer.' His father was sitting there with him. His father tapped him on the knee and said, 'Come with me.' They went outside, and Magic said his father said, 'Oh, yeah, you gonna take that $400,000.' So they went back inside, and Magic said, 'Mr. Cooke, we've reconsidered . . .'"

Smile

His religious mother disliked it, because it suggested the occult, but sportswriter Fred Stabley, who followed Johnson's high school team, first gave him the nickname Magic. Magic because of his beamer of a smile. Magic because of uncanny ability with a basketball. But mostly he was Magic because he somehow transformed good teams into great ones. He did that everywhere he played. At Everett High School in East Lansing. At Michigan State. And finally in L.A. Everywhere he went he displayed an uncanny leadership, one that had emerged long before.

CHRISTINE JOHNSON, MAGIC'S MOTHER: "I ran into Earvin's fourth-grade teacher in a grocery store. She laughed and started telling me a story about him. It was the first day of school in her first year of teaching, and the class was giving her fits. Spitballs were flying. Children were yelling. Earvin stood up and told his classmates to get in their seats, to behave, to listen to the teacher. She said everybody stopped and did just what he said to do."

JUD HEATHCOTE, FORMER MICHIGAN STATE COACH: "I'm asked a lot what was the greatest thing Earvin did. Many say passing the ball, his great court sense, the fact that he could rebound. I say the greatest things Earvin did were intangible. He always made the guys he played with better. In summer pickup games, Earvin would take three or four nonplayers, and he'd make those guys look so much better and they would win, not because he was making the baskets all by himself, but because he just made other players play better."

Johnson entered Michigan State in the fall of 1977 and 19 months later delivered the Spartans an NCAA championship victory. "I'd heard about him at Everett High School," Terry Donnelly, his college teammate, recalled, "and I'd even seen him play. But it didn't really hit me until I got in the backcourt with him, on the first day of practice. You're running down the floor and you're open and most people can't get the ball to you through two or three people, but all of a sudden the ball's in your hands and you've got a layup."

To his credit, Heathcote immediately recognized Johnson's unique talent. Although the Michigan State program was short on big men, the coach didn't hesitate to run the big freshman at the point.

JUD HEATHCOTE: "I still remember the first game that Earvin played. We were playing Central Michigan. I think he had seven points and about eight turnovers, and everyone said, 'Heathcote's crazy. He's got Earvin handling the ball in the break; he's got him playing guard out there on offense; he's got him running the break; he's got him doing so many different things. Nobody can do all those things.' It's just that Earvin was nervous playing that first game and he didn't play like he played in practice. Actually, he was very comfortable in all those areas. When he went to the pros and right away they had him playing forward, I said sooner or later they'll realize that Earvin can play anywhere on defense and he has to have the ball on offense."

The Lakers needed many things in the fall of 1979. They needed rebounding help for Kareem in the frontcourt, and as Heathcote projected, Magic filled in nicely as a power forward on the defensive end. The Lakers also needed help for Norm Nixon in the backcourt. And although Nixon was already a young, promising point guard, the Lakers eventually moved him to shooting guard, and as Heathcote also projected, they eventually gave Magic the ball at the point.

Yet the team's biggest need was enthusiasm. No one player needed this more than Kareem, who had carried the Lakers through five frustrating years. Each passing season had brought more noise about his failure to take the team to a title. The criticism had been particularly stinging when the Lakers were thumped by Seattle in the second round of the 1979 playoffs.

KAREEM ABDUL-JABBAR: "They fixed on me as the reason for everything bad. It was like 'our star can't do it all for us here in Los Angeles.'"

TED GREEN, FORMER *LOS ANGELES TIMES* WRITER: "At that time, Kareem seemed to be going through a peculiar questioning in his life. He seemed to be wondering if he wanted to continue playing basketball. He was often lethargic and apathetic on the floor. Many nights he operated on cruise control. One night in Madison Square Garden he scored 24 points and had only one rebound. I wrote a story and called him Kareem Abdul-Sleepwalker. He got very upset and didn't speak to me for several months."

His response to the circumstances was to pull even deeper within his shell. His already-cool approach to the game turned chilly. According to the story line, Magic then arrived and recharged the great center's competitive battery, an interpretation that irritates Abdul-Jabbar. Yes, Magic was influential, he would say time and again. But he contended that what really juiced him up was his new contract and the Lakers' decision to acquire two power forwards, Spencer Haywood and Jim Chones, to help him in the frontcourt.

Still, it was hard to deny that Earvin Johnson had all of L.A. jumping with excitement in 1979. The once sparsely attended summer league games in the balmy gym at Cal State Los Angeles suddenly opened to overflow crowds. The feeling grew from there and coursed through the whole season, pushed along by the verve of a 20-year-old. For Johnson, life was one big, joyful disco, a trip from one jam to another. All he had to do was pop on his Walkman headset, snap his fingers, and let the good times roll. Sometimes his youthful charm might be as ostentatious as wearing a full-length fur coat and chartering a helicopter as his personal limousine. Usually, though, it was as simple as his smile.

JAMAAL WILKES, FORMER LAKER: "His enthusiasm was something out of this world, something I had never seen prior to him and something I haven't seen since. It just kind of gave everyone a shot in the arm."

In training camp, Norm Nixon took to calling Johnson "Young Buck," later shortened to "Buck," because of his zeal.

Johnson's soul mate in this energy zone was a little-known second-year player out of the University of New Mexico named Michael Cooper who was fighting for his basketball life. He could execute spectacular dunks and had lots of raw athletic talent, but he was six-foot-seven and weighed only 185. Johnson would have breakfast with Cooper and tell him not to worry, that he had the team made. But the coaches had to choose between Cooper and another second-year player, Ron Carter out of Virginia Military Institute. The team needed some defensive toughness, and the coaches pondered which of the two would be more likely to provide it.

Assistant Paul Westhead recommended they keep Carter, but Jack McKinney chose Coop. Carter went off to work in the real estate business with Buss, and Cooper stayed around to play the vulture in Showtime's feared defense.

With a rookie leading the way, the Lakers charged out of training camp in 1979 and into a bright future. When Kareem won their opening game at San Diego at the buzzer with one of his skyhooks, Magic smothered him in a youthful celebration.

JIM HILL: "Everybody laughing and screaming and jumping up and down, and Magic runs over and jumps on Kareem and hugs him around the neck and is actually kind of choking him right out there on the floor. They get in the back and Kareem pulls Magic aside and says, 'Hey, we got 81 more of those. You don't have to hug me like that.' Magic with that enthusiasm and that passion says, 'I'll tell you what. You make that game winning hook shot like that 81 more times, I'm gonna hug you like that 81 more times.' Kareem, who had always had that stoic look about him, just had to break down and laugh himself."

BRENT MUSBURGER, BROADCASTER: "I did Magic's first game in the NBA in San Diego, the night he jumped in Kareem's arms. We kept taking tight shots and there were big smiles on his face. The smile never really faded."

MAGIC JOHNSON: "Everybody was shocked, but I was used to showing my emotions."

The first setback came just 13 games into that inaugural season. The Lakers opened with nine wins and four losses and were primed to scoot. Jack Mc-Kinney's offense offered something for everyone. It would obviously require adjustments, but the atmosphere was open and getting better with every game. Then McKinney suffered a serious head injury in a bicycle accident while headed to a tennis match with Westhead. For a time it appeared McKinney might not make it. At the very least, he faced months of convalescence. So Westhead, another Ramsay protégé, served as interim coach and selected Pat Riley, then serving as Chick Hearn's color man, to become his assistant.

PAUL WESTHEAD, FORMER LAKERS COACH: "It was difficult for many reasons. Jack was the reason I came to the Lakers. He brought me out to work with them. It was his team that he assembled in training camp. He put in all the fundamentals and the basic offenses and defenses. And we're off and running and playing pretty good. He has this disastrous bicycle fall and really isn't able to function for some weeks. He gets out of the rhythm of the team. So it was an incredible misfortune for Jack."

The Lakers resumed their pace in the aftermath of the accident. Westhead was just as big a proponent of the running game as McKinney. Still, there were problems. Johnson wasn't exempt from rookie growing pains.

PAUL WESTHEAD: "Because we had guys shooting the ball, Norm Nixon, Jamaal Wilkes, or Kareem. Magic would go get their misses and put it back, or give it back to them, so everybody loves somebody who's gonna go to the offensive glass and get your missed shot. Slowly, in year two and year three, he began to run the point, then slowly began shooting the ball more. He was smart enough to say, 'When I come in as a rookie, I'm gonna rebound the ball.' He was a power forward."

When Johnson did play the point, the veterans complained that he was controlling the ball too much, keeping it to himself. And his no-look passes kept catching teammates unaware.

JACK RAMSAY, FORMER PORTLAND COACH: "I didn't think Magic could be a point guard. Jack McKinney did, who was his first coach. Jack had been my assistant at Portland, then went down to the Lakers to take that job. He told me he was going to make Magic the point guard. I said, 'Good luck.' I thought he was going to be more of a small forward. But, you see, Magic worked on his game. His first year he couldn't dribble with his left hand. I remember a game in Portland we got nine turnovers from him by forcing him to the left side of the floor and making him play with his left hand. The next year you couldn't do that. Each year he added something to his game. Magic was such a great competitor he knew what he had to work on and did it."

Norm Nixon, who had run the point since being drafted by the Lakers in 1978, had rather selflessly given up that role and moved to shooting guard. Nicknamed Mr. Big, his presence took some pressure off the rookie and made his adjustment easier.

JACK RAMSAY: "In that rookie year, Nixon had more assists than Magic did. But by the end of that year, by the time they played Philadelphia in Game 6, Magic was doing everything."

KAREEM ABDUL-JABBAR: "You talk about people that weren't given their due. Norm could handle the ball as well as Earvin. Norm was faster up the court, and he had just as good a vision. But Norm couldn't get to the basket like Earvin because he didn't have the size. But when other teams tried to pressure Earvin and he gave the ball to Norm and let him run the break, then Norm and Jamaal, that was an incredible break right there. If the other teams tried to stop Earvin, that gave Norm and Jamaal the open court. They got us a lot of points. We went to two world championships that way."

RON CARTER, FORMER LAKER: "Magic and Norman don't get along. I mean they get along, but it's always about the court. So there's always this little petty inside thing going on. We're in Philly, Norm's late. The bus has to leave at 11, and Norm is a 10:59 kind of guy. Everyone's on the bus but Norm, and Magic is yelling from the back of the bus, 'Let's go. Let's go.' And somebody says, 'Well, Mr. Big's not here.' So Norm finally comes out, Mr. Cool, Mr. Last Minute, Mr. Never Break a Sweat. He gets on the bus, and somebody says, 'Hey, Big. The rook was trying to get you fined.' And Norm says, 'Well, yeah, he's young. I expect that out of young people.' This is the kind of stuff that's going on every day between Norm and Magic. Just little digs trying to get at each other. It got ugly. It manifested itself the latter part of that first season, when Magic played all the positions and did all the things that he did. I think it manifested in Magic's mind as, 'I don't need Norm. I can do this at the point guard. We don't need Norm.' We had two great point guards, and Norm took all the pressure off of Magic. But the problem was, in that locker room it was Norman's locker room. As long as Norm Nixon was there, it was gonna be Norm's locker room because of Norm's persona. It wasn't just about having the ball. It was always about, 'Who you gonna follow, me or Norm?' Kareem in a very discreet sort of way made it clear that Norm was his guy. Just subtly. Westhead might say, 'All right, run the play.' And Magic would grab the ball to run the play, and Kareem would slap it out of his hands and hand it to Norm. Just little stuff like that. You could see it irritate Magic. Eventually there was going to be this rift. You could see it coming."

"Magic had to learn to keep everybody in the game," Nixon told the *New York Times* later that season. "He was losing 'em. He had to make an effort, and he did. I like playing with him much more now. We complement one another."

PAUL WESTHEAD: "It was Jack McKinney's feeling that they should share the guard role. So they would play off each other. It was kind of an even deal. At least half the time Nixon was free to run the team."

Very quickly opponents realized that the Lakers had the best backcourt in the league. Combined with a dominant offensive center, they presented a formidable challenge. Kareem won the league's MVP for an unprecedented sixth time (Boston's Bill Russell had won five), and the Lakers topped the Western Conference with a 60–22 record.

Bird, meanwhile, had led the Celtics to a 61–21 finish. The Boston forward had averaged 21.5 points in helping his team to what was then the best turnaround in league history. The year before Bird arrived, Boston had finished 29–53. That upswing of 32 games resulted in Bird being named rookie of the year. It was an insult that left Johnson with plenty of incentive. During the regular season he had averaged 17.6 points, 7.7 rebounds, and 7.3 assists while shooting 52 percent from the floor. He upped those numbers during his 16 playoff games that spring of 1980 to 18.3 points, 10.5 rebounds, and 9.4 assists. With the team in synch and Kareem playing his best ball in years, the Lakers ditched Phoenix and defending champion Seattle on their way to the Western Conference championship and the Finals.

Bird's Celtics, meanwhile, had run aground against Julius Erving and the Philadelphia 76ers in the Eastern Conference Finals and lost 4–1. Coached by Billy Cunningham, the 76ers had finished 59–23, just two games behind Boston during the regular season. They brought a strong, veteran lineup to face the Lakers for the 1980 title. Julius Erving was still at the top of his high-flying game. "I don't think about my dunk shots," he had said during the Boston series. "I just make sure I have a place to land." But Kareem quickly overmatched Philadelphia's centers, Caldwell Jones and Darryl Dawkins, and put L.A. in position to win the championship. In Game 1 in the Forum he scored 33 points, with 14 rebounds, 6 blocks, and 5 assists, to push the Lakers to a 109–102 win. Nixon had 23 points and Wilkes finished with 20 while doing an excellent double-team job on Erving. "Every time I caught the ball I had two people on me," the 76ers star said afterward. Magic, too, was a factor with 16 points, 9 assists, and 10 rebounds.

In the earlier rounds of the playoffs, Westhead had begun playing Johnson at power forward on offense, while Nixon and sixth man Michael Cooper ran the backcourt. "That's our best lineup," the coach told reporters.

Kareem scored 38 in Game 2, but Philly's team effort was impressive. They virtually shut down the vaunted Lakers fast break and did it without fouling. The 76ers led by as much as 20 in the fourth period, but the Lakers raced back, trimming the lead to 105–104 late in the game. Then Bobby Jones popped in a jumper with seven seconds left, and that was enough for a 107–104 Philly win that tied the series at one-all.

The Lakers blamed the loss on the "distractions" of Spencer Haywood, who had fallen asleep during pregame stretching exercises. Once an ABA star and now a Lakers reserve, Haywood had been disgruntled most of the season, at one point saying that Westhead's reasons for not playing him more were "lies." The Forum fans loved Haywood, and he often encouraged their affection by waving a towel to urge their chanting his name. Game 2 brought the final straw, however, when he picked a fight with teammate Brad Holland. Afterward Westhead suspended Haywood for the remainder of the season, which left the Lakers thin in the frontcourt just when they needed the help.

Westhead made two key defensive switches for Game 3. First, he moved Jim Chones to cover Dawkins. With only the nonshooting Caldwell Jones to worry about, Kareem parked his big frame in the lane and dared the 76ers to drive in. Then Westhead switched Magic to covering Lionel Hollins on the perimeter, which stifled Philly's outside game. The result was a 111–101 Lakers win. Kareem had again given the 76ers a headache—33 points, 14 rebounds, 4 blocks, and 3 assists. And once again he got plenty of help from Nixon, Johnson, and Wilkes.

As expected, Philly lashed back for Game 4. The lead switched back and forth through the first three periods, then the 76ers took control in the fourth. Dr. J unleashed one of his more memorable moves, scooting around Lakers reserve Mark Landsberger on the right to launch himself. In midair, headed toward the hoop, Erving encountered Kareem. Somehow the Doctor moved behind the backboard and freed his right arm behind Kareem to put it in. It was pure magic, the Philly variety, and the 76ers went on to even the series at two-all with a 105–102 win.

All of which served to set up a marvelous Game 5 back at the Forum. L.A. clutched to a two-point lead late in the third quarter when Kareem twisted his left ankle and went to the locker room. At that juncture, he had 26 points and was carrying the Lakers despite an uneven performance from Magic. But the rookie took over with the captain out. He scored six points and added an assist as L.A. moved up by eight.

That was enough to buy time for Abdul-Jabbar, who limped back into the game early in the fourth period. His appearance aroused the Forum regulars, and despite the bad ankle, he acknowledged their support by scoring 14 points down the stretch. With the game tied at 103 and 33 seconds left, Kareem scored, drew the foul, and finished Philly by completing the three-point play. L.A. won 108–103 and took the series lead, 3–2.

That next morning, Thursday, May 15, the Lakers arrived at Los Angeles International Airport for their flight to Philly and learned that Kareem wouldn't be making the trip. His ankle was so bad, doctors told him to stay home and try to get ready for Game 7. Westhead was worried about the effect the news would have on the team.

In a private meeting, the coach told Magic he would have to move to center. No problem, the young guard replied. He had played center in high school and loved challenges such as the one he was about to face.

MAGIC JOHNSON: "Paul's fear was that we couldn't match up with Dawkins and Caldwell Jones. I told him I could play Caldwell Jones, and he looked at me like, 'Jesus, he's seven feet tall!' He couldn't believe that I could match up.

I told him, 'Coach, on the other end, what are they gonna do with us? Who's gonna guard the guys we're gonna have?' And that's what he couldn't understand. Because once we got the ball, we were gone. We beat Philadelphia in the transition game because they couldn't keep up."

When the team boarded its United Airlines flight to Philadelphia, Johnson plopped himself down in the first-class seat always set aside for Abdul-Jabbar.

TED GREEN: "It was like a sacrilege to sit in Kareem's seat."

PAUL WESTHEAD: "Kareem, as we called him, Cap, always sat in the first row aisle seat. Magic said, 'Well, Cap's not with us. I may have to take his spot.'"

JIM HILL: "People thought he was crazy. He looked back at everybody and said, 'Have no fear, EJ is here. We're gonna go win this game.' He sat back in Kareem's chair and started laughing. There are certain things you don't do. That was Kareem's domain. They were like, 'Young buck, you don't know what you're talking about.' Man, he went out that night and did what hardly anyone had ever done and probably what few people will ever do in this game."

Somehow the folks in Philly never really believed the Lakers would head into the game without their captain. Radio stations reported regular sightings of Kareem at the airport. One taxi driver even claimed to have taken the center to his hotel.

Billy Cunningham was just as distrusting as the man on the street. "I'll believe he's not coming when the game ends and I haven't seen him," the 76ers' coach told the writers.

The Lakers, meanwhile, were almost too loose, Westhead feared. Magic was his normal jammin', dancin' self. About the only thing that punctured his mood was reporters' questions about his thoughts for Game 7. It was perfect, he told his teammates. Nobody expects us to win here. In reality, most of the Lakers figured they didn't have a chance.

But when they arrived at the Spectrum that Friday evening they were greeted by the sounds of carpenters hammering out an awards presentation platform. The NBA rules required that Philadelphia provide some facility to present the trophy, just in case L.A. happened to win.

"It should be interesting," Westhead told his players before the game. "Pure democracy. We'll go with the slim line."

Which meant Magic, Chones, and Wilkes in the frontcourt while Nixon and Cooper took care of things up top. Kareem, who was sprawled on his bed back at his Bel-Air home, sent a last-minute message. Go for it. With that last blast pushing them sky-high, the Lakers took the floor.

PAUL WESTHEAD: "We were going out for the center jump and we said, 'Let's go.' The last thing, Jim Chones looked at me and said, 'Now, coach, I'm jumping center, right?' I said, 'No, Magic is jumping center.' We wanted it to appear that he was the center."

JIM HILL: "I remember Brent Musburger was doing the play by play. He started laughing. 'And the rookie Magic Johnson from Michigan State is going to be in the center circle to jump ball.' Next thing you know Magic's a center, he's a guard, he's a forward. He was just everywhere."

Magic grinned broadly as he stepped up to jump center against Dawkins. He lost the tip, but the 76ers seemed puzzled. L.A. went up 7–0, then 11–4.

PAUL WESTHEAD: "On the first play, he came down in the low post and took a turnaround hook shot. He took a Kareem hook shot. What happened the rest of the game, he played everywhere. He played guard. He played forward. Everyone sees him as playing center. It was a psychological thing. Everyone saw Magic as the center. That helped us. People forget Jamaal Wilkes had 37 points in that game."

Finally Philly broke back in the second quarter and took a 52–44 lead. Westhead stopped play and told them to collapse in the middle. Steve Mix had come off Philly's bench to knife inside for 16 points. The Lakers squeezed in and closed to 60-all at the half. Then they opened the third period with a 14–0 run, keyed by Wilkes's 16 points in the period. But the 76ers drew it close again in the fourth.

With only five minutes left, it was 103–101, Lakers. Westhead called time again and made one last attempt to charge up his tired players. They responded with a run over the next 76 seconds to go up by seven. Then Magic scored nine points down the stretch to end it, 123–107.

Alas, the Lakers were too exhausted to celebrate. Wilkes had a career-best outing, scoring 37 points with 10 rebounds. And Chones lived up to his vow to shut down the middle. He finished with 11 points and 10 rebounds. He held Dawkins to a Chocolate Blunder type of game, 14 points and four rebounds.

For the Lakers, even Landsberger had 10 boards. And Cooper put in 16 points. But the big news, of course, was Magic, who simply was. He scored 42, including all 14 of his free throw attempts. He had 15 rebounds, 7 assists, 3 steals, and a block.

"It was amazing, just amazing," said Erving, who led Philly with 27. "Magic was outstanding. Unreal," agreed Philly guard Doug Collins, who was injured and watched from the sideline. "I knew he was good, but I never realized he was great."

MICHAEL COOPER: "Magic made a pass one time in that '80 series against Philadelphia. He threw a bounce pass three-quarters of the court on the run to Jamaal Wilkes. He threw it between about five players, and to this day, I still don't know how he got it there. In training camp, he always used to say to the rookies, 'Whenever you get around the basket, keep your hands up,' because he'd knock your head off, because he'd get the ball there when you didn't think he could get it there."

PHIL JASNER, LONGTIME *PHILADELPHIA DAILY NEWS* BASKETBALL WRITER: "With Magic that night, you knew you were watching history. He didn't really play center; he jumped center. After a while his performance became psychological. He took that game over, whether he was bringing the ball up the court, rebounding, [or] blocking a shot. He was mesmerizing."

Despite Abdul-Jabbar's fine performance in the first five games, Johnson was named the series MVP. How had they done it without their center? Johnson was asked. "Without Kareem," he said, "we couldn't play the halfcourt and think defensively. We had to play the full court and take our chances."

Then in the postgame interview on national television, Johnson turned to the camera and addressed Kareem back home. "We know you're hurtin', big fella," he said. "But we want you to get up and do a little dancin' tonight."

Buss, in fact, was already jumping. He hadn't been a pro basketball owner a full year and already he was on national television, soaked in champagne and accepting a championship trophy. It was something he'd worked for a long time, he told CBS.

The Lakers partied all the way back to L.A., where Kareem and a cast of thousands greeted them at the airport. There were hugs and cheers and high fives all around.

Yet inside Kareem had been seething since he sat at home and watched stupefied as Johnson was named the MVP. Kareem suspected that CBS had tampered with the voting process so that there could be a presentation after the game. Johnson would later admit as much.

LON ROSEN, FORMER AGENT FOR MAGIC JOHNSON: "He was robbed of it. Kareem should have been the MVP."

KAREEM ABDUL-JABBAR: "I had to give away the MVP. I had won it. The writers voted me for the MVP, and then somebody from CBS went and asked them to change their vote so they could give it to Earvin. Earvin talked to me right afterwards. He said, 'Hey, I should give this to you. I didn't deserve this.' But I wasn't going to get into a thing with Earvin about that. I was thrilled with everybody else that he did what he did and we ended up with a World Championship. I was able to put it behind me, but it was one of the things that happened to me in my career that makes me bitter. It all came from me not being popular."

PAUL WESTHEAD: "It was a media selection. It had nothing to do with our team or our feelings. Magic was spectacular that night. If you were voting for the MVP that night, well he certainly deserved it. If you were voting for MVP of the series, we nonetheless would not have gotten that far if not for Kareem. If there was ever time for a co-MVP, that was the time to do it."

KAREEM ABDUL-JABBAR: "I kind of see it like the Chrysler Building. You can't build a building like that without an incredible foundation. My game was the foundation which enabled James and Earvin and Byron and Norman and all these guys to do their thing on the perimeter while I created what I created inside. We played off that, which is what teamwork is all about. Because of Earvin's special charisma the story was written a different way. It was always what he did. It got to the point that I had no real belief in the objectivity of the press. I guess I was a victim of my success, the team was a victim of its success, and Earvin was the victim of his success. We compounded each other's successes and difficulties. I should emphasize that I would rather be dealing with these problems than dealing with the problems of not ever winning a World Championship."

MICHAEL COOPER: "You know what? Magic had 42 points, 15 rebounds, and gobs of assists, but you forget that Jamaal Wilkes had a career-high 37 points, Michael Cooper had a career-high 16 points, Jim Chones had a career-high 14, 15 rebounds, so there was a lot of things that went on, but the limelight was on Magic because he made it fun for everyone."

Unable to enjoy the celebration was Jack McKinney, whose recovery from head injury had moved slowly. Against doctors' advice, he decided to attempt a comeback during the spring of 1980. When the Lakers questioned the wisdom of his move he became frustrated and criticized Buss in a newspaper story. After the championship series, the Lakers informed McKinney that Westhead would remain head coach. The decision left McKinney embittered at the team and Westhead, his longtime friend. McKinney later coached the Indiana Pacers and eventually acknowledged that the Lakers made the right decision, that he was still debilitated when he attempted to return.

BILL SHARMAN: "He had some memory loss for a while. It was just kind of a no-win situation for the team."

PAUL WESTHEAD: "It was difficult on one hand because Jack was an integral part of what we had done. Somehow he kind of got left aside on it. It was exciting because we won, so there were mixed emotions. The good and the bad mixed together. Jack McKinney was a key part of our team."

The McKinney situation notwithstanding, nothing could deter Johnson from savoring the special season. Over the years to come, he would treasure the videotape of his sixth game performance, playing it over and over again, almost weekly, even watching the old commercials, squeezing every moment.

MICHAEL COOPER: "I honestly believe this. If we hadn't won that championship I don't think we would have been as successful as we were. We would have won a couple of titles, but to win five within a ten-year period and to get to the Finals nine times, that's an impressive record. I don't think we would have been as successful because it would have hurt us mentally. What it showed us was that we could win under severe adversity. That's what it brought out. As Kareem went down, and Kareem was our main focus for the whole season, when he went down and we were able to get that game, we pulled together as a team. And we did it against a very talented Philadelphia team. Darryl Dawkins, Doc, Bobby Jones. By all rights, that Game 6 with Kareem not with us, that should have been their game and possibly their series. But we fought through that, and it showed us that if we worked together as a team and kept with the team concept, you could accomplish anything in this league."

MAGIC JOHNSON: "Game 6 was definitely a platform for everything else that we did. That's what ignited Showtime. That game actually coined the phrase Showtime, because our best dominant big man, the best big man in the game, was down. We're on the road against the most dominant team in the East, and we end up winning. We won because we ran up and down the court. That was the most unbelievable game that we all had been in because of the circumstances. We knew that we had to run and gun, and that's what we did."

9

Revolution

From the staid confines of Bobby Knight's program at the University of Indiana, Butch Carter came to the Lakers wonderland in the fall of 1980. He had just departed one of college basketball's elite teams to join the NBA champions. The difference was profound, as he learned in training camp.

BUTCH CARTER: "We had to run a mile after our first practice in Palm Springs. I'm a rookie trying to make the team. I mean I'm hauling ass; I'm trying to be first, trying to impress the coaches. And I couldn't catch Magic Johnson. This was a guy who had just earned the MVP of the championship series, and he's like 40 yards ahead of everybody else, and I'm asking myself, 'How do you ever make it up?' That's what I'll always remember about him. Not only was he the most talented, he was the hardest-working."

Once he made the team, Carter was in for more wide-eyed amazement as his veteran teammates lived large and enjoyed their status as champions.

BUTCH CARTER: "Every city we went to, there was a party for us, the defending world champs. They would provide transportation, everything. That was the tone in every city. What amazed me was our true stamina. People don't understand the godly gift some of these people have. They could stay out all night and be no slower the next day out on the floor."

If any owner in NBA history was ever suited for a championship party, it was Jerry Buss. He quickly endeared himself to players, media, or anyone else hanging around the Lakers.

JIM HILL, L.A. SPORTSCASTER: "Jerry likes to be at the big functions. I remember the first interview I did with him. He said, 'Oh, yeah, Jim, we're going to have a lot of fun.'"

JOE McDONNELL, LONGTIME L.A. SPORTS RADIO PERSONALITY: "When Jerry Buss bought the team, everything changed. You had an atmosphere like you were part of a rock and roll show. I can't tell you how many times we'd sit in the press room after a game with Jerry Buss and Bob Steiner and other media people and we'd play Trivial Pursuit till seven or eight o'clock in the morning. We'd walk out and the sun would be shining. Everybody was drinking and having a good time. Buss was just a really good guy."

RON CARTER, FORMER LAKER: "We're in Palm Springs in training camp. Norm Nixon and I sneak out to go to a club to hang out with Stevie Nicks. It's not late, maybe eleven. I'm like, 'C'mon, let's go back before we get caught.' So we're heading out of the club, and all of a sudden here comes Jerry Buss. So we run into the men's room. Buss has this entourage. He has television cameras following him. This is his first year owning the team, so he's living the life. He sends some guy into the bathroom and he says, 'Hey, Dr. Buss saw you guys run in here. And he wants you to come sit down and have a drink with him.'"

The owner exuded informality with his blue jeans and open-collared shirts. He fancied himself a playboy and took great delight in dating beautiful young women. Although he usually dated them only once or twice each, he liked to keep their pictures in photo albums, which he proudly showed to visitors and friends.

RON CARTER: "He liked the girls. The girls were always around. They were always very young. That took some doing."

JIM HILL: "We always said Jerry had a good eye for talent, not only on but off the court."

RON CARTER: "We went everywhere. We did everything. The girls, the jets, the fun. It was nothing for Jerry to say, 'Hey, I feel hot. Let's go to Vegas.' And get his pilot to crank up his jet and shoot over to Vegas. That kind of stuff. A crazy, crazy life. It was Showtime. Anywhere that we went, we were the party."

That quickly came to include the owner's skybox at Lakers games in the Forum. The owner's box became the ultimate place to entertain his real estate clients and new best friends among Hollywood's elite.

DOUG KRIKORIAN: "That was really fun up there. He'd bring young girls. I was single at the time. It was unbelievable, having dinner with Jerry beforehand at the Forum with all his celebrities, and then going up there to his box."

Always he wore the same outfits and sported a young girl on his arm.

RON CARTER: "Charlene, his secretary, and I used to always laugh, because Charlene would open up his closet and it would be the same jacket in about 12 colors and 12 sets of jeans. I said, 'Charlene, are we ever gonna do something about this?' And she said, 'I don't think so, Ron. I think we're stuck with this.' That was it for everything, for meetings, whatever. Blazer, silk shirt, jeans. That was the uniform."

Not surprisingly, Buss loved the L.A. club life and aspired to be a good dancer.

JERRY BUSS: "When I was in school, I loved a lot of dances, the cha-cha, the polka, the mambo. But the rage was the jitterbug. I loved it and did it all the time. Then the '70s came along, and I got caught up in the *Saturday Night Fever* craze. I took disco lessons and tried to imitate John Travolta [laughs]."

When Johnson joined the team as a rookie in the fall of '79, the owner began going to the clubs with his star rookie. "He would dance; I would dance," said Buss.

Buss had other favorites among the Lakers, but he soon learned a lesson about becoming friends with lesser players. It hurt too badly when they had to be traded or released. Johnson wasn't only a great friend; he was a safe one.

KAREEM ABDUL-JABBAR: "It kind of got to be like a family thing where Earvin got to be the favorite child. I think they did things to placate me. Up until the year I retired, I was the highest-paid player in the league. So I don't have any complaints. They paid me well; they appreciated what I did. But I never got to be a part of the family thing, because my own personal integrity made Dr. Buss uncomfortable."

Some observers believed that the stone-faced, seven-foot-two, 260-pound Abdul-Jabbar intimidated the owner. Others just thought their personal styles were simply different. Buss loved the high profile his association with the team brought. He packed his skybox with an array of impressive people. Actors. Lawyers. Executives. Intellectuals. Celebrities of all kinds. Afterward, he enjoyed taking them to the locker room to meet his stars. Kareem hated schmoozing and crowds and glad-handing. He wanted no part of Buss's celebrity games. Magic, though, loved the associates that the owner brought to the locker room. He set them at ease and made them feel welcome, while Kareem grabbed a shower and made a quick exit.

Buss also saw Magic as the great attraction for new investors in his real estate syndication deals. It would seem awkward under NBA competition rules for the owner of one team to engage in a business selling investments to players on other teams, but apparently that was not an issue in the early '80s. After being cut by the Lakers, Ron Carter went to work for Buss and his partner, Frank Mariani, and their real estate partnership, Buss, Mariani & Associates. To make matters even more interesting, Frank Mariani would come to own the Indiana Pacers in 1982, meaning that essentially one company controlled two NBA teams, another eyebrow-raiser.

RON CARTER: "Frank Mariani owned Market Square Arena and the Pacers. And Jerry Buss owned the Lakers. And they were partners in the same firm, Mariani, Buss & Associates. The league had to know. Because Mariani, Buss was the parent of California Sports [the Lakers corporation]. We were in a little dinky office, a two-story commercial strip building. The first floor was five retail businesses, and the second floor was Mariani, Buss."

As Carter explained, Buss was soon attracting players from across the NBA in real estate syndication deals.

JIM HILL: "Jerry Buss is like a swashbuckler, he's a daredevil, he's a risk taker, he's a visionary in his own right. He's also very, very smart."

RON CARTER: "Kareem wouldn't get into Buss's deals. He went with his agent, Tom Collins. Ralph Sampson, Alex English, a bunch of guys got caught up with Tom Collins. They were syndicating luxury hotels. We were syndicating luxury apartment buildings and single family dwellings. We'd accelerate depreciation on the buildings to get them their write-off every year. And we were accelerating the principal payments on the mortgage so we would own the buildings in seven, nine, eleven years. The idea was, when your career ends, you have this building spinning off tons of cash into your retirement. What happened, halfway into the program, Prime Ticket, his sports pay cable channel, took off, and Jerry started making tons and tons of money, and he was like, 'Sell the real estate.' We sold the stuff off, gave the guys their investments back plus some profit."

Kareem and those players who invested with Collins went on to lose millions.

RON CARTER: "The tax laws changed and that hurt Collins and the players on syndication. Luxury hotels is a tough business. Apartment buildings, that's stable, that's steady income. Plus we were building in Beverly Hills, Brentwood. Jerry had a real estate machine, and we were cranking out deals. Jerry made the transition out of heavy real estate into heavy television."

Buss didn't desert real estate altogether. In fact, his company was buying thousands of houses in Arizona, and he had grand plans for major arena ownership.

RON CARTER: "His strategy, and he almost pulled it off, was to own the Forum, Market Square Arena, and Madison Square Garden. Those were going to be his content engines for his television. The Madison Square Garden deal fell through when some knucklehead in Arizona, this state's attorney in Arizona, indicted Buss for racketeering."

The situation provided Carter the opportunity to watch Buss under pressure.

RON CARTER: "Jerry bought Pickfair—Mary Pickford and Douglas Fairbanks's place—and we called it a five million fixer-upper. It was a beautiful house. Once Jerry moved in there, we'd hold a lot of meetings at the house. When this story broke about racketeering in Arizona, we all met because we had to get to the bottom of it. Jerry had no idea what this prosecutor was talking about. He was so far removed from the deal. I was the one doing the deals. He wasn't involved in the day-to-day operations, but he got indicted. What was at the whole root of this thing was an issue of back taxes. We did the calculation and it turned out to be $1.3 million or so that we owed the state. He paid it, wrote the check the next day. And it went away. I remember that he was so cool. That has stuck with me. Here this man just got indicted, it's on national television, he's called a press conference at the mansion. When I get over to the house, I'm thinking this is going to be frantic, things are going to be crazy. But Jerry's just as cool as a cucumber. 'Hey, Ron. Come on in.' We sat down and talked a little bit. He looked at it like, 'We may have done something wrong in regards to Arizona law, but it wasn't our intention to defraud the government.' By the time they caught it, Buss had already made millions, so Buss was happy to pay it."

The publicity from the event soon passed, but it had paused long enough to prevent Buss from owning Madison Square Garden.

Ron Carter: "The local CBS affiliate in Los Angeles runs the story. Unbeknownst to that CBS affiliate and that reporter and that prosecutor in Arizona, Buss was in the throes of a deal with the CBS network in New York to buy Madison Square Garden. It was tossed out quickly, but it was enough to mess up the deal for the Garden."

Buss's publicity woes came to include persistent rumors, then a media report, that he was going bankrupt during the early '80s.

Doug Krikorian: "CBS did a whole thing on it that Jerry Buss was going broke. I heard that he was hurting at that time. There were fears that he was going to lose the Lakers, but as it turned out that didn't happen."

Ron Carter: "I'm in the front office with Mariani & Buss, and Norm Nixon is telling me that Jerry Buss is broke. He'd say, 'Aw, Ron, Jerry will be lucky if he can even make the payroll next month.' There were some cash flow problems. I knew that. I said, 'I wish I were as broke as Jerry Buss. Don't confuse cash flow with assets. I'm looking at a billion dollars worth of assets. So he's got latitude.' And right after I told Norm that, Jerry did the Great Western Forum deal. Great Western kicks in $20 million to put their name on the building, and then they give him a line of credit to do real estate deals. That was a big part of how he got out of the cash flow squeeze."

Doug Krikorian: "Jerry's kind of shy in some ways. In his box, he's very quiet, just kind of sits there. When he first came here he would talk, say anything. Then he learned to be much more reticent with the media, more circumspect. Much more. A lower profile as the years have gone on. At first, he used to be easy to talk to. Now, I seldom interview him anymore. I used to be able to grab him for an interview. Now you have to go through his PR people."

The Change

Despite their "godly gifts," the Lakers' good fortunes declined during 1981, their season of celebration. Johnson suffered a cartilage tear in his knee, then struggled back from surgery to rejoin his team late in the schedule, only to see the atmosphere disrupted by bickering. Nixon and Johnson sniped at each other in the press as the playoffs opened. The acrimony was relatively mild but clearly disruptive. More serious was the conflict between Kareem and Jim Chones, because it factionalized the team when Westhead decided to bench Chones. Nixon, Johnson, and others felt the coach made the move to keep Kareem happy. "We just lost our best inside player," Nixon told reporters.

PAUL WESTHEAD: "Injuries made it interesting. Magic goes down early in the year, one-third of the way through the season. He doesn't play for 40-plus games. We played very well that year. People forget that. We won 55 games, which is a lot. And our problem was, when we went into the playoffs we were still adjusting to Magic's return, getting into the flow of the game, mixing our old starting lineup with our new starting lineup."

The Lakers lost to Moses Malone, Mike Dunleavy, and a plodding Houston Rockets team, 2–1, in the opening round of the 1981 playoffs when Johnson, faced with a last-second shot to tie it, threw up an air ball.

PAUL WESTHEAD: "We had the misfortune of a three-game series. The league after that realized you really penalize a very good team by playing the best of three."

In the off-season, management shipped Chones, Brad Holland, and draft picks to Washington for power forward Mitch Kupchak, whose large salary served to keep the locker room stewing. By no means had the atmosphere cleared by the time training camp for the 1981–82 season opened.

News was leaked that in the off-season Buss had renegotiated Johnson's contract to a $25 million, 25-year deal, prompting an angry Kareem to call a press conference to question if Magic had become part of team management. "I'll tear up the contract if it's gonna cause problems," Magic said. Buss gave Kareem a new contract at $1.5 million per season to quiet the complaints. Yet observers wondered just how the guard and center would get along in the aftermath. Through training camp, the players bitched about Westhead's apparent attempts to slow the offense down.

PAUL WESTHEAD: "It's really hard to get inside what people were thinking and doing. Early in that season, Magic was still trying to work out some physical difficulties from his surgery. He didn't have the same quickness and movement that he'd had in the past, so he was being jammed up by defenders where normally it would be easy for him to control. I think he was both physically and emotionally distraught because he wanted to be and was the best."

The coach explained to the Lakers front office that he was merely trying to install a half-court offense so the team would have an option if the break wasn't available. But Westhead failed to make this clear to his players, who had been grousing about coaching since the '81 playoffs.

EDDIE JORDAN, FORMER LAKER: "That was Mitch Kupchak's first year, too. And Westhead wanted to incorporate Mitch into the offense. Now, we were out there running and Mitch didn't catch up so well [laughs]. So Paul wanted to get some post ups. I think he thought half-court basketball controlled the game. And it did for most teams, but not for those Showtime Lakers."

MICHAEL COOPER: "What we wanted to do was perform. We were more of a freewheeling team. We'd run, if we didn't get it, the ball was popped around. But now it became, 'Get it down and get it to Kareem.'"

Privately, Buss began planning to change coaches, but general manager Bill Sharman pleaded patience. Magic was among a group of players frustrated with Westhead's new offense. In mid-November, during a road win over Utah, Johnson and Westhead argued on the bench.

BILL SHARMAN: "Things came to a head in Utah. There was a miscommunication between Paul and Magic. The band was playing; Magic was toweling off and seemed not to listen. Paul kind of hollered at him and upset him."

JIM HILL: "When you have thoroughbreds, you let them run. I remember the night Magic told Westhead, 'You know what? You might as well trade me.' Magic wasn't used to that. He was a young man used to going and playing and having fun and not getting all caught up in the business aspect or the ego. So now Westhead is telling him, 'You gotta do this, and I don't want you doing that. And sit down and shut up.' And so forth. Magic said, 'Uh-uh. You might as well trade me.' And he was serious."

That night Johnson told reporters he wanted to be traded, saying he felt the new offense was stifling the team's creativity.

EDDIE JORDAN: "I was the first player to hear it. I went across the locker room and I told Norman, 'Norman, you and I are gonna be starting in the backcourt.' I had never heard a player say the coach has got to get fired or I have to get traded [laughs]. Then I told Kareem, and Kareem said, 'No, we'll straighten this out. Magic shouldn't have done it.'"

JIM HILL: "The next day we met them at the airport. Magic got off the plane, and I asked him if he felt the same way that he did the night before. He was so cool about everything. He said, 'I don't want to make further comment until I talk to Dr. Buss.'"

EDDIE JORDAN: "Walking off that plane the next morning, it seemed like the coach was fired in flight. We arrived in LAX, and the reporters were right there as soon as we came off the plane. The announcement had been made by the time we got to our homes. It was strange. You knew there were some grumblings, that [there] was some holding back of a team that really wanted to be let loose. But we didn't know it was gonna happen."

The next day Buss fired Westhead.

PAUL WESTHEAD: "We were on a five-game winning streak. People forget that. Usually you don't get fired for five-game winning streaks."

MICHAEL COOPER: "Yeah, but it was a very tough five-game winning streak. We weren't winning like we should have been."

PAUL WESTHEAD: "I think it was just something that management felt they wanted to do. I don't think it was necessarily just Magic, although it was laid on him by the media and the world. We had a little run-in after a game, after winning our fifth game in a row. I was fired the next day, so everyone said, 'Well, obviously it was Magic who did this.'"

MICHAEL COOPER: "This was not about me. It was not about 'I,' Magic. 'I want to score more,' or 'I want to do more.' After the championship year we had had, we were not doing the things that won us that sixth game. We were coming back and getting away from a lot of stuff. Again, it was a coach's decision, and he felt strongly about it. That was his opinion. We tried to work with it. As the owner saw it, he did what [he thought] was best for the team."

JOE McDONNELL: "When Magic spoke out, it wasn't because he was crazy or anything. It was because nobody else would speak out. This had been festering for the whole season. They just didn't like Westhead, period. Magic was no dummy. He knew that Jerry Buss would never trade him. It was just his power play, and he got him out of there."

BILL SHARMAN: "I defended him for a while. But it got to the point where, 'What'll you do?' Jerry West, Jerry Buss, and I all thought it was better to make a change."

JOE McDONNELL: "They all hated Westhead. Kareem was the only one who didn't talk too much about him on or off the record. One of the lines, I remember after a game, I was talking to Michael Cooper. And he said to me, 'You know what this fucking idiot did before the game?' I said, 'What?' He said, 'He tried quoting Shakespeare to us.' He said, 'Doesn't he understand the brothers don't give a shit about Shakespeare?'"

MICHAEL COOPER: "Paul did a wonderful job while he was here. I really like him as a person and a coach. I just thought that what was happening was supposed to be."

PAUL WESTHEAD: "The only thing I will say, that I want to attempt to clarify, was the explanation was that the team wasn't running as much. I said, 'Well, you can fire me for a million things. Take your pick. You didn't relate to the team. All the classic things. You weren't tough enough. You were too tough. But every practice of my coaching career has been running. So if that was the reason, that's not a reason, not an accurate reason. Fire me for other things then.' That's the only clarification that I requested. Not that it mattered. If you're relieved, then you're relieved. Ultimately, history will look back and see me as the mad scientist who ran more than any other coach, maybe in the history of the game. He might have lost a lot of games. He might have been fired more than anybody in the history of the game, but nobody ran more."

KURT RAMBIS: "For a player to come out and basically criticize the coach was something I'd never heard of before. If you're an athlete and you win, they forgive you for a lot of things."

The team was then caught in confusion over the identity of the head coach. Buss had wanted West, then a personnel consultant to the team, to return to the bench. West vehemently declined and instead offered to help the 36-year-old Riley adjust to being the team's boss. At the press conference announcing the coaching change, Buss told the media that West was the coach, only to have West deny it. Instead, West served as an assistant to Pat Riley for two weeks, until Bill Bertka was hired.

In the Lakers' next home game, Magic was stung by a chorus of boos from the Forum crowd. For months afterward he would hear extensive booing on road trips. "What you must do," Riley told him, "is ride it out and not break concentration. Just play your head off and you'll turn the crowd around."

The ensuing weeks brought round after round of condemnation from editorialists across the country who labeled Buss a meddlesome owner and Johnson a spoiled, overpaid crybaby. His new contract was cited as part of the problem. The *Los Angeles Times* called him a "glory hog," while the *New York Daily News* said he was a "spoiled punk."

KURT RAMBIS: "He got booed in a lot of arenas. People were coming down on him. The media was always down on him. So he went from being one of— if not the—NBA's favorite sons at that point to having to deal with a lot of criticism. Everywhere he went before that, everything was positive. Now half of it was positive, the other half negative. He had to grow and learn from that."

EDDIE JORDAN: "The change had been made. There was nothing you could do. Riley came in and he was good. Right from the beginning, he was good. I liked him a lot because he always said I was the fireman. I guess that's how he always thought of himself when he was a player. The fireman is always ready, whether he's called on every night or every third night, you're always ready to play. He had motivational techniques that were very new and innovative to the league."

In December, power forward Mitch Kupchak, for whom the Lakers had spent a bundle of cash, blew his knee out in a game at San Diego and was lost for the season. Just days after Kupchak went down, Kareem suffered a severe ankle sprain.

The injuries left the Lakers decimated in the frontcourt, and the controversy left them numb. Faced with this adversity, they responded with a short winning streak, much of it coming from Johnson's emotion. But it was clear that enthusiasm could only carry them so far. Even when Kareem returned they would face the same dearth of rebounding.

But then help arrived in two very unexpected forms. First came the acquisition of 30-year-old free agent Robert McAdoo, who while playing in Boston, Buffalo, and Detroit had been branded as selfish. Still, the Lakers were intrigued. McAdoo had a league MVP award and two scoring titles under his belt. Few people figured he would fit in, but he showed a remarkable willingness to play off the bench.

ROBERT McADOO, HALL OF FAMER AND FORMER LAKER: "I was coming off a foot surgery, and I wasn't even sure I was gonna be able to play again. Mitch had already gotten hurt, and they needed somebody to plug up that power forward position. When I first got there, every time they introduced Magic he was getting booed. I said, 'Wow, this team won the championship a year ago, and now they're booing one of the star players.' It took me all of a month before I felt any kind of condition. I was put in a game immediately, and I missed a fast-break layup. My timing was just bad. But after that month was up, I was up and rolling."

The other unexpected aid came with the emergence of power forward Kurt Rambis, the Clark Kent look-alike and free agent who reluctantly signed with the Lakers only after management assured him he had a solid shot at making the team. Not long after Kupchak went down, Rambis got an unexpected start and responded with 14 rebounds. He had a noticeable lack of athleticism. But the Lakers had enough of those properties. They needed his hustle, his defense, his rebounding, and his physical play. It seemed that the Lakers only needed direction to find their way out of the morass.

At first Pat Riley wasn't sure if he should take Westhead's place. After all, Westhead had given him the chance to be an assistant. Riley did not want to show disloyalty. He sought the advice of West, his old teammate. "Yes," West said. "Take the job."

"I was numb," Riley said later. "I thought the firing was horrible." Not to mention unfair. "Contrary to what people think, Paul was flexible. He was beginning to make changes in the offense. He was aware there were problems, but he was judged too quickly. It seemed to be the feeling of the media, the fans, the players, and the front office that it wasn't happening fast enough. I think it was more of an emotional decision than anything else."

Although confused, Riley agreed to take over the team and, more important, to make the fast break the team's top option. Still, there were problems aplenty. After Westhead's firing, the Lakers surged on emotion but fell back between January and March, barely playing .500 ball.

"Don't be afraid to coach the team," Jerry Buss finally told Riley in one meeting.

"I was giving the players too much responsibility," Riley explained later.

He began to assert himself. When the team lost at home to Chicago on March 12, he flashed his anger. "I got fed up," he said. "I didn't know what I wanted to do when I took the job. I looked at the players and I respected their games so much and I respected them as people. I gave them too much trust. I said, 'This is their team.' It was their team, but they needed direction. That's my job. It took me three months to realize it, but I have certain responsibilities to push and demand. They have to play. I have to coach. They were waiting for me to put my foot down. That's my nature anyhow."

Riley put his foot down, and no one shouted. In fact, the players seemed relieved.

EDDIE JORDAN: "We had Kareem and Magic and Jamaal Wilkes, Bob McAdoo, Mitch Kupchak, so with all that talent we still had to play together, still had to have a game plan and preparation. Riley was very good at that."

ROBERT McADOO: "Pat was new to the job, but he had done his homework well. He knew the talent because he had been around, seeing the guys from the booth, or seeing them from the bench. He knew what he had, but he kind of freelanced it a lot. He let us show our talents. He didn't get in our way, saying, 'You gotta be here on the court.' He didn't X and O us to death. Things were organized, but we were a freewheeling bunch, because there was a lot of talent out there on that floor. You look back now, I'm in the Hall of Fame, James Worthy's in the Hall of Fame, Magic's in the Hall of Fame, Kareem's. You had four Hall of Famers on one team."

Despite their struggles, they finished the regular season with a best-in-the-West 57–25 record. But more important, they were peaking as the playoffs opened. The team showed it was capable of using either Nixon or Magic to run the break, which doubled their potency.

ROBERT McADOO: "It was very nice to be able to get the ball off the board. You didn't have to really look for your point guard. You just turned and you just threw it. It was either Magic or Norm, either one of them. Whatever side they were on, or whatever side you turned to, you just threw it, and our fast break started through one of those two guys. Most teams your fast break started with one guy. In L.A., it was turn and go."

They won 21 of their final 24 games, fueled by Riley's decision to use McAdoo heavily.

ROBERT McADOO: "I had to adjust to coming off the bench for the first time in my life, which was very, very difficult. I was not playing a lot of minutes, which was also difficult. I just dealt with it. Nobody knew it, but I was probably the most frustrated that I'd ever been in my life. But I wasn't the type that was going to cause any problems. My main thing was winning a championship. I was just aching to win. I wasn't going to jeopardize that, even though I was used to playing 40 to 45 minutes a game. In L.A. I was playing maybe 15 minutes a game, and that was hard to deal with. Then we got to the playoffs and everything changed. I went from 15 minutes up to 30 to 40 minutes. It was crunch time. It was winning time, what I call pit bull time.

You put your best out on the floor. We had a playoff run that was just unbelievable."

From there, they would break loose, sweeping nine straight playoff games before finally closing out the championship with a record-tying 12 wins against only 2 losses. And Philadelphia proved a fitting victim in the Finals.

Suddenly Buss raised his eyebrows. The coach he hadn't particularly wanted was getting the job done. Much of the success, of course, was due to Johnson, who was getting reacquainted with his fans. "The crowds still get me going," he said toward the end of the regular schedule. "They still jack me up. And I still love the game. I don't think I'll ever lose that."

"Magic has become a great player," Jerry West told the writers. "I've watched him go from one level to another, higher level this year. He's become solid; that's the big thing. He's in control out there. He knows what he's doing every minute he's on the floor."

Despite a 63–19 record, the Celtics fell to Philadelphia in a seven-game Eastern Conference Finals. The Lakers watched this drama on the tube, having dispatched Phoenix and San Antonio, 4–0 each. Their last game against the Spurs ended a full 12 days before Philly finished off Boston. Rather than get rusty, they worked two-a-days in practice and battled each other to pass the time. "That's the best thing about this team," Riley said, "the work ethic."

Erving was 32 as the 1982 playoffs opened, and he was making his third trip to the Finals since coming to the NBA in 1976. Each time the 76ers failed, they had to fight the public perception that they were wasting Erving's bountiful talent.

ROBERT McADOO: "Once we got there, everybody was talking about Julius Erving and him getting his first championship. It was like I was the forgotten man. Nobody was saying, 'Bob McAdoo is trying to get his first championship.' I was like, 'Damn the 76ers and Julius Erving. I'm getting this championship here. I don't care who's in my way. If I'm able to perform and I'm out there on that floor, I'm gonna run through whoever it takes to get it.'"

Philadelphia had the home-court advantage in the 1982 Finals, but the Lakers had their nifty zone trap, devised by assistant Bill Bertka, which they produced at just the right time in the opener at the Spectrum on Thursday, May

27. Fresh from the battle of Boston, the 76ers worked their offense to precision until midway through the third period. At the time, Philadelphia led by 15. Then, over the next 11 minutes or so, the Lakers ripped through a 40–9 blitz. The bewildered 76ers fell, 124–117. In the postgame autopsies, Billy Cunningham called it both ways. He said the zone trap wasn't hurting his team all that much. Then he called it an obviously illegal zone.

Riley then decided to back off the trap a bit for Game 2. "The officials read the papers, too," he explained. Instead, he switched Magic to cover Erving on defense.

"I've always been his fan," Johnson said of Erving. "I respect him. I'm in awe of him." Perhaps there was too much respect. Erving brought the 76ers back with 24 points and 16 rebounds for a 110–94 win that evened the series at one-all. The Lakers, however, dominated the next two games in the Forum. Nixon led a parade in Game 3 with 29. Again the zone trap was Philly's undoing, 129–108. In fact, it worked so well, they employed it again in Game 4 to take a 111–101 win. Down 3–1, the 76ers seemed finished. But they lashed back in Game 5 to pin an embarrassment on Kareem, holding him to just six points, his lowest total since 1977–78 when he was tossed out of a game for punching Kent Benson. Afterward the Lakers center hurried from the locker room before speaking with the media. "They pushed and shoved a lot," he explained in a terse memo handed out to the writers.

Philadelphia had closed it to 3–2, but had to return to the Forum for Game 6, where the Lakers got the lead early. The 76ers held L.A. to 20 points for the third quarter and several times cut the lead to one. "I had a few butterflies about then," said Wilkes, who led six Lakers in double figures with 27. The Lakers then surged to boost their lead to 11 early in the fourth period. Philly again responded and with a little under four minutes to go trimmed the edge to 103–100. But Kareem completed a three-point play to put L.A. up by six. At the end, Wilkes got a breakaway layup to close it out, 114–104.

Riley and Buss smiled broadly as the Lakers owner accepted the trophy. "It seems like a millennium since I took over," Riley said of seven months as a head coach. Johnson with 13 points, 13 rebounds, and 13 assists in Game 6 was named the series MVP, an award that raised more than a few eyebrows. The Lakers, though, had had about all the controversy they could stand for one season. "There were times earlier in the year when I didn't think this would be possible," Wilkes said as champagne cascaded over his face. "We had so many unhappy people around here you wouldn't believe it."

Big Game James

Winning had made them all happy, at least for the time being. And they were soon set to get richer. Trading Don Ford to Cleveland during the 1979–80 season had brought them the Cavaliers' first-round pick for 1982.

Cleveland had finished last in the league, and the Lakers again won the coin toss with the worst team in the West, the San Diego Clippers. The decision was James Worthy, who had just come from leading North Carolina to the 1982 NCAA championship, or Georgia's Dominique Wilkins, "the Human Highlight Film."

JERRY WEST: "It looked like we were going to need a small forward first. I thought James and Dominique were the two players we should consider. It was very difficult not to take on Dominique Wilkins. Very difficult. Because we played in Showtime, and he was a Showtime player. And a great player."

Ultimately, the Lakers decided Worthy made a nifty fit into the Showtime review. His quickness to the basket was almost startling.

JAMES WORTHY: "I knew it was going to be special as soon as I was drafted. For two years I had watched Earvin just kill teams with his passing. I used to watch Jamaal Wilkes and Coop get out on the wing, and I knew I was gonna benefit from Earvin. I didn't realize then how much. But I knew it was going to be good running the break with somebody who could deliver it to you at the right time."

MICHAEL COOPER: "James Worthy was the next big six-nine player who played like a six-two player. Nobody had seen that. He redefined that 3 spot. Here he was a power forward, a Maurice Lucas type player, who was now playing a 3 position and every now and then he could slide to the 2 spot. That's what made it unique, was that he could still have that power forward mentality to get down in the low post and get it done."

JAMES WORTHY: "I had been a post-up player all of my life. As I grew older and got into college, I started playing against bigger post people, so I had to rely on quickness. I used just the basic fundamental drop steps and fake reverses and things of that nature. I just loved the game growing up. I watched the Carolina Cougars with Dennis Wycik and Billy Cunningham. And I used to see a lot of players come in to play them. So I used to imitate that pro style of play with the red, white, and blue ball. It was a matter of watching Dr. J and then going home and looking in the mirror and trying to do what they did."

The '82–83 Lakers boasted a deep roster. Johnson, Nixon, and Cooper in the backcourt. Rambis, Wilkes, Worthy, and McAdoo at the forwards. Kareem was in the last year of his contract and playing like a man who wanted to reap millions, the only problem being that his agent, Tom Collins, and Buss had fallen into nasty bickering over a new deal. Each day brought increasing speculation that Kareem's days as a Laker were growing short.

Yet no one could argue with the results. They ran off to a 34–9 record and had just finished a loss to the Celtics in Boston when the bad news came. Kareem's Bel Air mansion had burned to the ground, taking with it his personal sports memorabilia and vast collections of Oriental rugs, jazz albums, and books. His longtime girlfriend, Cheryl Pistano, and son, Amir, had escaped unhurt. But the loss was in excess of $3 million. Kareem took the next flight to L.A. while the team went on to Dallas. The media immediately speculated that the loss of his home would make it easier for Abdul-Jabbar to leave Los Angeles.

Riley and West figured that Kareem would miss at least a week while trying to get his personal life in order. But he flew to Dallas before that Wednesday's game and played, scoring a season-high 34 points. "It's absolutely incredible to me that he'd come here under these conditions," remarked West, who was traveling with the team. "You know why greatness endures when you look inside a person." Even more amazing was the fan response to the disaster. Beginning in Dallas that night and lasting months afterward, people would come forward in NBA cities to present Kareem with records and books to replace those lost. Josh Rosenfeld, former Lakers PR director, recalled Kareem being amazed that first night in Dallas when a young fan gave him an Ella Fitzgerald record. For years Pistano had been urging Kareem to seek a warmer relationship with his public. The fire had at last brought that about. "Kareem was showered with a lot of love and a lot of heartfelt concern for the first time in his entire career," Riley said. "I don't think he had ever seen that before."

Even with the support, the Lakers' momentum slipped after the fire. They finished 58–24, good enough for best in the West. But their hopes for a repeat championship dimmed a week before the playoffs when Worthy jumped for a tip-in against the Suns and landed unevenly on his left foot, causing a fracture of his leg just below the knee that finished him for the season.

Rambis, too, was hobbled by foot injuries and missed stretches of action. The Lakers were still deep enough to stifle Portland and then San Antonio in the Western playoffs. They were up 3–1 against the Spurs and should have ended it in Game 5 in the Forum, but they lost and had to return to San Antonio for a sixth game, where McAdoo got hurt. The cumulative damage doomed their hopes in the 1983 championship round against Philadelphia. Determined to win a title, 76ers owner Harold Katz had shipped Darryl Dawkins to New Jersey and acquired Moses Malone, the scoring/rebounding machine, from the Houston Rockets for Caldwell Jones. Thus armed, the 76ers ripped through the regular-season schedule with a 65–17 record. When writers asked Malone how the 76ers would fare in the playoffs, he uttered his famous "fo, fo, and fo" prediction. They had come close, sweeping the Knicks in the Eastern semifinals and losing a single game to the Milwaukee Bucks in the conference Finals before moving on to the NBA Finals for the third time in four years.

The Lakers quickly found more trouble in the championship round; Nixon went down with injuries. Without help, Kareem found himself in a situation similar to the one that had frustrated him so during the late '70s. Malone dominated the boards, outrebounding Kareem 72–30 over the course of the series, and the Lakers fell in line with the 76ers' other victims. Each game they would lead at the half, yet each time the 76ers would power ahead.

ROBERT MCADOO: "When you lose it, you feel like you're just another team, like you weren't even in the championship, just an empty feeling all summer long. Depressed. I really believe that if we had healthy people we'd have won that championship four years in a row. In '83, Worthy had broken his leg and Norman had a shoulder separation. I had a pulled thigh muscle. It was just too much for us to overcome with three of us out of the lineup. We were fast. They called us the greyhounds, and we were up and down the court. You have a tendency to pull muscles when you're all-out sprinting all the time. Everybody always thought we were smooth and finesse, couldn't match up with the

East bullies. Well, you saw them change their games a lot when we came to town. They would brutalize you to get offensive rebounds, but against us those Celtics and Philly teams wouldn't go to the boards because they were afraid we would get that ball off the boards. They knew we had the better sprinters baseline to baseline. We were one of the fastest teams in the history of the league."

Redemption

With each passing season, Norm Nixon's relationships with the Lakers' front office had grown more tenuous.

RON CARTER: "Jerry Buss personally liked Norm. Norm was a Buss kind of guy. Jerry wished he had Norm's whatever it was—charisma. He was a female magnet. Norm was real cool. Jerry liked that. But they never had a good relationship because Norm never trusted Jerry."

The aftermath of the sweep in the 1983 Finals was not pleasant. That summer Nixon, long a thorn in the side for Lakers management, said he suspected that the team was having him investigated for drug use. Specifically, Nixon believed that West, who had replaced Sharman as general manager, was out to get him. The two had not been close since 1978, when West was coach and Nixon his rookie point guard.

TED GREEN, FORMER *LOS ANGELES TIMES* REPORTER: "Nixon was West's personal whipping boy. Norm hated it. The day after the 1978 season ended, Norm and I were standing curbside at LAX, and Norm said, 'I put up with his shit a whole year because I was a rookie, but I'm not taking it anymore.'"

RON CARTER: "Norman fed it, too. Norman would say things to stir the pot. I don't know why. That's just in his nature. For example, Norm broke one of many of West's records. And the reporters came and said, 'Did you know you just broke Jerry West's record?' Norm knows the script: 'I am so proud to have my name mentioned with the great ones like Jerry West.' C'mon, Norm, you know the script. Say the script. But Norm said something to the effect that 'I never saw Jerry West play, so it doesn't mean that much to me.'"

For his part, West saw a talented young player in need of heavy tutoring, as young point guards often are. The position was about decisions, and if you wanted to play it, you had to live with a coach's second-guessing.

DOUG KRIKORIAN: "Jerry pushed him. Jerry wanted him to be like him. And Norm was not like him. Norm was at that time, shall we say, a modern athlete. And I'm not sure Jerry approved of his particular lifestyle."

The Nixon lifestyle improved dramatically after he met dancer/actress Debbie Allen.

RON CARTER: "We all met in that movie, *The Fish That Saved Pittsburgh*. She was one of the dancers or cheerleaders. There were probably about 30 to 40 guys from the league who were in the movie. The climax was the Lakers playing this fictitious team, the Pittsburgh Pisces, for the championship. Debbie and Norm got real serious."

Nixon went on to build a reputation as an excellent guard and a team leader over the ensuing seasons. His teammates thought highly of him, but from time to time his fiery personality clashed with players, coaches, and management alike.

KAREEM ABDUL-JABBAR: "Norm was a very cocky little guy and not afraid to voice his opinion. He was a team player, but he could also disagree with you. That summer he just got into it with them [management]. When you're winning, nobody cares. When you lose like that . . ."

JAMES WORTHY, FORMER LAKER WHO CONSIDERED NIXON A MENTOR: "He was conscious. He was aware; he was tapped into all categories and aspects. Not your average jock."

But the situation worsened as camp opened that fall. There were trade rumors that Nixon was gone, and there was talk around other teams that he had a drug problem. Nixon saw the drug talk as West's attempt to manufacture an excuse to get rid of him. As camp opened, West told him to relax and play. But the issue ate at the guard. Former Lakers staffer Lon Rosen said, "Norm said that he'd had enough, that he wanted to go." During the exhibition season, West triggered a deal sending Nixon and Eddie Jordan to the Clippers for the center Swen Nater and the rights to unsigned draft pick Byron Scott.

KAREEM ABDUL-JABBAR: "I think Jerry West made it easier on himself and the team. That's what general managers are supposed to do. Norm went over to the Clippers and was an All-Star and had a good career. It would have been a lot better for him to finish with the Lakers. But he did okay."

RON CARTER: "Norm wasn't happy about being traded to the Clippers, and that's understandable. There was the premise under which it happened, and that was that he somehow was a bad seed. It wasn't nice. It wasn't very nice."

JIM HILL, LONGTIME L.A. SPORTSCASTER: "That was a move that West really agonized over. You had this young stud Byron Scott that you could get. Plus he had a six-nine Magic handling the ball. No one had ever seen anything like that before. And once Jerry was convinced that Magic could handle those duties, the ballhandling duties, there was no question. You've got to do it."

DOUG KRIKORIAN: "I liked Norm. I had a good rapport with him. He was a good ballplayer. I hated to see him leave. But that's what made Jerry West such a good general manager. He saw ahead. He saw that Magic had to have the ball. And they weren't good at sharing. Norm liked to bring the ball up. I remember Magic would reluctantly, reluctantly give him the ball and let him bring the ball up, which was ridiculous."

JIM HILL: "Magic has always said he learned a lot from Norm. At his retirement speech at halftime at the Forum, Magic said then that one of the people he wanted to thank was Norm."

The deal meant that rookie Byron Scott faced difficult circumstances when he joined the Lakers with two exhibition games left.

BYRON SCOTT: "I caught a lot of trouble. Norm had been traded, and the people in Los Angeles weren't happy about it. And the team didn't seem real happy. They thought they'd been betrayed and were losing a friend. It all came down to me, a rookie who had nothing to do with it. Earvin and Cooper were the two that gave me the most trouble, because Norm was very close to both of them. Mostly it was just pushing and shoving, things like that. Taunting and talking, trying to make me upset. As a rookie you have to do what they say. Go get water. Get this and that. I think they took it a little bit overboard, but I never complained and kept doing what I could until one day Coop threw an elbow and I told him, 'You throw another one, I'm gonna throw one back.' After that, they started to respect me a little bit. Earvin told me they had done it number one, to see if I could play; number two, to see what kind of heart I had; and number three, to see if I could fit in. He told me I passed all three with As."

Scott was not as good a ball handler as Nixon, but his presence didn't complicate the offense with two guards wanting the ball. An excellent shooter, he knew the role of off guard well. He spotted up, waited for Johnson to drive, then caught the kick pass when Johnson drew the double-team. From there, it was merely a matter of hitting the open shot, which Scott was born to do.

By January the Lakers had assimilated him into the lineup and were on their way to compiling a 54–28 record, once again the best in the West. Along the way, Kareem passed Wilt as the game's all-time leading scorer in an April game against Utah in Las Vegas. With a smiling Johnson making the assist, Kareem racked up a total of 31,421 with a skyhook over Utah's Mark Eaton. "I'd like to give thanks to the great Allah for gifting me," he told the audience afterward. "I'd like to give thanks to my parents, who are both here tonight for inspiration and a lot of courage and support. I want to give my best to my family, and lastly, I want to thank all of you fans for your tremendous support."

The 1984 season marked a turning point in the NBA for a variety of reasons.

RUSS GRANIK, NBA VICE PRESIDENT: "I think '83–84 was a watershed year for the league. David Stern became commissioner in '84, and at the end of '83 we got our first agreement with the players association that had a salary cap and an antidrug agreement, which I think was critical for the development of the league. That's when we really started to become a national event on television. Then Larry and Magic met in Finals, Michael Jordan was drafted and played on the Olympic team. Isiah Thomas had that great playoff series with the Knicks. It was an incredible time. Obviously Larry and Magic coming in together, it all fueled a lot for us."

It was also the year that the Lakers hosted NBA All-Star Weekend, which brought a promotional trial by fire for Lakers staff member Lon Rosen. He first signed Lionel Richie to sing the national anthem for the Forum event.

LON ROSEN: "We had to ditch those plans the week of the event. A league official asked me, 'Who's Lionel Richie?' I got Marvin Gaye as a replacement."

Rosen then watched in horror the day before the game as Gaye ran through a five-minute version of the national anthem with the rhythm track to "Sexual Healing" as the backbeat.

LON ROSEN: "I knew there was no way that CBS would put up with a five-minute national anthem. So I had to go up to Marvin and ask if he could trim it down. I was worried, so I asked him to show up an hour early tomorrow to do a run-through."

Gaye frowned and mumbled something about being at the Forum at 11:30. The next day 11:30 passed, then noon. With the 12:37 game time looming, it was panic city for Rosen.

LON ROSEN: "I didn't think he was gonna show, so I got this Forum usher who said she could do it. I was about to take her to center court at 12:25 when Gaye and his entourage of five showed up."

He strolled to the mike and turned out a two-minute, 24-second version of pure soul sweetness.

LON ROSEN: "People started to clap, players were dancing to it."

But upstairs at the Forum offices and in New York at the CBS switchboard, the phones were ringing. The national anthem and "Sexual Healing"? People were outraged. Fortunately, Rosen saved the soundtrack, and when Gaye was killed months later, the Lakers played it as a tribute to him. Years later the

NBA included Gaye's anthem on its *50th Anniversary* soundtrack, then featured it at the 2004 All-Star Weekend in Los Angeles.

One Last Boston Embarrassment

For four seasons they had danced around each other in the NBA, meeting only twice each year in regular-season games. Still, Larry Bird and Magic Johnson were always aware of each other. They searched the headlines and kept their eyes on the standings and the box scores. They were trying to find some way of measuring who was best, and both would later admit that they wanted to meet for a championship. In 1984 it finally happened. Bird's Celtics versus Magic's Lakers.

"It's like the opening of a great play," Jerry West told the writers just before the 1984 Finals. "Everyone's waiting to see it." Pro hoops had never enjoyed such media hype. As Scott Ostler and Steve Springer pointed out in *Winnin' Time*, it was a clash of symbols. Bird versus Magic. West versus East. Showtime versus Shamrocks. L.A. Cool versus Celtic Pride. But beneath all the symbols and media hooks, at the heart of everything, were two guys with immense confidence, supreme talent, and a mutual desire to dominate.

JERRY WEST: "With Magic, it was a macho thing. He wanted to be better than everybody else."

The same was true with Bird. "The number one thing is desire," he said, "the ability to do the things you have to do to become a basketball player. I don't think you can teach anyone desire. I think it's a gift. I don't know why I have it, but I do."

JAMES WORTHY: "Bird talked as tough as he played. He'd always say, 'Get down!' or 'In your face!' or 'You can't guard me!' Whatever he could use to throw you off balance. That was his biggest weapon over the years. Back then, when I was young and didn't know any better, I thought he was a jerk. But after reflecting back, I realized that was just part of his game. He was measuring and analyzing his opponents, and he would do it from the moment he stepped on the floor. In the layup line, he'd be looking down there at you, just checking out your tendencies and your mannerisms and your posture. He could tell if your confidence wasn't right. He could tell. He could sense the vibe. If you came out on him and really didn't bump him or weren't aggressive with him, he knew. He knew he had you. If you showed any signs of doubt, you were through with Larry."

These forces of pride and ego collided in the 1984 championship series, and the league was ever so thankful for it. The Boston/L.A. fling in the Finals was the juice that grew the NBA. Over Bird and Johnson's first dozen years in the league, television rights money alone zoomed from roughly $14 million per year to more than $100 million. In sports bars, living rooms, and cocktail lounges across America, the competition spawned a running debate as to who was the greatest. Bird would be named the league MVP for three consecutive seasons, 1984–86. On the heels of that, Red Auerbach went so far as to declare him the greatest basketball player ever, even greater than Bill Russell, a five-time MVP.

Yet even as Bird claimed his awards, plenty of observers, including Chamberlain, thought Johnson was being shortchanged. "I don't know if there's ever been a better player than Magic," Wilt said. Bird himself readily agreed. "He's the perfect player," he said of Johnson.

It was a nice public statement, but in 1984, as both teams were fighting their way to the championship round, the two superstars held an abiding dislike for each other, which meant that they were more than eager to prove something on the court.

JIM HILL: "It was an intense rivalry, almost a hatred."

The Lakers finished off the Phoenix Suns and took the Western Conference title. Once again, they were lucky to be there, having overcome injuries and other problems. Johnson had missed 13 games early in the schedule with an injured finger. Then in February, Jamaal Wilkes had contracted an intestinal infection that would hamper him the remainder of the season. Still, they possessed a solid confidence as they prepared for the Celtics. Kareem was no longer dominant, but he still gave the Lakers a formidable half-court game when they needed it. Beyond that, Worthy had quietly come into his own as a forward. He had brilliant quickness, and once Johnson got him the ball in the low post, the result was usually a score. He took delight in faking one way, then exploding another. And he continued to add range to his shot, building consistency from 15 feet out.

And the Lakers again got good frontcourt minutes and scoring from McAdoo. In the backcourt, Michael Cooper had found his identity as a defensive and three-point specialist, while third-year guard Mike McGee contributed 9.8 points per game.

MAGIC JOHNSON: "We were just pushing that ball up and down. We didn't give you a chance to rest at no time in the game. We utilized everybody's talent. Kareem would get the rebound and say, 'Okay, you guys just run on down the floor. Now if you don't score, you call me down and I'll come down and shoot the skyhook.' But first you go for option number one, that's me. Option number two, that's James Worthy. Number three, probably Byron. Number four, Kurt, or whoever is trailing. But we were gonna go through all those options before we said, 'Big fella, come down and save us right quick 'cause we couldn't score.' But we wanted to run at every opportunity. Made basket. Missed basket. Coach Riley had a saying, 'It may not have no effect in the first quarter. The running game may not have no effect in the second quarter, but by that third quarter and the end of that third quarter, it's going to have some effect.' And sure enough, we would usually take over that game by the fourth quarter because you would be so tired. It was beautiful basketball."

Once Johnson put his finger injury behind him, they won 56 of their last 61 games, including a nice little roll through the early rounds of the playoffs. As the Finals opened, there was a sense that L.A. was the better team. But the Celtics had ended their conference Finals series on May 23, while the Lakers didn't wrap things up until Friday night, May 25. With the first game of the Finals set for Sunday, May 27, in Boston Garden, the Celtics' four days' rest seemed to be a major factor. It had been 15 years since L.A. had last faced Boston in the Finals, yet old-timers needed no reminder of the numbers. Seven times the Lakers had met the Celtics for the championship, and seven times they had lost.

JAMES WORTHY: "We had heard a lot about the Boston jinx, but it wasn't something we worried about. We knew we could win. There were fire alarms at two or three o'clock in the morning every night in the hotel, so you didn't sleep well, and the humidity in Boston Garden was terrible."

KAREEM ABDUL-JABBAR: "There was the phantom person, whoever it was, who would come to the hotel where we were staying and set a fire in the stairwell early in the morning. That started happening in Philly in '83. Then it happened again in '84. We had to leave the hotel in Philly. The alarm went off at four or five in the morning. I just went down and sat on the bus and waited two hours on the bus."

It was a long-held Lakers suspicion that Red Auerbach was responsible for these things. In the locker room before Game 1, Byron Scott reached over to pick up some tape on the floor and felt warm air coming out of a vent. The Celtics were heating the locker room, he concluded.

LON ROSEN: "The Celtics did all kinds of dastardly things. It was all Red Auerbach. The guy is classless. That's old-time bullshit."

The schedule required the Lakers to make three cross-country trips. With each visit they changed hotels, hoping to avoid the harassment. To no avail.

JOSH ROSENFELD, FORMER LAKERS PR MAN: "The Boston papers and TV stations were publicizing our hotel locations."

Hours before Game 1, Kareem was wracked by one of the migraine headaches that had troubled him throughout his career. Team trainer Jack Curran worked the center's neck and back an hour before game time, at one point popping a vertebra into place. That seemed to do the trick on the 37-year-old captain. He walked out and treated the Garden crowd to 32 points, 8 rebounds, 5 assists, 2 blocks, and a steal. He made 12 of his 17 shots from the floor and 8 of 9 free throws. He did all of that only when the Lakers slowed down. They spent the rest of the time running their break in one door and out another for a 115–109 win. Kaput went Boston's home-court edge.

Game 2 then became a Worthy showcase for the first 47 minutes or so. He hit 11 of 12 from the floor and scored 29 points. Even better, the Lakers had come from behind to take a 115–113 lead with 18 seconds left. McHale went to the free throw line for two shots but missed both. Thoughts of a sweep crossed 14,890 Boston minds. But the Lakers picked that particular moment for a snooze. Pat Riley had told Johnson to call time-out if McHale made the shots. But Johnson misunderstood and called time-out after the misses, which gave Boston time to set up the defense. Inbounding at midcourt, Johnson then tossed the ball to Worthy, who spied Byron Scott across the court and attempted to get the ball to him. Lurking in the background praying for just such an opportunity was Boston's Gerald Henderson. He stepped in, snatched the fat pass, and loped down the court for the layin. The game was tied, but again Magic made a mistake. He allowed the clock to run down without attempting a final shot.

"The other players never did anything to help him," Riley would say later in defense of Johnson. "They stood out on the perimeter and didn't get open. Kareem moved with 12 seconds left, which meant he was open too early. Magic got blamed."

ROBERT McADOO: "Magic had the ball, and I was screaming at him not to call a time-out. But we were ordered to call a time-out. Pat talks about it, that he made a mistake, too, that he called a time-out. Nobody thought McHale was gonna miss the free throw. We didn't need to call a time-out. All we had to do was hold it, and they'd foul us and we'd shoot the free throws and go home. You don't forget those. You've got to win 'em when you can because disaster happens."

Late in overtime, Celtic reserve forward Scott Wedman hit a jumper from the baseline to give Boston a 124–121 win and a 1–1 tie in the series.

Afterward Riley was haunted by the steal. "What will I remember most from this series?" he asked rhetorically. "Simple. Game 2. Worthy's pass to Scott. I could see the seams of the ball, like it was spinning in slow motion, but I couldn't do anything about it."

JAMES WORTHY: "I had the first big blooper of my career. I threw the ball to Gerald Henderson. We could have gone up 2–0. That set the tone for them."

The Lakers quickly recovered back home in the Forum. Johnson had a Finals record 21 assists, and Showtime rolled to a 137–104 win. Bird was outraged at Boston's flat performance. "We played like a bunch of sissies," he said afterward.

The next day the L.A. papers began touting Worthy as the series MVP, a development that infuriated the Celtics. Coach K. C. Jones adjusted the Boston defense, switching Dennis Johnson to cover Magic. Regardless, the Lakers took an early lead and seemed poised to again run off with the game. From the bench, Boston's M. L. Carr vociferously lobbied for the Celtics to become more physical. Kevin McHale complied in the second quarter when he clotheslined Kurt Rambis on a breakaway, causing a ruckus under the basket. The incident awakened the Celtics and gave the Lakers reason to pause. Later Riley would call the Celtics "a bunch of thugs."

Maxwell, on the other hand, was overjoyed with the development. "Before Kevin McHale hit Kurt Rambis, the Lakers were just running across the street whenever they wanted," he said. "Now they stop at the corner, push the button, wait for the light, and look both ways."

Still, L.A. held a five-point lead with less than a minute to play in regulation. But Boston's Robert Parish stole a bad pass from Johnson, and the Lakers point guard later missed two key free throws, allowing the Celtics to force an overtime. Late in the extra period, Worthy faced a key free throw. But Carr hooted loudly from the bench that he would miss. Worthy did, and Maxwell stepped up and greeted him with the choke sign. The Celtics vaulted to a 129–125 win to tie the series again and regain the home-court edge.

JAMES WORTHY: "Cedric Maxwell and M. L. Carr would try to talk you out of your game. They'd do a good job of it. They made me mad with the choke signs. I really didn't say anything, except, 'Forget you,' or something like that. But they were good at taunting you and keeping you disoriented."

The free throw misses and the turnover would trouble Magic for a long time. "I thought the free throws more than the pass were mistakes," he would say later. "Those were things I—not the team—I should have taken care of."

The Celtics realized they were on to something. The Lakers could be intimidated.

GERALD HENDERSON, FORMER CELTIC: "We had to go out and make some things happen. If being physical was gonna do it, then we had to do it. I remember in the fourth game that was the turnaround. We had to have that game or we were gonna be down 3–1. We had to have it."

BOB RYAN, *BOSTON GLOBE* COLUMNIST: "Riley's epiphany that took place during the 1984 Finals. In Game 4, Kevin McHale took Kurt Rambis down, almost violently. At that moment, Riley swore he'd never get out-toughed again. All at once, a strong team became much tougher mentally."

The Celtics found their mental and physical tactics worked. The series hinged on Game 5 in Boston, where the Lakers sought an edge with oxygen tanks on the bench.

BOB RYAN: "The so-called 'heat game' in 1984. It was 97 degrees in the Boston Garden, and the one player that you could have predicted turned this game into a positive was Larry Bird. The Lakers were sitting there sucking on oxygen, and Bird is saying, 'Hey, we've all played outdoors in the summer. We've all played on asphalt. We've all done this. Why should this be different? It's just because we have uniforms on and it's a national television audience.' That game and that performance summed up Bird to me as much as anything else he's ever done."

In that crucial match, Bird was 15 for 20 from the floor for 34 points as Boston won, 121–103. Kareem, meanwhile, appeared to be just what he was—a 37-year-old man running in sweltering heat. How hot was it? a reporter asked. "I suggest," Kareem replied, "that you go to a local steam bath, do 100 push-ups with all your clothes on, and then try to run back and forth for 48 minutes. The game was in slow motion. It was like we were running in mud."

"I love to play in the heat," Bird said, smiling. "I just run faster, create my own wind."

"He was just awesome," Riley said of Bird. "He made everything work."

The Lakers then answered the Celtics' aggressiveness in Game 6 back in the air-conditioned Forum. In the first period, Worthy shoved Maxwell into a basket support. From there, the Lakers rode their newfound toughness and an old standby. Kareem scored 30, and L.A. pulled away down the stretch for a 119–108 win to tie the series at three apiece. As Carr left the Forum floor, a fan pitched a cup of liquid in his face, enraging the Celtics. Carr said afterward that the Lakers had declared "all-out war." Bird suggested that the Lakers had better wear hard hats on the bench for Game 7 in the Garden because the fans might get wild.

The entire city of Boston was juiced up for the event that Tuesday night, June 12. The Lakers needed a police escort just to get from their hotel to the Garden. Carr came out wearing goggles to mock Kareem and told the Lakers they weren't going to win. Not in the Garden.

Cedric Maxwell further ensured that, presenting a high-action, low-post puzzle that the Lakers never solved. He demoralized them on the offensive boards. He drew fouls. By halftime, he had made 11 of 13 free throws. When they tried to double-team him, he passed them silly. He finished with 24 points, 8 assists and 8 rebounds. Bird had 20 points and 12 rebounds, Parish 14 points and 16 rebounds. And Dennis Johnson scored 22 while covering Magic.

Even against that barrage, the Lakers fought back from a 14-point deficit to trail by just three with more than a minute left. Magic had the ball, but Dennis Johnson knocked it loose. Cooper recovered it, and Magic again went to work and spied Worthy open under the basket. But before he could make the pass, Maxwell knocked the ball away yet again. Later the vision of Worthy open under the basket would return to Johnson again and again.

At the other end, Dennis Johnson drew a foul and made the shots, spurring the Celtics to their 15th championship, which was celebrated deliriously by the Garden crowd. Kareem had made the mistake of retrieving a rebound as the final horn sounded and was caught up in the rush.

KAREEM ABDUL-JABBAR: "It all came down to one bad pass that James threw. And then there was the sweatbox game. That was a classic Celtics win. I was really annoyed at how we had lost it. Certain things had happened. I got mugged after the last game on the court. Someone snatched my glasses."

One fan jumped on Rambis's back and would later file suit after the Lakers forward slung him off.

JOSH ROSENFELD, FORMER LAKERS PUBLICIST: "There was no crowd control, and they just went nuts."

In the Celtics' locker room, Auerbach enjoyed yet another of his very fat, very special cigars as Commissioner David Stern presented the league trophy. The Celtics president clutched it with satisfaction and asked, "Whatever happened to that Lakers dynasty I've been hearing so much about?"

Reporters packed the tiny visitors' dressing room waiting for Johnson and Cooper, who sat on the floor of the shower too disconsolate to come out. Johnson's friends Mark Aguirre and Isiah Thomas waited, too.

Josh Rosenfeld: "Finally they went back to Earvin and told him, 'Why don't you get this over so we can get out of here?'"

Then the Lakers tried to escape the bedlam in the streets outside the arena, but the crowd spotted their bus headed down the exit ramp.

James Worthy: "It was a slow exit from the arena down that ramp. The crowd was shaking and hitting our bus."

Rudy Garciduenas, longtime Lakers equipment man: "People were throwing stuff at the bus and banging on the windows. There was this one guy in a wheelchair shooting us the bird. I remember people laughing at him. He was smiling and flipping everybody off. He was just sitting there so out of it about the Celtics."

Breakthrough

Unfortunately, the Lakers couldn't get out of town after the 1984 Finals. They had to spend one more night in their hotel, trapped inside of Boston with the Celtic blues again. Needless to say, it was a sleepless night. Owner Jerry Buss chain-smoked. Michael Cooper spent the time in deep and miserable mourning sequestered in his room with his wife, Wanda. Riley quickly put away the white tuxedo he had planned to wear for the championship celebration and began thinking about next year.

Joined by Isiah Thomas and Mark Aguirre, Johnson talked the night away. About music. Cars. Old times. Anything but the series. Occasionally the conversation would drift that way, but they'd steer it away. It was too tender a subject.

Isiah Thomas: "We talked until the morning came, but we never talked about the game much. For that one night I think I was his escape from reality."

Early the next day Kareem had agreed to appear on the CBS morning news.

JOSH ROSENFELD: "When we showed up at the studio, Cedric Maxwell was there. The producer's idea was to have Cedric and Kareem on together. We were there about 10 minutes, and Cedric was sitting across from Kareem. Cedric had said a lot of things during the series. Kareem asked the producer, 'Is he on first, or am I on first?' She said, 'Oh, no, we want the two of you on together.' Kareem got up and very politely said, 'Thank you for inviting me. I can't do that.' This poor girl, the producer, she was frantic. She was in tears. She followed us out to the limo and said, 'We can reformat the show. You can go on after Maxwell.' Kareem said, 'No, I'm not in the mood anymore, but thank you.' Then he explained to me, 'Maxwell accused Worthy of choking. I can't be seen on national TV with him. It would be offensive to my teammates.'"

The Lakers' humiliation would remain for months. Johnson returned to California, where he was set to move into his new Bel Air mansion, only the furniture hadn't arrived. His palace sat as empty as his heart, so he hid out for three days in his Culver City apartment. His mother, Christine, phoned to see how he was doing. He told her he just couldn't talk about it.

Yet everywhere he turned there seemed to be something to read about it. The Celtics were having fun with their victory. McHale even dubbed him "Tragic Johnson." Asked about the 1984–85 season, Bird said of the Lakers, "I'd like to give them the opportunity to redeem themselves. I'm sure they have guys who feel they didn't play up to their capabilities." Asked if he meant Magic, Bird replied, "You think we don't love it? Magic having nightmares."

Johnson retorted that he had no need for redemption. Even worse than the Celtics cockiness was the trashing he took from the L.A. newspapers. "I sat back when it was over," he said later, "and I thought, Man, did we just lose one of the great playoff series of all time, or didn't we? This was one of the greatest in history. Yet all you read was how bad I was."

MICHAEL COOPER: "Magic has had his trials and tribulations throughout his entire NBA career. That's the thing I've always admired about him. He's always met them head-on and conquered them to the best of his ability."

His meeting the challenge began when the Lakers returned to Palm Springs for training camp that fall.

BYRON SCOTT: "When we walked on the floor that first day of camp, we saw it in everybody's eyes. This was going to be a serious year."

Especially for Riley.

GARY VITTI, LONGTIME LAKERS TRAINER: "Pat was screwed down pretty tight, like a spring. And it escalated from there."

BYRON SCOTT: "Riles made us aware of exactly what he wanted. He let us know from day one, 'I'm gonna work you from the first day of camp to the last day of the playoffs.' He didn't let up. That's the main reason we kept going all year, because we had a coach who wouldn't let us stop."

Riley later explained that his team's psyche was fragile. They had won two championships on their talent, but the Celtics had challenged them with psychological warfare and won. The Lakers would have to either form as a team and fight back or fall apart.

KAREEM ABDUL-JABBAR: "That first series that we gave them in '84 really seasoned us. It gave us the mental tenacity that we didn't always exhibit. We couldn't outrun everybody. We had to understand that sometimes there were other ways to skin the cat."

It was something that Paul Westhead had lost his job trying to tell them. By the 1985 playoffs the Lakers had regained their composure and their strength. The frontcourt was bolstered by the return of Mitch Kupchak and Jamaal Wilkes to go with Kareem, Worthy, Rambis, McAdoo, and Larry Spriggs. The backcourt showed Magic, Scott, Cooper, and McGee. As a group, they were driven by their '84 humiliation.

"Those wounds from last June stayed open all summer," Riley said as the playoffs neared. "Now the misery has subsided, but it never leaves your mind completely. Magic is very sensitive to what people think about him, and in his own mind I think he heard those questions over and over again to the point where he began to rationalize and say, 'Maybe I do have to concentrate more.' I think the whole experience has made him grow up in a lot of ways."

After all, Johnson was a mere 25, and at a time when most pro players were just beginning to feel comfortable in the game, he already owned two championship rings. Across pro basketball, observers sensed that he was about to add to his jewelry collection. The Celtics, however, were conceding nothing. With a 63–19 regular-season finish, they had again claimed the home-court advantage. The Lakers had finished 62–20. And neither team dallied in the playoffs. Boston dismissed Cleveland, Detroit, and Philadelphia in quick succession. The Lakers rolled past Phoenix, Portland, and Denver.

For the first time in years, the Finals returned to a 2-3-2 format, with the first two games in Boston, the middle three in L.A., and the last two, if necessary, back in Boston. The situation set up an immense opportunity for the Lakers to steal one in the Garden, then pressure the Celtics back in L.A. Yet on the eve of the Finals they were struck by old doubts.

JAMES WORTHY: "We really weren't sure of ourselves. We got back to the Finals and said, 'Golly, we got the Celtics again. How're we gonna do it?' We just came out and played like a bunch of women, really. Didn't have any aggressiveness. No killer instinct. We paid the price for it."

Which was one final, profound embarrassment. Game 1 opened on Memorial Day, Monday, May 27, with both teams cruising on five days' rest. The Lakers, however, quickly took on the appearance of guys who had just come off two weeks on the graveyard shift. The 38-year-old Kareem, in particular, slogged up and down the court, while Robert Parish seemed to glide. Often Kareem would just be reaching the top of the key to catch up when all of a sudden the action raced the other way. He finished the day with 12 points and three rebounds. And Johnson had only one rebound. Meanwhile the famed Showtime running game had been slowed to a belly crawl.

And the Celtics? They placed a huge red welt on the Lakers' scar from the previous year, 148–114. "It was one of those days," K. C. Jones said, "where if you turn around and close your eyes, the ball's gonna go in."

Abruptly, the Celtics quieted their trash talking, as if they sensed that they had gone too far. "It's definitely time to back off," Maxwell said. "It's not like backgammon or cribbage, where if you beat someone bad enough you get two wins."

The next morning in the Lakers' film sessions, Kareem moved to the front row, rather than recline in the farther reaches as he usually did. And the captain went to each of his teammates later and personally apologized for his effort.

KAREEM ABDUL-JABBAR: "That horrible game, the Memorial Day Massacre. That was mainly me. I remember watching the film of that game. The camera would follow the ball, and I would always be at the back of the pack. I'd be out of camera range, always bringing up the rear. I realized I simply wasn't keeping up with the play. I had worn down over the course of the playoffs. So we had like three days before we played. The massacre was on Sunday, and we didn't play again until Thursday. And I did like a mini training camp. I just made myself get my cardiovascular back to where it should be. I told everybody, I promised, that whatever happened on the next game I would give my best, whatever that was. Pat was trying to accommodate me minute-wise, but I don't get into shape unless I work myself into shape. I got to play. So the more time I spent on the bench, it really wasn't getting the job done. We needed a different way of approaching it."

JAMES WORTHY: "A lot of the discussion was pointed at Kareem. But it was all of us, because none of us played well. But he was our leader. He made a contract with us that it would never happen again. Ever."

PAT RILEY: "That game was a blessing in disguise. It strengthened the fiber of that team."

JAMES WORTHY: "That set the tone. That game was the turning point in Lakers history, I think. We came back strong and Kareem led the way. Riley, too. He stepped forward. It was the turning point in his career, too. He took his coaching to another level. It brought the last development of his coaching technique. It was to utilize all aspects. After that particular game it wasn't pretty. It was factual. It was the truth, and it was presented to us in a way we couldn't deny. We had to go out and do something about it."

Before Game 2 on Thursday, Kareem went to Riley and asked if his father, Al Alcindor, could ride on the team bus to the Garden. Riley consented and thought of his own father.

GARY VITTI: "Pat talked about when he was a little boy. His big brothers would take him down to the playground. He was the smallest guy out there, and he'd get beat up every day and go home crying. They'd take him home, and his father would say, 'Take Pat back down there tomorrow.' And the big brothers would say, 'Dad, the guy's getting beat up.' His father said, 'Take him back. At some point, you gotta plant your feet, kick some ass, and make a stand.'"

Just before he died, the elder Riley had reminded his son that to survive you had to make that stand. Riley recalled those words to his players in his pregame talk.

GARY VITTI: "That's why Pat is what he is today, those types of influences. Riles is an inspiring guy. I mean after hearing him, I wanted to go out there and kick some ass, too."

And the Lakers did. Kareem, in particular, reasserted himself with 30 points, 17 rebounds, 8 assists and 3 blocks. Cooper hit eight of nine from the floor to finish with 22 points. And just like that, the Lakers evened the series, 109–102. Best of all, they had stolen a game in the Garden and now returned to the Forum for three straight.

"They expected us to crawl into a hole," Lakers assistant Dave Wohl said of the Celtics. "It's like the bully on the block who keeps taking your lunch money every day. Finally you get tired of it and you whack him." They hosted the Celtics on Sunday afternoon and really whacked 'em again, returning the favor of Game 1, 136–111. This time Worthy was the man, with 29 points. But Kareem's presence was felt again, too. He had 26 points and 14 rebounds.

At one point, Boston had led, 48–38, but Worthy dominated the second quarter and L.A. charged to a 65–59 edge at intermission. The Lakers ran away in the second half, during which Kareem became the league's all-time leading playoff scorer with 4,458 points. Bird, meanwhile, had fallen into a two-game shooting slump, going 17 for 42. He had been troubled by a chronically sore right elbow and bad back, though some speculated his real trouble was Cooper's defense.

As with '84, the series was marked by physical play, although this time it was the Lakers who gained an edge. "We're not out to physically harm them," Kareem offered. "But I wouldn't mind hurting their feelings." Before Game 4, the NBA's vice president of operations, Scotty Stirling, warned each coach that fighting and extra rough play would be met with fines and suspensions. Riley told his players of Stirling's warning, but K. C. Jones chose not to. With their uninhibited play, the Celtics stayed in it, and the game came down to one final possession. Bird had the ball but faced a double-team, so he dumped it off. From there, Dennis Johnson drilled the winner with two seconds left. Boston had evened the series and regained its home-court advantage, 107–105.

Game 5 two nights later in the Forum was another showdown. The Lakers went on a 14–3 run at the close of the half to take a 64–51 lead. They stretched it to 89–72 after intermission, until the Celtics closed to within four at 101–97 with six minutes left. But Magic hit three shots and Kareem added four more, giving him 36 on the day, as the Lakers walked away with a 3–2 lead, 120–111.

"People didn't think we could win close games," Johnson said afterward.

From there it went back to Boston. Jerry West didn't dare make the trip for fear of spooking the proceedings. Across the country old Lakers held their breath and watched the tube. After eight painful losses, this seemed to be the best chance yet to end Boston's domination. The Celtics would have to win the final two games. With a mere 38 hours' rest between games, that just didn't seem possible.

Kareem was there again, this time with 29 points, 18 of them in the second half when it mattered. The score was tied at 55 at intermission.

Kareem sat much of the second period in foul trouble while Kupchak did admirable work at backup. The Celtics had played only seven people in the first half, and Magic could see that they were tired. Riley told him to keep pushing it at them, not to worry about turnovers. Just keep up the pressure. He did.

And the Celtics did something they had never ever done before. They gave up a championship on their home floor, on the hallowed parquet, 111–100. McHale had kept them alive with 36 points, but he got his sixth foul with more than five minutes left. And, thanks in part to Cooper's defense, Bird was closing out a 12-for-29 afternoon. "I thought I'd have a great game today," he said afterward.

In the end, the Lakers' victory was signaled by the squeaking of sneakers in the deathly quiet Garden as the crowd slipped away. It was the same crowd that had so riotously jostled the Lakers the year before. "We made 'em lose it," Johnson said with satisfaction.

KAREEM ABDUL-JABBAR: "They fought as dirty as they could until they realized they were gonna lose. Then they came back with Celtic pride and all this crap. Being able to shut those people up in Boston Garden—that was so satisfying. Even though we came back to L.A. and lost a game, we didn't lose any momentum. That was the first year where James really just started to dominate. He just emerged in such a spectacular, wonderful way. It was a nice thing to see. He could finish the break and he could post up. He was just so versatile. And we had Mitch Kupchak and Bob McAdoo on the bench. It was just great stuff."

Kareem was named the MVP. "He defies logic," Riley said of the 38-year-old Lakers center. "He's the most unique and durable athlete of our time, the best you'll ever see. You better enjoy him while he's here."

Johnson's trophy was the sweet redemption he had said he didn't need. "You wait so long to get back," he admitted afterward. "A whole year. That's the hard part. But that's what makes this game interesting. It's made me stronger."

JERRY BUSS: "The Garden was nearly empty with the reporters taking notes in the locker rooms and writing their stories. Hampton Mears, one of my old friends, and I slipped out to the center of the Garden parquet. We giggled and exchange high fives. The most odious sentence in all of sport—the Lakers have never beaten the Celtics—wasn't true anymore."

Across the country, old Lakers felt a weight lifted.

In the wake of the '85 title, the Lakers decided to ditch two old favorites. They waived Jamaal Wilkes and declined to pick up the option on Robert McAdoo's contract. Both were popular with their teammates.

MAGIC JOHNSON: "Without a doubt, that was the Lakers' greatest moment. Those years with McAdoo, that team was awful close. We were all so tough-minded. We would go on the road and just say, 'Okay, how many games we got?' We'd see there was six. 'We're gonna win all six.' And then we'd go and win all six. We would push each other to make sure. Coop would be on me. I would be on Coop. If the game got tight, Coop would say, 'Buck, take over.' And I'd take over. Or I'd say, 'Kareem, it's time for you to dominate. Take over the game.' And it was just that way. Or we could get on one another. 'Man, your man's beatin' you! What's up?' You would get so mad, you'd just shut 'em down. That was the respect we had for one another. That was the sign of a true championship team, that we could get on one another."

To bolster the frontcourt after McAdoo's departure, the team signed veteran bruiser Maurice Lucas. It was figured that he would give the roster a little toughness, but it didn't work out. A veteran, Lucas expected the perks of one. He expected a first-class seat on planes but was told they belonged to the Lakers' inner core of veterans, most of whom had far less time in the league than Lucas. He fumed at the snub, and Riley tried to explain. "These guys have been together a long time," he told Lucas. "Are you gonna be the guy to break that up? You gotta look beyond yourself to the team."

The friction, however, persisted and became one of several factors in the Lakers' ultimate failure.

GARY VITTI: "Winning the '85 title took tremendous energy from our guys. It was really mentally fatiguing to break that Celtic barrier. That next year, we needed an injection of something and it just wasn't there."

The end came abruptly against Houston in the first round of the 1986 play-offs. They fell 4–1, finished off by Ralph Sampson's last-second shot in the Forum that bounced up and in.

BYRON SCOTT: "We beat them the first game and thought it was going to be a cakewalk. Then they caught up and got us in Houston and we never recovered."

GARY VITTI: "Houston was playing great, and we were going through the motions."

Once again the Lakers sat back and watched Boston defeat Houston for the title. Jerry Buss didn't like it. He was convinced they should trade Worthy to Dallas for Mark Aguirre. But Jerry West talked him out of that deal, saying no team wanted to make a trade based on emotions. Bird and his Celtics had held their breath, hoping that Buss would break up the team. The owner's anger at their lackluster play eventually cooled, and Pat Riley began looking for answers.

Under Pressure

Kareem Abdul-Jabbar was 40 years old heading into the 1986–87 season. As long as anyone could remember, he had been the focus of the Lakers' offense. But the center's retirement was inevitable, and coach Pat Riley wanted to begin shifting the burden to other players. He wanted Magic, and to a lesser degree James Worthy, to become the focus of the offense. So the coaches began roughing out their ideas of how this transition should work. They took their notions into training camp that fall and were promptly confronted with confusion and frustration.

Kareem Abdul-Jabbar: "By then [Magic] kind of felt he was the team. When we lost in the playoffs to Houston, I was the failure and Earvin was the answer. I was being written out of the mix."

With Westhead's demise in the back of his mind, Riley had second thoughts and told longtime Lakers assistant Bill Bertka that maybe they should junk the idea. No, Bertka replied, now is the time to make the change.

Magic Johnson: "This was Kareem's team. He was the dominating type. I played my role, and it was great. I didn't mind it, but it was other people saying things. They figured I couldn't dominate like Kareem."

Despite the clash of egos, the players found their comfort zone in the new system. Kareem personally reassured Riley that everything was working fine. Johnson's play over the season would confirm it. He became the first guard since Oscar Robertson to win the league MVP award. His scoring zoomed to a career-high 23.9 points per game, and he was tops in the league in assists, at 12.2 per game.

He didn't do it alone, of course. Kareem, Worthy, Byron Scott, Cooper, and rookie A. C. Green—all of them wanted to establish their superiority. They had the opportunity to prove themselves as one of the greatest teams in basketball history. And they were about to get better.

The big boost arrived February 13, when the front office acquired Mychal Thompson from San Antonio. Larry Bird was heartsick at the news. How could the Spurs give Thompson to the Lakers? he asked. The 6-foot-10 Thompson gave the Lakers just what they needed up front. He could play backup to Kareem at center, and he was a solid power forward. Better yet, he was an excellent low-post defender, and having played with McHale at the University of Minnesota, Thompson knew better than anyone how to defend against Boston's long-armed forward. It was, Kareem said later, West's most brilliant move as general manager, because it made them championship contenders again. With Thompson, the Lakers surged to a 65-win regular season, the best in the NBA.

GARY VITTI, LONGTIME LAKERS TRAINER: "We rolled in 1987. It was almost a piece of cake. It was like, 'Who's next?' Every night we knew we were gonna win. All we had to do was keep it close. Then they could just turn it on and finish."

It had been 18 seasons since a team had won back-to-back championships in the NBA. The 1986–87 Celtics had hopes of being the first modern team to stretch to that achievement. Standing in their way was a tall, skinny guy with an inferiority complex. For several seasons Michael Cooper had shown the league that he was Showtime's defensive backbone. The '87 season finally brought his recognition as the NBA defensive player of the year. He had made Larry Bird his personal challenge, spending hours studying the Boston forward on videotape, even going so far as to take the tapes on vacation.

RUDY GARCIDUENAS, LONGTIME LAKERS EQUIPMENT MANAGER: "Coop just drove himself. He wanted to be the best. His wife, Wanda, used to give him hell all the time because that's all he did was watch tape. He didn't pay attention to her or the kids when he was home."

JAMES WORTHY: "Larry didn't talk as much with Coop. Coop would be right back in his face. Most of the time, Coop would get the first lick in. He would come out on the floor and say, 'Nothing tonight, Larry. Nothing for you. I'm sorry.' Then that would get it started right there."

MICHAEL COOPER: "I never once thought that I got into Larry's head. And he never showed it. That's the thing I loved about Larry. There were situations where he was doing some things to me, and I couldn't let him see the frustration, because if you let that set in, you know the guy's getting to you."

JAMES WORTHY: "I learned a lot from Coop in that aspect, because there wasn't any backing down. If you got 55 points against him, it was gonna be the toughest 55 you had ever gotten. Coop and Larry had that same talent, because if Coop saw you weren't ready or you weren't gonna work hard, it was history. He'd shut you down in a minute."

MICHAEL COOPER: "I think it was the mental toughness that frustrated me about Larry. His shot—he could probably go 1 for 16—but you knew there was going to be that one point in the game where he was going to hit that shot. The same defense, hand in his face, and he knocks it down, and he had this look like he had hit 6 or 7 in a row. Here I am with a look in my eyes like you just missed 10 or 12 in a row."

GARY VITTI: "It wasn't just Bird. Coop talked to everybody out there. The guy was 175 pounds. He was nothing. He was like a feather. He was afraid of no one. We weren't a bunch of bruisers. We were a finesse team. But when there was a fight on the court, Michael was always a part of it."

Cooper was the best athlete in the Showtime retinue, in Vitti's opinion. His quick first step. His speed. His timing. The hand-eye coordination. And what the trainer called his "kinesthetic sense—knowing where his body is in space."

GARY VITTI: "One of the greatest things to watch in those days was Coop baiting somebody on the breakaway. Coop would give 'em a step and they would go to the hole, and Coop would be a step behind and time it perfectly to leave his feet and block the shot. It was a vintage thing. He knew what they were gonna do before they even did."

Michael Cooper: "I came into this league primarily known as a defensive player, but runnin' and jumpin' and dunkin', that's what I liked to do. I think people kind of liked that."

Gary Vitti: "The other thing was his mental toughness. It was like Coop was so insecure about his body and size that everybody had told him he couldn't make it. He was too thin, too small. He wasn't strong enough. That's why he was so great, because he had to prove to himself that he was."

This mental toughness was something Cooper extended to his teammates.

Gary Vitti: "Magic's motivation in many, many ways came from Michael Cooper. He motivated Magic. We play too many games. We have too many practices. You cannot be 100 percent mentally and physically ready every single day in this league. When Magic wasn't there, it was Coop that was grabbing him by the jersey saying, 'C'mon, Earvin! C'mon, Earvin!' They really thrived off each other in a verbal sense. Kareem and Magic maybe thrived in a mental sense. They were on the same wavelength, but they didn't have to talk to each other. Coop and Magic talked to each other a lot on the court, getting in each other's face."

Rudy Garciduenas: "Coop was probably the most superstitious player in the league. You had to come to understand Coop and accept him for his oddities. He had to have his socks pulled all the way up to his knees. If he was going through a slump, he would walk in one day and everything had to be new. His socks, his jocks, his wristbands. He shaved his face. It was like he would cleanse himself of everything and that would break his slump."

As a young player, Cooper was an acrobatic leaper and quickly became a Forum favorite executing his "Coop-a-loop," the alley-oop slam dunk that fired up the fans. But as he aged, his legs diminished, and he made himself into a great defensive player and a solid three-point threat.

Michael Cooper: "As the years went by—Magic and I talked about this—the one thing we had to do was diversify our game. Every year other teams were getting better and different. And we had to become like that. That's what we used to tell all the people. Every year people like Larry Bird could do other things that you couldn't do the year before. So eventually I got to be the backup point guard. And that wasn't my original role. I was brought in to be a slasher/semi-shooter/defensive stopper, playing just the 2 and 3 positions. From like '85–86 on, I was playing 1, 2, and 3. That's great because the more positions you can play the more times you got a chance to be out on the floor."

Best of all, he had an iron will, reflected in his streak of 556 straight games played, which ended fittingly enough in January 1988 when he was suspended one game for fighting.

The Lakers scorched the earth as they moved through the 1987 playoff field. Denver fell 3–0 in the first round. Then Golden State dropped out of sight, 4–1. Seattle, the opponent in the Western Finals, went down, 4–0, meaning the Lakers concluded their conference work on May 24, while the Celtics and Pistons fought through a seven-game series. Faced with a week off, Riley set up a minicamp in Santa Barbara to keep them focused. They had a pancakes-and-strawberries breakfast buffet on Saturday, May 30, and watched the Celtics advance with a 117–114 win over Detroit.

Three days later, on Tuesday, June 2, the Finals opened in the Forum before a crowd peppered with celebrities. The regulars, Jack Nicholson and Dyan Cannon, were there, but the series attracted many more. Bruce Willis, Don Johnson, Whoopi Goldberg, John McEnroe, Johnny Carson, Henry Winkler, and many others. Their presence only seemed to inflame Pat Riley more. He had begun stewing with the end of the Eastern Finals, when the press described the injured Celtics as a blood-and-guts brigade. Riley threw this up to his troops as an affront. The Celtics get all the respect for being hardworking, while the Lakers are packaged as a bunch of glitzy, supertalented guys who glide through their Showtime without much character or thought, Riley alleged.

And he considered the presence of all the celebs just another reason for the press to underestimate his team. "A bunch of glitter-group, superficial laid-backs," Riley spat. "This is the hardest-working team I've ever had, but regardless of what we do, we're minimized . . . we're empty people . . . and most of us aren't even from California."

The tirade brought puzzled looks from reporters, but most of them figured he was looking for something to whip his team to the next level. Either the

Celtics would come in game-sharp and take it to the Lakers, or they would come in weary from two straight seven-game battles. The latter very quickly established itself as the operating format for the day. Their tongues wagging, the Celtics could do little more than watch the Lakers run weave drills up and down the floor. "The Celtics looked like to me like they were keeping up pretty good," Mychal Thompson quipped, "just at a different pace."

Johnson led the rout with 29 points, 13 assists, 8 rebounds, and no turnovers. On the receiving end of many of Johnson's passes, Worthy had 33 points and nine rebounds. The Lakers ran 35 fast breaks in the first two quarters and led by 21 at intermission. They settled into a canter thereafter, finally ending it 126–113.

The Celtics knew they were reeling and to catch themselves they had to stop Johnson. Which they did in Game 2, but in the process they allowed Michael Cooper to switch specialties, from defense to offense. Boston trailed by seven in the second quarter, when Cooper pushed the Lakers through a 20–10 outburst, accounting for all 20 points himself by either scoring them or assisting.

Kareem Abdul-Jabbar: "He was so invaluable. Coop could come in for a few minutes and really change everything in a game."

When it was over, he had laced in six of seven trey attempts. And the Celtics had spent another day gasping in pursuit of the Lakers break. "One of the Laker Girls could've scored a layup on us," backup center Greg Kite said later. Kareem flicked in 10 of 14 shots for 23 points, while Magic put up nice boxy numbers, 20 assists and 22 points. In Coop's big second quarter, he racked up eight assists, tying a Finals series record. His six treys broke a playoff record as well. It all added up to a 141–122 rout, Boston's sixth straight road loss in the playoffs. The L.A. papers enjoyed these developments thoroughly and took to calling the Celtics "Gang Green." Before doubt crept too far into Celtics minds, they righted themselves in Game 3 with a 109–103 win. "We're just too good a team to be swept," Bird said.

The pressure of Game 4 shifted to the Lakers, which made Riley's mood even blacker. During a closed L.A. practice in the Garden, Riley told the cleaning staff to leave the building. "Maybe he thought they had VCRs in their brooms," the Garden security director quipped.

When they weren't playing cloak-and-dagger games in the Garden, the Lakers were sequestered in their hotel rooms, waiting on nightmarishly slow room service and jumping at the fire alarms that always greeted their stays in Boston. Riley expected the worst. He sure got it. Boston went up by 16 just after the half. Jack Nicholson, who had wormed a seat in the upper press area, spent most of the evening getting choke signs from Boston fans. "There was one guy," Nicholson said. "He was giving me the choke sign so hard, I almost sent for the paramedics. He was wearing a gray sweatshirt, and his face turned almost as gray as his shirt. I couldn't believe it."

At one point, Jack allegedly mooned his tormentors.

RUDY GARCIDUENAS: "I was surprised he didn't get arrested. But the Boston fans loved him being there. He gave them somebody to jeer at."

LOU ADLER, LONGTIME LAKERS FAN AND NICHOLSON SIDEKICK: "The fans were so onto Jack that we wore steel helmets for a couple of the games. Hardhats. Then finally they moved us into those steel cages up above the arena. It was safer. I think the Celtics fans at that point didn't realize just how good the Lakers were and just how much of a real fan of basketball Jack was."

Shortly thereafter, relief came to Nicholson and the Lakers. L.A. cut the lead to eight with three and a half minutes to go in the game. From there, the conclusion, the series actually, came down to one Magic sequence.

With half a minute left, the Lakers called time to set up a pick for Kareem. But Johnson told Kareem to fake it as his defender, Parish, attempted to fight through the pick. When Parish tried to fight through, Kareem should roll to the basket, Magic said.

He did. The pass was there, and the Lakers took a 104–103 lead. But Bird grabbed it back at the 0:12 mark with a three-pointer, putting Boston up 106–104. On the next possession, Kareem was fouled and went to the line, where he made the first and missed the second. McHale grabbed the rebound, but Mychal Thompson gave him a gentle push and the ball went out-of-bounds. McHale signaled Boston ball and had the boys in green headed back to the other end until the officials got their attention and notified them that it was Lakers ball.

What followed of course was another of those plays for the ages. Magic took the ball on the inbounds pass at the left of the key and at first contemplated a 20-footer, but McHale came out to change his mind. So Magic motored into the key, where Bird and Parish joined McHale in a trio of extended arms as Magic lofted a hook. Parish almost brushed it. But the ball rose up and then descended to a swish. K. C. Jones, watching in a standing twist from the Celtics bench just feet away, felt his heart sink into an abyss.

MAGIC JOHNSON: "See everybody thought I couldn't score. I had said, 'You know, I'm just gonna go along, and one of these days it's gonna be my show.' That shot proved it to everybody, and that was the year I won the MVP. That's the year Pat said, 'Okay, Earvin, I want you to take over.' And that's what happened. After that, people said, 'It *is* Larry and Magic,' instead of 'Larry can do this, and Magic can't do that.' You always had to fight that."

The Celtics got a time-out with two seconds left, and the Lakers even left Bird open for a shot, which went partially in. But it didn't stay down, and Magic ran off happily, having stolen Game 4, 107–106.

Red Auerbach, however, was anything but happy. The Celtics boss chased veteran official Earl Strom off the floor, and in front of the press contingency and the television cameras he made pointed, disparaging remarks, suggesting that Strom was a gelding, that Strom had given the game to the Lakers. Strom ducked into the officials' dressing room, then stuck his head back out to tell Auerbach, "Arnold, you're showing the class that you always have."

Auerbach later explained that he chased Strom in an attempt to fire up his team. "People say, 'Relax, the game is over. The game is over.' Well, the game is never over," he said.

Alas, Red was wrong. The game was most definitely over, and Magic had retired to the locker room to be lost in his eternal joy. He dubbed the shot "my junior, junior, junior skyhook."

"You expect to lose on a skyhook," Bird said with a sickly smile. "You don't expect it to be Magic."

At one point during Game 5, the Lakers staff iced down several cases of champagne. But the Celtics had incentive enough. They got their second win, 123–108, and the series jetted back across the continent.

Kareem arrived for Game 6 with a shave job on his balding head. And for a time it seemed L.A. was intent on cutting it close. Magic had only four points by the half, and the Celtics led 56–51. But like Kareem's pate, the Lakers glistened after intermission. Worthy finished with 22, and Kareem had 32 points, 6 rebounds, and 4 blocks. Mychal Thompson had 15 points and 9 rebounds. And Johnson led them with all-around brilliance. His 16-point, 19-assist, 8-rebound showing brought him the MVP. And the Lakers claimed their fourth title of the decade, 106–93.

"Magic is a great, great basketball player," Bird conceded. "The best I've ever seen."

Johnson saw the reflection of his special talents in the team. "This is a super team, the best team I've played on," he said. "It's fast; they can shoot, rebound, we've got inside people, everything. I've never played on a team that had everything before. We've always had to play around something, but this team has it all."

Bird had to agree. "I guess this is the best team I've ever played against," he said.

Bird's assessment was nice, but the major questions about the Lakers remained unanswered. How deep? How good? How tough? Would they live up to their promise?

Riles

The lines in his face suggest the price of being forceful. They run deep, particularly the furrows cutting perpendicular to his mouth, framing the jutting chin and leaving him gaunt, almost haggard. It's a hard look, but then again, Pat Riley is a hard guy.

On many nights he would stand at courtside, arms folded, waiting intently for his Lakers to demoralize another opponent. The tension would tighten his face until he looked like he might gnaw the leg of the scorer's table. "I'm still the kind of coach to get jacked up for a regular-season game," he explained once. "I'm not searching for the meaning of life in the NBA, okay? But it gives me a feeling of being totally alive every time I'm out on the floor."

JACK KENT COOKE: "I take great pride in Pat Riley. He was the 12th man on a 12-man squad. We didn't know what to do with him, so finally we made him a broadcasting assistant to Chick Hearn."

As Showtime wore on, the Riley image came to be a trademark. The intense, chiseled face. The folded arms. The $1,500 Armani suits. The slick hair. Ah, that hair. Riles guarded it jealously.

RANDY PFUND, FORMER RILEY ASSISTANT: "Most people focus on Pat's image. They don't comprehend his intensity."

Riley played for Adolph Rupp at the University of Kentucky, where Riley was an All-American forward in 1966.

PAT RILEY: "He was the ultimate when it came to discipline. He had a system, he had a great philosophy, and he made you believe in that philosophy. He had a great plan that got him great results. He taught us to take great pride in it, which I do. You do it the same way every day of your life. He was the most repetitious man I've ever been around. Every day we did the same drills. When I was a player, I probably hated him. There's a lot of his philosophy in mine."

There were other influences. Riley's wife, Chris, a psychologist, has had a profound impact. Riley also studied John Wooden's writings, his "pyramid of success," and the UCLA coach's near-mystical approach to the game. From there Riley fashioned his own paradigm, the "three commitments." The first, he said, was "commitment to your life plan, to family, retirement, things like that." Second came the "Lakers plan," a total commitment to winning and all the little extra efforts it required. The third, the one he constantly hammered into his players' minds, was unity.

PAT RILEY: "You gotta totally get out of yourself and into the unity of the team. The spirit of unity does not guarantee you anything, but without it you can't be successful."

Riley's personal transformation was one of the fascinating developments of Showtime.

DOUG KRIKORIAN: "I covered him when he was the lowest-paid player among the Lakers, the most humble nice guy. I've never known anyone since I've been covering sports to change more dramatically than Pat Riley. He became like this aristocratic, philosophical, serious person. He was just a regular guy, beer-drinking, nice, typical guy, a jock, and all of a sudden he became this very effete person, espousing all this philosophy and principle."

Riley's father, Leon, was a big leaguer, and later Leon became a minor-league coach. But he then went into business and failed, requiring that he work late in life as a school custodian, a station that Riley recalls his father carrying with dignity. The youngest son, Riley was a strong-armed high school quarterback in Schenectady, New York, and Bear Bryant wanted him to play football at Alabama. But Rupp talked him into basketball in the bluegrass. From Kentucky, Riley went on to a nine-year pro career over which he averaged 7.7 points.

PETE NEWELL: "Pat made up for his lack of speed with hustle and drive."

He injured a knee in 1975, and the Lakers dealt him to Phoenix. "I felt betrayed," he said. "My only pro blood is Lakers blood. They were the only team I cared about or had a passion for." A year later he ended his career and found himself an ex-jock caught in the throes of postpartum funk. Finally Chick Hearn saved him from this purgatory with an offer to be his broadcast assistant. Riley tackled the job with relish, until 1979, when Paul Westhead asked him to serve as assistant coach. Two years later, he was thrust into the head job and had to learn, at Jerry Buss's urging, to exert his will over the team. Once he learned, he came to relish the struggle for unity.

A. C. GREEN, FORMER LAKER: "He does know how to put a team together. That's always been his biggest asset. He makes the nucleus jell. He takes the players' strengths and potential and tries to bring it all together and make it work for everybody."

Sort of like hard-boiling an egg. This unity extended from the players right down to the coaches and staffers. Riley kept the group small, the dozen players and four or five staffers.

LON ROSEN: "He called it the family."

GARY VITTI: "It meant that you fit into a slot and everything was done for the good of the team. Pat drove that home. That was the philosophy. He didn't care if you had to stay up all night to do your part."

As trainer, Vitti worked closely with Riley for five seasons and learned to live with his drive. "He thrives on intensity," Vitti said. "He thrives on it. There was always pressure, always pressure." It stemmed from a desire to win matched only by Earvin Johnson's. "They will sell their souls, sell your soul, whatever it takes," said Vitti. "Pat will claw and scratch. He will rip your eyes out." Riley became fanatical about every little detail with the team. The staffers had to report everything to him, because it was the little things that led to winning.

LON ROSEN: "Behind his back, Kareem began calling him Norman Bates."

GARY VITTI: "If somebody makes you be your best all of the time, puts that pressure on you all of the time, there's going to be resentment. I respect Pat because most of us aren't tough enough to do that. We're not tough enough to piss people off to get 'em to be their best."

Frank Brickowski came to the Lakers in the fall of 1986 and was quickly awed by the team dynamic.

FRANK BRICKOWSKI: "I've never encountered anything like it before or after. Riley was intense, but Magic and Kareem only let him get away with so much stuff. When it came to a point of drawing a line, they would not have a part of something. The first day I was there, they had just gotten done playing back-to-back preseason games. We were sitting in a circle at the start of practice, and Riley said we'd go for two and a half hours and get out of there. Magic stood up as we were ready to break and said, 'All right, an hour and a half and we're outta here.' Riley said, 'No, I said two and a half hours.' Magic said, 'Oh, I thought you said an hour and a half because we're tired because we played the last two nights.' There was a dead silence. Then Riley said, 'All right, if we do this and that, we'll be out of here in an hour and a half.'"

Promises, Promises

Even before the Lakers had put the wraps on their 1987 title, Pat Riley had begun plotting the course for next year. It would begin with a reporter's question. Riley waited until someone got around to asking if this Lakers team could repeat as champions. "I guarantee it," he said flatly. The reporters, the players, the staffers all stopped in their tracks.

His players were instantly infuriated. The game was tough enough without asking for trouble. Championship pro basketball is essentially a matter of taking on the pressure that builds over the course of a long season, the goal being to conquer that pressure and ultimately eliminate it. The greater the player, the greater the ego; the greater the ego, the greater the pressure. The reward, for truly great players, is a summer away from the pressure, a time in which they can say that they've lived up to their potential.

GARY VITTI: "In '87, we win the thing, and then Pat turns right around and lays all that pressure right back on them."

BYRON SCOTT: "Just when we thought we'd done everything we could do, Riles makes this guarantee. I thought he was crazy."

Nineteen seasons had passed since the Celtics had won consecutive championships in 1968 and '69. Many observers had come to the conclusion that the feat couldn't be accomplished in the modern NBA. Riley rejected that notion. He believed that winning again was a test of will, that greatness was available to the team with the mental toughness to fight for it. He knew the Lakers were a team of mentally strong individuals. They just needed someone to drive them to greatness. He was that person. Ultimately, Riley got away with it because the Lakers remained haunted by their missed opportunities. 1981. 1983. 1984. 1986.

GARY VITTI: "The fact is, we had teams that could've and maybe should've won all those years."

Beginning with training camp the next fall and throughout the following season, Riley pushed them like a man obsessed. He was Captain Ahab, and the back-to-back championship was the elusive great whale. On occasion the crew came close to mutiny, but then he would read their mood and lighten up just enough to keep them going.

The biggest factor, of course, was the team itself. They had the image of Showtime, of Magic's smile and the electraglide fast break, of run and gun and fun. But all in all they were a serious lot. Kareem, Worthy, and A. C. Green were as businesslike as they come. Johnson, too, had his fun face, but he had hardly been frivolous in his pursuit of basketball excellence over his career. As a team, they practiced like accountants. Detail mattered. Distraction wasn't tolerated. They had to be tough. They had to work. And they didn't slip often, but when they did, Riley was there to remind them, to irritate them with his professorial tone and his mind games. In the end, the Lakers' intensity became a way of life. And quite simply, the Boston Celtics couldn't match it.

The Lakers' 1987 championship season had only confirmed that the Lakers would need Worthy's low-post game if Riley's obsession was to be realized. With the 1987–88 season, Kareem would be 41, and while he was still the presence that the Lakers needed in their half-court game, he simply couldn't carry the load that he once had. Much of that burden would fall on Worthy's shoulders.

Heading into his sixth NBA season, the former North Carolina forward had come to enjoy a reputation for consistent excellence. In every facet of his life and his game he seemed to opt for quiet dignity and grace rather than for flash and fame. It wasn't that he disliked the Hollywood aspect of playing for the Los Angeles Lakers. He just didn't immerse himself in it. At six-foot-nine, Worthy was incredibly quick and swift. No man his size in the league could stay with him. Without a doubt, Johnson was the guard who drove the Show-time machine, but Worthy was the forward who made it go. "Earvin can push the ball up-court at an incredible tempo," Riley once explained. "But he needs someone even faster than himself to break for the wing and fly up-court. James is the fastest man of his size in the NBA. In terms of finishing the fast break creatively and swiftly and deceptively, no one else compares."

And when the game slowed down a bit, Johnson liked to send the ball to Worthy in the low post. Then, the guard said with a smile, it would be over in a matter of seconds. "His first step is awesome," Maurice Lucas said.

As a veteran pro, Worthy showed an array of moves, a repertoire of head fakes and twitches and shifts that he used to reduce his defenders to nervous wrecks. "He'll give a guy two or three fakes, step through, then throw up the turnaround," Riley said. "It's not planned."

That season would mark the crescendo of Worthy's career, sealing his reputation as "Big Game" James. He would lead the Lakers through the postseason, earning himself the playoff MVP distinction in the process.

Other Lakers stepped forward as well. Byron Scott had labored to find his shot during the 1987 Finals, but the 1987–88 season brought new confidence. He led L.A. in scoring, averaging 21.7 points over the regular season while shooting .527 from the field. Also vital was A. C. Green at power forward. He didn't shoot much, but when he did the selection was good. He rebounded well and continued to learn the intricacies of low-post defense.

Johnson once again showed consistently brilliant play, although he missed 10 games at midseason due to a groin injury. If there was a problem for the Lakers, it was Kareem's age. His decline was marked throughout the season, yet Mychal Thompson's presence off the bench provided just enough patchwork to make the Lakers effective in the post. They started the schedule with an 8–0 run, the finest opening in their history, but from there it became a test of survival.

GARY VITTI: "The season was a trainer's nightmare. We didn't know who was gonna play from one game to the next."

Worthy's knees ached. Byron Scott was plagued by patellar tendinitis. Johnson had his groin injury. And Cooper got hammered.

GARY VITTI: "Coop sprained his ankle badly in March in Houston. He was never the same after that. That was really the injury that slowed him down. When he came back from that injury, Karl Malone threw him into a press table and bruised his foot. He still played every single game after that, but he was hurting."

Somehow they overcame these ups and downs to claim the league's best regular-season record at 62–20. "Guaranteeing a championship was the best thing Pat ever did," Byron Scott said as the schedule drew to a close. "It set the stage in our mind. Work harder; be better. That's the only way we could repeat. We came into camp with the idea we were going to win it again, and that's the idea we have now."

To do so, they had to face the ultimate test. They dumped San Antonio 3–0 in the first playoff round but then had to fight their way through three consecutive seven-game series to win the title, something that no team had done before. Next came Utah and a full series battling Karl Malone, followed by seven games with Dallas.

They arrived at the Finals to meet the Detroit Pistons, who had put down the Celtics in six. Isiah Thomas's team had acquired the sobriquet "the Bad Boys" because of their penchant for hard fouls and rough play. Despite this newfound toughness, the Pistons weren't projected as much of a problem for the Lakers. Maybe the series would go six games, the observers figured. Maybe it wouldn't.

JOE DUMARS, FORMER PISTONS GUARD: "We were the peasants, and they were the royal family at that time. They did carry themselves with a tremendous air of confidence, a swagger. But I understood that. I didn't take that as a slight. When we got to winning titles we had a little swagger of our own."

It opened at the Forum on June 7 with both sides professing determination to win a championship. Yet it was all tempered a bit by the sight of Magic and Isiah holding hands and kissing before the tip-off of Game 1. It was a display of brotherly love, they explained. That didn't stop it from wearing a bit thin as the matchup intensified.

JOE DUMARS: "If you knew Isiah, if you knew Magic, the kiss was no big deal. They were going through some tough times because they were both trying to dance with the same girl. And there was only one partner."

Detroit wasted little time casting doubt on L.A.'s repeat plans. The Pistons' Adrian Dantley stepped forward, making 14 of 16 shots from the floor, enough to lead the Pistons to a shocking 105–93 win. Suddenly, the Los Angeles press noticed that the Lakers bore a remarkably striking resemblance to the Celtics: they looked old and tired.

ADRIAN DANTLEY, FORMER PISTON: "We thought we should have won it when we won the first game. But their will took over. The first thing we had to worry about was Magic. He had a great series. He had a little bit of a tough time with Dennis Rodman. Dennis played Magic very well defensively."

Playing with the flu, Johnson scored 23 points in Game 2. Worthy scored 26 while Scott had 24, and the Lakers evened the series with a 108–96 win. "I don't think there's any doubt Earvin Johnson showed the heart of a champion," Riley said afterward. "He was weak. Very weak. But this is what I call a hope game—you hope you get through it—and we got through it."

The site then switched to the Pontiac Silverdome, the football arena where crowds of 40,000 or more were expected. Ignoring the crush of fans, the Lakers shoved past the Pistons to take the third game and a 2–1 lead, 99–86.

Which put the pressure on the Pistons for Game 4. Johnson repeatedly used his size and strength to get to the basket, and Detroit's answer was to try to knock him down, which left him fuming and complaining. "Magic is tough because he likes to penetrate," Detroit's Dennis Rodman said afterward. "But I try to distract him, and hopefully he won't be able to look up the court and make one of those great passes."

The tactic worked, and Johnson was obviously frustrated. At one point, he knocked Thomas to the floor with an elbow. By then it was too late. Detroit blew past the Lakers and won by 25 points, tying it at two-all.

Determined to counter, L.A. opened Game 5 with a fury of physical intimidation, scoring the game's first 12 points. But that approach soon stalled, then backfired into foul trouble. The Lakers got away from what they do best—rebounding and running. "We couldn't contain anyone on the boards," Riley said. "We had [two] defensive boards in the fourth quarter, and they had 10 offensive boards. You're not going to beat anyone with that."

The Pistons won, 104–94, and took a 3–2 lead. Riley's dream seemed to have gone gray. But Detroit would have to claim the championship in the Forum, and that wouldn't be a cakewalk. The Pistons fell behind, 56–48, early in the third quarter of Game 6. Then Isiah Thomas scored the next 14 points in trancelike fashion—two free throws after a drive in the lane, then a five-footer off an offensive rebound, followed by four jumpers, a bank shot, and a layup. But, with three minutes to go in the period, Thomas landed on Cooper's foot and had to be helped from the floor. Despite a severely sprained ankle, he returned 35 seconds later and continued the assault. By the end of the quarter he had hit 11 of 13 shots from the floor for 25 points, setting an NBA Finals record for points in a quarter and driving Detroit to an 81–79 lead. That momentum boosted the Pistons down to the wire, and with a minute left in the game, they held a 102–99 edge. They were a mere 60 seconds from an NBA title, the franchise's first ever. The league trophy was wheeled into the Pistons' locker room. Iced champagne was brought in. CBS requested the presence of Detroit owner Bill Davidson to receive the trophy. Minutes later, those plans were rapidly disassembled, the trophy taken away before Davidson could feel it.

"A minute is a long time," Johnson would say later. "A long time. It's just two scores and two stops and you're ahead."

The first Lakers score came on Byron Scott's 14-foot jumper, to bring L.A. within one, 102–101, at 52 seconds. Detroit struggled for the right shot on its possession and failed when Thomas missed an 18-footer. At 14 seconds, Kareem positioned for his skyhook from the baseline, but Detroit's Bill Laimbeer was whistled for a foul. Kareem made both free throws, giving L.A. a 103–102 lead. The Pistons had the ball and a chance to win it. At eight seconds, Joe Dumars took the shot for Detroit, a six-foot double-pumper. It missed, the rebound slipped through Dennis Rodman's frantic hands, and Byron Scott controlled the loose ball. The Lakers were smug again.

ADRIAN DANTLEY: "We had 'em on the ropes, but we couldn't get 'em down."

There was only one major question for Game 7. Would Thomas play with the bad ankle? He answered with relative ease: "I'm playing—period," he declared.

JOE DUMARS: "The amount of intensity and focus was unlike anything I'd ever seen before. The tension was thick out there. I mean thick. Nobody wanted to give an inch. Attitudes were everywhere. And it was great [laughs]."

The ankle took Thomas to the third quarter and no further. Despite limping badly in warm-ups, he scored 10 points in the first half, leading the Pistons to a 52–47 lead. But the downtime between halves brought on stiffness, and he could no longer be effective.

The Lakers, meanwhile, got going behind Worthy's low-post scoring and raced to a seemingly insurmountable lead, 90–75, in the fourth quarter. Seemingly headed down in a blowout, the Pistons fought back with a pressure lineup that consumed the Lakers' lead in gulps. At 3:52 Detroit's John Salley knocked in two free throws to close to 98–92, and the Lakers were in obvious panic. At 1:17, Dumars hit a jumper to make it 102–100. Then Magic scored a free throw off a Rodman foul, stretching it to 103–100. Detroit had an opportunity, but Rodman took an ill-advised jumper at 39 seconds. Scott rebounded and was fouled. His two free throws pushed the lead to 105–100. Then Dumars made a layup, Worthy hit a free throw, and Laimbeer canned a trey, running the score to 106–105 with six seconds showing. Green finished a layup, making it 108–105, and although the Pistons got the ball to Thomas at midcourt with a second remaining, he fell without getting off a shot.

Riley could only give thanks. "It was a nightmare to the very end," he said. "I kept saying, 'Please don't let this end in a nightmare.' We were a great team trying to hold on."

JOE DUMARS: "Kareem walked over to our locker room after they won Game 7, congratulated us, and said, 'You'll be world champions one day.' He was the only guy who walked over and congratulated each and every guy and shook everybody's hand. That stuck with me. I thought, 'Wow, look at this professionalism here.' To the people who want to short him for his supposed lack of communication, their criticism is a reflection on them, not him. His credit is due based on what he did on the court, not on whether he was gracious enough to stand around and chat with reporters. That doesn't diminish what he did. He showed a tremendous amount of class to us."

Worthy had racked up 36 points, 16 rebounds, and 10 assists, the first triple-double of his career. For that and his earlier efforts in the series, he was named the MVP. Self-effacing as usual, Worthy said he would have voted for Magic. The big news, though, was the team. At last, the league had a repeat champion. The Lakers had grasped the greatness about which Riley had rhapsodized so often.

BYRON SCOTT: "He pretty much got it all out of us that year. We went seven games every series and ended up winners."

The three-peat pressure began immediately and swirled throughout the 1988–89 season, mixed with night after night of Kareem's retirement tour. He was 42 and announced that this campaign was his last. It was a painful year. His skills obviously diminished by age, he labored through many nights, which led to a flurry of media questions as to whether he was just playing for the money. In retrospect, it seems a little odd that a team going for a third title would have to weather such scrutiny. But some of Kareem's nights were difficult. There were even discussions with Jerry West about an abrupt departure. However, wisdom prevailed. Kareem stayed, and the Lakers prospered. With each day that spring, hope grew that they could send Abdul-Jabbar out with another ring. They finished with a 57–25 record, once again the best in the West, yet short of the Pistons' 63–19 march. The Lakers, though, had confidence that they could win in Detroit and leave no doubts as to their supremacy.

The Lakers furthered the notion, sweeping their way along an 11–0 run to the Finals. Portland, Seattle, and Phoenix—each had gone out with the dustpan. The wins meant that Pat Riley needed only one more victory to become the winningest coach in playoff history. As it turned out, that achievement was far more remote than it seemed.

Detroit, too, had made a sweep of the first two rounds. In Boston, Larry Bird had spent the season on the sidelines after undergoing heel surgery in November. As a result, the Pistons easily pushed aside the Celtics in the first round, 3–0. The same fate befell the Milwaukee Bucks in the second round, 4–0. Only Michael Jordan and the Chicago Bulls interrupted this trend. They won a pair of games from Detroit before falling, 4–2. Left to wait while Detroit beat Chicago, Riley took the Lakers to Santa Barbara and worked them hard. They cursed him for it.

BYRON SCOTT: "The thing that upset us more than anything was how hard we worked. It was like training camp all over again. We didn't feel that we really needed that."

DOUG KRIKORIAN: "The '89 Lakers team was the best I ever saw. They were 11–0 going into the Finals against Detroit. Magic was in his prime, just primed to go. Orlando Woolridge was playing great ball. They had Mychal Thompson playing great ball. Byron Scott had his great season. They were tremendous. Riley should never have taken them to Santa Barbara."

The Pistons' worries—not to mention the dramatic possibilities—began to soften before Game 1 in Detroit, when Scott suffered a severe hamstring injury. He wouldn't return. Suddenly the hard workouts became an issue in the Lakers' minds. Without Scott to help contain the Detroit guards, the Lakers faced an onslaught. With six minutes to go in Game 1, Detroit led, 97–79, and they glided from there to a 109–97 win. The Lakers then targeted Game 2 as their opportunity. Sure enough, they snapped right back to pound the boards and take a 62–56 lead at intermission. Cooper was hitting, and Johnson had that look in his eye. But events turned upside down in the third period. With about four minutes left, Detroit's John Salley blocked a Mychal Thompson shot, starting the fast break. Johnson dropped back to play defense and, in so doing, pulled his hamstring. Sensing immediately that the injury was serious, he flailed at the air in frustration. "I felt a twinge early in the third quarter but thought everything was okay," Johnson said later.

Even without him, Mychal Thompson led an L.A. comeback. Down 106–104, the Lakers had the ball with eight seconds left when Worthy was fouled and went to the line. He missed the first and made the second, leaving the Lakers short at 106–105. Thomas hit two free throws with a second remaining for the final, 108–105. Down 2–0, L.A. was short on options. The immediate speculation centered on Magic. Could he play in Game 3 in the Forum? He tried but left the game in the first quarter with the Lakers leading 11–8. "I wanted to play so bad, but I just could not," Johnson said later. "I could not make the cuts, defensively, that I had to make."

Without Johnson, the Lakers still did a fair imitation of a championship contender. Worthy scored 26, and Kareem played out of his 42-year-old body, scoring 24 points with 13 rebounds. The only veteran in the backcourt, Cooper had 13 assists and 15 points. Grand as it was, that didn't do it. The Pistons won a third time, making the ending a foregone conclusion.

The crowd came to Game 4 expecting an event, Kareem's final game. The big center conducted his final warm-up, his bald pate glistening a regal green and red from the Forum lights. He was composed, spending much of the session standing silently in a half-slouch, his hand on his hip. He did one final finger roll in the layup line and headed down to the bench. With that signal, the team followed, igniting a growing applause that spread across the arena. Riley told Worthy that he would have to up his game a few notches and get them a win. Worthy responded with a championship effort—40 points on 17 of 26 from the floor. But the Pistons weren't about to let up.

The Lakers held a 78–76 lead at the end of the third, but the Bad Boys turned the chores over to James Edwards, who slammed and picked his way along, giving Detroit the lead in the process. The Lakers appeared drained.

When Detroit got the ball back with 3:23 left and leading 100–94, the crowd rose to a standing ovation, not to try and pull a miracle out of exhaustion, just a note of thanks. At 1:37, Kareem executed a neat spin move and bank shot, his last NBA points, bringing the Lakers to 100–96. In the closing seconds, with the game clearly over, Riley sent Lakers sub Orlando Woolridge in for the Cap, a bittersweet hug time for the Lakers. Johnson came out to meet Kareem. The crowd's applause was large and warm, and the Pistons all stepped onto the floor, faced the Lakers bench, and helped out. Then Isiah Thomas went to the line to shoot two final free throws. Nobody even noticed if he made them. "Kareem! Kareem! Kareem!" the crowd intoned over and over.

Some would argue that the curtain closed on Showtime with his departure. Others would say that Magic's style and personality defined the era.

Burnout

In nine seasons Riley shoved and pressured the Lakers into four championship performances and got them close to three others. But by 1990, the human possibilities had been exhausted. Publicly, Riley sought to make it appear that he made the choice to leave, but veteran Lakers beat writer Mitch Chortkoff believes that Riley was forced out. Regardless, the circumstances of his leaving remain somewhat mysterious.

In his first few seasons with the team, Riley kept a low profile. But as the Lakers won championship after championship, he harvested a bundle in endorsements and motivational speech royalties. "The players started thinking that he was profiting from their work and success," explained a Lakers staffer.

During the celebration of their back-to-back championships in 1988, Byron Scott led the fans in a chant. Gary Vitti recalls the words as "Three-Repeat!" But other Lakers staffers says Scott used the phrase "Three-peat!" Riley soon filed a trademark on the term, a move that infuriated some players, who believed he had appropriated Scott's creation.

GARY VITTI: "Pat made you be the best you could be, so you looked for things to be mad about. You think anybody was gonna look themselves in the mirror and say, 'I'm mad at Pat because he made me be the best that I could be?' No. But you could look in the mirror and say, 'I'm mad at Pat because he copyrighted *Three-peat*.' Nobody cared about that. It was an excuse to be angry."

Still, there is ample evidence that Riley's leaving followed a shipwide mutiny and that West was faced with keeping order. West believed pro basketball to be a players' game. The coach had to give the players freedom to be creative. Yet West fielded many complaints over the 1989–90 season that Riley's iron will was choking the life out of the roster.

BYRON SCOTT: "It got to the point where we'd heard this speech before and to the point where he got tired of saying it."

With Riley flashing his anger and stamping his feet on the sideline, the Lakers powered their way to a league-best 63–19 record that spring of 1990. It was their first season without Kareem, and Riley was determined to make the transition. But the acrimony thickened with each passing day, until the Phoenix Suns closed down the Lakers 4–1 in the second round of the playoffs.

JAMES WORTHY: "By the end of the season, the fire was not there. As far as the team was concerned, the locker room was dead. For the first time since I had been with the Lakers, it was a job."

"That year was ugly," one Lakers staffer said of 1990. "By the end of the year, Byron and James wouldn't even talk to the guy. Pat would come in the locker room and ask a question, and they wouldn't respond. It was his personality. Then he finally left, and it was like everyone in the whole organization rejoiced."

When the season ended, Riley told reporters that he was considering leaving his post. Lakers staffers figured the coach was fishing for entreaties to stay from West and Jerry Buss. Neither, however, was about to suggest that, because both had had enough. Seeing he had no support, Riley knew it was over, explained one Lakers staff member.

DOUG KRIKORIAN: "Pat Riley was a great coach who wore out his welcome in L.A. and was fired. He did not go out on his own. It was not Jerry West. It was the players. They rebelled against him. They said they did not want to go on another season with him. Magic went to Buss. Pat was fired. They gave him some money and everything and told him goodbye. Riley went to New York and made a lot of money, and now he's a multimillionaire down in Miami. In the NBA, when you're a driving coach like him, the players can only take it so many years."

MARK HEISLER, RILEY BIOGRAPHER: "Riles started to get a lot of credit in '88, and I think he did start taking himself very seriously. He was withdrawing too. And he was getting really, really into the job. The team was getting older and couldn't perform the way he wanted it to. And the older they got, and the more they slowed down, the more he was kickin' them."

Yet any rejoicing over Riley's leaving was mixed with mourning. An era had ended. And after they had time to reflect on it, his players would realize something special had passed through their lives.

BYRON SCOTT: "We didn't see eye-to-eye on a lot of issues, but I respected him because of what he had done. And he gave all of the players respect. Now that I look back on it, I even respect him more because of what he helped us achieve. Looking back on all that, I say he's probably the best coach in the game."

Riley ushered them through the next season and resigned to become an NBC broadcaster for a season, to be replaced by Mike Dunleavy. Coop left, too, asking to be waived so that he could play in Europe.

Dunleavy had Johnson, Worthy, and Scott to go with the crop of young players West had brought together. They began with a losing streak to open the 1990–91 season, but Dunleavy frantically righted the team and coached them to the Finals yet again. The Trail Blazers had ruled the regular season in the Western with a 63–19 finish, but the Lakers survived in the playoffs, ousting Portland in the conference Finals, 4–2.

For most observers, the Finals seemed a dream matchup: Michael Jordan and the Bulls against Magic and the Lakers. Many, including Riley, then at NBC, figured the Lakers' experience made them a sure bet. L.A. was making its ninth Finals appearance since 1980 and had five titles to show for it.

"The Lakers have experience on us," Chicago's Scottie Pippen conceded as the series opened in Chicago Stadium, "but we have enough to win."

The big negative for the Lakers was Worthy's ankle, sprained in the Western Finals against Portland, which took away much of his mobility. Some insiders figured Worthy's injury would cost the Lakers the series. Game 1, however, seemed to confirm Riley's prediction. The Lakers won, 93–91, on a late three-pointer by Sam Perkins. The Bulls got the ball to Jordan, but his 18-foot jumper with four seconds left went in the basket and spun out.

BYRON SCOTT: "We won the first game, we said, 'Hey, we can beat these guys.'"

The only problem, said Gary Vitti, is that they forgot to win the rest of the games. The trainer remembered telling the young Lakers on the roster that year, "You guys just don't understand. You join the Lakers, you see the history, you think that this is part of the deal, that every year we'll play for a championship. This may be the only time you will ever be in this position in your life, and you must win. You have to win because you may not ever get another chance."

The Bulls, however, found success by pressuring Johnson's ballhandling over the next four games. And the Lakers could find no means of helping him out. The tumble started with a Chicago blowout in Game 2, 107–86. The Bulls starters shot better than 73 percent from the floor, with guard John Paxson going eight for eight to score 16 points. "Does Paxson ever miss?" Sam Perkins asked.

In Game 3, Jordan hit a jumper with 3.4 seconds left to send the game into overtime. There, the Bulls ran off eight straight points for a 104–96 win and a 2–1 lead. Jordan was elated, but he refused to dwell on the victory. The Lakers had plenty of experience in coming back, he said.

But experience proved no match for the Bulls' young legs and determination. For Game 4, the Bulls harried the Lakers into shooting 37 percent from the floor, good enough for a 97–82 win. The Lakers' point total was their lowest since before the shot clock was adopted in 1954. They managed a total of 30 points over the second and third quarters. Perkins made just one of his 15 shots.

"I didn't even dream this would happen," Magic said.

The Bulls then took their third straight in the Forum to close the series on a Wednesday night, 4–1. It was a finish without glory for L.A., but the Lakers weren't cut too deeply. They had had plenty of glory over the past dozen years. Besides, they expected to get another shot at the title next year. Wasn't that the way it always happened?

No one, least of all Earvin Johnson, would have believed it at the time, but the 1991 championship series was the swan song for Showtime. The golden era had ended.

12

The Reckoning

It was just before World War II that the English writer Aldous Huxley took a stroll on the beaches southwest of Los Angeles with his good friend, the German writer Thomas Mann, and their lady friends. As they strolled in the sunlight talking of Shakespeare, it was the women who first noticed the small white creatures. There were millions of them, strewn across the sand as far as the eye could see, strange diaphanous creatures. What were they?

Upon closer examination, the couples discovered in surprise that they were used condoms, millions of them, washed up from the untreated sewage the city dumped into the ocean daily—which helped explain why the lovely beach was so deserted. The distinguished visitors probably shouldn't have been surprised. As Jessica Hundley and Jon Guzik write in their guidebook, *Horny Los Angeles*, "From the very beginning, Los Angeles was built on a history of scandal and intrigue, feats of sexual perversion, prowess, and seduction that would make your mama blush." Hollywood and its stars, of course, had been on the Coast but a short time in the early 20th century before they began wallowing in sexual excess and scandal. Film legend Mae West in the early days of the industry was known for an immense sexual appetite that drove her to bed a wide array of male stars, including Cary Grant and George Raft. Clara Bow, another sexually liberated starlet, was rumored to have exceeded even West's dalliances by taking on the entire University of Southern California football team. Many Hollywood historians scoff at that claim. Regardless, the tendency toward frivolity—not to mention statistics—was well established.

There's little wonder then that California led the charge into the American sexual revolution. As fate would have it, Bob Short moved his team into the midst of this stirring pot just as that revolution was surging over the ramparts.

In all fairness, it should be pointed out that hypersexuality evidenced itself in other sports and pastimes, in other cities. Hot Rod Hundley (now what was the genesis of that nickname?) freely admitted to doing his best to bed the female population of Minneapolis/St. Paul before the Lakers ever made their move west.

L.A., though, clearly provided the opportunity for the team's stars to explore an array of sexual options, with decidedly mixed results, evidenced by more than a bit of heartbreak. From Wilt Chamberlain's claim of making love to 20,000 women, to Magic Johnson's surprise announcement that he was HIV positive, to the prostitution solicitation charge against James Worthy, to the 2003 rape case against Kobe Bryant that garnered international attention, the Lakers have made scandal a persistent part of their image. Jeanie Buss, the daughter of Lakers owner Jerry Buss, posed nude for *Playboy* in the team offices in 1994. Buss himself has long been known for serially dating hundreds of beautiful young women (and proudly keeping a photo collection of them). True to his playboy image, Buss has even fathered two children with younger women.

MIKE MONROE, *SAN ANTONIO EXPRESS NEWS* SPORTS COLUMNIST: "You know what Lakers mystique is? It's an owner whose daughter has appeared nude in *Playboy*."

STEVE BULLPET, *BOSTON HERALD* SPORTSWRITER: "Celtics mystique is championships and black sneakers and the parquet floor. Lakers mystique is Jerry West and Kareem Abdul-Jabbar and Magic Johnson and women with boob jobs lining the front row. Their history of success follows the whole idea of the West Coast lifestyle."

RON CARTER, FORMER LAKER: "When we were in college and our teams played each other in the NCAA tournament, Norm Nixon and I went out after the game. And we couldn't get a date. Couldn't get in a club. Two years later we were laughing because two women were fighting in a nightclub over Norm one night. I said, 'Norm, what happened?' He said, 'You know, Ron, it's an amazing thing, but when you sign a Lakers contract you become awfully good looking.'"

DOUG KRIKORIAN, LONGTIME L.A. SPORTSWRITER: "Even back in '68 and '69, we'd get off the bus and go in the hotel lobby, and there'd be a bunch of women in there looking at Johnny Egan, who was a straight Catholic boy who would never play around on his wife, straight as a string. Even then these guys would be besieged with women."

Nixon and Carter came to the Lakers in the late '70s when the climate around the team had been stewing for more than a decade. The '60s may have unleashed the sexual revolution, but the '70s turned it into a fest, especially for the Lakers, which left the team's front office struggling to deal with blatant sexual frivolity.

PETE NEWELL, FORMER LAKERS GENERAL MANAGER: "We were reluctant to get involved, although we were all appalled by the women who just flaunted themselves. The players just kind of passed these gals around. There was no deterrence about AIDS and sex in those days. The players just didn't have as much to lose."

RON CARTER: "The women were very aggressive. Very aggressive. We were very promiscuous. That was the pre-AIDS era. The big thing then was herpes; you might contract herpes. Other than that, unprotected sex was very, very common. We were coming right off of the free-love era."

Looking back on the times in his 1990 book, *A View from Above*, Chamberlain claimed to have slept with better than 20,000 women during his career. His claim was designed to sell copies of his book, but Chamberlain very quickly came to regret it.

RICK TELANDER, *CHICAGO SUN-TIMES* COLUMNIST: "Wilt's was a body of work that transcended L.A., but he probably did 80 percent of his work right there in L.A., under the big retractable roof, in the circular bed, or whatever he had."

KELLY TRIPUCKA, FORMER NBA PLAYER: "Thank you, Wilt. We can all tip our hat to Wilt. He paved the way, not only on the court, but off the court as well. It was a 10-lane highway for Wilt."

Part of the reason for Chamberlain's regret was that he felt his claim led people to view him differently. Suddenly his off-court activities overshadowed his real accomplishments. However, there was another reason as well. Some of his associates doubted his claims.

DOUG KRIKORIAN: "Complete hyperbole. I spent many a Saturday night where Wilt would call me and say, 'Let's go out and have dinner together.' He was the worst guy I've ever seen trying to hustle women. That thing should be debunked. Trust me. I saw firsthand. Yes, he might have had his share of women, but as a slick hustler, please. No."

LOU HUDSON, FORMER LAKER: "I was there when Wilt was there, and I didn't see that. That's an exaggeration on Wilt's part. That's like one-and-a-half to two people per day, every day. There are days you travel all day, days you play, days you spend time with your family. I do know some people who came close for maybe a year or a month, but you don't do that for 12 years, every year. Nobody does. If they do, they've got a problem. That's beyond the realm of fun. That's the realm of a nymphomaniac, the same for men as for women. If somebody does that, he has a sexual disorder. It just wasn't that way. We did things, but not to that extent."

DOUG KRIKORIAN: "There's married Lakers players who had a lot more sex than Wilt did. I don't want to go further than that. There was one, I won't name him, who made Wilt look like an amateur."

While some observers have implied that the scale of NBA sexual activity was related to ethnicity, that's hardly the case. The women absolutely loved Jerry West, according to team sources from that era. And Gail Goodrich also enjoyed immense popularity, as did other Caucasian players. Clearly the '70s presented an equal-opportunity environment.

Ron Carter recalled coming to the team in 1978 and being stunned by the veterans' attitudes and sexual habits. "All the old school guys—these guys were like sex addicts. They were crazy with it. It was there and it was available. Actually, it was a part of the mentality that the veteran players would teach you how to manage the women. Kobe could have used some of that."

Understandably, the circumstances made players from other teams eager to visit L.A. Some observers said it was the Lakers' true home-court advantage.

KELLY TRIPUCKA: "That was a big distraction for teams. You're going out to L.A. and coaches worried about that. You're so hyped up to be into it and to play against Showtime, and you're sitting over there looking at whoever may be walking by, and your head's doing a little swivel. You're not concentrating. You're not into the game. You really had to have blinders on like those horses at the track across the street. As far as coaches, they really sweat it, playing the Lakers in that particular environment. If you didn't have your team's entire concentration for 48 minutes, you could get embarrassed out there."

FRED CARTER, FORMER NBA PLAYER: "The Forum was kicking in the seventies, too. It was just a different time. The hype wasn't there. But the feeling, the enthusiasm was still there. We had our East Coast clothes and our West Coast clothes. And when you're married, all of a sudden your wife wonders, 'Why are you wearing that out there?' Some things you had to hide. You didn't let your wife pack your clothes."

Likewise, the Lakers would go on the road and find the female populations of other cities more than eager to welcome them.

RON CARTER: "These women would come to the hotel. First of all, it always amazed me that they could figure out where we're staying. But they'd be there when we got there. They'd have the team roster. 'Can I speak to Magic Johnson?' 'I'm sorry, ma'am, that line is busy.' 'Can I speak to Kareem Abdul-Jabbar?' 'Sorry, that line is busy.' 'Can I speak to Jamaal Wilkes?' They're reading down the roster. They are there to get a Laker. I used to get down. I was the eleventh call. Every other guy would go in the room and take their phone off the hook, so it rings busy. I'd keep a phone on the hook. I'm waiting for the overflow."

The Buss Factor

The team's sexuality quotient took a huge jump in 1979 when Jerry Buss bought the team. He wanted to revolutionize basketball marketing by dressing pretty young girls in skimpy outfits so that they could perform sexy dance routines during time-outs.

JOE MCDONNELL, LONGTIME L.A. SPORTS RADIO PERSONALITY: "Jerry Buss . . . never did any marketing. His marketing was all on the floor. He used sex to sell the Lakers. He wanted the Laker Girls and the uniforms and Showtime and having a guy like Magic with a great infectious personality as the main guy. Was it a novel idea to have cheerleaders? No. But to dress them like that and make them an important part? A very novel idea."

JERRY COLANGELO, FORMER PHOENIX SUNS OWNER: "[Jerry Buss] was a newcomer to say the least without any background whatsoever in basketball. But he had his own MO, his own style. He's made great contributions to the game in Los Angeles and on a national scope as well. His record speaks for itself. It's tough to say that would have been the same script in another market. Certainly it was the appropriate script in L.A. I think Jerry hit a grand slam."

Lon Rosen was a young marketing assistant for the team who soon found himself in charge of Buss's new idea. It was clear the Laker Girls were at the heart of the owner's plan for charging the atmosphere at the Forum. They weren't cheerleaders, per se. They were dancers, among Southern California's best. Buss wanted them visible.

So Rosen sat and watched the bump and grind, the step and slide, and called on his expertise to make the selections. That was how he tabbed an 18-year-old choreographer named Paula Abdul in 1983. Later, the team would turn the chores over to a dance professional, but in those early days of Showtime, the pleasure was all Rosen's. Yet when the time came to give it up, he wouldn't complain.

LON ROSEN: "I was getting married. And the Laker Girls can put undue stress on a relationship."

The Next Level

It didn't take Magic Johnson long after he arrived in L.A. in 1979 to learn that he had taken up residence at the prime end of the world's casting couch. Hollywood offered an abundant supply of beauties, many of whom were eager to get to know a basketball star. Back then Norm Nixon was the reigning ladies' man, and Johnson was an inexperienced understudy. Butch Carter came to the Lakers as a rookie in 1980 and found Johnson marveling at Nixon's popularity. One day Johnson walked through a hotel lobby and three women gave him their phone numbers—to take up to Nixon's room. Nixon had such a smooth rap that his teammates took to calling him "Savoir Faire," or "Wa" for short.

BUTCH CARTER: "At the time, Norm Nixon was the king of L.A. When we'd go out somewhere, the women would ask, 'Where's Norm? Where's Norm?'"

It wasn't too long, however, before Johnson was making his own time. Taking the Lakers to championship after championship, he lit the incandescent lamps of his own stardom. Captivated by his smile, by the career shortcut that an association with him might offer, those Hollywood ladies began asking, "Where's Magic?"

His excesses became the stuff of legend. He would later estimate that he had sexual relations with 300 to 500 women annually. Even more amazing was the discretion with which he rang up these numbers. Outside of a small inner circle of Lakers staffers and players, few people knew exactly what he was doing.

RUDY GARCIDUENAS, LONGTIME LAKERS EQUIPMENT MANAGER: "When I first started with the team, it was astounding. But it was an existence, a way of life with Earvin. I came to understand Earvin and the way he did things, his love for women. When you're a person of that stature, it's almost expected. All the movie stars get the same attention. It's part of the business. It's difficult to imagine, but Earvin was used to doing anything he wanted. And people loved Earvin so much that nothing he did was wrong. It was never really hidden from anybody, what Earvin did. He was always pretty up-front with it. That was part of him. You had to learn to accept it."

JOE MCDONNELL: "You would go to the end of the tunnel, and the women would be handing their phone numbers to the ball boy, or Magic would have seen somebody that he liked. 'Bring her in, and bring her in.' Everybody knew what was going on back in the weight room and everything else. The women were just ridiculous. Not only the ones with Buss, but the ones who came to hang around just to try to be part of the scene."

This phenomenon, of course, wasn't exclusive to Johnson or the Lakers. The modern professional athlete in all major sports has discovered that physical prowess, fame, and fortune attract large numbers of women. "I could tell you Dodger stories for a year and tomorrow about stuff going on down in little rooms at the clubhouse before the games," said McDonnell. "It's prevalent in all sports. In baseball, it can happen during a game. In basketball, it always happens after a game."

The Atlanta Hawks' Dominique Wilkins once enjoyed a reputation as a ladies man. "They want the thrill of being with an athlete," he told *Sports Illustrated*. "And they don't want safe sex. They want to have your baby, man, because they think that if they have your baby, they're set for life. That's the hard fact of it, because if they had a life, they wouldn't be hanging around the hotel or showing up at the back door of the arena trying to pick up a player."

LORIN PULLMAN, FORMER LAKERS PUBLIC RELATIONS ASSISTANT: "They act like these women are such a problem for them. But the guys perpetuate the behavior."

By the time Norm Nixon left the Lakers in 1983, Johnson was well on his way claiming a role as the team's most sexually active player. He had even begun playing the role of social director, introducing players from visiting teams to some of his favorite ladies.

LORIN PULLMAN: "I couldn't believe how they all shared notes in the locker room. 'My God,' I thought, 'this is like they're still in high school.'"

Some went so far as to keep stats, although the results were often much disputed, what with the male ego showing a propensity for overestimation. But for Johnson, keeping score was almost moot. There was, however, a code for Johnson. He never allowed a woman to stay overnight with him. That was reserved for his college sweetheart, Earleatha "Cookie" Kelly, who would become his wife in September 1991 after years of stormy relations over his womanizing. She couldn't bring herself to break off her relationship with him, although she tried for several months. Yet she also couldn't stomach the scene in L.A., so she remained in Michigan during his first decade in the league. Johnson was unrepentant about his indulgences, and his token acknowledgment of her was that he booted his partners out of bed before sunrise.

Besides, he had always told Cookie that his first love was the game. And for the game, he saved himself. No sex before tip-off. None. He wanted nothing to keep him from performing his best. Sex was the game *after* the game. And the Forum Club comprised a large part of the playing field. Basketball had never seen anything quite like it, and probably never will again. Before Lakers games, it was the spot for power dinners with L.A.'s elite. After games, it was transformed into a swinging singles bar, throbbing with energy and celebrity and celebration. At the height of Showtime, the Lakers lost only four or five home games a season, meaning that the Forum was a place to see and be seen with winners. Players from both teams would hustle to shower and don their Armani suits for a swing through the crowd to scope the lovelies.

BYRON SCOTT, FORMER LAKER: "Any athlete who walked in there was already spotted. He's got three, four, or five girls who already spotted him, and it depends on which one he wants to go with."

The atmosphere was so thick with women that Lakers wives and regular girl-friends were often forced to make an appearance just to check out their competition.

LORIN PULLMAN: "They had to do that to make sure these women knew their guy was accounted for."

Away from L.A., the hotel lobbies generated another level of excitement.

BYRON SCOTT: "When our bus would pull up to a hotel you'd see 60 people out there waiting and 40 of them would be women. It was like going around with a rock group. It was just amazing."

The "road" left the wives and girlfriends at a distinct disadvantage. Under coach Pat Riley, the Lakers had an "excess baggage" rule barring wives and girl-friends of players from traveling with the team because they created a dis-traction. Riley would later explain that his "excess baggage" distinction didn't mean the wives. Yet the ban against them was so strongly implied that when wives did travel to away games, they would hide from the coaches. Which meant that players faced 50 to 60 nights per season alone on the road.

LORIN PULLMAN: "I always felt that contributed to the excess. If you wanted your wife or girlfriend along, what was wrong with that? You're not going to walk through the bar or lobby looking for women if your wife is upstairs in your room."

Many times, though, the Lakers didn't have to go to the action in the lobby. It came to them. In 1989, Pullman was traveling with the team during Abdul-Jabbar's retirement tour. Somehow the front desk in one hotel got her room number mixed up with Johnson's. She returned that evening to find messages from six different women slid under her door. As AIDS fears gained prominence, Gary Vitti, the team's trainer, began carrying condoms and distributing them to the Lakers.

GARY VITTI: "I made a point of always asking [Magic] if he was protecting himself. He'd say, 'Yeah, everything's cool.'"

Vitti would ask this question frequently, and he knew Johnson was fibbing. It would later haunt Vitti that he didn't confront his friend. In that regard, Vitti came to consider Johnson's fate his fault. After all, he reasoned, he was the trainer, the person most responsible for the players' well-being.

GARY VITTI: "I felt I let him down. I let myself down. I didn't do what I was supposed to do. Somehow I should've made him more aware, made him understand."

With Johnson's appetite, Lakers players and staff marveled at his durability. And in a sense, they came to believe in his infallibility. After all, wasn't he the Magic man? Wasn't he the person with the special gifts and the broad smile? Wasn't he the deliverer of miracle plays and championships?

Things Fall Apart

Johnson was on vacation in August 1991 when he phoned Cookie Kelly. I'm ready to get married, he told her. "I think it's time." They had been through this several times before, only to have their plans fall through. So Kelly was understandably cautious. Are you sure? she asked. "This is it," he said. "I want to do it." Now.

HERB WILLIAMS, FORMER NBA PLAYER AND LONGTIME JOHNSON FRIEND: "They had to hurry it up. So she didn't get time to set up a big wedding or anything."

There was time, however, to negotiate and sign a prenuptial agreement in which Kelly gave up claims on his estimated $100 million in wealth. Such harsh details aside, they assembled a quick wedding in Lansing.

HERB WILLIAMS: "It was a small wedding. Me and Isiah Thomas and Mark Aguirre were there. So was Darwin Payton and Dale Beard, two of Earvin's old friends. Cookie had a lot of joy on her face. She's a nice girl. She's got a nice head on her shoulders. She had a nice job. I mean she could have had a whole lot of other guys, whoever she wanted. But she had always been there for him, no matter what."

Two weeks later, the Lakers opened the season with an abbreviated version of training camp in Palm Desert, California. Johnson arrived there in poor shape, with the idea that he would work himself into condition during the team's twice-daily practices. From there, the Lakers jetted to Boston for two quick exhibition games with the Celtics, then on to Paris to play in the McDonald's Open, where they played another two games, barely beating a Spanish team, Joventut Barcelona, for the championship. It was in Paris that Cookie Kelly Johnson learned she was pregnant.

By then the grind of playing himself into shape while crossing time zones had begun to show on Johnson, and the 14-hour plane trip home offered little relief. He arrived in L.A. with a face drawn and tired. But there was little time to rest. Back home, the Lakers faced two more exhibition games in the GTE Everything Pages Shoot-out, where they again beat Boston, then lost to the Milwaukee Bucks. The schedule then called for them to fly to Utah for another game, before heading off to Vancouver, British Columbia, for yet another game the next night against the Seattle Supersonics. From there, they were scheduled to fly back to L.A. that night to hold practice the next morning at the Loyola Marymount University gym, their regular practice facility. It was an idiotic schedule, Johnson thought. Boston. Paris. Los Angeles. Utah. Canada. What a terrible way to start the season. He didn't want to go to Utah and he was vocal about it. But he went.

The Lakers had just checked into their hotel in Salt Lake City that afternoon of October 25 when Johnson got a message from Lon Rosen, his agent, stating that he had to return to Los Angeles immediately.

GARY VITTI: "I couldn't believe it when he told me. My first thought was that he had arranged a doctor's excuse to miss the rest of the trip. Then I thought, 'Nah, Earvin wouldn't do that.' So I called Micky Mellman, one of our team's doctors, and asked him what was up. He said, 'I can't tell you about it at this point. Something has shown up abnormal on Earvin's physical exam. He has to come home.' A superstar never gets called home from the road. I knew something was wrong, and I always knew everything that was going on, so this was driving me crazy. I thought it might be a heart condition. Earvin's tall, and heart trouble develops in tall people. But he'd had batteries of stress tests and passed with flying colors. It wasn't his heart. I spent hours wondering, what could be wrong? In the middle of the game with Utah that night, I realized what it was. It was like somebody hit me in the head with a sledgehammer. Bang. He's HIV positive. I didn't know for sure. But I *knew*."

Johnson treated Vitti like a brother, coming to dinner at his house, taking time to be nice to Vitti's parents. Most NBA trainers didn't get such respect and attention from stars. But Johnson was loved by all the Lakers staffers. Many pro ball players are so focused on their own grand existence, they often fail to notice the people around them doing the little things that make their worlds go round. Not Johnson. He always noticed. Every staffer at the Forum. The ushers. The scorekeepers. The custodians. The public relations people. He knew them by name. What's more, he liked them, and they knew it. After all, they inhabited a special world together at the Forum. He made all of them feel a part of Showtime. If a ball boy needed a car for the prom, Johnson knew it. Here, kid, take the keys and don't scratch the paint. If a public relations assistant was stuck in a low, blue mood, Johnson wasn't above having a bottle of champagne sent over. Just like that, a bottle of Dom. The idea of such a gesture would never occur to most NBA players.

The Lakers lost in Utah that night, and as the players boarded the team plane for Canada they all wanted to know what was wrong with Magic. Vitti told them he didn't know. But he did.

GARY VITTI: "At eight the next morning, my phone rang in Vancouver. It was Mellman. I told him, 'Mickey, you don't have to tell me a thing. I already figured it out. Earvin is HIV positive isn't he?' He told me, 'I knew you would figure it out. Earvin wanted you to know. We're only telling a few people. No one else is to know. No one. No coaches. No players. Absolutely no one.'"

Vitti's and Johnson's immediate concern was how to handle the news. Johnson needed time to talk to counselors, to lawyers, to doctors. He needed to examine his options.

GARY VITTI: "We came up with this bullshit that he had the flu. The media were told that he would miss some practice and games. That story would buy us about 10 days, which would be time enough to figure out what to do."

These stories may have held off the media, but they didn't add up for Dunleavy, the team's 37-year-old head coach. Concerned about the strange situation, he went to Kupchak's office.

MIKE DUNLEAVY: "I told Mitch, 'Something's not right here. If Earvin has cancer or AIDS and you know it, you'd better let me know. I've got about a week before the season starts, and if he's not going to be in the lineup I've got to start making some plans.'"

Dunleavy was told that something very bad had come up, that it would have a major impact on the team.

MIKE DUNLEAVY: "I knew from that standpoint that I had about a week to prepare. So I began immediately changing our plays around, running different things for different guys. Some players were scratching their heads, wondering what the hell I was doing."

Fortunately, the team had traded for veteran guard Sedale Threatt during the off-season. Threatt was an NBA journeyman known for his smooth shot. But over most of his eight pro seasons he had rarely played more than 15 minutes a game. Suddenly Dunleavy found himself placing the burden of running the Lakers, with their flock of $500-per-night fans, on the shoulders of a career reserve.

MIKE DUNLEAVY: "I thought, if nothing else, this'll be interesting."

Amazingly, Johnson's circle of friends, family, and advisers kept their secret for almost two weeks. Johnson's family knew. Cookie Kelly's family knew. Plus the doctors and a few other select counselors. But few in that group understood the implications of the news. Least of all Johnson.

For most of the time, he and the people around him thought that testing HIV positive meant that he had AIDS. They would soon learn the difference, but at that moment there was much to sort out. For Johnson, the question was what to do with the information. His first inclination was human. It was his body, his infection, his business only. He was not going to tell anybody that he had AIDS. That was a gay disease, and people would think he was gay. But he didn't have to think long about it to realize that his infection could not remain his own dark secret.

GARY VITTI: "He absolutely had to go public with it because of the thousands of women that he'd had sexual relations with. . . . He had a moral and ethical responsibility, so he went up there like a man and did what he had to do."

Once Johnson faced the inevitable, his advisers began making plans for a press conference. First, Johnson met privately with Dunleavy. His voice breaking, Johnson told the coach that his career was over, that things would be all right, that he would get through the circumstances as best he could. From there, Johnson turned to his next great task—telling his teammates.

GARY VITTI: "He came in. He had on a blue suit and a white shirt, and he looked really good and distinguished. I can just see him so vividly. He told the team that he had this virus, you know. 'I got this virus.' You know the way he talks. 'I can't play basketball anymore.'"

Weeping as he spoke, Johnson paused to talk about the "wars" he had been through with his longtime teammates Worthy, Scott, and A. C. Green, and how special those wars had been. Then he went around to each of the players and the coaches and Vitti and Garciduenas and hugged them and spoke privately with each one.

BYRON SCOTT: "To have him confirm it was like somebody had just reached in and grabbed my heart and pulled it out."

MIKE DUNLEAVY: "The guys broke down crying, the whole room. Everybody felt for Earvin. We felt like we had lost somebody, and yet he was still there."

Assistant coach Bill Bertka, who had been with the Lakers in one capacity or another for parts of three decades, took the news hard. In his sixties, Bertka, affectionately known as Bert, was a father figure to Lakers players and coaches alike.

GARY VITTI: "I really tried to be strong for Earvin, because he's so strong. Bert was next to me. I was the last guy. Bert's a stoic, Scandinavian kind of rock, icy type of guy. He's a pillar of strength. Earvin put his arm around Bert, and Bert's knees just buckled. To see that man, who's like the toughest guy I know . . . I just came unglued. Earvin came over to me. I was trying to gather myself up."

Upstairs, a throng of media was waiting for Johnson, with CNN and ESPN planning live feeds of the press conference to their audiences.

GARY VITTI: "Earvin went in the bathroom and washed his face and went upstairs and got in front of those cameras like it was nothing. He went from this huge emotional scene to going up there and standing in front of the world, like the strongest man that ever lived. He did what he had to do."

"Good afternoon," he told a worldwide audience moments later. "Because of the HIV virus that I have attained, I will have to retire from the Lakers today. I just want to make clear, first of all, that I do not have the AIDS disease. I know a lot of you want to know that. I have the HIV virus. My wife is fine. She's negative, so no problem with her.

"I plan to go on living for a long time, bugging you guys like I always have. So you'll see me around. I plan on being with the Lakers and the league, and going on with my life. I guess now I get to enjoy some of the other sides of living that I've missed because of the season and the long practices and so on. I'm going to miss playing.

"I will now become a spokesman for the HIV virus. I want people, young people, to realize they can practice safe sex. Sometimes you're a little naive about it, and you think it could never happen to you. You only thought it could happen to other people. It has happened. But I'm going to deal with it. Life is going to go on for me, and I'm going to be a happy man. . . .

"Sometimes we think only gay people can get it, or 'it's not going to happen to me.' Here I am, saying it can happen to anybody. Even me, Magic Johnson."

The Lakers players and staffers watched these strange events unfold, heard the follow-up questions from the overflow crowd of reporters, and sat around numbly as the session wound to a close.

GARY VITTI: "Then we all just went home and turned off our phones."

Friends

Friendship is a strange concept in the exclusive little world occupied by celebrities. Most, of course, are mere acquaintances arranged for career strategies. In 1989, Johnson threw a thirtieth birthday party for himself and invited 500 of his "closest friends." But when his big trouble struck two years later, he had no trouble paring that group down to a short list of people who needed to be notified before the news broke. The list included Michael Jordan, Pat Riley, Arsenio Hall, Larry Bird, Michael Cooper, Abdul-Jabbar, Isiah Thomas, and Kurt Rambis. Johnson asked Rosen to make the calls.

LON ROSEN: "A lot of people came together for Earvin. Norm Nixon was there, and he and Jerry West even talked and spent some time together."

In the United States at that time, AIDS was thought to be largely a disease for gays and serious dope shooters. Of the 45,506 new AIDS cases reported to the Centers for Disease Control in 1991, approximately 52 percent involved homosexual males.

The news flash that Thursday in November gave hoops junkies around the world reason to pause. Was Magic gay? On playgrounds in every city, in every small town, the balls stopped bouncing as the debates began. Magic Johnson, one of the two or three greatest players in the history of the game, is sweet? No way, Jack.

LON ROSEN: "Earvin hated that people would think he was gay. He wanted to go on Arsenio Hall's talk show that Friday night. And we decided to do an interview with Jim Hill and to do an article for *Sports Illustrated* with Roy Johnson. We knew that by going to the people Earvin felt comfortable with, people who would protect him, the message would get out."

Among several pointed questions, Hall asked if Johnson was gay. Johnson replied that he wasn't, and the studio audience applauded enthusiastically. He also called for people everywhere to practice safe sex, a plea that later brought broad criticism because Johnson hadn't pointed out that the best protection against sexually transmitted disease was abstinence. Johnson quickly tailored his future messages to include that option.

In the dressing room at Hall's show, Johnson also did his interview with Hill, then sat down and talked with Roy Johnson for the *Sports Illustrated* piece. "By now I'm sure that most of America has heard rumors that I am gay," he wrote. "Well, you can forget that. . . . I sympathize with anyone who has to battle AIDS, regardless of his or her sexual preference, but I have never had a homosexual encounter. Never."

His doctors had said from the very start that they wanted him to continue exercising. He had begun taking AZT, the medicine thought to help slow the spread of the virus, and his physicians were eager to see how he adjusted. Johnson began having more and more thoughts about a retirement tour to celebrate with his fans one more time.

Soon Johnson was seriously thinking about returning to the Lakers for the 1992–93 season. But Rosen found a way of stalling him, hoping he would realize the futility of the impulse. In the days after the announcement, the agent had flown to New York for a parley with the NBA's top executives—David Stern and assistants Gary Bettman and Russ Granik. Earvin will want to play in the All-Star Game in Orlando, Rosen told them. After all, his name is on the All-Star ballot, and this will be an excellent farewell.

Stern and his associates immediately agreed. That would be a very good idea, they said. After all, Johnson had been the linchpin of the league's success. There wasn't one good reason not to let him play.

Activism

With his revelation, he had announced his intention to become "a spokesman for the HIV virus." He would quickly discover that this role was far more complicated than he imagined.

To his credit, he studied hard, learned about the disease, and played his part. Asked if the virus had brought him "bad days," Johnson replied, "I'm not a bad day person. Every day I wake up, I'm happy. I'm ready to go do something. The virus can only make you have a bad day if your frame of mind is like that. So I'm not down about it. I'm not trying to say, 'Why me?' I'm going on. It's happened, and I'm dealing with it. But it hasn't stopped me from living and enjoying life."

In the days after his announcement, AIDS hotlines across the country had been jammed with callers seeking information and counseling. The cards and letters to his foundation filled a large storeroom at the Forum, where the bags of mail were packed to the ceiling. It would take platoons of volunteers weeks to open each piece, discarding the small amount of hate mail to focus on the frantic pleas for help from some writers and the support offered by others. In the first two weeks after the announcement, his Magic Johnson Foundation took in more than $500,000 in unsolicited donations. (NBA player Rex Chapman alone sent a $50,000 check, even though he hardly knew Johnson.)

The outpouring of public love encouraged him and, to some degree, all AIDS victims. It was said time and again that surely God must have selected Magic to fight this disease. Who else could rally the public against fear, against centuries of prejudice toward the victims of contagion?

Thus inspired, Johnson moved quickly to make good on his promises to join the AIDS fight. In addition to setting up the Magic Johnson Foundation to raise money for AIDS research, he lent his name to a book, *What You Can Do to Avoid AIDS*. And he and Arsenio Hall produced an AIDS awareness video, *Time Out*. Beyond that, he joined broadcaster Linda Ellerbee for a well-received AIDS special for children on the Nickelodeon network (which Nestlé supported, thus atoning for canceling his commercial shortly after the announcement).

Johnson said he especially wanted to reach "the young people, because I'm trying to make sure that what happened to me doesn't happen to them."

All-Star

The announcement that Johnson would play in the NBA's 42nd All-Star Game in Orlando in mid-February 1992 was hailed as another great step forward for enlightenment. Suddenly, it wasn't just another boring All-Star Game. It was Magic Johnson's grand finale, the farewell event, the greatest public relations opportunity that AIDS awareness campaigners could imagine.

The game would be broadcast worldwide in 90 countries, and more than 960 journalists would be there, to see an HIV-infected athlete compete against the world's best basketball players. If only for a brief time, AIDS victims worldwide could emerge from the shadows to feel a bit normal. One of their own was playing in the big game. Unfortunately, many NBA players didn't quite see it that way. They were worried that playing against an infected opponent could have disastrous results. After all, it was a brutal sport. Players fought for rebounds and loose balls. Scratches, cuts, fat lips were a part of every game.

LON ROSEN: "Earvin was at a low point in January. He was shooting around alone before a game at the Forum with Miami. Rony Seikaly [then the Heat's center] came up to him and asked if they could play one-on-one. Earvin was surprised. The best part was that Seikaly was competitive with him, pushing him around for rebounds and stuff. Earvin didn't know him very well, but he knew that Seikaly was just letting him know that he supported him, that things would be okay. Earvin wouldn't forget that."

MAGIC JOHNSON: "He took me right out there and played. People were putting fear in other people's minds. He had no fear at all. We just played."

While his close friends were expressing doubt, here was someone Johnson hardly knew, telling him everything would be all right. The NBA, too, went to great lengths to make things all right. Part of the strategy was a massive information campaign, for both athletes and the media. In the coming months, the league would establish a policy for bleeding players. If someone sustained a cut or scratch in a game, time would be called and the player removed until the bleeding was stopped and the wound bandaged. Team trainers would treat all such cases while wearing latex gloves.

Afterward, only one question remained for the players: "If it's so safe for us to compete against an infected player, then why is the trainer wearing the gloves?"

The All-Star Game in Orlando proved to be the NBA at its marketing best. The league teamed with Walt Disney World to throw a rousing party. On Friday night of All-Star weekend, the Magic Kingdom was opened to the media and the NBA's special guests. There were marching bands and Disney characters and free shows and an endless flow of booze and seafood and hors d'oeuvres.

During his preliminary press conference Johnson talked about how wonderful Sunday was going to be, how it would be a triumph for AIDS victims everywhere. "No matter what negative comes, I've always been a positive person, always been upbeat," he said. "As long as you have your family and friends supporting you, that's all you need. I have to be out there for myself and I have to be out there for a lot of people, whether they have disease or handicaps or whatever, and let them know that they can still carry on."

HERB WILLIAMS, FORMER NBA PLAYER AND JOHNSON FRIEND: "On Friday night of All-Star Weekend, I dropped by Earvin's room. Isiah was there laughing and talking with Magic. I figured that Earvin had come to Orlando to put in a cameo appearance, that he was gonna take a bow, enjoy the weekend and get out of the way. But he told us that night, 'I'm winning the MVP.' I said, 'What you mean?' He told me he'd had the guys at his sports club running five-on-five. He said, 'My game is right. I feel good. And when I leave here I'm taking that trophy home with me.'"

When Johnson appeared courtside to shoot around that Sunday before the All-Star game, Jerry Buss worked his way through the crowd to greet him. He shook the owner's hand, draped a long arm over his shoulder, and gave a squeeze. For the past dozen years, they had celebrated championships and weathered hard times together. Those times had been easy compared with the news about Johnson. Buss had gotten word the very day Johnson learned he was HIV positive.

LON ROSEN: "In a lot of ways, Buss took it worse than anybody else. Every day he would phone me to check on Earvin and every day he would always break down and sob. He'd say, 'Just tell me what I can do for Earvin.' I told him, 'Why don't you call him?' But he said he couldn't do that. He said they needed to meet in person."

When they did, Buss was again torn with grief. He assured Johnson that although the agreement was unsigned, his new megacontract was good. Many people offered Johnson support in this low period. But none was bigger than Buss. And no one was happier to see Johnson playing at the All-Star Game. Buss didn't have to say much standing there at courtside. They both knew what it meant to each of them.

Before all big games, Johnson was nervous, sleepless, anxiety-driven. The All-Star game was no different. He had not played against pro competition in almost four months. He was a proud man and did not want to make a fool of himself in front of the world.

JAMES WORTHY: "I told him to relax. I said, 'Just kick it, man. Don't worry about messing up. If you shoot an air ball, people are going to boo. Just laugh with 'em and have fun.'"

Johnson did just that, and the Orlando Arena that afternoon answered with an outpouring of love, 23,000 people showering him with their appreciation. It began as he took the floor and lasted all afternoon.

Soon after it began, the game was over, at least from a competitive standpoint. The West quickly outclassed the East, leaving much garbage time, but easily the sweetest garbage time in the century-old history of basketball. For the record, the West won, 153–113, but the Magic moment had nothing to do with the outcome. With just under three minutes to go in the game, Johnson first played Isiah Thomas one-on-one as the other players cleared out of the way. He stopped Thomas on defense, then hit a three-pointer at the other end as the crowd whooped.

On the next possession, he found Dan Majerle of the Phoenix Suns with a patent no-look assist, again to the crowd's great delight. Finally, he matched up one-on-one with Michael Jordan, stopped the superstar on defense, then lofted in yet another trey at the other end, setting off yet another tumultuous celebration.

With 14 seconds left, Isiah Thomas grinned broadly and picked up the ball. The game had to end on Johnson's big shot. For his style and charisma and 25 points and nine assists, he was named the game's MVP, just as he had predicted on Friday night.

"I will cherish this the rest of my life, no matter what happens," he said. "I'm in a dream right now, and I don't ever want to wake up."

Johnson said he hoped to capture the weekend in a bottle, cap it, and never let it go. Instead just the opposite happened. His life escaped with a rush after that. The eyes were hardly dry from the All-Star Game when a week later the Lakers retired his number 32 in another emotional ceremony at the Forum. In the aftermath of the two events, he again felt an overwhelming urge to return to playing. But again his advisers and friends urged him not to, and he listened. Instead, he turned to serving as a broadcast analyst for NBC.

The Lakers, meanwhile, labored on without Magic as Worthy, forward Sam Perkins, and center Vlade Divac all missed great chunks of the season with injuries. Regardless, Sedale Threatt, the journeyman backup, delivered solid, steady play at point guard, a pleasant surprise for the team's management, although his effort went largely unnoticed by many in the Forum crowd who were paying high prices to see a superstar. Simply, the fans were used to seeing Magic Johnson, and no matter how good Threatt was—and he was pretty good—it wasn't the same.

As for his playing urges, Johnson focused his attention on the upcoming Olympic Summer Games in Barcelona, where he would play on the "Dream Team," the first American men's basketball team to be comprised largely of professional players. Johnson had won a championship at every level, but his trophy case lacked an Olympic gold medal. He wanted one badly.

Again there were some rumblings about an HIV-infected athlete competing, but those were minor. Still, there were plenty of other major distractions. In April, L.A. erupted with urban riots, creating a holocaust that was broadcast live by the networks, particularly CNN. The fires and violence and looting left more than 50 people dead and resulted in billions of dollars in damage. The violence spread within blocks of the Forum, with some Lakers players and staffers watching television inside the arena's offices as the bizarre events unfolded outside. In that regard, the concrete shell of the Forum became a bunker. But even it wasn't considered safe enough. With Threatt's leadership, the team had managed a late win that miraculously put the Lakers in the playoffs for the 16th consecutive time. And the riots forced the team to move its home games to Las Vegas in the first-round series against Portland. The Lakers lost three games to one, which immediately turned the focus to next season. Would Johnson attempt a comeback? The answer was a resounding maybe.

In early June, his NBC broadcasting schedule for the playoffs conflicted with the due date of Cookie's pregnancy, so they agreed to induce labor, which allowed Johnson to perform as Lamaze coach during the delivery. The result was Earvin Johnson III, a fat, wide-eyed son, complete with all his fingers and toes and an HIV-negative blood test. Much elated and relieved, Johnson returned to his busy schedule. His autobiography, *My Life*, with cowriter William Novak, was on a rushed schedule. Charged with advance promotion, Johnson attended the American Booksellers' Association convention in Anaheim, where he hobnobbed with the publishing industry's power buyers. He was greeting a line of well-wishers at a reception when a 43-year-old woman gave him a pair of her daughter's ballet slippers to sign. When he complied, the woman was obviously thrilled. She thanked him, turned, walked a few feet, and collapsed, instantly dead of a heart aneurysm.

LON ROSEN: "Earvin was shaken. He kept asking, 'Did she die because of the excitement of meeting me?' I told him that wasn't the case. He wrote her family and offered his condolences. We started wondering what could happen next."

Dream Team

Of the thousands of athletes at the Olympics, it was Johnson who loomed over the games. Crowds everywhere in Barcelona greeted him with the familiar chant, "*Ma-jeek. Ma-jeek.*" His answer was to avoid them and the media throng's endless questions about AIDS. The first day in Barcelona he told them he would answer health questions just that once and from then on it would be only basketball.

Still, it was difficult. He was a world-class player at the world's competition. And he was infected with the world's disease. The populations of Africa, Asia, Europe, and North America were threatened by the spread of AIDS, according to the World Health Organization. And Johnson was easily the most visible of all the victims. Wherever he took a step, they took a step. Whenever he played, they played. The only real question seemed to be, did he empower AIDS victims or trivialize them? The answer seemed to be that he did both. But the major result of his participation was again positive. The world watched in early August as he stood on the awards platform with Jordan, Larry Bird, and his other teammates to receive the gold medal in men's basketball.

As his turn came to receive the medal, the crowd roared. He acknowledged them with a bow, smiling, not too broadly, a tight smile, packed with happiness. The noise grew when he bent to have the medal draped about his neck. Then he rose with the applause, punched the air in exhilaration and unleashed the full smile, a bright beam to the world. A soon-to-be AIDS victim had just claimed the gold. He, who wanted to win everything, now possessed the only trophy he hadn't owned. This one felt the best of all, he said. It was "the greatest feeling I've ever felt winning anything."

With the Olympics over, Johnson finally faced the question. Would he play again in the NBA? He originally planned to make his decision two weeks after the Summer Games. Instead, he dragged on for eight weeks, unable to make up his mind, which left general manager Jerry West twisted in knots. If Johnson wasn't coming back, West needed to sign a first-rate guard to strengthen the backcourt. Sedale Threatt had worked out well, but the team needed a point guard, a ball handler to run the offense. If Johnson didn't play, that opened a position on the team under the NBA's salary cap rules for another big-money player. Free agent Rod Strickland was available, and he was just the kind of guard West was looking for. Strickland seemed eager to come to the Lakers, but he couldn't wait for Johnson's decision.

LON ROSEN: "Every day Jerry would call me to bitch about Earvin not making up his mind. I told him, 'Jerry, you're only happy when you're crazy.'"

The general manager fussed, but he didn't put any real pressure on Rosen, even as he watched Strickland give up on the Lakers and sign with Portland.

JERRY WEST: "I believed all along that Magic would come back. And I knew if he did come back we could be a great team, that we had a chance to win another title."

Johnson was in the final stages of renegotiating his contract with team owner Jerry Buss. Normally, West was the tough guy negotiating all Lakers contracts. But Buss and Lon Rosen had been discussing a new agreement for several years. They had first begun talking at training camp in Hawaii in 1990, although under league rules the deal couldn't actually be signed until after the 1992 playoffs.

During the 1991 off-season, Johnson and Rosen had gone to Spain for a promotional appearance for Campofrio, the Spanish meat company. While there, Johnson was offered $20 million to play a season for a Spanish pro team. In September 1991, Rosen met again with Buss at the owner's house to discuss the new contract.

Lon Rosen: "I used the Spanish offer as leverage. I asked Buss for a lot more than $20 million. It was a huge figure. Jerry said, 'That's very high. A lot of money. More than I'm willing to pay him. But we'll keep talking.'"

Buss did not want his superstar playing for another team, even if he was at the end of his career. The nature of Buss's dealings with Johnson had always been love/business. In 1981, the owner had given Magic what seemed like an incredible deal, $25 million for 25 years. But spiraling player salaries soon dwarfed those numbers. In 1987, Joe Smith of Capitol Music-EMI had helped Johnson renegotiate the deal into a $2.5 million annual package. Seemingly miffed at Smith's involvement, Buss pointed out that he could easily take away Smith's floor seats at the Forum. "Of the 128 seats out there, 96 belong to lawyers," Smith told him. "So if you want to deal with them instead . . ." Buss said he was only kidding. But the lesson in his toughness didn't escape Johnson's advisers. The owner may have loved Magic, but he meant business.

Rosen and Buss had planned to resume contract discussions in November 1991. But then Johnson's test results came back positive, which left the owner in a deep emotional funk, forcing him into virtual seclusion.

Lon Rosen: "Just before Earvin announced to the world that he was HIV positive, Jerry pulled me aside and said, 'Look, I'm still giving him his contract.'"

By then, the matter was no longer a business deal. Buss was operating on pure emotion. In fact, the new contract made absolutely no business sense, because it jammed the Lakers against the salary cap for another three seasons, making it more difficult for West to arrange trades and other player deals.

LON ROSEN: "Jerry Buss had no obligation whatsoever to do that for Earvin Johnson, but that's the way he is."

Buss had a history of generosity toward other people involved in the Lakers' run of championships. James Worthy, former coach Pat Riley, Michael Cooper, even West, all had gotten fat contracts and bonuses from Buss. But the league's salary cap had prevented him from doing the same for Johnson.

JERRY BUSS: "People told me I was crazy for giving him that contract. But I don't think people looked at the way Magic handled himself. At no time in his career did you see that he was unhappy with his contract. For a while that first big contract allowed him to be among the best-paid players. But then basketball contracts went into the stratosphere and Magic was left behind."

Buss had always told Johnson that he would be the highest-paid player on the team. But making that happen within the salary cap had been impossible. Johnson never complained, although Buss sensed that he expected something to be done. Sometimes Magic and Buss went to prizefights at the Forum.

JERRY BUSS: "He enjoyed the fights, and we'd have dinner together. A lot of the talking Magic and I do is at the fights. I told him in one of those talks that I would take care of it. He could have complained about his pay. He could have caused a lot of problems. But Magic Johnson is too professional to do that. Because he treated me so honorably, I returned the favor."

The "favor" was a whopping one-year, $14.6 million contract extension, bringing Johnson's guaranteed income to $19.6 million. It was the largest single-year contract in the history of pro basketball.

LON ROSEN: "To get that figure, Jerry and I looked at Lakers payrolls from the past to find out just how much Johnson had been underpaid. This was Buss's way of paying Earvin back for all those years."

Johnson didn't say he was coming back to play, but everybody around sensed he was. New Lakers coach Randy Pfund sensed it. Jerry West sensed it. Johnson's doctors did not advise for or against playing, although they suggested that if he did play, not to attempt to cover the full 82-game schedule. He planned to avoid back-to-back games and long, grueling road trips, anything that might weaken his immune system and hasten the onset of AIDS. Johnson hoped to play about 60 games on the schedule.

RUDY GARCIDUENAS: "A lot of people didn't know what to expect. But a lot of people knew that Earvin couldn't be without the game."

Cookie knew, too, and finally she consented as well. "I'm back," he announced, with his wife and Dr. Michael Mellman at his side at a news conference at the Forum on September 29. God had put him here to play basketball, he said, admitting that at first his doctors had been opposed. "But they've never dealt with anyone as big and strong as I am. I continued to work out and do what I was supposed to do, and now I'm in a position to come back and play, so here I am. I'm back, baby."

Rejection

The first stone in his path back to NBA stardom came just as training camp opened in October when columnist Dave Kindred of *The Sporting News* urged Johnson "to tell the whole truth about how he acquired the AIDS virus . . . He said unprotected heterosexual sex did it; numbers say that's highly unlikely." If Johnson was hiding the fact that he acquired the virus through homosexual activity and his lie caused research money to be diverted into the wrong areas, then that lie would be "reprehensible," Kindred wrote.

Kindred, a well-respected sportswriter, had based his column not on any specific information that Johnson was bisexual, but on statistics of the disease in America. The odds are roughly one in 500 that a man can get the virus through unprotected heterosexual activity, Kindred quoted one study as showing.

However, AIDS worldwide is largely a heterosexual disease (at the time, 75 percent of the millions worldwide who had contracted it had done so through heterosexual activity). In Africa, India, and Asia, an estimated 98 percent of all victims had caught the virus heterosexually. That, health officials had told both Johnson and Rosen, was an important message in the United States, where AIDS was wrongly considered just a gay problem.

The *Sporting News* story would be followed by others on the issue, and within days Jan Hubbard, *Newsday*'s NBA writer, would produce a story saying that a prominent NBA player was spreading rumors about Johnson's sexual preference.

Within hours, the issue had been ignited and tossed onto the media's agenda.

At every turn in the exhibition season, there were new questions to be answered. It soon became apparent that the only practical solution was to hold a press conference before each preseason game, which Johnson quickly came to detest. Next, Phoenix Suns owner Jerry Colangelo weighed in against Johnson's return.

Midway through the exhibition season, Johnson told a small group of writers that a well-known NBA player was smearing him around the league as a bisexual. Johnson said he had confronted the player twice and each time the player denied it. "If you're gonna be a man, be a man," Johnson told the writers. "If you're gonna say something behind my back, then when I come to you, be a man. Say you said it."

By the time the Lakers reached San Diego on October 23 for an exhibition against the Sacramento Kings, news reports had identified Isiah Thomas as the prime suspect in slandering Johnson. Lon Rosen would later be accused of tipping off the press, which the agent strongly denied. Actually, the rumors themselves were an old item in NBA gossip circles.

After whipping the Kings in San Diego, the Lakers headed east for their final three exhibition games, the first being another meeting with the Kings in St. Louis. Johnson, however, passed on this game and instead flew to Chicago with his wife and Rosen for a taping of the "Oprah Winfrey Show." The appearance marked the opening of his promotional efforts for his new book, *My Life*. His unofficial agenda was to defend his sexuality, and the book provided a good basis for that with a brief account of his many encounters. This would soon prove to be a disaster, as in several key interviews Johnson told far more than the book revealed.

GARY VITTI: "He was surrounded by so much controversy it destroyed the hero. I mean the hero is still there, but for a lot of people it has been destroyed. When he started talking about six women at a time on the "Oprah Winfrey Show" and stuff like that, he lost a lot of people. He felt he had to say these things about [having sex with] six women. He felt he needed to defend himself. He didn't want people to think he was gay."

LON ROSEN: "I remember watching him doing an interview with ABC's 'PrimeTime Live' when he started talking about the same stuff, all this sex. His face looked really different. He looked so sad. I felt really bad for him. We had talked about him limiting what he had to say about the sex stuff, but Earvin's his own man. He's always been good with the media, but that became a problem when he went into explanations and descriptions of this stuff. He said it, and I knew it was gonna cause a lot of shit."

Shortly thereafter, Rosen informed Random House that Johnson would have to discontinue his promotional efforts. Other things were planned, but the publicity wasn't in Johnson's best interest.

LON ROSEN: "We were in Chicago and we were waiting for him to tape Oprah's show. We both read where Jerry Colangelo was saying more about his return. Earvin couldn't figure it out because he had always considered Colangelo his friend and now Colangelo's attacking him and campaigning against him. He gave me the newspaper. I got really pissed. I phoned Russ Granik, the NBA's deputy commissioner, and I asked him to say something to Colangelo. He called Jerry, but then Russ called me back and said that it didn't work, that Colangelo had a right to speak his mind. They couldn't stop him."

The baggage Johnson carried to North Carolina left him weary. That night another two dozen reporters awaited Johnson in the press room at UNC's Smith Center, where the Lakers were scheduled to play the Cleveland Cavaliers. "The most amazing thing is that everything you say now will be printed," Johnson said, laughing hard at his answer.

The exhibition game began just like hundreds of other Lakers road games. Ready to broadcast, Chick Hearn sat courtside, his left hand on his stopwatch as he read over stats. As usual, Johnson examined the game ball, bouncing it near the Lakers bench, rolling it in his fingers, then pausing to eye its roundness. Satisfied, he passed it to official Dick Bavetta at midcourt. Then came the player introductions, and as usual, the applause for Johnson was the loudest. But it was far from deafening on this Halloween night. The 21,500-seat arena had 9,000 unsold seats. Those who did attend quickly realized it was not one of Johnson's best nights. About midway through the first period, he attempted to back Cleveland's Craig Ehlo down near the goal. Working from the right side, Johnson reversed left and right while Ehlo leaned in and snatched at the dribble. Going to his left, Johnson suddenly whirled about-face, and Ehlo hit his right forearm. Foul. As he walked to the free throw line, Johnson examined first one arm, then the other. Watching from the bench, free agent Sean Higgins told Gary Vitti that Johnson had gotten scratched.

GARY VITTI: "Moments later, during a time-out, I decided to look at Earvin's right arm myself. He sits down, and I get kinda nosy. I turn his arm over. I see this small scratch. No bigger than a fingernail. I could easily have looked the other way. But you're supposed to cover open wounds. I pull a 4-by-4 gauze pad out of my jacket pocket. I hand it to Magic. I said, 'Put this on your arm and wipe away the perspiration.' I got a cotton-tip applicator and sprayed some benzoin on it, which is a sticky, adhesive substance. I painted his arm with it. Never put my fingers on the wound. Yeah, I held his arm, but I never put my fingers on the side of the wound. I made it sticky so we could put a bandage over it. Then he went back out and played."

With about three minutes left in the half, Vitti decided to put a sweatband over Johnson's small, clear bandage as additional protection. Later, the Occupational Safety and Health Administration would cite Vitti for a safety violation for failing to wear latex gloves during the bandaging.

GARY VITTI: "I didn't forget to put the gloves on. I chose not to. It was a non-bloody wound in a controlled situation, one that was so small the official couldn't see it. There was a lot of controversy about players playing with Magic. I felt this was the perfect opportunity to make a statement. If I put the gloves on, that would have sent a mixed message to all of these players. 'Gary, you're telling us to play with Magic Johnson because we can't get HIV. But now he has this fingernail scratch. It's a non-bloody wound and you're putting gloves on? Now if I can't get it, why are you putting those gloves on? What are you trying to say? It's okay if he bleeds on me, but not on you?'"

This whole scenario played itself out with most people in the arena failing to notice. Neither public relations director John Black nor the Lakers broadcasters noticed it. Nor did most of the reporters in attendance. Photographer Brad Isbell on the baseline took pictures of Johnson receiving treatment, but outside of that, little attention was paid to it.

LON ROSEN: "Earvin got cut while he was playing in the Olympics. It was another small cut on his finger. They covered it with a Band-Aid, and nobody even noticed or said anything."

Properly bandaged, Johnson continued play, but the results were mixed at best. With Johnson playing 28 minutes and making just one of 10 shots, the Lakers lost. Afterward, a crowd jammed the hallway outside the dressing rooms, and about two dozen media people came in to interview Johnson. "You kinda got nicked a little on the arm?" a writer said. "Is that a problem at all?"

"No. No-o-o-o," Johnson said. "Everybody, anybody who gets cut, not just me, anybody, you just go, get it fixed. Boom. Come right back."

"Nothing special to worry about?" the writer asked.

"No," he said. "That's everybody. Not just me. Everybody in the league."

Then he was asked what kind of impact he'd have as the first NBA player with HIV. "The impact will be just that. I'm just happy it was me," he said, bubbling into laughter.

"I'm like a guinea pig," he added, his voice turning suddenly serious. "I like challenges. It's fun. It's no fun when you don't have challenges. This is one of them."

It was his role to fight that blindness, he said, and playing basketball helped him do it. "Look at this. I'm in North Carolina right now. Boom. The message is out. I'm here. I'm playing. I'm talking to you. Boom. It'll be in the papers tomorrow. Next time I'll be in Philly. I'm gonna be in Cleveland. In Chicago. See? So the message gets out even bigger."

Playing in the Olympics helped broadcast the message? someone asked. "Oh, man," Johnson said. "That's the whole forum. That's what I wanted. So I got the whole forum. We educated them," he said, his eyes gleaming.

Heartbreak

The next night, after he got home, Earvin Johnson phoned Lon Rosen and told him he was retiring. Again. For good.

LON ROSEN: "I was stunned. I told him, 'If you're retiring because you got cut, you're a chickenshit.' He told me, 'No, it's not that. It's no fun.' He said it wasn't right for him. He said he could see that his presence was changing the game. Because players from other teams feared him, they might not play as hard as they could. He didn't want that. He told me that would hurt the game, and he didn't want that. He said he didn't want to let down all the children with HIV. Earvin knew how many had written him and told him they were counting on him to keep playing. As long as he played, he knew they could play, because other kids wouldn't have an excuse for keeping them out. But he couldn't do it anymore."

The next day, the agent phoned team officials to inform them that Johnson was ending his comeback attempt. He later held yet another press conference at the Sports Arena before the Lakers played. "I definitely want to come back," he said, "but I won't . . . It's a different hurt this year."

He spoke in a crowded side room just as the game was set to begin. The national anthem blared in the background. "I'll never disappear," he promised as the session closed. "I don't know how to. I love to live. When you disappear, you stop living."

13
Aftermath

To his credit, Randy Pfund didn't try to mimic Pat Riley's intensity. First of all, when he took over as Lakers coach in 1992, Pfund didn't have Kareem and Magic, the two great pieces of the basketball puzzle that Riley had. Second, Pfund knew a hard-driving approach wouldn't work with his veteran players. As Riley's assistant, Pfund had seen the Lakers wear down under the constant push. James Worthy readily agreed, saying he much preferred Pfund's cooperative style to Riley's pressure treatment.

Yet the results were mixed, and it became increasingly clear as the 1992–93 season progressed that, fair or not, Pfund's coaching future was hanging in the balance. After struggling early, the Lakers opened 1993 with more of their strange cadence, losing to teams they should have beaten, then producing inspiring upsets of the Bulls in Chicago and winning their third game against Portland.

They closed January with a solid 3–3 record on yet another eastern road trip, defeating Charlotte, Boston, and Washington while falling to Utah, New Jersey, and Indiana. However, a sense of foreboding settled on the coaching staff. Pfund gave up his plans for a major move toward the motion offense. After the Indiana loss, the usually quiet Sedale Threatt had groused to reporters that the Lakers needed to run. Pfund agreed, and they made the effort to break more often. But to run, they needed great defensive rebounding, and the Lakers never made that commitment.

So they persisted in their weird ways, out of synch some nights, just getting by on others, with their moments of inspiration coming at odd intervals. "This is a tough team to figure out," West conceded.

"When you don't have a leader on the floor, you get lost," assistant coach Larry Drew observed in late January. The situation left them all wishing Johnson had fought off the criticism to resume his playing career.

LARRY DREW, FORMER LAKERS ASSISTANT COACH: "Earvin was one of those guys to challenge people individually. He would set the tone in practice, and once he set the tone, it was up to everybody else to follow the lead. If you didn't, he let you know. That's why he was so successful. Teams would die to have people like that on their roster. It was just unbelievable. I've been with teams where we thought we had leaders. But when I came with the Lakers, Earvin started in training camp. He just demanded perfection."

JAMES WORTHY: "There were 9 or 10 points gone from my game just from his passing ability, just from his getting the ball to you in unique situations. His leadership qualities were unique. Here's a guy who didn't mind getting on you. Some guys can do that; most can't. Plus Earvin had energy all the time. Energy at shootaround, energy on the bus, energy in the locker room, energy while he slept. He was just that type of guy. He would not let you get down. He would not let this team lose."

With every game the Lakers had grown more desperate for a player to step forward.

JAMES WORTHY: "We had energy, but we didn't have Earvin Johnson. We didn't have that same level. We were trying the best we could, but we didn't have that special talent that he had."

West grew increasingly displeased with how unorganized the team seemed. Pfund, of course, countered that the club was clearly one in transition, that it was impossible to get much more out of the roster than he did. Worthy, in particular, struggled with his declining skills and with his waning passion for the game. Trading him, however, had become an impossibility because of the balloon contract with which Jerry Buss had rewarded him, a deal that paid him a reported $7 million per season over the final two years of the agreement.

This problem, and the team's lack of leadership and a point guard, seemed to have Pfund locked into a course for failure over the spring of 1993. The Lakers suffered through a record six straight home losses at the Forum in March (they would finish 20–21 at home, their first losing home record since moving to L.A. in 1960). They finished the year at 39–43, fifth in the division, yet somehow managed to make the playoffs, where their first-round opponent was the top seed, the Suns with Charles Barkley, the team with a league-best 62 wins and the momentum for a championship. The Lakers were figured to be a mere speed bump on the Suns' roll to the 1993 NBA Finals. Yet, the circumstances somehow stirred something in Pfund's players, particularly Worthy. Playing with a fire not seen all season, the Lakers came out and promptly claimed the first two games in Phoenix. Never in NBA history had an eighth-seeded team taken the first two games on the road against a top seed. Better yet, never in league history had a team fallen behind 2–0 in a five-game series and survived it.

Unfortunately, the Lakers hosted the next two games, and the Forum had been quite friendly to the Suns in recent seasons. Barkley bore down, and like that, Phoenix evened the series with two wins in Los Angeles. With Game 5 in the Suns' brand-new America West Arena on May 9, the Lakers seemed finished. But once again, they came out strong, hitting a team playoff record 7 of 15 three-point attempts, and seemed on the verge of a stupendous upset until they lost their lead in the last minutes of regulation and went to overtime, where Barkley and the Suns finally found an edge for a 112–104 win.

The series performance was just enough to save Pfund's job. But the 1993–94 season was doomed to be yet another phase of transition. In the '93 draft, West went for North Carolina forward George Lynch with the 12th pick of the first round, but the real prize was Nick Van Exel out of the University of Cincinnati with the 37th selection in the second round.

Most pro scouts had seen talent in Van Exel but worried about his shot selection and questioned his attitude and character. Part of the problem stemmed from Van Exel's seeming reluctance to visit certain teams that were interested in him.

West had often said that if you don't have a top pick you have to wait around and hope that other people make mistakes. With Van Exel, the entire NBA made a mistake in 1993. Soon after Van Exel came to work, the Lakers realized they had a rare, rare find, a rookie who could start and excel at point guard.

He was, however, just that—a rookie—and that contributed to an immense problem for Pfund. The Lakers began the season with a starting lineup that averaged just 23.4 years in age, the youngest in the league. Plus, the team still lacked strong rebounding and a leader. West had hoped that Lynch, whose defense and rebounding had helped Carolina to the '93 NCAA title, would contribute in those areas. But Pfund seemed unimpressed with the rookie, who had a power forward's game in a small forward's body. The

Lakers needed scoring and rebounding from the small forward slot, and Lynch's jump shot was suspect. But where Lynch struggled, Van Exel immediately found a comfort zone and a job as the team's starting point guard.

Unfortunately, the roster was again strangely unmotivated, which frustrated both rookies, not to mention Pfund. The Lakers opened the season with a losing month, then proceeded to stack up the kind of forlorn defeats not seen since their dark days in Minneapolis.

NICK VAN EXEL: "It was tough. There were a lot of games where we'd go out and see guys who really didn't want to play and were not giving their all. That really hurt the most because we know they could do better."

Sitting and watching this lack of effort was particularly tough on the immensely proud and workmanlike Lynch.

NICK VAN EXEL: "George didn't lose many games in his college career, and he's won a national championship. It was hard for him losing so many games. He felt there were a lot of games where we should have won, where people should have tried harder."

A rash of injuries opened up playing time for Lynch, and he showed that he could play with intensity. Yet when a team has to draw on rookies for its strength, there's trouble. And there was plenty of that for Pfund. Strangely, the Lakers picked March, the team's only month with a winning record, to release the second-year coach. Buss and West first extended his contract an additional year in early March, although their decision was already made. From there, the Lakers went on a rare winning streak, claiming a 6–1 record from March 7 up to their March 23 game against the Mavericks, before which management relieved Pfund and assistant Chet Kammerer of their duties.

For two games, Bill Bertka ran the team until new coach Magic Johnson and assistant Michael Cooper could get situated. The emotion and excitement of Johnson's return generated renewed interest in the Forum, where ticket sales had sagged through the miserable season. Those feelings grew when Johnson won five of his first six games. Yet it soon became clear that his presence on the bench was a halfhearted experiment, and the problems that had plagued the Lakers remained very malignant.

The end of the season was quite ugly, a 10-game losing streak, the longest in franchise history. The losing gained momentum after Johnson announced that he wouldn't take the job on a long-term basis. Frustrated by the lack of concern among key players, Johnson reportedly smashed a player's beeper against a wall when it went off during practice. He wanted full commitment to winning, and they weren't willing to make it. Johnson himself wasn't ready to take on the challenge and stress of coaching. Instead, he acquired a minority ownership of the team and settled in as a vice president not long after the Lakers finished 33–49 and out of the playoffs for the first time in almost two decades.

Someone else would have to do the coaching. For that, West turned to Del Harris, a well-traveled veteran known for his slowdown offenses. Actually Harris had been a proponent of the push game during his days in Houston. But he slowed down the Rockets' offense to match the skills of then-center Moses Malone, and that resulted in a trip to the 1981 NBA Finals against the Boston Celtics. The Rockets lost, but Harris' record for flexibility was established among keen observers. Which is why West could hire him with a clear conscience before the 1994–95 season. West knew that Harris wasn't wed to any one system and would find the style of play suited to the young roster.

The other big holes for the Lakers included a small forward who could score and rebound consistently and a superstar. For years that had been James Worthy's domain, but his declining game and the sudden death of his mother led to retirement in the fall of 1994. To fill the small forward spot, West struck a deal with Phoenix that brought in Cedric Ceballos, a fifth-year forward with strong offensive skills and a mild interest in defense.

Added to that was the selection of Eddie Jones out of Temple with the tenth overall pick in the '94 draft. Teamed with Van Exel at the point, Ceballos at small forward, Elden Campbell at power forward, and Vlade Divac at center, Jones proved he could contribute immediately as the Lakers' off guard. As a result, they were one of the NBA's big surprises in 1994–95.

That was especially true of the development of the young guard tandem. "We're one of the best teams in the league," the 57-year-old Harris said unabashedly eight weeks into the season. "I think Nick and Eddie Jones have got to be the most exciting backcourt in the league," he added. "I mean these kids are 23 years old and they play like salty veterans. We are really blessed."

Since Johnson's abrupt retirement in 1991, the Lakers had drifted along without a leader. That helped explain why Van Exel's intense competitiveness and leadership abilities were so welcomed in Los Angeles.

LARRY DREW, FORMER LAKERS ASSISTANT COACH: "If you find a guy with a passion to win, you got yourself something special. Nick was very passionate. He wanted to win badly and got frustrated when he didn't."

NICK VAN EXEL: "I got a lot of competitive relatives. All of my aunts, when they were growing up, played softball and were great competitors. My dad, my uncles, everybody in my family always wanted to win."

ANTHONY PEELER, FORMER LAKER: "The Lakers gave him the ball as a rookie and told him to run the team. As a rookie, Nick was just witnessing a lot of stuff that he couldn't really do anything about."

His second year, though, Van Exel had more power and he had the benefit of frequent talks with Magic Johnson.

NICK VAN EXEL: "The Lakers gave me a lot of confidence to be the leader, and it was a role I wanted."

Del Harris and the fiery young point guard, however, soon hit the first of many bumpy spots in their relationship. The coach quickly downplayed a playing time disagreement they had during a game in Portland that second season. The incident, Harris said, "was a nothing kind of situation. I love working with him. He's a special player."

Lakers fans quickly latched on to Jones and Van Exel as a guard tandem. Harris and West both projected a great future for Jones, who at six-foot-six, 190, had the body and temperament to play both big guard and small forward. The Lakers spent much of his rookie season building his confidence and skills, with Drew schooling him on his midrange jumper and Michael Cooper teaching the nuances of tough defense and stopping the pick-and-roll.

EDDIE JONES: "Jerry West came to me several times and said, 'Man you can be great.' He's like the basketball guru, the best of scouts. So that just made me want to work so I could perform to his level of expectation. I just tried to do my best to play my heart out."

There was little question that Jones did that, although his coaches thought he was too reckless in taking the ball to the basket and challenging the league's bigger, stronger inside players. Sure enough, Jones' fine rookie season was interrupted when he injured a shoulder dunking. Losing his scoring and defense could have been disastrous, except that Anthony Peeler, long in management's doghouse and slowed by a series of injuries, came through with a tremendous spring. The young Lakers closed out the schedule with a show of strength, winning 48 games and finishing in fifth place in their conference. Better yet, Van Exel proved to be an immense factor in the playoffs, guiding the Lakers to a first-round upset over fourth-seeded Seattle.

In the second round, they were derailed 4–2 by David Robinson and the San Antonio Spurs, winners of a league-best 62 games. But there was little doubt that the young Lakers had put the league on notice. With Divac having developed into a solid center and Ceballos offering all-star caliber play at small forward, Harris's club had a bright, bright future. And Jerry West was spinning his wheels, trying to find the next infusion of great talent.

Among his first thoughts, though, was an old answer. Since his failed comeback in 1992 and his brief attempt at coaching in 1994, Magic Johnson had struggled with the idea of attempting a second comeback. Those feelings intensified as the 1995–96 season neared, but Johnson didn't give them voice until the campaign started oddly and meandered into January.

Then he and West began discussing a comeback. The team clearly needed him, and the climate for an HIV-positive player now seemed less controversial.

JERRY WEST: "I told him that his time was running out. It was getting to a point when he needed to make a decision and I think he felt the same."

When he finally did step into uniform for a late January home game against the Warriors, he was greeted with magazine covers hailing his return. Now 36 and decidedly heavier, Johnson answered with nearly a triple-double (19 points, 10 assists, and 8 rebounds). The next game brought a drubbing from the dominant Bulls (with an amazing 40–3 record on their way to a 72–10 finish that broke the mark set by the '69 Lakers), but Johnson's reappearance brought a winning surge and a boost to sagging tickets sales.

The team had posted a 24–18 record before Johnson's return (he led the team with 6.9 assists per game and averaged better than 14 points), but with his help the Lakers zoomed off to a 29–11 finish. The numbers generated big thoughts about the playoffs until a series of April incidents dampened the team's outlook. Johnson's impatient presence had a mixed impact on the young roster, led by Van Exel. Many of the players remained from the group that Johnson had criticized just months earlier when he was coach. He struggled with his role and coach Del Harris's approach to the game. Yet all of that might have been overcome had Van Exel not been suspended for bumping an official in an April game. Johnson hadn't more than completed his upbraiding of Van Exel, when Johnson himself was suspended for a similar incident two games later.

The Lakers finished with a surprising 53 wins, but they were disconcerted and lost in the first round against the defending world champion Houston Rockets. The experience convinced Johnson to retire for good, but the most significant product of the season came with further deterioration of the relationship between Harris and Van Exel.

DEL HARRIS, FORMER LAKERS COACH: "We kept Nick Van Exel for four years. He hated me. He was my point guard for four years. Jerry West was able to massage him along."

West had always played a large role with the team, but his chores now shifted. Not only was he looking for the next infusion of superstar talent for his Lakers, West was also charged with keeping the peace.

The Logo

Reporters who covered the Lakers over the years had long been amazed and amused by Jerry West's tortured persona as the team's top basketball executive. Perhaps the largest of many ironies in West's life is that he's the NBA logo—his graceful, slashing silhouette is the centerpiece of the red, white, and blue logo. As much as he'd like to forget it, he and everyone else associated with the NBA is reminded of his playing career at virtually every turn. The NBA logo is plastered everywhere and he's revered accordingly.

Understanding West had always been the key to understanding the Lakers. He was the mystic who molded this team, working, as he explained it, "in my own weird way."

MARK HEISLER: "Jerry West is one of the wackiest guys I've ever covered in sports, and I've covered Al Davis. Jerry, as wacky as he is, can function in the world, whereas Al has to retreat to wherever and work from his cave. I'm a Jerry West guy. I thought he did an incredible job for the Lakers. But his nervous system, it's just wired a little tighter than most of them, or any of them."

KAREEM ABDUL-JABBAR: "Jerry always seems like he's having a terrible time, or something bad is impending. He's always worried. He reminds me of the pilots in *Catch-22* who are about to fly off into combat. He has this sense of foreboding and anxiety."

J. A. ADANDE: "In the '80s, there were two things you could be sure of. Magic would do something to bring the team a victory, and Jerry West would make the right move to bring the right players in. Those were the two things as a Lakers fan that you always knew were going to happen. For Jerry to come through time and time again, to always make the right move, whether it was Bob McAdoo or Mychal Thompson, it always seemed like he knew what to do to keep that franchise on top."

By and large, West got far more agony than satisfaction from his job. During games he would become a bundle of nervous energy and sometimes wind up out in the Forum parking lot while the outcome was being settled. Or he could be seen standing near section 27, peeking past the ushers at the action, his body twisted with tension.

When he did sit, he sometimes watched the game with Chick Hearn's wife, Marge. Usually West could determine in the first three or four minutes how the Lakers were going to do. If the prognosis was bad, he was up quickly, stepping on poor Marge's toes as he made an early exit. He would retreat from there to his office, where he watched the rest of the game on television. There he could express his disgust in solitude. West was easily offended if the game wasn't played right.

J. A. ADANDE: "The amazing thing is that he is so insecure and so uncertain of things. Here was this great team that he had put together, and he could barely even watch it. He'd disappear down the tunnel during games. This team he put together—his lasting tribute to L.A.—his last couple of years he wasn't even watching it. He was driving up to Santa Barbara. That stuns me more than a bit. Obviously the guy was Mr. Clutch as a player. Here he was with the game on the line, and he was the calmest guy on the court, wanted the ball in his hands. He could control everything and always come through in the end and make the shot. Here was this guy who was so cool under pressure and yet sitting in the stands he would crumble. He was a mess."

MARK HEISLER: "Jerry's one of these guys, if he thinks it he'll say it to somebody. And it'll get out. Another guy who's like him is Doug Collins. When I covered the Sixers we used to call him Scoop for the same reason. Always knows what's going on, always wants to know what's going on, always interested. Jerry is really a smart guy, plus he's really a live wire. I was doing a book on Pat Riley. Jerry knew I was doing it, and I was curious about how much he was gonna have to say. The Lakers were in training camp, and he was making eye contact with me, kind of inviting me to come over. So I sat down with him at the swimming pool at the Royal Hawaiian. I got my tape recorder out and we talked for about a half hour. He didn't lay Riles out or anything. He didn't take the hide off of him, but he gave me some very interesting stuff. So about two months later, and I think Riles is calling around and asking his friends not to be all that helpful, so West calls me up and says, 'Are you doing a book about Pat Riley?'"

Reporters told such West tales yet quickly acknowledged he possessed the best mind in the business. His West Virginia background loomed as the root of his stubborn streak, his ability to persevere as an NBA executive, a complicated job that very few do well. Most people who have tried running pro basketball teams soon find themselves sunk in confusion and despair. West, though, was clearly tougher and more determined than his peers. Anyone dealing with him on trades and other NBA deals soon learned that underneath the courteous exterior he possessed a toughness hardened by his coalfield upbringing.

MARK HEISLER: "Jerry had tremendous power by deign of his prestige and experience and his standing with Buss and his standing in general. Jerry West's passion was the passion of the Lakers. Nobody ever expected more of himself than Jerry did, and more of everybody around him. That's why he was so successful, and that's why the pressure was so high with the Lakers. There were no standards, there was no accomplishment except for winning a title."

JERRY WEST: "Being a general manager is competitive, but it's so different. Being a player, it's a wonderful feeling to win an important ball game, to compete against the best players. Being a general manager is so much more subtle, so much more frustrating. It's a completely different feeling. Every once in a while, when you get something done as a general manager, you really feel good about it. You really do. Finding and drafting players and watching them develop, that's where you get your satisfaction."

West's relationship with Lakers owner Jerry Buss had been punctuated by disagreements over the years, sometimes followed by West considering attractive offers to take over other franchises. But he could never bring himself to leave. Since his rookie days he had been a Laker in one capacity or another, except for two seasons of bitter feuding with then-owner Jack Kent Cooke in the 1970s.

He suffered from ulcers and sleepless nights in the early 1990s, particularly after games, when he would twist and turn, running back every play in his mind. At the end of the 1989 season, a spot mysteriously appeared on his lung, frightening West and his family. It later went away, but doctors weren't sure what it was. The fear made him appreciate his family more, but it didn't dull his drive.

"I do think this job is wearing," he said at the time. "There's a lot of pressure on you."

The translation, of course, was that he put tremendous pressure on himself, and indirectly on the coaches and players.

JERRY WEST: "It makes no sense that I'm not happy. I should be happy. The reason I tend not to be happy is goal setting. You want to stretch yourself. You want to stretch your players and make them try to take that last step, and that's to end their season with a win. If you do that, you're gonna have a fun summer."

His every move was haunted by the same old questions: What does it take to close? What does it take to finish? What does it take to win? In the wake of Johnson's second and final retirement, those questions took on an added urgency, with strong financial overtones.

SID HARTMAN, MINNESOTA NEWSPAPER COLUMNIST WHO RAN THE LAKERS IN THEIR EARLY YEARS: "We paid Maury Winston $15,000 for the franchise in 1947. Bob Short bought the Lakers in 1957 for $150,000. He in turn sold them to Jack Kent Cooke in 1965 for $5.2 million. Cooke sold it to Jerry Buss in 1979 for $67.5 million."

By the mid 1990s, the franchise was escalating toward a worth of more than $300 million. *Los Angeles Times* columnist Mark Heisler projected that Buss and his associates annually pulled as much as $40 million in profit from the team, the Forum, and the associated sports ventures. How had the franchise maintained this lofty perch over the years? By having star players and winning championships, a mix of star quality that attracted Hollywood's and the world's interest.

The tentative nature of that formula had made itself known since Magic Johnson's first retirement. "Since I came here in 1960," West said at the time, "the Lakers have always had one or two players that have been at the top of the league in talent. In perpetuating this franchise, our next move is, where do we find another one of those guys?"

Admitting that any franchise would be lucky to have one Magic Johnson in a lifetime, West nevertheless became obsessed with finding the next great one, "that one unique player who can get through the tough losses and come back and compete the next night. Those players are rare in this league. They'll play hard every night. They'll play in every building. They'll play in every circumstance. That kind of person is the most difficult to find."

Seeing the athletic talent would be easy, he said. The hard part would be identifying what couldn't be seen. He knew this would be nearly impossible, particularly when he didn't see it in Johnson the first time around.

JERRY WEST: "I felt he would be a very good player. I had no idea he would get to that level. No idea. But see you don't know what's inside of people. You can see what they can do physically on the court. The things you could see about Magic, you loved. But you wondered where he was gonna play in the NBA. But just through hard work he willed himself to take his game to another level. I don't think anyone knew he had that kind of greatness in him."

Identifying that player, seeing the unseeable, was just the first part of West's impossible task. After that, he had to manipulate the NBA's Byzantine personnel structure so that the Lakers could get the rights to that special player. That had become nearly impossible with the league's salary cap and expansion.

Despite his determination, that replenishing process had stalled as the franchise sorted through an array of players and coaches, trying to find a competitive mix. Meanwhile, the Lakers plodded through one unproductive season after another. While the situation stretched his patience, West busied himself by acquiring the finest complementary players he could find, so that he would have the pieces in place for adding the prize talent for which he was searching.

Finally, early in the 1996 off-season, Jerry West found that two very special opportunities presented themselves. Both a talented young amateur and the most impressive of veterans were available. But getting them would require a huge gamble, meaning that if he miscalculated, all of his hard work of the last five years would be wasted. It was a risk that would cost tens of millions, but after years of yearning to compete for a championship, both West and Jerry Buss were willing. That the two developments converged so nicely almost made them seem preordained.

The Art of the Deal

Because he was 17 and there were so many concerns about his suitability for NBA life, Philadelphia high school star Kobe Bryant agreed to perform an unusual number of workouts for teams as the 1996 draft appeared. He jetted from point to point on the NBA map, hoping to show teams just why they should take a chance on someone so young.

In Los Angeles, Bryant found an organization that immediately understood his potential. His workout left West raving. The Lakers scouting staff may have questioned Bryant's willingness to involve teammates, but West watched him move and shoot during the workout, then saw him battle assistant coach and former Laker defensive star Michael Cooper. There was length, there was strength, there were physical talents, but to go with them was a beautifully polished set of skills, the kind of skills that a 17-year-old could possess only after long hours of dedicated work. The skills themselves said much about the issue of work ethic and that hardest-to-read factor, the player's heart. It was the single best workout West had ever seen. "He has the potential to be an All-Star," he excitedly told people within the organization.

BILL BERTKA, LONGTIME LAKERS ASSISTANT COACH, SCOUT: "It was the first time in the history of the franchise that we'd ever had anyone as young as Kobe. I can remember the day that we worked him out at the Inglewood YMCA. As soon as the workout was over, Jerry West said, 'This guy's special. He's very special even though he's a high school player.'"

KOBE BRYANT: "At that point I really didn't think Jerry West liked kids coming out of high school coming into the NBA."

There didn't seem to be much of an immediate opportunity for Bryant to become a Laker. His father, Joe Bryant, had done his research and figured that his son would go somewhere in the top 15 picks. The Lakers were drafting much lower than that.

Unbeknownst to the Bryants, a very large development was already bringing a shift in the course of events. Shaquille O'Neal had grown disenchanted with his team, the Orlando Magic, and had filed for free agency. At 7–1, 330 pounds, he presented an intimidating package of strength and athletic ability and seemed certain to net an offer worth tens of millions as a free agent.

Some observers were stunned that O'Neal would think of leaving Orlando and the opportunity to play with gifted young guard Anfernee "Penny" Hardaway. ESPN declared that there was no way O'Neal would be foolish enough to go, because playing in Orlando presented the best opportunity to win championships.

Other observers, though, began to question the Magic's chemistry. There were whispers that Hardaway's immensely successful "Li'l Penny" marketing campaign had created a persona so large that it crimped even O'Neal's style.

Another factor was his team's losses in the '95 and '96 playoffs. In Orlando, it was O'Neal, not Hardaway, the coaches, or his teammates, who bore the pressure for those losses, both sweeps. In '95, the Magic fell 4–0 to Houston in the NBA Finals. In '96, it was the Bulls who took them 4–0 in the Eastern Conference championship series. O'Neal wept after both of those series, the only times in his life he had cried over basketball other than a loss in the state championship game his junior year that abruptly wiped out an unbeaten season.

The losses, the negative publicity in Orlando, his rumored differences with coach Brian Hill, his ill feelings about Magic management, all contributed to his decision to opt for free agency.

Much later, O'Neal himself would pinpoint a perceived lack of support from Orlando management in his having to deal with what he saw as negative media.

SHAQUILLE O'NEAL: "The media in Orlando are very small-minded. Very stupid. For example, when I was having a baby, instead of asking me, you know, who the girl was—it was my girlfriend for five years, and we were planning on getting married—they tried to flip it. They asked, 'Is it a white girl?' Stupid shit like that. 'Is it a girl he met on the road?' they asked. 'Is it a whore? Is it a stripper? Because we know those guys go to strip clubs.' Just stupid shit like that. Nobody upstairs [in the team's front offices] really ever stuck up for me. I did the Shaq's dinner for the city. I went to the hospitals to visit children, gave kids clothes. I did a lot for the city on my own. Nobody upstairs ever said, 'Leave Shaq alone.' They treated me like I was one of those young prima donnas that was always getting in trouble, drinking and driving, doing drugs, bullshittin' around. And I wasn't. I was a model athlete."

Whether Orlando management could have exercised much power over the media wasn't clear. What was clear was that the Lakers were a team with a history of taking special care of players. West, in particular, had been a superstar himself. He knew the pressures, the misunderstandings, the problems that players of stature face. It could be argued that no NBA executive went to the effort that West did to protect and nurture young stars.

Then there was the Lakers tradition. Their Hollywood affiliations, their aura in the Forum were real attractions to O'Neal. Working in Los Angeles meant he could take advantage of the Hollywood connections to his off-court interests, his rap music production and feature film making.

West and his staff saw that they had a shot at signing O'Neal but that it could cost them as much as $100 million, a figure large enough to frighten off most suitors. The situation left West struggling to find room under the salary cap to sign the big center.

"If you have to give up your entire team for a cornerstone player such as Shaquille you'd consider it," West said.

It soon became clear that he could have a shot at both players, Kobe Bryant and O'Neal, if he could trade Lakers center Vlade Divac and his $4 million salary to Charlotte for the rights to Bryant. The only problem with that strategy was that the Lakers would be sunk if they traded their center for Bryant only to later discover they couldn't swing the final deal for O'Neal. Besides, Divac had been a Laker for seven seasons and in that time he had evolved into one of the best centers in the game and a fan favorite. Without hesitation, West and Buss pulled the trigger on the trade.

"It really was a gamble," Jerry Buss said at the time. "We could have been left high and dry. We laid it out there and could have lost just as easily. From the time we traded Vlade we were out on a limb. We were either going to be very sorry or ecstatic."

West figured he would have to come up with a $95 million offer to get his prize. But ultimately that would prove to be many millions short of what was needed. Buss, however, urged him to keep trying. To create more room under the salary cap over seven seasons, West practically gave away guard Anthony Peeler and reserve forward George Lynch, sending them to Vancouver.

"The Lakers could have folded," said O'Neal's agent, Leonard Armato. "They may have been on the verge of it a few times. But Jerry West wouldn't do that. He was Mr. Clutch as a player and again in these dealings."

The Orlando offer jumped to $115 million, then a little more. The anxiety climbed to unbearable levels for West and his staff. Buss, though, didn't blink. To push their offer to $123 million, they renounced seven players, including Magic Johnson and Sedale Threatt. Dumping their roster of players seemed to border on lunacy. If O'Neal stayed in Florida the Lakers would be forced to bring in a host of low-rated talent to fill the gap.

The Magic could have paid more to sign their own free agent, well above the Lakers' $123 million. But it became apparent that, as O'Neal claimed, money wasn't the key factor. Actually, the Orlando deal was frontloaded with as much as $20 million in cash the first year, but O'Neal looked west.

SHAQUILLE O'NEAL: "They're a basketball organization. When I made my decision to move, it wasn't on money, it wasn't on movies, it wasn't on rap. I just wanted to feel appreciated, that's all."

For the fourth time in the franchise's illustrious half century of history, the NBA's glamour team had managed to snare the game's most physically dominating presence by signing the 24-year-old O'Neal.

"Los Angeles, shorn of Magic Johnson and Wayne Gretzky, torn by earthquake, riot, and the murder case of the century, took a giant step in its comeback in the size 22-EEEEE shoes of Shaquille O'Neal," declared columnist Mike Downey in the *Los Angeles Times*.

"If this had gone much longer, we were dead," West, who bordered on nervous exhaustion following days of anxious maneuvering to get O'Neal, told reporters after announcing the deal. "To get this prize," he said, "I think is something that when I look back on history and the time that I've spent with this team, this might be the single most important thing we've ever done."

If his efforts had failed, the tightly wound Lakers executive said he might well have jumped out of the window of O'Neal agent Leonard Armato's high-rise offices.

A similar sentiment settled on the executive suites of the Orlando Magic. "I think he had a better chance to win here than in L.A." said Magic executive Pat Williams. "It came down to the aura of Los Angeles."

By moving from Orlando to Hollywood, O'Neal stepped into a long line of great Lakers centers, including George Mikan, Wilt Chamberlain, and Kareem Abdul-Jabbar. If nothing else, history had shown NBA teams just how important it was to have a dominant big man. More than 75 percent of the championships in league history had been won by clubs that relied on power games featuring big, bad post players. Having such a player was particularly important in Los Angeles, where marquee value ranked at the top of the food chain. Certainly O'Neal had plenty of that with a budding career as an actor, movie producer, and rap recording artist. But it was his backboard-shattering play in the post that mattered most to the Lakers.

With the team's tradition came the expectations in the Great Western Forum, where Hollywood stars paid $700 nightly for courtside seats to be entertained by basketball's best. With O'Neal's contract those ticket holders knew prices were headed up. Indeed, they would move up over $1,000 a game. The size of the deal brought an immediate gasp.

How, critics asked, could one player command so much money, particularly one with 54 percent free throw shooting in four NBA seasons? O'Neal's clunkers at the line had allowed opponents to defend his slam dunks with fouls that dared him to make the foul shots. This characteristic—and the fact that he never led his LSU club to an NCAA title—drove comparisons to Chamberlain's star-crossed career.

The Lakers did admit to being concerned about O'Neal's free throw shooting. O'Neal's perspective was that he had come to Los Angeles to team up with Kobe and Eddie Jones and Nick Van Exel and Elden Campbell, all of them young and talented and seemingly poised on the verge of greatness, immediately if not sooner.

That certainly was the hope in Los Angeles, where happy endings were concocted daily in the celluloid screening rooms of the film industry. Making them happen on the court, however, proved to be a bit more problematic.

14

Air Balls

Days after announcing that he would go to the NBA directly from high school, Kobe Bryant signed a promotional contract worth approximately $10 million with Adidas, the shoe and clothing giant. Jerry West and his staff, meanwhile, engaged in a bit of fretting over how the organization would deal with having an 18-year-old in the fold. Having seen what the Hollywood life had done to Magic Johnson, the Lakers tried to think of ways of softening his adjustment to pro life. But that proved to be very little of a problem initially. Shortly after their son's being drafted and traded to the Lakers, Joe and Pam Bryant packed up with younger daughter Shaya, who withdrew from LaSalle, and moved to Los Angeles to inhabit a six-bedroom seaside home in Pacific Palisades with Kobe. They were there to provide the support he needed in this period of adjustment to life in pro basketball.

From Bryant's first contact with the team, he presented an aloof front, leaving teammates to guess at exactly who he was. In his early days in Los Angeles, he accepted an invitation from O'Neal to go out to dinner.

KOBE BRYANT: "It was good. It was cool. I just didn't like to go out that much."

It wasn't a scenario that would be repeated. The 24-year-old O'Neal enjoyed the L.A. club scene and nightlife, something that held little appeal for his workaholic younger teammate. Instead, Bryant enjoyed time with his family, or spent hours alone in his new room. There, in his retreat filled with stereo equipment, video game gear, a computer and video monitors, he could study basketball to his heart's content or even write poetry. If he tired of his virtual nightlife, he could get up and gaze out on the silvery Pacific or cast his thoughts to the sparkling lights of L.A.

With a new rookie salary structure in place, he signed a standard three-year, $3.5 million contract with the team, then made a brief appearance on "The

Tonight Show" with Jay Leno. From there, his focus turned to playing for the Lakers' developmental team in the Fila Summer Pro League, one of several leagues that NBA teams use for summer work.

Many observers suspected that O'Neal's high-profile arrival in Los Angeles would help to obscure Bryant's introduction, thus taking some of the public pressure off the young rookie. But hopes of that evaporated with his first appearance at the Long Beach Pyramid, the 5,000-seat arena where the summer league held games. Usually there were plenty of empty seats, but his first night brought an overflow crowd, and 2,000 fans were turned away.

Larry Drew, former Lakers assistant coach: "I remember the first day he arrived, all the media and all the people that were there chanting his name. It was a packed house. The first day he came he didn't even get to dress to play, but there was a lot of electricity in the air about him being there."

Usually the Lakers used the league games to help prepare their rookies and young players for adjustment to the team.

Larry Drew: "In summer league, we normally get five or six days to practice and to get the players used to what we want to do. He came in right as the games were being played, so he was just kind of out there, kind of playing on instinct. He was like a little puppy let out of a cage. He was bouncing all over the place. Everybody could see that he was gonna be a special talent. You could see the swagger about his walk. He was a confident kid who didn't shy away, who had no fears about going against pro players."

The star quality that West and Jerry Buss were desperate to see made itself known immediately. He scored 27 in his first game, 36 in another, and over the four-game schedule averaged 25 points and five rebounds.

Kobe Bryant: "I felt that I could always do what I did in high school, that it wasn't that hard."

To do that, however, he would need playing time, which would require that Del Harris have as much confidence in him as Kobe had in himself. Harris, however, concluded that Kobe was a kid who needed a more realistic view of the team and his role in it.

Harris would later explain to some Lakers staffers that the team's manage-ment had given him directives that Kobe had to receive playing time in order to learn. The staff member got the distinct impression that Harris would have preferred to keep the 18-year-old on the bench.

DEL HARRIS, FORMER LAKERS COACH: "It was a tough growing up process for Kobe, but I let him work his way through the thing. I didn't give him any-thing, and I know that he resented me for that. Maybe one day he'll realize that that was the way it had to be. We already had a good team before he got there, and the other players on the team, they wanted to make sure he earned everything that he got, that the coach didn't just give him something because the fans wanted to see this young phenom play."

Regardless, Bryant's plans for immediate stardom suffered a setback. In early September he broke his wrist while playing an outdoor pickup game at Venice Beach.

DEREK FISHER: "The first thing I heard about Kobe was that he had injured his wrist playing at Venice. I just couldn't believe that a guy would be play-ing up at Venice Beach."

Publicly, some Lakers staffers offered admonishment for Bryant's stooping to play pickup ball. West, though, could see true passion in a player. "This guy will play in a Little League tournament," he said of Kobe. "It doesn't bother me. He loves to play basketball. He's one of the more dedicated players I've ever seen."

KOBE BRYANT: "I went up to tip dunk the basketball. The ball was bouncing on the rim and dropped in. I made the mistake of not holding onto the rim, grabbing the rim and coming down slowly. I just tried to back off in the air."

Fortunately, the injury didn't require surgery, but it meant that he wouldn't be ready for the opening of training camp in October. For a rookie to miss training camp was a huge blow, especially as the Lakers adjusted to their new center.

Complicating the situation was the fact that Bryant had no one position but was viewed as a combination of a point guard, an off guard, and a small forward and would play at all three positions during parts of the season. His size and quickness were the core of a tremendous versatility. Missing training camp meant that he would develop it at a slower pace. Beyond that, the camp brought an adjustment for rookies and veterans alike, now that the Lakers had their new post weapon.

TRAVIS KNIGHT, LAKER ROOKIE WITH BRYANT: "Everybody had to learn to play with Shaq, to face the basket and when to cut."

DEREK FISHER, LAKER ROOKIE WITH BRYANT: "That first day of training camp Kobe was injured and everything, but he still wanted to be out there, trying to do two-line layups and do everything that he possibly could to still be involved with practice and be a part of the group."

Establishing himself as part of the team was clearly important to Bryant, yet as time went on his teammates found that he kept them at a distance, answering questions about anything not related to basketball with one- or two-word replies. He seldom initiated any personal conversations at all, Fisher recalled, an approach that Kobe would maintain in the months and years that followed.

DEREK FISHER: "He really is to himself, so you don't know exactly how he feels. You don't know what makes him happy, what makes him sad. So it was hard for us early on to understand what he was going through, what he was trying to do, and that he was really trying to be a part of the team. But the way he played was just the way he knew how to play."

SHAQUILLE O'NEAL: "They knew what they were getting into. They should have nipped it in the bud in the beginning. I told them when he came, 'I'm not gonna be babysitting. I'm not gonna be arguing. I'm a man of few words.'"

As the situation wore on and the hard feelings deepened, Fisher decided that as a point guard he should try to break through to Bryant.

DEREK FISHER: "I just kind of started thinking that we possibly could be the backcourt of the future for this organization and that it was going to be really important for us to have some type of bond. We may not raise each other's kids and be godparents and do things like that for each other's families, but we have to have a working relationship. And that's when I kind of started. Even though he wasn't necessarily reaching out, I kind of started reaching out, trying to be more talkative, just trying to maybe spark conversation about anything just to get to know him a little better."

Over time, Fisher came to the conclusion that Bryant's silence was merely a defense mechanism. It was almost as if he feared that taking a more personal approach with his teammates might open him up to being swayed away from his dreams and his goals.

DEREK FISHER: "From day one, he knew the things that he wanted to accomplish in his career. Things that he's wanted to achieve, he already had that in mind. Because of his talent level, it's almost like a self-fulfilling prophecy for him. If he sees something, he can go and get it. Most other players, even most stars, didn't have that power."

From the very start, Kobe's Lakers teammates didn't know how to take his extremely high confidence, which was unusual for even a veteran player, much less an 18-year-old.

DEREK FISHER: "The more you experience time around him and get to see him in different situations, the more you understand that that's all it is, is confidence. It's not arrogance. It's not his personality. He's not a selfish person. He's not a guy that only thinks of himself. He's just a guy who has an immeasurable amount of confidence in his ability to play the game."

In the fall of 1996, however, that information wasn't available to his Lakers teammates. And later, even when it was available, some still struggled to see him as more than arrogant. Without question, Bryant's decision to have minimal personal relationships with his teammates would factor heavily into the team's chemistry for seasons to come and would serve to vex players, coaches, and staff members alike.

Clearly, though, Bryant's rookie season proved to be the best in terms of relationships with teammates. First, the Lakers had brought longtime veteran Byron Scott back to the team, and with his warm personality and vast experience he proved to be a solid mentor. Bryant wanted to soak up everything he could about Scott's days with Johnson and the Showtime Lakers.

KOBE BRYANT: "Byron told me how important it is during the season to keep your work habits. You have to keep working on your jump shot, your physical preparation. At this level, you always have to be working to improve your game or you'll get left behind."

It also helped that first year that Kobe had a friendship with Lakers guard Eddie Jones, whom he had first met five years earlier in Philadelphia. Then 23, Jones was heading into his third season with the Lakers after an outstanding start to his career. He had been ready with friendly advice when he learned Kobe was going to be his teammate.

KOBE BRYANT: "Eddie said I had to prepare myself mentally because L.A. can be very distracting."

O'Neal, too, stepped forward with a good-humored friendship. "There's clearly a looking-after-him attitude on this team," Kurt Rambis, a Lakers assistant that season, explained. But in time, each of those relationships would become strained by the circumstances. Bryant's intensity simply burned with an all-business approach.

DEREK FISHER: "That's why people really misinterpreted him a lot of times as a guy who really thinks only of himself."

In time, Bryant would be asked if he had any kind of personal relationship with any of his teammates. "Not really," he replied. "All that matters is what we do on the court."

Into the Breech

His injury finally healed, Bryant snared his first playing time that October 16 in a preseason game played in Fresno and responded with 10 points and five rebounds. Two nights later, the Lakers played their first game of the preseason in the Forum against Bryant's hometown 76ers, which certainly factored into his hyper approach. Late in the game, he tried to force a dunk and collided with Philly reserve center Tim Kempton. The impact sent Bryant plummeting to the floor and left him with a badly strained hip flexor and yet more down time.

It was obvious that Bryant took special delight in getting to the basket to dunk in the face of taller players, but in the aftermath, Eddie Jones advised him to ease up on trying to dunk so often and so spectacularly, especially when a three-foot bank would do the job. The hip flexor meant that he got no playing time in the home opener, a Lakers win over Phoenix. The next game, against Minnesota, he played briefly, had his shot blocked and racked up a turnover. "I'm sure he would have liked to make a more auspicious debut," Harris told reporters. "It's okay. We already know he can play."

Like most pro coaches, Harris took a wait-and-see approach with rookies. Bryant was no different, except that Harris took even more caution because of the age factor. Besides, the coach had plenty of other problems on his hands. Stripping the roster to get O'Neal meant that the team had undergone the largest single turnover of players in franchise history. Of the 16 athletes on the training camp roster only five—point guard Nick Van Exel, center Elden Campbell, forward Cedric Ceballos, forward Corie Blount, and Jones—had been Lakers the previous season.

As a result, Harris would spend most of the season searching for the right mix around O'Neal. The situation was further complicated by the fact that halfway through the schedule Ceballos was traded to Houston for Robert Horry. Then West added another veteran forward by trading for George McCloud.

EDDIE JONES: "That told us right there that we were serious about winning, about playing defense, when they traded for Robert Horry. Getting Robert was a big step in changing that team."

Indeed, Horry's presence would prove a huge factor over the coming years. Even with the headaches, the Lakers started 3–0, including an impressive road win over New York, the start of their first extended East Coast trip. But soon their losses would include unfathomable defeats at the hands of Toronto and Charlotte.

Of his team's problems, Del Harris said, "We're just totally out of rhythm offensively, and our execution is very weak. We don't set or use screens very well, and we have a tendency to bog down in our ball movement."

It would prove to be a blueprint for all that bothered the Lakers teams in the late 1990s. The other unspoken factor was that Harris didn't hold marvelously organized practices. Traditionally, the Lakers had been a franchise that prized practice, with Pat Riley conducting the sessions with a tightly packaged fervor. Yet even Harris's defenders would later concede that he had that old-style NBA attitude of just rolling out the ball for the veterans.

KOBE BRYANT: "A lot of times with Del people just did what they wanted. Guys wouldn't even practice at all."

The other side to that argument was that the NBA was never meant to be a league for developing talent. With a schedule that called for three or four games a week, there wasn't the time.

The circumstances presented a harsh reality that grew more worrisome to Bryant with each passing week. Over the course of the season, he would play in 71 games and average a little better than 15 minutes a game playing time, good enough to rank him only eleventh on the roster.

KOBE BRYANT: "My father told me, 'Your time will come.'"

Adapting

Despite the newness of their relationships, they found a groove that December of 1996, winning seven of their first eight games that month. O'Neal in the post presented a troubling problem for their opponents. At the point, left-hander Nick Van Exel displayed an unbridled bundle of moxie and quickness. Eddie Jones was a defensive terror on the wings. And Elden Campbell provided power and flexibility as either a forward or backup center.

Little did anyone realize at the time that this promising group would peak so short of expectations. In retrospect, they would come to be viewed as a misdirected lot, and when the members would later be shipped out of town one by one, the veteran sportswriters covering the team were happy to bid them good riddance.

The Lakers centered on the growth of Van Exel as a point guard. He had been forced to alter his game with the arrival of O'Neal as the 1997 schedule rolled by. The center knew that the development of his relationship with Van Exel would be a main key to the Lakers' championship potential.

SHAQUILLE O'NEAL: "When I first talked with him, he told me his goals. He said, 'Look, I don't care about scoring. I don't care about anything. I just want to lead the league in assists, and I want you to lead the league in scoring.'"

Then in his fourth NBA season, Van Exel's development had come at the constant pleading and fussing of Harris, leading to flashes of anger between the two. "They've got problems there with Nick and Del," former Laker George Lynch, who had been traded to the Grizzlies from the Lakers over the summer, had alleged in a Vancouver newspaper interview. "When you get in a tough game down the stretch, you've got to have your coach and your point guard get along. If they don't it's not going to work."

That season, the Dallas Mavericks had sought to trade point guard Jason Kidd for Van Exel, but it was Harris who didn't want to make the trade because he didn't think Kidd could shoot nearly as well as Van Exel. Later, the failure to make that deal would leave some Lakers insiders shaking their heads.

Harris, though, seemed to relish the challenge of making Van Exel harness his game to blend with O'Neal. It was the same transformation that he hoped to see Bryant make, once playing time became available.

Van Exel admitted that the offense had sputtered during the team's adjustment to playing with O'Neal. "I think at times we're too stagnant," the point guard said. "Everybody is standing around and watching when we throw the ball into the post. There's no movement. Everybody's watching to see what the big guy's gonna do. Then there are a lot of times when we're just careless with a lot of turnovers."

That assessment would become a refrain among Lakers players over the coming months. The circumstances would trouble no one more than Bryant, who wanted playing time badly only to realize once he got that playing time that he was trapped in a stagnant offense. Early in the season, O'Neal had taken to calling Bryant "Showboat" because of his flashy offensive play.

MITCH CHORTKOFF, VETERAN L.A. SPORTSWRITER: "When they played Sacramento, Kobe stole the ball from Billy Owens, looked around, saw nobody was near him, so he did a 360-spin for a dunk. That brought the crowd to its feet. That's an example of why Shaq made up the name "Showboat." The night before, Kobe blocked a shot by Mitch Richmond at the end in a close game, and then at the other end the Lakers missed, but Kobe got the rebound with his back to the basket and put it back in over his head."

Chortkoff pointed out that Bryant had a key turnover that cost the Lakers in a game against Portland, which made Harris anxious about playing him. Chortkoff had advised Harris that he would just have to live through those things as Bryant developed.

KOBE BRYANT: "My rookie year I had no clue. I figured it would work out and I would realize my dream, but I didn't know how. I kept thinking about it all the time and wondering, 'How? How is it going to happen? How are the pieces going to fall in place?'"

What wore on him most was Harris's seeming inconsistency. Kobe would play well and just when it seemed like he would get more time, Harris would hold back.

KOBE BRYANT: "I felt like I was playing with one hand tied behind me. One of the hardest things was not knowing whether you're going to play or how many minutes you're going to play."

Since childhood he had been used to five-star hotels and in-room dining, so the hermitlike existence of an NBA rookie seemed to his liking, as long as room service could deliver the apple pie à la mode he craved. On buses and the team plane, he read or tuned the world out by stuffing his head between earphones.

There were other adjustments for an 18-year-old in the land of big paychecks. One of the most challenging was Los Angeles itself. "Because of the lifestyle," he explained. "With there being so many distractions."

Asked about off-court entanglements, he said, "Sure the groupies come after you. Living in L.A., how could you not be approached by women like that? They tend to be older, but some are younger. You have to handle it in a professional manner. I've learned all about that growing up."

Setback

In Orlando, O'Neal had acquired a reputation for shirking team leadership, but in his first months in Los Angeles his coaches and teammates saw little evidence of that.

Del Harris: "He was a better leader than I was informed. Again, maybe that was because he was young. Perhaps it was a function of maturing, but whatever, he was a nice leader on our team."

Yet, just as the young team was making progress in its adjustment to playing with O'Neal, the center missed 30 games with knee injuries. Suddenly the team had to shift back to its old identity, built around Elden Campbell on offense and its pressure defense. The situation expanded Bryant's role only slightly. Even so, he still had found a means of reaching the spotlight, in snowy Cleveland of all places.

He, Travis Knight, and Derek Fisher had all been invited to play in the rookie game at the NBA's annual winter carnival, the All-Star Weekend. What made the 1997 event so special was the fact that the league was celebrating its 50th anniversary that weekend and honoring the game's 50 greatest players over its first half century. The rookie game presented an opportunity for young players to show their stuff before the game's legends, and Bryant took every advantage during the 30-minute exhibition. Philadelphia's Allen Iverson used his quickness to score 19 and led the East team to victory. But Bryant led the charge from the West with 31 points, many of them delivered with his trademark flash.

About an hour after the rookie game he was scheduled to participate in the Slam Dunk contest. First devised as an attraction during the last ABA All-Star game in 1976, the event had been revised by the NBA in 1984 and was used to showcase some special high flying by Jordan, Dominique Wilkins, and a host of other players. The league selected an All-Star panel of judges that included Julius Erving, Walt Frazier, and George Gervin. Bryant's sense of the game's history gave him more than a little extra buzz for the event. His nervousness apparent, Bryant barely the made the round of four finalists for the event, but from there he trotted out a spectacular finish, good enough to claim the slam dunk trophy. From the left side he attacked the basket, switched the ball between his legs and whirled in to find the rim, a finish that ignited the building, bringing Dr. J and the other judges to their feet. The event only raised more questions about the weapon Harris was keeping on the bench.

Del Harris: "We brought him along a little slowly during the regular season—very slowly, actually—because we had a 50-plus win team and he did not have training camp and was injured twice. But his progress was gradual and obvious and definite."

Finally, over the final weeks of the regular season Harris let him play a little and Bryant responded by averaging 11 points per game. Still, it was too little too late in the eyes of Kobe's family and friends. Strangely, Harris chose the playoffs to shove the young rookie into pressure situations with the season on the line. Bryant himself would never complain about the circumstances. He was glad for every opportunity to learn. But Jeremy Treatman, one of Bryant's high school coaches, watched the situation unfold and was dumfounded.

JEREMY TREATMAN: "It was almost like Del Harris was setting him up to fail. He hardly played him during the year, then put the ball in his hands with the season on the line."

O'Neal returned from his knee injury April 11 and immediately helped the Lakers to four straight wins, bringing L.A.'s record to 56–26, their best record in seven seasons. With O'Neal scoring 46 points in Game 1, the Lakers quickly took control of their first-round playoff series against Portland, then did the same thing in Game 2. It was obvious the Blazers had no means of contending with O'Neal and fell by the wayside, 3–1.

The next round brought the veteran Utah Jazz, routinely a tough matchup for the young Lakers, but in their late season run the Lakers had dispatched the Jazz 100–98 with 39 points from O'Neal. The outcome was enough to give Harris and his staff hope that they could turn the circumstances around in the playoffs. The Jazz, though, wasted little time in dispelling those notions with a 93–77 win in the Delta Center. For Game 2, the Lakers managed to mix their post and perimeter games, with O'Neal scoring 25 and Robert Horry finding his range with seven consecutive three-pointers. The effort earned the Lakers a shot to win it at the buzzer, but Karl Malone blocked Van Exel's shot for a 103–101 win and a 2–0 series lead.

Game 3 in the Forum brought a Lakers blowout, 104–84, fueled by 17 fourth-quarter points from Bryant. In all, he would finish with 19 for the game, the team high. He made 13 of 14 free throws, a tremendous display of poise down the stretch for an 18-year-old.

Unfortunately, the afterglow lasted only briefly. Malone answered furiously in Game 4, scoring 42 points to give his team a 3–1 series lead with the venue returning to Utah. There, in Game 5, the Jazz jumped to an 11-point lead and seemed set to cruise. The Lakers had lost Horry to a third-quarter ejection, weakening their defense. Still, they managed to roll back into contention and even held a one-point lead with about nine minutes to play. From there the lead shifted back and forth until O'Neal fouled out with just under two minutes to go. Then Utah's John Stockton managed to blow past Bryant for a tying layup.

With the score knotted at 87 with just under a minute left in regulation, the teams went into a final flurry of fruitless possessions. Eddie Jones had a shot blocked, Malone missed a jumper. Then with 11 seconds to go Van Exel got a steal, which set up a last possession for Los Angeles. During the ensuing time-out, Harris decided that the ball and the shot should go to Bryant. The plan? Spread the floor and let him attack.

Questioned repeatedly about the decision later, the coach explained that Bryant's one-on-one skills made him the best choice to get off a solid shot. "I spent over half of the year being criticized for not playing Kobe," Harris said. "Now I'm getting criticized for playing him."

According to plan, Bryant got the shot, a decent look at the basket from 14 feet, with the defense in his face and the Delta Center crowd pounding down the noise. The building exploded when it fell an air ball. Overtime would only extend his nightmare. With O'Neal out of the game and with an offense that offered little structure or little plan, the Lakers found themselves putting the extra period in Kobe's hands. Each of his three deep air balls goosed the home crowd to delight. The loss sent the Jazz on their way to the conference championship and effectively ended Phase 1 of Kobe Bryant's NBA education. After the debacle, he sat quietly for a time, composed himself, then answered reporters' questions. Sure it hurt, but he would keep the memory as motivation, he said.

"He's a young guy, and this is all new to him," Stockton told reporters. "He's played with a lot of confidence in this series, but he was asked to make some tough shots at the end, and he just didn't come up with them."

DEL HARRIS: "I'd give him that shot again, then, now, and forever. First of all, at that stage in Nick's career you don't put him up against John Stockton.

He wouldn't have been able to get it, at that point. We couldn't even get him open to get the ball in to him when Stockton was guarding him. Eddie Jones had had the last two shots. I wasn't going to go that direction again because they might be expecting it. They had blocked his last shot. I thought, 'Well, they'll be looking for Eddie again, and they won't be looking for Kobe. They won't think that Kobe will get this shot.' The score was tied, and I was saying that the most important thing with six seconds to go was to get a shot. Now, if it goes in, he's gonna know that I believed in him when he was an 18-year-old kid. If it doesn't go in, he's still gonna know I believed in him, and we're gonna go to overtime and we'll see what happens. He got a shot. I've seen hundreds of times in that situation where a team doesn't even get it inbounds, much less get a good shot. He got a 17-foot open look off that right elbow. I can still see it. It just didn't go."

15

When Trust Was Spent

The Boston Celtics gambled during the 1997 off-season and released Rick Fox, their versatile team captain, with hopes they could sign him later. But the Cleveland Cavaliers rushed in and offered Fox better than $20 million, the riches of a lifetime. He stunned all of basketball by turning them down and taking a deal with the Lakers that paid him a mere $1 million a season.

RICK FOX: "They wanted me to wait three months, but then Cleveland offered me all that money. I just wanted to see how the other side did it. I had grown up in the '80s, when the Celtics and the Lakers were what basketball was all about, that championship excitement. After Larry Bird and Kevin McHale retired, the Celtics had gone on a slide for five years as an organization that left me wanting a change, wanting to win. When I looked out here to the West, I saw Shaq and a group of talented young guys to grow with. I took what everyone thought was a risk beyond being sensible about your life. I guess it was, but I was happier making a million dollars for two years."

Fox's decision was made easier by the presence of Jerry West in the Lakers' front office.

RICK FOX: "Jerry, having been Mr. Laker and Mr. NBA for his career, represented everything I wanted to be a part of. He would do everything he could to convince his owner to put the players on the floor to win a championship. He spent every waking hour thinking about how he could make the Lakers better. I knew that if I joined a team where the general manager was as committed and focused as he was, then eventually something positive was going to happen."

West liked Fox, a University of North Carolina product, because of his complete skills. He was bulky, but could shoot, pass, defend, rebound, and even work off the dribble a bit. Plus Fox had a little age on him at 28, something the Lakers needed. Their roster boasted the youngest team in the league, with Bryant at 19, Van Exel and O'Neal at 25, Derek Fisher at 23, and Jones at 26.

The well-spoken Fox, already a working actor, figured living in Los Angeles would boost his film and TV career, not to mention his love life. He would soon marry entertainer Vanessa Williams. He joined Shaquille O'Neal, Kobe Bryant, Nick Van Exel, Eddie Jones, Elden Campbell, Robert Horry, Derek Fisher—all of them in place just one year after the wild maneuvering to sign O'Neal. Yet it proved to be a gnarly mix of egos, playing styles, and experience levels, all pushed along by O'Neal's giant dissatisfaction.

RICK FOX: "I don't think we could have been more talented. Sometimes talent will overshadow the experience that's needed."

The young Lakers didn't know how to play together to win. As the young giant of the game, O'Neal faced the same type of expectations thrust upon Wilt Chamberlain four decades earlier, only now those expectations seemed magnified by exhaustive media coverage.

JERRY WEST: "What surprised me about Shaquille during his early days in Los Angeles was how frustrated he got. He was not fun to be around. The shortcomings of our team and his teammates made him angry because he knew he was going to be judged on how much he won."

Much of that frustration found its target in Bryant, but he wasn't the sole focus for O'Neal's anger. Van Exel and Eddie Jones both felt the center's fire. Part of O'Neal's anger could have been self-directed, but it wasn't. He possessed amazing power but had never made the full effort in developing his offensive game.

HERB WILLIAMS, LONGTIME NBA PLAYER: "I felt his power a couple of times when he was just a kid down in Orlando. And I used to tell Patrick [Ewing], 'Let me tell you something, once this kid learns how to score over the top with either a jump hook or a turnaround jump shot that he can hit on a pretty consistent basis, you can shut it down, because the game's over.' Back then he had to get beside you or around you to dunk it. He was limited by that. But once he learned to score over the top, you could forget it.

You couldn't play him. He's too agile. A guy his size, as mobile as he is, it's almost unfair."

SHAQUILLE O'NEAL: "I began learning that in Orlando. I kept developing it in Los Angeles. That changed my game a lot."

Until his skills and his team developed, O'Neal presented a substantial challenge for any coach.

RICK FOX: "Getting it together sometimes is easier than making it all work. A great general manager such as Jerry West putting together a team that you perceive to be a championship team, it may not always equate to that. A lot of that has to do with the coaching of the talent, and the individuals' understanding how sacrifices have to be made from the individual standpoint. The team has to come first."

Given the opportunity, Del Harris would have slowed things down for Bryant's second NBA season, but the playoff embarrassment had spurred the player to work even harder over the summer of 1997.

The effort began with his flight home from Utah after the Lakers' Game 5 exit and Bryant's passel of air balls. He was up the next morning in the gym, shooting shot after shot, attacking the visualization of his failure. He also reviewed the end of Game 5 at Utah, the 17-foot air ball, and asked himself why hadn't he just gone to the basket and torn the rim down with a jam or forced the Jazz to foul.

"I can beat that buzzer anytime," he told himself, "gimme the ball in the last 10 seconds, I can wait till decimal time, I'll still hurt you, tick, tick, tick, tick . . ."

Later, as training camp opened, he would have to view the sequence again. He laughed at it. The only thing that would have hurt, he later told a reporter, is if he had chickened out and passed the ball, if he had not taken that pressure on himself.

DEREK FISHER: "I remember being very disappointed in the decision to put him in that position, not because I didn't think he was capable of doing it. I felt that Nick Van Exel would have been a better choice if you had to pick one guy. The thing I remember most vividly is Shaquille basically putting his arm over Kobe's shoulder and talking to him as we walked off the court, telling him there'd be another day."

Bryant knew the great ones wanted the ball at the end of the game. Jordan had set a standard for that. Soon it would become common belief that he wanted to be the next Jordan.

NICK VAN EXEL: "I gave him a highlight tape of Mike, and I ain't seen it yet."

Over the first few months of the 1997–98 season it would become clear that Bryant had spent quite a bit of time studying the tape, because he had just about all of Jordan's moves down pat, even the famous post-up gyrations where Jordan would twitch and fake his opponents into madness. "He's got a lot of 'em," Jordan himself would admit later.

A lot of Lakers fans had come to the same conclusion and wanted to see Harris play him more. The Lakers coaching staff, however, wanted Bryant's thinking to run in another direction during the 1997 off-season. He was directed to again play for the Lakers team in the L.A. summer league, where he was told to put his focus on improving as a team player and learning where to send the ball when he drew double-teams. Larry Drew again coached the team, and Kobe again turned to his instincts, using his superior conditioning to blow past the competition. Neither Drew nor West liked what he saw. On one occasion Bryant crossed words with Drew, who accused him of "playing like the old Kobe." Bryant's main reluctance in following the Lakers plan was that he didn't trust Del Harris's offense and was never quite sure what to make of Harris himself.

KOBE BRYANT: "I decided just to leave it alone. He was the coach."

Harris, though, faced increasing questions about his young player. "It causes a rift between us because I'm trying to get him to give up the ball, and he feels that his game is to take on the world," Harris told reporters.

DEL HARRIS: "The other players on the team, they wanted to make sure he earned everything that he got, that the coach didn't just give him something because the fans wanted to see this young phenom play. They all knew that he could have been playing more, that he could have done more. But I made him earn every minute he got. I did that for his own good, and I did it really so the players, I thought, would respect me for being that way. I don't know that it worked out that way."

Bryant was aware that he needed to fit better within the team, but his efforts to do that were often frustrated by turnovers. He considered the offense unorganized. The ball usually went first to O'Neal in the post. If the center was impossibly double-teamed, he then sent it back out to the perimeter, where things often seemed to break down for the Lakers.

And there was another factor. Like a young Jordan, Bryant always considered himself the best opportunity for his team to score. The Lakers staff considered it a habit that needed breaking.

Bryant, however, saw it as much more than a habit. He saw it as the essence of who he was as a basketball player, and that was why he vowed, "I will not let them break me."

For the time being, Bryant accepted that his station in life was to come off the Lakers bench and provide scoring whenever it was needed. Harris had given up on the notion of using him as a backup point guard and decided his minutes would come spelling Eddie Jones at the two guard, or as a backup to Rick Fox at the small forward.

The regular-season schedule opened with the Lakers entertaining Utah, and Bryant entertaining the crowd. He scored 23 in a confidence-boosting win. But he didn't play up to Harris's team standards in the next two games, both wins. It wasn't until the fourth game, yet another win, that he broke out again with 25 points against Golden State. A late ankle sprain kept him out of action for a three-game road trip to Texas, where the Lakers racked up three more wins, bringing their start to seven straight victories. Bryant returned for a romp over Vancouver, then put the exclamation mark on the month in his team's first visit back to Utah since the playoff debacle. This time he blocked a three-point attempt by Utah's Bryon Russell in the closing seconds and sailed in for the clinching dunk. With that, the Lakers were 9–0, and Bryant was the talk of the NBA, a buzz that sizzled among the local media in every city the Lakers visited as Thanksgiving came and went and November gave way to December.

"I don't want to sound blasphemous," Kings director of player personnel Jerry Reynolds told reporters, "but he really can be like Jordan."

The Lakers had run their record to 11–0 when O'Neal pulled an abdominal muscle against the Clippers, an injury so painful that it would keep him out for weeks. Suddenly the team needed Bryant's scoring even more, and he was so happy to oblige, upping his average to better than 19 a game, big numbers for a nonstarter. The Lakers, though, saw a dip in their fortunes as they adjusted to O'Neal's absence. Their 11–0 start soon sagged to 15–5. It was obvious that Bryant was too aggressive many times, too far away from team concepts. "I don't think he's aiming for triple-doubles yet," Rick Fox told reporters in reference to Kobe's paucity of assists. "He definitely sees himself as a scorer."

Looming on the schedule was a road trip to the Midwest and a matchup with Jordan, a development that boosted the buzz about Bryant into a small-scale media frenzy. The matchup attracted reporters from virtually every magazine and news show, all of them sensing some sort of coronation.

How would Bryant do matched up against Jordan?

While the outcome was a 20-point win for the Bulls, the contest between master and student generated a few sparks. Jordan scored 36, and Bryant produced a career-high 33. It was a night for highlight clips with both players dancing in the post, draining jumpers from the perimeter, and weaving their way to handsome dunks.

"I felt like I was in the same shoes of some of the other players I've faced," Jordan explained. "He certainly showed signs that he can be a force whenever he's in the game. He has a lot of different looks. As an offensive player, you want to give a lot of different looks, so that the defense is always guessing."

Jordan pointed out that just like himself as a young talented player, Bryant had to learn to make sure that his "taking over" didn't take away from team effort.

"Man, that's the hardest part about ball," Bryant agreed, saying that the urge to challenge Jordan individually was gigantic. He admitted that the power to score was something he had to learn to control. "You have to just hold it back sometimes," he said.

The buzz of the Chicago game begat headlines which begat a bubbling pot of interest in Kobe Bryant. That, in turn, translated into All-Star votes. Dennis Scott, then playing for the Dallas Mavericks, had told reporters that within a matter of a couple of years Bryant "could be the man of this league."

Hundreds of thousands of fans agreed with that assessment as the votes for the All-Star game stacked up in the final days of December. It would prove to be an unprecedented response, with fans choosing a 19-year-old substitute as an All-Star starter. With their votes, the fans said they preferred Kobe's potential to the accomplishments of a whole range of established veterans, including Sacramento's Mitch Richmond, Utah's Jeff Hornacek, Houston's Clyde Drexler, Dallas' Michael Finley, and the player who started in front of Bryant on the Lakers, Eddie Jones. Before Bryant's election to the game, the youngest All-Star starter in league history had been a 20-year-old Magic Johnson.

Clearly, it helped his cause that the Lakers were a team afire, even without O'Neal. Coming out of the Chicago loss, L.A. won four straight with Bryant leading the team twice in scoring with 19 points. After a loss to the Celtics, the Lakers ripped through another streak of five wins against one loss. By the first of January, O'Neal had returned, sending Bryant back down the Lakers' list of offensive priorities. Regardless, they rolled through January at a 9–4 pace with O'Neal averaging 29 points a game and earning NBA Player of the Month honors.

Once the Western Conference coaches had decided the substitutes, the Lakers found themselves with four All-Star representatives, with Van Exel, Jones, and O'Neal joining Bryant on the roster. Held at New York's Madison Square Garden, the 48th NBA All-Star game opened its publicity assault by drawing hundreds of media representatives from around the world to a hotel ballroom for the opening interview sessions on Friday afternoon. Each All-Star player was positioned at a table around the massive ballroom, but it was Bryant's table that immediately attracted a major throng of reporters, all squeezing in around him to videotape or record his comments.

"Kobe has taken the league by storm," Orlando's Anfernee Hardaway said as he watched reporters crowding around the Bryant table.

"All this is incredible," Bryant said into the bank of microphones in his face. "My body's numb. My heart's racing. I don't know what to think. It's cool."

It seemed as if overnight, Bryant's image was everywhere. In full-page newspaper ads promoting the All-Star Weekend and its broadcast events. On magazine covers and international news feeds. On cable sports shows.

Then, on Sunday morning before the game, he appeared on "Meet the Press" with NBA commissioner David Stern and other players. And later when NBC broadcast a promotion for an upcoming Lakers/Rockets game, it was Bryant's image, not O'Neal's, that got top billing.

Watching the swirl of Bryant mania, Detroit's Grant Hill shook his head. "It makes you mature fast," he said. "It's good, but it's also a curse."

Starting the game matched up against Jordan, Bryant flashed his creativity with an array of first quarter aerials that included a 360-degree slam and an alley-oop dunk on back-to-back possessions. Jordan replied with a pair of fallaway jumpers, one of which caught Bryant in a fake and earned an added free throw.

"I came down being aggressive," Bryant told the assembly of reporters afterward. "He came back at me being aggressive. That's what it's all about. I can use it for my knowledge in the future. He hit those two turnarounds. I was like, 'Cool, let's get it on.'"

Bryant's enthusiasm for the individual matchup, however, was not something that pleased Seattle coach George Karl, who was in charge of the West team. Bryant also left Karl Malone fussing by motioning him off when the Utah veteran stepped up to set a screen. Also in that third period, Bryant dropped in a three-pointer to pull the West within 12 points. At the end of the quarter, the East held a 101–91 edge. In the personal showdown, Jordan had 17 points, 3 rebounds, and 4 assists in 24 minutes. Bryant's numbers were 18 points, 6 rebounds, and 1 assist in 22 minutes. It was Karl, however, who promptly ended the battle by benching Kobe for the entire fourth period while Jordan continued playing to claim Game MVP honors with 23 points, 6 rebounds, 8 assists, and 2 turnovers, all good enough to propel the East to a 135–114 victory.

Later, some West veterans expressed surprise that Karl kept Bryant out of the game. Others pointed out that Karl was known for using the All-Star setting to teach young players a lesson. In 1994, the Seattle coach had sent a swarming defense at Shaquille O'Neal, then playing for the East, to prevent him from having an impact on the game. Such a defensive effort was highly unusual for the All-Star game, and it left O'Neal fuming.

Asked about his decision to bench Bryant, Karl explained, "I thought we tried to be too entertaining." It was as if Karl and Del Harris were of one mind.

Harsh Lessons

The dark clouds wasted no time in descending on Bryant's career after the All-Star Weekend. The excitement and nonstop media interviews had left him exhausted, but there was no time for rest. The Lakers' first game after the break was in Portland, and Eddie Jones was out with the flu, meaning that Bryant would get his first and only start of the season. The Lakers immediately fell in a hole, then battled back to within four at halftime, only to see Portland open the third quarter with a 20–4 run to take a 117 to 105 win.

Although Bryant finished with 17, Harris was incensed at what he considered selfish play. Two nights later, back in Los Angeles, Jones remained ill, but Harris chose to start little-used Jon Barry rather than Bryant. Owner Jerry Buss appeared to be infuriated by the move and had heated words with Harris in front of reporters after the game, but the message got through clearly to Bryant.

Not surprisingly, the team as a whole also spiraled into trouble, losing seven out of the first dozen games on the schedule after the break. After the loss to the Blazers came disappointments against the Sonics, the Houston Rockets, and the Phoenix Suns. To make matters worse, Van Exel was sidelined by a knee injury on February 18th that required surgery.

Officially, Bryant became the backup at both guard positions. But his seemingly unshakable confidence began to quiver. Soon he began talking about "hitting the wall," the NBA term for when young players reach a level of physical, mental, and emotional exhaustion. In one stretch he made just 30 of 100 shots, setting in motion what *Sports Illustrated* described as "the first rumblings of an anti-Kobe backlash."

The end of that February brought the Lakers an East Coast road trip in which he shot terribly, going 3 for 12, 1 for 8, 4 for 12, and 4 for 15 from the field through one four-game run. "This is the toughest stretch I've ever gone through," he said at the time. "I'm hating it, but I'm loving it. It's part of the challenge."

Yet even his optimism irritated teammates. O'Neal, in particular, continued to point out that he wanted to win a championship immediately and didn't have time to wait on Bryant to grow up.

DEL HARRIS: "I felt like the NBA and NBC used him to his detriment. He was a willing participant, but when he came back, he was more one-on-one oriented."

KOBE BRYANT: "I wanted eventually to be one of the best players in the league. I just didn't know that other people would urge me to be that right away. Everybody was expecting me to be the next Michael. I thought I was going to sneak through the back door."

DEL HARRIS: "I know it was hard for Kobe, when he was just 18 and 19 playing for me, to come off the bench and not be a starter on our teams. We won 56 and 61 games when he was 18 and 19, and Shaq was 24, 25. I told him at that time that his day would come, that he was going to be a special player. I knew that, and he knew that. But being young and competitive, he wanted it right then. We just couldn't work it that way. Eddie Jones and Nick Van Exel and Rick Fox were ahead of him. Having said that, there were a number of times that I went to him for important shots because I knew that his day would come."

In a dozen different small ways, the Lakers season quickly fell into a finger-pointing session. Soon the L.A. papers were running stories that the players had met and voted 12–0 to ask that Harris be fired. The team downplayed those reports, but on their East Coast trip they had the look of a group about to come apart at the seams.

The Letter

Probably the most accurate assessment of Kobe Bryant's second NBA season could have been measured in Jerry West's stomach acid. Earlier in the campaign the team's guardian had negotiated to trade Eddie Jones to the Sacramento Kings for Mitch Richmond, a powerful two guard with a polished veteran game, the idea being that Richmond provided just the type of tough leadership and scoring that the young club needed. But Jerry Buss nixed the deal, pointing out that Richmond would soon be 34 and needing an expensive new contract.

Buss's decision was a bitter defeat for West, and as the season wore on and began to unravel he spent late nights agonizing at his Pacific Palisades home, poring over every detail of the season. He even went so far as announcing that he would step down as executive vice president by the end of the 1999 season. Sensing a coming transition, Buss began sending his son, Jim, on scouting missions with West and GM Mitch Kupchak.

Like many sports executives and their owners, West and Buss had always managed to survive the thorny aspects of their relationship. But as time wore on, it was clear that they shared many thorns and few roses. West thought he had Kupchak, a solid basketball mind, in place to groom as his successor, but the increasing presence of Jim Buss left him with the fear that a non-basketball executive could be poised to take over. West loved the game and loved the Lakers too much to see that happen.

As the playoffs approached, reporters speculated about his future, and West put them off by saying he wouldn't make a decision until August. "I want to get myself calmed down," he told them, "where I don't have to worry about wins and losses, where I don't have to worry about injuries. Let somebody else worry about that."

If the timing didn't seem right, the circumstances certainly did. The Lakers' talented but temperamental young roster was clearly high maintenance, so high that West had wearied from untangling their complaints about Harris and about each other. The game was simple enough, but they were all making it so complicated. He wanted to tell them "to not make the super play but the smart play. Not make the home run but hit a single. Make one pass that will lead to another pass that will lead to a basket instead of making one pass and a shot. Simple little things."

"I've had a number of players—and they were all young—say, 'I want to win an NBA championship,'" West confided to a reporter, "and I asked them, 'Do you know how difficult it is to win an NBA championship?'"

Clearly, as February became a chamber of horrors, these young players hadn't the slightest clue how to win. And West began to suspect that neither did Harris, at least not with this group.

"Talent and character win in this league; effort doesn't always win," he confided to *Los Angeles* magazine. "We win games sometimes when we're simply more talented. What I would like to see is for us to grow up more, become more professional in our approach to the game."

Wanting to tell them these things, he composed a letter to his young Lakers and delivered it to them soon after they returned in the early days of March from their trip East. "Each of you is on the verge of letting this season slip right through your fingers," he wrote. "You need to be thinking 'winning' 24 hours a day. You need to be consumed with Lakers pride. . . . You need to have personal pride in knowing that you are the best team players that you can be. . . . Only one team will be champion. . . . That team will be a machine that's fueled with compassion, desire, determination, drive, devotion, and pride. . . . That team could and should be the Lakers."

JERRY WEST: "I thought it was important for someone to make a statement to our players. I didn't want them to ever be accused of not giving their best, and my best guess, from watching the games and being objective, which was my job, was we weren't giving that."

Perhaps it was because he had never been a rah-rah guy that the note struck a chord. After their loss in Washington on March 2, the Lakers came home, read West's letter, and began winning. They started with six straight victories, then suffered a loss to Seattle, then healed it with another five straight wins. A loss to Utah punctured their euphoria at this turnaround, but they quickly jump-started another six-game winning streak, the bulk of which came on yet another trip to the Eastern Conference.

When it was over, they could look back on an amazing run of 22 wins against 3 losses. Better yet, they had surpassed West's hopes of a 60-win season with a 61–21 finish.

DEL HARRIS: "I know our players, when I was there, were really more concerned about pleasing Jerry than they were about pleasing me. I always knew when I was there I was coaching Jerry's team. It wasn't my team, and I knew the players were loyal to him. The proof of that is the night we won our 60th game, my last full year there, the headlines the next day were, 'West Might Retire.' And then on the second line, they had a little line that we had won our 60th game. To put that in perspective, no team won 60 games in 2001. It's not easy to win 60 games. The players were saying, 'If Jerry leaves, I'll leave. I don't know if I'll stay.' It should have been one of the highlight moments of my life, winning my 60th game. Instead, it was this other story. It wasn't a team event at all, and the players were saying they weren't sure if they wanted to be on the team."

Their record left them third best behind the 62 wins of the Utah Jazz and Chicago Bulls. But across the NBA there was an increasing chorus that the Lakers were poised to claim the league championship. They had been only the third team since the deployment of a shot clock in 1954 to lead the league in scoring while holding their opponents under 100 points.

All of this was accomplished with Bryant taking a remarkably low profile. Harris kept him on a short rope, using him as a defensive pressure point with Eddie Jones but always watching to yank him back to the bench if his offensive efforts displayed a hint of the Jordanesque. Even on that tether, he managed to finish the season with an impressive 15.2 points per game scoring average.

During the playoffs, an L.A. TV station would come up with the nifty idea of running a poll to see if fans thought the Lakers were better with or without Bryant. Fifty-five percent of the respondents said they were better without. Soon the subject was humming on talk radio and in newspaper columns. Sensing the opportunity, playoff opponents seized that notion and began talking it up. The idea had crossed Del Harris's mind long before.

In Game 1 of the Lakers' first-round series against Portland, Bryant scored 11 points down the stretch in the fourth quarter to forge a 104–102 victory. He hardly played the next two games before hitting for 22 in a blowout that sealed the series for Los Angeles.

Seattle, also a winner of 61 games, came next. Bryant hardly played in a blowout loss in Game 1. For Game 2, he had the flu and didn't play. The Lakers won, and three days later Harris decided that he would keep Bryant on the bench for Game 3.

KOBE BRYANT: "What people didn't realize is that I could have played in those games. Del just didn't want me to play. You never knew what he was going to do."

DEL HARRIS: "I know he felt he could have done more during those years, if I had allowed him to do more. And he could have. It's just that we didn't need that at that time. If we'd had a team in the lower half of the standings, then we would have opened it up more for him."

Game 3 brought yet another blowout win for the Lakers, leading Seattle's Sam Perkins to say that the Lakers didn't need Bryant, adding, "It seems like they're more at ease without him."

For Game 4 Harris played Bryant 3 minutes and then 11 minutes in Game 5 as the Lakers closed out the series.

KOBE BRYANT: "More than anything it made me so anxious, made me so hungry just to play every aspect of the game. I'd be sitting on the bench hearing the coaches say, 'Man, we've got to get some rebounds.' And it made me mad that I couldn't contribute. Besides seeing what the team was doing positively, it just made me hungry to go out there and help them any way I could."

With the win, Harris's team had advanced to the conference Finals to once again face the Utah Jazz. Before the series, the coach explained that the team was playing well and Bryant might see little playing time again. That wouldn't prove to be the issue. In Game 1, the Jazz jumped out to a 40–15 lead, and the Lakers' confidence plummeted. With no double-teams on O'Neal, the focus shifted to the Lakers perimeter players. Van Exel shot 28 percent for the series, Fisher 34.8 percent, Bryant 36.7 percent, Elden Campbell 21.4 percent, Horry 36 percent, and Fox 40 percent.

MITCH CHORTKOFF, VETERAN L.A. SPORTSWRITER: "Harris kept expecting the guards to warm up, but it never happened."

On defense, the Jazz executed the screen and roll to perfection.

NICK VAN EXEL: "We could never stop their offense. They ran it the way they wanted the whole series."

And the Lakers fell in four straight games.

The *Los Angeles Times* would reveal that during a practice leading up to Game 4, Van Exel committed an offense that finally erased what was left of team chemistry. As practice closed, the players moved in to clasp hands and break from their huddle. Instead of yelling the usual "Lakers!" on the break, Van Exel supposedly improvised and shouted, "Cancun," the implication being that he was ready for vacation.

Furious, O'Neal reported the incident to West and told reporters, "Guys have to find out what is important to them. If they don't want to play, then get off my team."

DEL HARRIS: "The day we got swept by Utah, Jerry Buss came in the offices and he said, 'Nick Van Exel and Elden Campbell have played their last games for the Lakers.' It turned out that was true on Nick. On Elden, it took them into the next season to trade him."

The sweep ignited speculation that Harris would be fired, but the coach had a year remaining on his contract at $1.1 million. The cash-strapped Buss couldn't afford to pay two coaches.

DEL HARRIS: "Buss told me, 'Don't feel bad, coach. You tried your best. I'd still rather had you coaching than anybody I've had. You're the best last-two-minutes coach I've ever had.'"

Harris, though, had hoped for a contract extension, and none was offered.

DEL HARRIS: "When I won 61 games, I had a year left on my contract, but Jerry Buss did not give me an extension. We had won 48, 53, 56, 61 games. I had never gotten a raise. I had never gotten an extension. I was Coach of the Year. They signed me to a two-year contract with a year at their option. They said, 'Oh, way to go, coach. By the way, we're gonna exercise our option.' But there was no raise or nothing."

Smack Daddy

The 1998–99 NBA season was delayed by an owner lockout, which closed down the league until a new collective bargaining agreement could be reached. The financial standoff between owners and players wasn't resolved until January 1999. Even as negotiators ironed out the final details of a new labor agreement, players from each team got together for informal sessions in advance of when their teams could officially begin practice.

In that spirit, Shaquille O'Neal, Derek Fisher, Corie Blount, and Bryant found themselves playing a little two-on-two in mid-January. It remained obvious that Bryant's struggles with his teammates the previous season had cut deep into their relationships. His basic strategy in dealing with the other Lakers was to talk as little as possible.

DEREK FISHER: "There were times you'd ask him a question, and he'd say yes or no. And that would be it. Other times he'd be a little more expressive. But Kobe did such a good job of never allowing people to know what's going on with him, how he's feeling or what he's thinking."

Fearing that continuing the cold relations would damage the team, Fisher had begun approaching Bryant during the 1998 off-season, using small talk as a way to get to know him better, because, after two years, Fisher knew very little about him.

DEREK FISHER: "I tried to find ways that we could just talk. Talk about things not even related to basketball, how his family was doing, things like that. I knew one of his sisters had gotten married and was pregnant. I'd ask how she was doing. He was fairly responsive."

Bryant viewed Fisher's efforts with a raised eyebrow. But in the off-season the two players sometimes trained at the same times and places. Bryant saw how hard Fisher was working on his shooting and his conditioning. And that in turn led him to feel more comfortable in January 1999 when the opportunity arose to play two-on-two with Fisher and Shaquille O'Neal and Blount. Since his days as a youngster battling his father one-on-one, Bryant had always been a physical practice player, the kind of guy to use elbows, hip checks, hard box-outs, or any other advantage to challenge opponents. His Lakers teammates didn't approach the game the same way.

The only one seemingly capable of battling Bryant and not getting upset was Eddie Jones. He and Bryant would have furious battles in practice yet never feel the need to carry it beyond that. "I'm gonna bust your ass," Kobe would tell Jones during their battles, which only drove the intensity higher. Other Lakers, however, harbored an intense dislike for Bryant because of the way he attacked practices.

DEREK FISHER: "That really was the way we all should have been competing. With Kobe's spirit."

It didn't work out that way, though. And the Lakers' troubles in 1999 would begin with that January pickup session. More than five weeks later, word of the conflict would leak into the L.A. newspapers, that Shaq had slapped Kobe during practice. The reports didn't detail when the incident happened or what was involved, but it would be cited as a sign of their growing dislike for each other.

DEREK FISHER: "It had just been physical. Both guys had gotten tired. Neither guy really started it. It started just from them both being physical. Some true feelings came out. They didn't really say all that much, but it was done in an extremely negative way. You could tell the guys had negative thoughts for each other. It was clear those feelings weren't going away any time soon. It would always be remembered."

Although the lockout meant that the 1999 NBA regular season would be shortened to 50 games, the Lakers suffered through a crazy mishmash of a campaign that in effect was four different seasons crammed into one. First, there was the preseason and opening 12 games that Del Harris coached the team. The second season began when Harris was fired and assistant Kurt Rambis promoted to the job on the same day that the team added strange agent Dennis Rodman to the roster. That second season, in effect, lasted another 11 blissful games until the team decided to work a major trade, sending Jones and Elden Campbell to the Charlotte Hornets for what would essentially be Glen Rice and J. R. Reid. After a month of turmoil adjusting to the trade, the fourth season would begin with the abrupt release of Rodman, after which the team would settle into a new and different round of internal conflict.

During each of these seasons within the season the Lakers would suffer through a blur of frustration, but there would always be one constant—the team's dislike of Bryant. The tension within the team would require a series of meetings trying to deal with chemistry problems, yet the malignancy was never addressed frankly.

"It was all sort of beating around the bush," explained a longtime Lakers staff member. "The whole thing is about Kobe. The whole failure of the team is about him."

DEREK FISHER: "That's the way I perceived it. That was the way that it was. There were a lot of people who felt that way. Nobody ever really came out and said that they felt Kobe's selfish play was our problem. But that's what everybody felt."

Bryant's friends and family would see the response as an intense case of envy, for his status and for the $71 million contract he signed before the season opened. The situation would grow so bad that some in Kobe's camp wondered if his teammates were intentionally failing to let him know when opponents were setting screens on his blind side. Asked about the situation, Kobe acknowledged that he had no real relationship with any teammate. "All that matters is what we do on the court," he said.

Time had revealed that the most tenuous and most critical facet of Jerry West's plans for building a championship contender was the relationship between Shaq and Kobe. O'Neal was a huge, fun-loving man. After Del Harris was fired, the coach would tell associates that the center was perhaps too fun-loving, too much of a comedian, to be an effective team leader. He had a great sense of humor and loved to amuse himself and others with it. In his first season in Los Angeles, O'Neal used that humor to nudge Bryant toward being more of a team player. The center even composed a ditty, set to the tune of "Greatest Love of All," aimed at Bryant.

In the locker room, Shaq would croon: "I believe that Showboat is the future/Call the play and let that motherfucker shoot . . ." He'd sing a verse, then come back with the next a little louder: "I believe that Showboat is the future . . . ."

Bryant wouldn't exactly fall in stitches at the derisive performance, but he wasn't thin-skinned about it either. They were simply different in their approach to life. O'Neal enjoyed the nighttime, the clubs, the L.A. music scene. Bryant had a different agenda, namely his ambition. "I feel weird going out, on the road, knowing that you have a game the next night," he explained when asked about the matter. "That's not handling your business."

For years rumors had persisted that the reason O'Neal left Orlando was the envy he held for Penny Hardaway, who had enjoyed tremendous success with the creation of his L'il Penny marketing alter ego. Kobe's presence in Los Angeles posed a similar threat. His number 8 Lakers jersey outsold O'Neal's in sporting-goods stores around Southern California, just one of many points of marketing competition between the two in which Kobe had taken the upper hand.

"People say Shaq is jealous. That's way far from the truth," Derek Fisher said. "All Shaq wants to do is win."

"I want him to get all those commercials and do all that stuff," O'Neal volunteered during an interview when asked about Bryant. "Because with marketing, when they see Kobe, they see me. And when they see me, they see Kobe."

At one point during the 1999 season, O'Neal would point at Bryant across the Lakers locker room and tell reporters, "There's the problem."

Beyond that first slap, though, the season held little direct confrontation, due in large part to the efforts of Rambis and the Lakers coaches to keep the rumblings from flaring into the kind of trouble that could never be repaired. "Shaq and I have never even talked about it," Kobe said when asked about their difficulties. "We communicate about it through the media mostly."

Which meant that if it was discussed at all the subject was raised as innuendo. Asked if he had tried to help Kobe through his growing pains, O'Neal replied, "I try not to help guys out too much. Experience is the best teacher. Kobe really didn't go to college. He went to high school, and he's different. Kobe's a great player, and he's gonna get a lot of press. He's a new, up-and-coming kid."

One person who didn't understand Bryant was Ruben Patterson, the Lakers' 23-year-old rookie from the University of Cincinnati. A second-round pick making the NBA minimum wage, his fiery personality clashed immediately with Bryant in practice.

DEREK FISHER: "Between Ruben and Kobe something was always going on and escalating. Ruben wouldn't back down. It got out of line a couple of times, because of Ruben's nature. Kobe can get into a tussle and still not take it across the boundary. He can push and shove and fight for position and not react emotionally. On the other hand, Ruben was a rookie, a guy always trying to establish himself and he wasn't gonna back down."

Somehow even these confrontations factored into the players' sense that there was a double standard for Bryant, a Lakers staff member said.

DEREK FISHER: "As players, we had to deal with Kobe's success and the way the organization viewed Kobe. It was clear the organization was satisfied with how Kobe played as was the coaching staff. It was clear they were not gonna hold him back or slow him down from the player that he wanted to be. Shaq also benefited from the star system. That's the way the NBA works. But it can be demoralizing to a team, demoralizing to the players making the sacrifice."

Kobe Bryant was potential personified, Jerry West told reporters. "To some degree, he has to be looking over his shoulder. He's a 20-year-old kid who has more energy than the whole team put together. When he looks at his game, all he needs to do is slow down, read situations, and not take the whole thing on himself. He's a big draw, and he's one of those guys you just sit back and say, 'Hmmm, I wonder what he's going to be like when he's 25?'"

Riding the Whirlwind

West himself was caught in the throes of a financial standoff with Jerry Buss. Supposedly, the owner had promised the team's executive VP a $2 million bonus, then held off in delivering it. Faced with Buss reneging, West began hinting to reporters that he was thinking about leaving the Lakers to work for another team, which had O'Neal himself offering veiled threats to leave the team via free agency.

"If Jerry West would leave for health reasons that would be understand-able," O'Neal told reporters. "If he would leave for any other reason I would be very, very upset. Jerry West is the reason I came to the Lakers."

"Had I left I would have been careful to say I was resigning rather than retiring," West told them. "I don't know any other work."

Eventually, the bonus was paid and West was given a fat new contract, set to kick in with the 1999–2000 season. At least part of Buss's reluctance in pay-ing out monies stemmed from the reshuffling of the team ownership struc-ture to include Rupert Murdoch's Fox entertainment conglomerate as a minority partner and plans to move the Lakers into the Staples Center, a $300 million building under construction in downtown Los Angeles, for the 1999–2000 season.

Because the labor lockout had cut more than three months out of the 1998–99 schedule, the NBA was forced to cram 50 games into 89 days—and three games into three nights on some occasions. Usually training camp and eight or nine preseason games are scheduled across the month of October for each team, but the 1999 season didn't start until February, meaning that teams had just two weeks to prepare.

From the start it was an uphill climb. Attendance and television ratings drooped. So did scoring and shooting percentages. And injuries were up. Across the league, fans, players, and coaches found themselves trying to cope with a strange season.

However, Bryant's extensive off-season conditioning work and his focus on offensive footwork meant that he charged out of the gate with a burst of energy. Through the Lakers' first 10 games he posted averages of 20.6 points, 9.3 rebounds, 1.4 steals, and 1.3 blocked shots and shot 46.4 percent from the field, up from 42.8 percent the previous season. The situation prompted *USA Today's* David DuPree to ask West what if Bryant had gone to a team that used his offensive skills constantly, much as the Chicago Bulls had done with Michael Jordan in 1984. "If he had played in a situation like that, it might be really remarkable where he might be today," West admitted. "But I think that in the patience, the setbacks, the good nights and the bad nights, and the criticism that he's faced in this situation will help him. He's faced an awful lot of criticism at an early age. And how he handles that, along with his quest to be the best player, will determine just how good he'll be. I'm just glad he's on our side."

Through the first games of the season, O'Neal continued to call publicly for management to sign a power forward. This in itself indicated just how great the pressure was on the 26-year-old center. He had played six years in the league without winning a championship, a factor that his critics pointed to whenever discussions of his game, his leadership, and his free throw percentage arose on talk radio. "Ultimately he will be judged by how many championships he wins," Harris told reporters. "That's how all the big guys are judged."

After the Lakers lost to Utah in the second game of the season, O'Neal told reporters that he not only needed Dennis Rodman at power forward but that the team needed better perimeter scoring. Jones, the starting two guard, had struggled to open the season in the wake of several reports that he would soon be traded. The tension in the locker room thickened once O'Neal began openly campaigning for a new scorer to replace Jones. "We need a great shooter," O'Neal said. "We have good shooters; we need someone who's known as a shooter."

Speaking of Utah's Stockton and Malone, the Lakers center said, "They have a great one-two punch. We have a one-and-sometimes-two punch."

Nick Van Exel, who had been traded to Denver in the off-season after O'Neal's complaint, smiled at the situation when the Lakers visited Denver the fourth game of the season. "If they don't win a championship this year, I wonder who they're going to blame it on," he mused.

Seizing on O'Neal's public comments, fans at the Forum had begun chanting, "We want Worm" during games.

With this nasty chemistry and an uneven schedule lurking, the Lakers had the feel of a team headed for trouble. Strangely, Del Harris didn't smell it. He had coached 14 seasons in the NBA, long enough to distinguish himself as one of just 20 people to win better than 500 games. The totals were quite impressive. But his young Lakers could not beat the Utah Jazz in the playoffs, meaning that Lakers management decided to fire him after three straight February losses. At age 61, Harris saw his effort to mold Shaq and Kobe into a team come to an abrupt end.

DEL HARRIS: "They fired me with no severance pay. I lost my insurance. I was stuck out there with no money coming in, no insurance, no nothing. Jerry Buss's comment, when West went to him for severance pay, was, 'We don't owe that guy anything.' I don't know the reason. Never in my four years there did I ever have anything but a positive conversation with Jerry Buss. It all hit me out of left field. I should have realized when he didn't give me an extension over the summer. I had two job offers, big money, and Jerry Buss said I ought to take them because he was never going to pay big money for a coach. And I said, 'No, I can't leave a championship team. I'll take my chances.'"

West had noticed the Lakers quitting in a fourth quarter loss at Denver, and he concluded that Harris had lost the ability to motivate them. West and Mitch Kupchak announced the move at a news conference. "The thing that makes it so tough," said West, "Del Harris has been a friend of mine for years and someone who's done just an absolute incredible job here. The nature of these jobs here, they're fragile."

DEL HARRIS: "In the end, Jerry West didn't fire me, Jerry Buss did. Jerry West was very sad about it, and Jerry Buss knew he was gonna fire me because he thought that Kurt Rambis was gonna be the next great young coach in the NBA."

Staggered

Just months earlier, Kurt Rambis, the young Lakers assistant coach, had been the man seemingly everybody wanted to hire. There was the head coaching job of the Sacramento Kings, his for the taking. Or the Los Angeles Clippers, less desirable with the Clippers culture of despair, but an opportunity all the same.

Rambis, though, was given reason for pause by the Lakers. For a while it had seemed that longtime assistant Larry Drew was poised to take over if head coach Del Harris was fired. But the demand for Rambis had driven Lakers management to covet him as well. Rambis was clearly a coaching talent, and the Lakers didn't want him to get away. The message Rambis got was that he, not Drew, would be next in line if Harris was fired or resigned.

So Rambis passed on the other jobs that summer and decided to wait, to see what his future held. After all, the Lakers roster was stocked thick with talent. It offered the opportunity to move in and coach Shaquille O'Neal and Eddie Jones and Kobe Bryant.

Later, when Rambis had all the time in the world on his hands, it would be easy to look back and see that the karma was wrong from the start. The coach who replaced Harris wouldn't have the opportunity to begin the season in training camp. It was there that a new coach had the time go over his system with the players, to do all the work necessary to instill his philosophy with the team.

Once an NBA season begins, there is precious little practice time for making changes. Rambis knew this would be a problem. He knew that if he accepted the job he was faced with inheriting Harris's lax practice approach and an offense that the players often failed to execute. But Rambis assumed that after this transitional short season he would have a full training camp the next fall.

Having earned his millions in real estate, Jerry Buss had always been a gambler. He loved poker and was known to refer to his assets, even the players on his Lakers teams, as his stack of chips. Rambis didn't exactly realize it at the time, but when he took over the Lakers in February 1999, he was one of Jerry Buss's chips. Buss didn't consider the gamble on Rambis a wild one. After all, he had made the same bet in late 1981 on another young coach named Pat Riley. So it seemed reasonable nearly two decades later that Buss would again decide to gamble on a young assistant with no head coaching experience. Like Riley, Rambis had been a valuable role player for Lakers teams that won titles. He had that understanding of the game. Rambis even possessed enough of an offbeat image to remind some observers of a young Phil Jackson. Rambis also had connections that ran deep in the organization. A California guy, he had been a teammate of Lakers minority owner Magic Johnson, and he was liked by West. Better yet, Rambis's wife Linda and Jerry Buss's daughter Jeanie, who had taken on a management role with the team, were close friends. Rambis's main flaw was that while he was lucky, he wasn't lucky enough. To start at the top of the NBA and succeed, you have to be very lucky.

The Lakers soon demonstrated there was little luck to be had in 1999. That, however, didn't deter Jerry Buss from going aggressively against the odds. While he was betting on Rambis, Buss decided to raise the ante, shoving more chips onto the table with the signing of oddball forward Dennis Rodman. The volatile Rodman had always proved to be a challenge for a variety of NBA coaches, but from his very first moment on the job, Rambis was faced with adding Rodman to a roster already debilitated by bad chemistry and dissension.

Rodman's basketball smarts and rebounding brought a dizzying ascent. Rambis won his first nine games as coach of the Lakers and then a bunch more. While the atmosphere around the Great Western Forum grew giddy, veteran observers harbored a sense of caution, even foreboding. And with good reason.

Not satisfied with things merely going well, Buss decided to roll the dice yet again, this time a blockbuster trade. Everyone involved had felt the sense of foreboding over the rumors. According to insiders, the deal had been drawn up and awaited only the final details that would send Eddie Jones and Elden Campbell to Charlotte for Glen Rice, B. J. Armstrong, and J. R. Reid. Rice, the key player in the deal from the Lakers' perspective, had been out of action more than a year after arthroscopic surgery to remove bone spurs from his right (shooting) elbow.

Surely, the front office wouldn't dampen this winning streak, observers said. But Buss in particular wanted to trade Campbell because the big center was paid $7.5 million as the reserve behind O'Neal.

Jones would supposedly be thrown into the deal to make it work from a salary cap standpoint, but some in the media doubted that was a necessity. Instead, West himself implied that he had come to believe that Jones would want a huge pay increase when his contract ended in a year. So Jones, a strong fan favorite with a tremendous defensive ethic, had been factored into the deal. But would the Lakers agree to it? The constant rumors about the trade had worn on Jones all season long.

EDDIE JONES: "I mean there were days where I could have sat around and just cried my eyes out. Once I started feeling like that, I just wanted to work on something, do something, that would totally take my mind off what was happening."

KOBE BRYANT: "I'd known Eddie a long time. I could tell it was bothering him. It couldn't help but bother him. You hear it so many times, it has to affect you. But he kept his head. He never talked about it here in the locker room. He never moped about it. He just went out there and played."

EDDIE JONES: "The trade talk became a total distraction to me. It came in abundance. The first few times I heard it, I was like, 'Well, I'm not gonna worry about it. Maybe my play will show these people how good I am.' Then you hear it again and again, it was like, 'Well, I gotta go out and show them again.' Then you show 'em, and then you start hearing it again."

Later, it would become clear just how important a role Jones played in the Lakers team defense. Beyond that, another unseen contribution was his ability to smooth out the relationship between O'Neal and Kobe.

EDDIE JONES: "When you're in a situation with two great players, there has to be somebody who's the mediator. I used to always be the guy who would say, 'Hey, man, we're gonna get this guy the ball.' I would say it. I could take somebody looking at me strange."

Although Jones and Kobe were clearly not as close as they had once been, theirs was the kind of relationship that worked smoothly on the court.

EDDIE JONES: "Kobe understood. He knew I knew the game. He knew I wouldn't do anything that would do him wrong. He knew I would do all the right things to make our team work."

Indeed, more than any other Laker, Jones had no hesitations about nudging O'Neal away from his defensive laziness.

EDDIE JONES: "I would tell him anything. To challenge shots. We needed to challenge shots. 'Do it. Let's get it going.'"

Bryant's associates said that his large contract seemed to bother Jones immensely. And then there was the obvious factor that while he could play small forward, Kobe's best position was the one that Jones played, the two guard. Still, that potential conflict mattered little to the two of them.

EDDIE JONES: "We were playing against each other in practice each day. We competed hard. We enjoyed each other's talent. We made each other better. He loved the way I competed defensively. And offensively, I loved the way he competed. I told one guy, I said, 'Let me tell you something about that kid. He might be probably the most talented player I've ever seen in my life.' I mean he can do wonders with a basketball that people haven't seen yet. I'm serious. The things he used to do in practice, things that he would spend hours before practice started and practiced on, those things were incredible. I was in awe, man."

With the Rodman frenzy and the team's success, many observers thought there was no way the trade would go through. Rodman's rebounding and hustle drew loud, raucous responses from the Forum crowd. Although he hardly spoke to his teammates off the court, they said it didn't matter. On the court, he had brought them together by sitting at the back of the defense, talking them through situations. The entire team's enthusiasm could suddenly be measured in their new intensity. Solid proof of that came with their seventh straight win, in Utah's Delta Center of all places, where the Jazz had a 20-game home winning streak. (Utah had won 5 straight over Los Angeles and taken 13 of the previous 16 games.) The Lakers claimed a win over the Clippers that Tuesday, March 9. The next morning news reports said Jones and Campbell had been traded.

EDDIE JONES: "I never told anybody that I wanted out, but I did. I didn't want any of the fans to feel like I wanted to leave L.A., to leave them. But the situation that I was in, I wanted out. Whether I was at the two guard, or Kobe was at the two guard or the three, I knew that we could be together on the court. I know how to play the game. I know to step off my game when I see someone else doing well. He understood that, so I think we could have lived together. I don't think the trade was made because of that. I knew they couldn't get rid of Elden without me. I knew that. If they wanted to get something, they were gonna have to throw me in with the deal. I was like, 'Let it happen.' I didn't care where I was going. I just wanted to get out, because I felt mistreated. I felt disrespected."

JERRY WEST: "A player our owner really wanted to move was Elden Campbell. He didn't want to watch a guy come off the bench at $7 million a year. People talk about the loss of Eddie Jones, but Elden was a big factor for us. We lost another big guy, somebody to replace Shaq when he comes out. In exchange, we took a player who had not played in nine months."

DEL HARRIS: "Just think where they'd be if Buss hadn't panicked. He alienated Jerry West. He started listening to other people. It was so good to have Elden as a backup. He was also good against Portland and San Antonio. Shaq missed 53 games the two years I had him, and Elden averaged 18 points and eight rebounds during those games when Shaq was out. That's pretty good. Jerry Buss panicked. He got rid of Elden. And he felt Eddie Jones was standing in Kobe's way, that they couldn't play together. Plus Jerry said he wasn't going to pay that third salary. He knew he was gonna pay Shaq and Kobe, but he was never gonna pay that third salary. So he got rid of Eddie and Elden for Rice, and then he got rid of Rice because he didn't want to pay his third salary. He got rid of me, and ended up having to pay all that money for Phil Jackson. I would have worked for a lot less. Just think how good their team would have been now if they had Eddie Jones in there with Kobe and Shaq and Fisher and Fox. And Elden Campbell, too. After all that, he really didn't listen to Jerry West. There were just so many things that happened. The trust was broken, and Jerry West won't admit it. The trust was broken between him and Jerry Buss."

The supposed upside of such a trade was the teaming a shooter of Rice's caliber with a post weapon like O'Neal. On paper, it made an unbeatable combination. But no matter how fine the prospectus, trades always take time to work in pro basketball because it's nearly always impossible to produce an instant chemistry, or to predict if there will be a chemistry at all. Players need time to adjust to each other, to the new styles of play.

Yet if there was one commodity that Kurt Rambis didn't have in the whirlwind spring of 1999, it was time. Even with the chaos of management's moves, he somehow kept the club moving mostly in a positive direction, despite the fact that he faced one crisis after another as March turned to April.

Rambis wondered about the reasoning behind the flurry of moves, but he never really had the time to sit down with management to discuss them. They clearly had a destabilizing effect on his team, and worse, the moves only exacerbated the sour relationship between O'Neal and Bryant. With the trade, Bryant moved from small forward to shooting guard, a huge defensive transition to make in midseason.

JERRY WEST: "I felt he was doing great at small forward. He was defending incredibly well."

With the team struggling in the wake of the trade and Bryant trying to find a defensive footing, O'Neal took to issuing furtive criticism of his young teammate for not producing. Yet other observers, including former Lakers great Wilt Chamberlain, took Shaq to task for his own obvious defensive shortcomings, most notably a laziness about getting back. Still, there's no question that the trade and the subsequent pressure it put on Bryant further alienated him from O'Neal and some teammates.

JERRY WEST: "He was so young and had had a lot of success. A lot of that success had come before his actual accomplishments. Guys like John Stockton and Karl Malone paid a high price trying to be champions. Most of the players who have attained greatness, they've had a lot of personal sacrifice and a lot of pain. But no matter how much you put into it individually, it's very, very difficult. Kids today have so much success at an early age. They arrive in the NBA and think it's gonna be easy. It's not easy."

With the turmoil, Rambis found himself forced to spend way too much time talking with players' agents and parents and assistants, all of them seeking to be coddled and reassured over every little concern about playing time and shots and personality conflicts. As the difficulties unfolded, Rambis made an effort to talk with each of the team's three stars, with O'Neal, Bryant, and Rice. What confounded him was that each one of the three offered a radically different perspective on what was needed to make the team work. He was stunned to realize that his team's three stars were not remotely on the same page. Worse yet, the three talked hardly at all with each other, meaning the team was caught up in an undeclared tug-of-war over playing styles. And as an interim coach, Rambis had little or no real power to deal with it.

As the season wore on, Rambis came to see Rice as a one-trick pony, a marvelous shooter who was unwilling or incapable of doing the multifaceted things needed on a championship team. Rice wanted the coaching staff to devise and run plays for him that allowed him to shoot coming off screens set by teammates. This, of course, came into immediate conflict with O'Neal, who wanted to receive the ball in the post and shoot it or draw double-teams and throw it out to open teammates on the perimeter.

Beyond that, Rambis was alarmed by the energy he had to expend in keeping the hard feelings between Bryant and O'Neal from flaring into open warfare. Rambis went to O'Neal and implored him to be more accepting of the 20-year-old Bryant. Rambis reasoned that O'Neal should change his attitude because he was the team leader, the one player capable of pulling the group together. You can heal this rift; you can reach out to Kobe, Rambis told his center. Bryant was young and hardworking and just learning the game, the coach pointed out, and the center should make a move to reconcile with him. The coach later recalled that O'Neal's only answer was a blank, cold stare. Nothing more. That, Rambis would come to understand in retrospect, would be the moment, his one chance to heal the relationship, to bring an end to the team's deep division.

It wasn't going to happen. Instead, the season played itself out in a sad drama, with Rodman being released in April after a drunken appearance at practice. Even with the distractions, Rambis coached the Lakers to 25 wins against 13 losses and a first-round playoff victory over the Houston Rockets. But then things fell apart against the San Antonio Spurs in the second round. For the second year in a row, the Lakers were swept from the playoffs. It was a bitter, ugly defeat, one that filled the players, especially O'Neal, with a deep anger, the kind that would linger for months. The big center left Los Angeles without bothering to attend the team's season-closing meeting and returned to his Orlando home, where he stewed in frustration.

The loss to the Spurs was so humiliating that forward Rick Fox decided afterward he had lost all love for the game.

16
Triangle Days

From all indications Jerry West was prepared to retain Kurt Rambis as the team's coach, until a groundswell of support developed for a change. The name most commonly tossed about as a replacement was Phil Jackson.

Jackson, who had coached the Chicago Bulls to six championships, had actually sent up the first trial balloon for the job in the spring of 1998. He had published excerpts from his diary in *ESPN The Magazine* in which he mused about coaching the Lakers and wondered if O'Neal would be smart enough to play in Jackson's triangle offense. Like others around the NBA at the time, West had been irritated by Jackson's boldness.

West had been a friend of Bulls general manager Jerry Krause since the late 1970s when Krause worked as a Lakers scout. The two men would often commiserate over the difficulties of their jobs. In 1989 and '90, when West's relationship soured with coach Pat Riley, West would unburden himself on the phone, telling Krause about the intense level of dislike that had flared up between Riley and him. Later, when Krause began having his difficulties with Jackson, he would tell West about how Jackson's manipulation and ego had troubled the Bulls organization.

Jackson had walked away from the Bulls after the team's 1998 championship, leaving Michael Jordan behind in disappointment. Jordan would later explain that he believed Jackson would remain with the team if he managed to convince Bulls chairman Jerry Reinsdorf that the team should not be broken up. Reinsdorf ultimately agreed with Jordan, but then Jackson walked away anyway, saying he needed a sabbatical.

Jackson had spent the 1999 season on the speech circuit and working for the Democratic presidential nomination campaign of Senator Bill Bradley, his former Knicks teammate.

Longtime Jackson assistant Tex Winter explained that Jackson would come back into the league only if he found a team with the right level of talent. Jackson coveted the idea of coaching the Lakers, Winter said. To do that, however, Jackson would have to gain the blessing of West, which seemed unlikely.

On the final weekend of the 1999 season, as the Lakers were about to be swept by the Spurs, West was sitting in the nearly empty Great Western Forum when this book's author mentioned Jackson.

"Fuck Phil Jackson," West said.

Thinking that he had been misunderstood, this writer again mentioned Jackson. "Fuck Phil Jackson," West repeated, emphasizing the words and his disdain.

West wasn't alone in his opinion. While Jackson was wildly popular with millions of NBA fans, many coaches and team officials around the league openly loathed him. In New York, feelings against him had turned particularly strong that spring. Jackson had been cast as a potential replacement for Knicks coach Jeff Van Gundy and had quietly agreed to discuss the job with the team's front office. That decision blew up in controversy when the story broke in New York newspapers that the Knicks were talking employment with Jackson even as they had a coach under contract. Center Patrick Ewing responded to the news by declaring that he wouldn't play for the former Bulls coach. Ewing said he'd rather be traded.

Other coaches around the league chimed in on what they saw as an underhanded move. The uproar was strong enough that it played a role in Knicks executive Ernie Grunfeld leaving the team.

WALT FRAZIER, KNICKS BROADCASTER AND FORMER JACKSON TEAMMATE: "That whole thing blindsided Phil. Coming from some of his peers. From guys in the coaching profession making derogatory comments. But it was more jealousy than anything, because he's been so successful. This is a business. Someone's going to make you an offer and you're not going to listen?"

As if the Knicks fiasco wasn't enough, in one of his rare 1999 interviews, Jackson commented that the 1999 championship would be undervalued because it was a shortened season, a statement that further angered his colleagues around the NBA. Then, in early May when he was honored by the Bulls at halftime of their final regular-season game, Jackson held a press conference beforehand and made reference to Rodman's release by the Lakers. He offered the opinion that Rodman hadn't gotten the same support in Los Angeles as he had gotten when he played for Jackson in Chicago. Although Jackson was seemingly referring to Rodman's off-court support, from agents and other professionals, West took Jackson's comments as criticism of the team's management itself. "Apparently we don't do things right," West said angrily, adding that the Lakers had done everything they could for Rodman, including paying the salaries of his two security guards.

TEX WINTER, JACKSON'S LONGTIME ASSISTANT: "At the time, it seemed Phil had burned his bridges around the league. It was unfortunate. With the success he'd had there was bound to be some natural jealousy. It behooved him to be humble and complimentary of other people. I think there was a lot of resentment in the league because of the success he had in Chicago. People seemed to feel that Phil was lucky to coach Michael Jordan. I don't think they gave Phil the credit he should have received, but at the same time Phil should have been a little more humble. There was the impression that Phil rubbed it in."

Clearly West was Mr. Laker and was set to begin a new contract in 1999–2000 as team vice president. There was little question that his presence as an executive added huge pressure and expectations to the people coaching and playing for the franchise.

TEX WINTER: "You also had Magic Johnson looking over everybody's shoulder. He's another icon. That was a tough situation. As long as Jerry West was there, it seemed it would be tough for Phil."

The only hope for Jackson in Los Angeles rested with Jerry Buss, who had long expressed an interest in Jackson. The team was moving into the new Staples Center for the 1999–2000 season and had expensive skyboxes and season tickets to sell. Jackson would obviously be a marquee name in that regard. Buss, though, seemed understandably reluctant to force the issue. His efforts to get involved in the Lakers' management had backfired disastrously.

To West the idea of hiring Jackson seemed like another Buss gamble. West was the guardian of the team. He wasn't about to turn it over to a Machiavellian force. Still, clearly Jackson had star quality, something the franchise had always needed to operate in Hollywood.

West had assembled a collection of talent, but in his frustration Buss had begun trading it away. And the team's play had left fans with empty feelings.

Quite simply, the Lakers had played without conviction in the 1999 play-offs, and the team had gone nearly a decade without contending for a championship.

Something had to be done to get fans excited about the 2000 season. Could the Lakers do something to bring in a player? the team's management asked. Buss had long disdained the idea of paying a coach a big salary. But it became clear to Buss and his managers that they couldn't spend $6 million on a player and generate the kind of excitement that hiring Jackson would bring. There was no player available at such a price tag whose presence would make people go out and buy tickets, or make corporations purchase skyboxes.

In fact, spending $6 million a year on Jackson would be a tremendous savings and they would sell a lot of tickets. Later these financial considerations would be explained to Rambis. Even the deposed coach had to admit it. The skyboxes in the new Staples Center had to be sold, and hiring Jackson was the quick way to drum up interest. In that sense, Rambis became a victim of the building and of his owner's gambling.

Capitulation

In the end, the decision to hire Jackson was left with Jerry West. The team vice president put away his anger and looked at the circumstances. He could rehire Rambis, who had promise as a coach, but Rambis remained untested, and if he was retained the team could well find itself looking for yet another coach the following the season. There had been enough change, West said. The team needed a veteran coach to deal with its internal strife.

Both O'Neal and Bryant had offered as much in encouraging West to hire the 53-year-old Jackson. O'Neal had even indicated he might leave the franchise if Jackson wasn't hired. West knew the center wouldn't walk away from his huge contract, but he also knew Jackson was the right choice, despite his personal misgivings.

In mid-June, West announced Jackson's hiring at a press conference, ending speculation that had dragged on more than a month, since the end of the season. Jackson had been in Alaska, finishing up a fishing vacation with his sons, and got off a boat one day to learn from an Eskimo boy that he had been hired as the Lakers coach.

There would be discussions and brief negotiations, but the matter was a foregone conclusion. Asked about Jackson, West told L.A. reporters, "What

Phil talked about was how to get players really to trust themselves, how to get everyone to share the ball. And in the offense he plans to run, everyone has to do that, or no one's ever going to score. That to me is the most important aspect of having him here. I don't think we have to worry at the end of the season about coaches anymore."

The Lakers were going to use the triangle offense, Jackson said. "When you have a system of offense, you can't be a person that just is taking the basketball trying to score. You have to move the basketball, because . . . you have to share the basketball with everybody. And when you do that, you're sharing the game, and that makes a big difference."

Running the triangle meant that he wanted Winter as his assistant coach. Jackson also brought in former Bulls assistants Frank Hamblen and Jim Cleamons, plus he retained Bill Bertka of the previous Lakers staff.

Asked if he also planned to bring in his old team, Jackson replied, "My old players? I'd like to have them all. Obviously, we had the right crew there in Chicago. But most of them are under contract and Michael's retired and Dennis [Rodman] has gone into some other ozone. . . ."

Although Jackson and the staff wanted the front office to obtain former Bull Scottie Pippen from the Rockets, West emphasized that he was against it. Besides, the real question on people's mind was Jordan. He immediately insisted he had no plans to return to the NBA as a Los Angeles Laker. He did, however, have some kind words of advice for the young Lakers who soon would be working with Jackson. The Lakers should keep an open mind about Jackson's quirky approach to coaching, including his use of Zen Buddhist philosophy, Jordan said. "It can relieve a lot of tension in your life, and I'm pretty sure they got a lot. Actually I think they're gonna be happy with Phil. He's gonna give them a certain structure and a certain guidance that they probably need. They got the talent. It's always been there. It's just how you utilize the talent in a focused situation. And I think Phil is good at that."

There was immediate speculation that the triangle would be difficult to install in Los Angeles. In recent years, three NBA coaches had attempted to install the triangle offense to help rid their teams of offensive stagnation. The three—Jim Cleamons, Quin Buckner, Cotton Fitzsimmons—all lost their jobs after players revolted with complaints that learning the system was too difficult, too unnatural.

Set offenses had often been greeted with disdain in Los Angeles. The previous season, Rambis had attempted to install some plays that would allow new offensive weapon Glen Rice to shoot coming off screens. O'Neal tried them for a few weeks, then informed Rambis after a players' meeting that the plays would have to cease.

"If I'm on a team where we come down and call plays every time, then it's time for me to quit," O'Neal confided later. "Then I'm not gonna be an effective big man no more. I don't want to play like that. I want to run and get crazy and look at the fans and make faces."

STEVE KERR, FORMER JACKSON PLAYER: "I talked to Phil about it before. I said, 'If you had Shaq would you run the triangle?' He said, 'Absolutely.' He said he felt like the offense was adaptable. He would give Shaq more post-up opportunities in the triangle. He thought it would be perfect."

Kobe Bryant said he was eager to use the triangle. But would O'Neal and the other Lakers have the patience and take the time to learn the offense?

STEVE KERR: "Phil told me he thought it would take two years to learn the triangle. You tell me what NBA coach has two years to fiddle with an offense? Most of them get fired before then."

Jackson's success in Los Angeles would depend on O'Neal. The center's adjustment to the offense would be so much better if the coaches had someone who understood every element of the triangle and could be a coach on the floor. The discussion came back around to Scottie Pippen, who had expressed his eagerness to join Jackson in Los Angeles, so much so that he was trying to force his trade away from the Rockets. West put together the deal to acquire Pippen. All the Lakers had to do was pull the trigger. But Buss declined, saying that Pippen's huge contract was too expensive.

The Portland Trail Blazers, though, were owned by Paul Allen, the cofounder of Microsoft who had many billions in the bank. Allen was eager to spend money to make Portland better. So Allen gave Blazers GM Bob Whitsitt permission to ship six reserves to Houston for Pippen, who had just passed his 34th birthday. The vastly wealthy Allen didn't mind paying Pippen's four-year, $54 million contract, which boosted the Portland player payroll to more than double the league's $34 million salary cap.

Jackson had badly wanted Pippen, but suddenly the player became his old coach's worst nightmare. Suddenly, the opposition in Portland had a player who understood Jackson's system. Worse, Pippen was motivated. He wanted to win a seventh league championship after winning six with Jackson, Jordan, and the Bulls.

Jackson would explain later, "Sometimes, it's a matter of economics . . . When it happened, I was able to say, 'We let our biggest opponent step into the gap and supply themselves with a player who could eventually end up costing us, big-time.'"

The new coaching staff was immensely disappointed. With Pippen out of the question, Jackson turned in earnest to the job of teaching the Lakers the offense.

When Jackson moved to Los Angeles, wife June had stayed behind in New York. The couple had worked to regain their relationship following the revelation that Jackson had committed infidelities in Chicago. If he had elected to end his pro basketball career, they might well have succeeded in repairing the damage, several friends observed. "She wants to get out of the shadow of being an NBA wife," Jackson acknowledged.

The bicoastal circumstances would soon bring an end to his marriage. In the spring, the *Chicago Sun-Times* would receive a tip from someone affiliated with the Bulls that Jackson was romantically involved with Jerry Buss's daughter Jeanie. The union of the new coach with the team owner's daughter left both West and Jerry Buss taken aback. Jackson had experienced numerous problems with ownership and management in Chicago. His quick move with Jeanie led critics in Chicago to suggest that he had finally found a way around such problems—sleeping with the owner's daughter.

The Different Drummer

His Lakers players soon discovered that Jackson beat a tom-tom on game days. The instrument had routine purpose in the lives of the Native Americans, and he was determined it would have the same for his players.

DEREK FISHER: "I guess the drum was basically for gathering in terms of Indian customs. They would hit the drum so that people would come together. Whether it was time to eat or time to meet or whatever. He just did that on game days when it was time for us to go in and watch film. It was different. But that's part of who he is, his life experiences. He chooses to share that with his teams."

On occasion Phil Jackson also burned sticks of sage. He had done the same during his time in Chicago, where he would walk around the Bulls' locker room with the burning sticks waving them about when his team was struggling or facing a tough playoff foe. He would pause in front of each player's locker moving the smoking stick up and down.

DEREK FISHER: "That's done to drive away the evil spirits. I think everybody kind of knew that he enjoyed doing different things. And he kind of touched on the things that he would like to do when he first talked to us."

At first, when they heard the drum and saw Phil Jackson chanting, many Lakers fought to suppress their snickers.

KOBE BRYANT: "It kind of caught me off guard. I didn't know about that. I smiled. I laughed, as a matter of fact. It was funny. He said, 'You guys gotta get your hearts going. Just like warriors preparing for battle.' I said, 'Okay, Phil. All right.' Phil said, 'Is your heart beating a little faster?' I was like, 'No, Phil. No.'"

In Chicago, Jackson had not beaten the drum as insistently. It wasn't necessary there. Over his years with the Bulls he had come to share a great intuitive feel for the game with Pippen and Jordan. From that shared intuition, Jackson developed an abiding love for his Chicago teams. Even the Bulls employees who did not like him—and there were a few—could sense this love for his team, and they admired him for it.

Among his frustrations in Los Angeles was that his young stars showed little intuitive depth when it came to basketball. As a result, the coach found himself trying hard to love this Lakers team. In Chicago, Jordan had found great benefit to Jackson's Zen approach and to the mindfulness sessions provided the Bulls, no matter how unusual they seemed, even though he himself had sometimes kept his own playful distance from them.

JOHNNY BACH, FORMER JACKSON ASSISTANT: "Michael would always have some pithy or irreverent statement to make when Phil tried these things. It was nothing disrespectful. Phil is very able to handle relationships like that. I kind of enjoyed Michael's irreverence. It wasn't harmful, wasn't nasty. Michael's humor added that little spark in the coach/player relationship. It was exciting. We would all ask, 'What did Michael say?'"

Jackson searched for that same spark in his Lakers players. Some of them did not understand him. Others were intimidated by him. But they all extended a measure of respect to him based largely on the fact that his Bulls teams had dominated professional basketball. The Lakers quickly came to see that the coach and his assistants brought an immaculately detailed approach to their work. As Fisher explained, it was the detail, all the little things, that made them an absolutely great coaching staff. So that made it easy for the players to accept the tom-tom, as strange as the drumming seemed to them, as part of the package of that detail.

DEREK FISHER: "It was funny to see him and hear him walking through the locker room chanting and beating on his drum. Sometimes he was smiling, sometimes he was chanting. Sometimes he was just hitting it."

ROBERT HORRY: "I wondered what he was doing. Everybody said he always does crazy things, so I was like, 'This must be Phil being Phil.'"

His eccentricities and offbeat approach masked a coaching style completely grounded in discipline and fundamentals. "I do unusual things, yes, but I'm very, very sane," Jackson said in 1990, in the midst of his first season as an NBA head coach. "I'm a very centered person. I feel very much in control."

Shaquille

Perhaps no player in the game wielded more power than Shaquille O'Neal. A gifted giant with a mammoth contract that averaged better than $20 million per season, O'Neal had been known to throw that weight around by demanding a coaching change or even the trade of a teammate. Yet, as soon as Jackson took over as coach of the Lakers in 1999, the center gave his unconditional cooperation.

BRIAN SHAW: "Not to take anything away from the other coaches that Shaq's played for, but it was the first time that I think he really bought into what a coach was selling and what it takes to win. Some of the coaches, because Shaq is who he is, didn't get on his case when Shaq wasn't doing what he was supposed to. And Phil did. If Shaq wasn't doing the job, Phil was the first one to point it out. He said, 'Hey, you're not doing this, you're not doing that. Get your ass up the court and do it.' I think Shaq respected that. I played with Shaq three years in Orlando. Shaq was really the one making the adjustment. Phil didn't have to make any adjustments. He's coached the greatest players to ever play in Michael Jordan, Scottie Pippen, and Dennis Rodman. They've won championships. They bought into his system and what he preaches. Shaq had that respect for him just based on that. Michael Jordan listened and executed. If he did it, then there's something to it."

JOHN SALLEY, PLAYER FOR JACKSON IN CHICAGO AND L.A.: "Phil understands the game better than most people. And he expects certain things that he knows his guys can give him. He knows when to push his players, when not to push 'em. He knows who to yell at, who not to yell at. He knows who can take it. And he treats you like a man, as opposed to downplaying you, or talking to you like you're less than him because of his position. He's a great coach. He laughs and smiles at life."

BRIAN SHAW: "From the outside looking in, I always thought he was intimidating. Real serious all the time. But playing for him, I found he joked around and was real lighthearted. He wanted you to come in and put in your work. He allowed you to have input. I liked that about him. Some coaches, it's like, 'I'm the coach. I'm the man with the power.'"

Many coaches, Shaw said, seem to tell their players, "I'll do the thinking; you don't have to think." Jackson, though, wanted his players thinking and questioning. Rather than put his '60s counterculture experiences behind him like many of his Baby Boom contemporaries, Jackson had gloried in them as a coach, gaining notoriety for mixing Zen and Native American philosophy with proverbs from his fundamentalist Christian upbringing, and clinging to the Grateful Dead, Timothy Leary, and other icons of the period. It was well known that he loved preaching to his players about the great white buffalo or giving them obscure books to read or having them pause amid the looniness of the NBA for a meditation session.

PHIL JACKSON: "I believe that there is a tenuous trial sometimes between coaches and players. I've found that I have the confidence of my group, so that they feel comfortable. And it's not anything where if I try experimental things that they feel threatened or can't deal with it. It's sort of something where I've had an open working forum to try a variety of styles and approaches, all of which seem to be enjoyable to them. The only thing they don't like is monotony and constancy. But we still make one thing constant, and that's fundamentals. The one thing that we always strive for is to make fundamentals and execution a part of our game."

TEX WINTER: "I'm amazed at times in the course of the game how he sits back and lets things happen. He likes people to be able to solve their own problems, and so he gives his players the reins. On the other hand, when he sees they're out of control, then he starts to pull them in a little bit. I think this is his strength, the way he handles the players and his motivation, his personal relationship with the players. That's borne out by the fact that they'll accept his coaching, they'll accept the criticism, even though sometimes it's pretty severe with certain players. They accept that because it's who he is, because he's Phil."

One of the fascinating elements of the Jackson story was how Tex Winter had factored into it. The two first got to know each other in 1986 when Jackson joined the Bulls as an assistant coach. Over his decades on the bench, Winter had been the head coach at five colleges—Marquette, Kansas State, Washington, Northwestern, and Long Beach State—and had served as head coach of the San Diego/Houston Rockets in the 1970s. His specialty was the triangle offense, a system of team basketball that required stars to share the ball with lesser players. His Kansas State teams of the late 1950s and '60s hovered atop the national polls, and Winter enjoyed success against the rival Kansas Jayhawks. In fact, it was Winter's K State team that defeated Wilt Chamberlain's team in the Big Eight conference in 1958, leaving the gifted giant so frustrated that he decided to leave Kansas early to play with the Harlem Globetrotters. For Winter, it was the ultimate victory of team basketball over the brilliance of an individual player.

Winter was mostly retired in 1985 when Bulls GM Jerry Krause, a longtime friend and admirer, lured him to Chicago with a handsome salary to be "the coach's coach." Winter helped guide Jackson when he made the transition to head coach in 1989 and was delighted that Jackson chose to use the triangle for the team's offense. As the seasons of success unfolded, the older coach soon came to serve as something of a Merlin to Jackson's King Arthur.

When Jackson moved to Los Angeles, one of his first requests was that Winter move with him. It didn't take long for the Lakers players to understand why.

BRIAN SHAW: "He's seen so much basketball and all the players through the years and he's seen all the coaches coach."

Indeed, Winter had once played junior college ball against Jackie Robinson and later wound up at Southern Cal, where we was a teammate of Bill Sharman and Alex Hannum playing basketball for the legendary Sam Barry.

Lakers players got an indication of Winter's vast experience after watching him spin through a jump rope routine in his first days with the team. Most of them only knew him as the old guy who always sat next to Jackson during all those championship runs in Chicago, but the Lakers soon discovered a surprisingly nimble sort who was ready to challenge them or Jackson at every turn.

BRIAN SHAW: "We were practicing in Denver, and Phil had one of those heavy medicine balls. Tex was sitting on a table on the side. Phil took the ball and threw a bullet pass to Tex. The ball was coming right at him, and he jumped out of the way real quick. Then he got up and picked the ball up and fired right back at him. He was like, 'Oh, you wanna fire the ball at me?' Derek Fisher and I were sitting there, and we just started cracking up. We couldn't believe that he could move that fast. I hope that if I'm fortunate enough to make it to 78 that I can have as much spirit as he does."

That spirit had often evidenced itself in Winter's determination to criticize modern NBA athletes about their play. Winter considered himself a guardian of the game, an assistant coach so ancient and untouchable that he could say whatever he wanted to a high-salaried young player.

Winter hadn't been in Los Angeles long before his frankness chafed the supersensitive O'Neal, who would get angry at the criticism Winter offered about his play. Quietly fuming, the center would refuse to speak to the coach for several days. "He just kind of grunts his answers," Winter said. "He's got a heart of gold, but he gets mad at me and won't talk. He's very sensitive."

Winter acknowledged that this confronting of players was just one of the pressures he has taken off Jackson over the years. "I make his job easier," Winter said. "Phil knows that."

"They complement each other," said Bill Wennington, who played on three of Jackson's championship teams in Chicago. "Tex is the one that's gonna yell at you all the time. He's the one getting on you about the offense, so Phil doesn't have to do that."

Jackson himself was quite capable of leveling his own criticisms at players, but the more strident evaluations often fell to Winter, who grew so bold during the final years of his Bulls tenure as to fuss because Jordan's chest passes needed to be more fundamentally correct.

Winter also took it upon himself to regularly challenge Jackson himself, although it didn't take him long to bump up against Jackson's legendary stubbornness. If the head coach seemed too willing to sit passively on the bench without calling a time-out or making an adjustment, it was Winter who jumped in his ear, saying, "You better get off your ass and do some coaching."

Winter had often marveled at his friend's intensely psychological approach to building a championship team. He said the key to Jackson's success lay in his ability to orchestrate relationships with his players, his assistant coaches, his fellow employees, the media, his opponents, in fact just about all the parties inhabiting the rare environment of the NBA.

"Phil is a master manipulator," explained a longtime Bulls employee who worked daily with him. "You're talking about the media, the players, the staff, everybody."

Most important, Jackson possessed an uncanny ability to measure the impact of what he said and did on those around him, Winter said. "There's method in his madness. Always. If you see him do something you can figure it's calculated. He might be impulsive every once in a while. After all, he is human."

For the most part, though, if Jackson said or did something, it was a move intended to elicit a specific reaction from his players, from the opponent, from the media. Just the amount of effort and intelligence such an approach required was almost mind-boggling in itself, said guard Derek Fisher after watching Jackson renovate the Lakers.

The same could be said of Jackson's dealings with opponents, a practice that had drawn heated criticism over the years. His mind games with the other team usually involved sly comments made to the media, such as using the nickname "Van Gumby" for New York Knicks coach Jeff Van Gundy during the 1996 playoffs, or his labeling Sacramento Kings fans as "rednecks" during the 2000 playoffs. Less obvious to the public was the way Jackson crept into the minds of opposing players. Sacramento backup center Scot Pollard watched some of his Kings teammates fixate on Jackson's comments during their first-round playoff battle with the Lakers in 2000.

"He's great at working the media, I will say that," Pollard said. "If nobody who was playing in the games, or coaching the games, or refing in the games, paid attention to the media then there would be no head games, then he wouldn't be doing that."

But others do pay attention to the media, Pollard said. "People read that. If he says the other team doesn't do this well, then the other team reads that and they start thinking, 'We gotta prepare for this, because Phil says we don't do this well. So we gotta do this.'"

On more than one occasion over the years, Jackson had sat back during the playoffs and watched an opponent chase its tail over things he'd said.

"I chuckle quite a bit at it," Tex Winter said. "He's an amazing coach. He's unorthodox. He likes to play those mind games, the way he comments about the things that happen during a playoff series. He likes to get a point across, likes to jab it into the opponent. The things he presents in his media sessions, he's calculating."

He used all the devices of propaganda, including strong suggestion with his own players in the playoff scouting tapes they review over the course of each series. Jackson adopted from Bulls assistant coach Johnny Bach the technique of splicing snippets of other information into those scouting tapes, including bits of Three Stooges skits and other images, all used to suggest and emphasize points to the players. Jackson then expanded this process by showing entire feature films, spliced in pieces around scouting tapes, during the playoffs each year. "He'll splice in little scenes from movies to try to send a little message," explained former Bull Steve Kerr.

For the first round of the 2000 playoffs, he used the film *American History X* starring Edward Norton, about the lives of neo-Nazi youths filled with racial hatred. The film concluded with a moving passage about the futility of hatred and included an appeal for people to listen to the better angels of their nature. This message reemphasized Jackson's season-long efforts for O'Neal to take a kinder view of Bryant.

But Jackson also played games with the film's starker images, juxtaposing shots of the skinheaded Norton with his swastika tattoo alongside shots of Kings point guard Jason Williams, a white player with a shaved head. There were even allegations, based on a report in the *Washington Post*, that Jackson used shots of Sacramento coach Rick Adelman with his mustache to suggest Adolph Hitler.

Another activity conducted in private that Jackson fiercely guarded was the mindfulness sessions provided by psychologist and meditation enthusiast George Mumford. These efforts were in large part responsible for Jackson's image as a Zen master, a tag he disdained because it elevated his status to that of those who have spent a lifetime engrossed in spiritual endeavors. Jackson was certainly serious about his beliefs, but he was no priest.

Mumford's sessions, however, made immense sense for professional athletes because they were aimed at reducing the stress of competition by using a mix of meditation, tai chi, yoga, and common sense. When Jordan spoke of playing "in the moment" as he performed spectacularly in carrying the Bulls to their later championships, he was voicing the theme of these sessions.

Jackson said he considered the Mumford sessions a competitive secret and usually declined to discuss them in detail. Many of his players, however, raved about them, except for some veterans, such as Lakers forward A. C. Green, who gave the sessions a lukewarm response for religious reasons.

BILL WENNINGTON, FORMER JACKSON PLAYER: "George is pretty much there to relax your mind and body. To try and help you resolve the stress that's involved with everything. He tries to get your basketball life, your whole life, in a peaceful, relaxed state so that you can compete. You can't worry about what just happened, the basket you missed, the foul you made two minutes ago, because it's over. You can't worry about what's gonna happen the next time down the floor. You have to be right there in the moment. It's most important especially in the playoffs."

The Jackson approach also facilitated his teaching of the triangle offense, which posed a challenge for players trying to learn its complexities. Jackson had taught Jordan to share with his teammates in Chicago. Now the coaches faced a similar task of convincing O'Neal and Bryant of a new approach. Jackson knew exactly what he had to do to move things in the right direction. In Chicago, Tex Winter had watched in amazement as Jackson built a strong relationship with Jordan.

TEX WINTER: "When you have a relationship that strong with the star player, the rest of the team just kind of falls in line. Phil worked very hard at cultivating that relationship with Michael."

Jackson began building a similar relationship with O'Neal. Winter explained that Jackson knew that O'Neal was motivated by the opportunity to score lots of points, so he fashioned a trade-off with the big center. If O'Neal would show the leadership that Jackson wanted, then the triangle offense would provide him the opportunity to score large numbers of points.

This, of course, got down to the basic conflict between O'Neal and Bryant. When Jackson was hired, Bryant had purchased *Sacred Hoops* and gone up to his hotel room in Los Angeles to greet him. Later, O'Neal would travel to Montana to visit with Jackson. Obviously, both were eager to please their new coach, even to curry favor with him.

It was O'Neal who would take top priority in Jackson's plans. The coach began by placing responsibility squarely on the center's seven-one, 330-pound frame. "This team should be looking to win 60 games," Jackson told the L.A. media as training camp opened. "That's a realistic goal."

He paused in the middle of that thought and looked at O'Neal sitting nearby. "The ball is going into Shaq," Jackson said. "And he's going to have a responsibility to distribute the ball. It's going to be good for the team, and good for him."

O'Neal would go on to average 29.7 points per game while operating out of Jackson's triangle offense that first season, good enough to lead the league in scoring and to earn O'Neal's first MVP honors. In an acceptance speech he had been polishing for years, O'Neal would dub himself "The Big Aristotle."

For all the excitement over the big offensive numbers, Jackson reminded O'Neal and his teammates early and often that it was defense that would distinguish them. To play it, Jackson wanted O'Neal in shape and filled with desire to block shots and defend the basket. "Maybe I could play a little defense from the bench, who knows?" Jackson joked in that first press conference from training camp.

Jackson's initial disappointment over not getting Pippen led him to forecast a 5–5 start for his team in November. And that came before an October 13 injury forced Bryant to miss the first 15 games on the schedule. Yet even a setback such as Bryant's broken right wrist proved to be a blessing. It allowed the coaches to mold the team identity, then to add Bryant's frenetic energy to the equation in December, like some sort of super-octane fuel.

It would also allow time for the rift between Bryant and O'Neal to calm. On that issue, Jackson wasted little time. "I'm going to stop some of the gossiping, stop some of the rumor-mongering among the personnel here," he promised that first day.

At the time, Jackson and his coaches didn't realize just how deep a divide they faced. After the season, Winter would confide that he was shocked by the level of hatred O'Neal expressed for Bryant when the coaches first arrived on the scene.

TEX WINTER: "There was a lot of hatred in his heart. He would speak his mind in our team meetings. He was saying really hateful things. Kobe just took it and kept going."

O'Neal's main message to anyone who would listen was that the team could not win a championship with Bryant. It was an opinion that the center regularly expressed to management. Like West, though, the coaching staff saw Bryant as a Jordanlike player. His hands were smaller than Jordan's, but the athletic ability, the intelligence, the desire, were prodigious. What wasn't clear was whether Bryant would grow to possess the Alpha male nature that made Jordan so dominant in his late 20s. Bryant was still so young, it was hard for the coaches to see that. He certainly possessed the drive and work ethic.

But Jackson elected not to form a close relationship with Bryant. The coach reasoned that O'Neal's nature craved such a relationship, and Jackson turned just about all of his attention to O'Neal. Early in the season, Bryant would point out that he had yet to sit down for an in-depth conversation with Jackson. Bryant kept expecting that conversation to occur. But it never would. Jackson kept his time for O'Neal.

Some on the coaching staff pointed out that Bryant could have approached the coach about such a talk, but the young guard had such a strong sense of team issues that he seemed happy to let Jackson focus his efforts on soothing the center's harsh feelings.

For much of the healing between the center and guard, Jackson and Winter relied on their triangle. The main idea was that because the offense was so structured, it would make the relationships between O'Neal and Bryant smoother on the court. Still, the coaches found there was much residual anger on the part of O'Neal and other veterans against Bryant, so much anger that Jackson had to spend months counseling O'Neal on how to get over it.

The danger, said Winter, was that O'Neal seemed to influence the entire team against Bryant. So he and Jackson worked regularly on changing that attitude.

DEREK FISHER: "The coaches voiced to us that they weren't seeing the same things we were seeing when they watched film and when they watched what was going on. They didn't see the same selfishness or one-on-one play that we saw. What I tried to tell some of the other guys is that this is our fourth year now. Me, Shaq, Robert, Rick, Travis [Knight], so we still had issues that we had dealt with before this year. It was kind of similar to a relationship between a man and a woman where you get upset with all of these things from the past that come up. That's really where a lot of this stuff stemmed from. The coaches saw that a lot of this stuff would come in due time. But we were so impatient because we had dealt with it before."

For a time, it seemed that no matter what Bryant did, O'Neal and other teammates wanted to find fault with it. Winter revealed that he finally put together a videotape to prove to O'Neal that Bryant was doing just what he was supposed to do.

TEX WINTER: "I think Kobe really leaned over backward to get the ball into Shaq that first year. If there was a problem there, it was that I don't think Shaq appreciated what Kobe was trying to do to help his game."

And so it became easy for the coaches to take Bryant's early injury as a blessing. The guard's absence allowed the team's entire focus to fall upon O'Neal, which worked nicely into Jackson's plans. He had named O'Neal captain and spent considerable time talking through a new approach to the game. Jackson wanted more leadership, conditioning, and defense out of O'Neal.

Jackson also regularly called O'Neal's hand if he failed to do the right thing. Jackson, in fact, told *Sports Illustrated* that he doubted whether O'Neal could be a leader because his poor free throw shooting meant that he couldn't deliver at the end of games.

JOHN SALLEY: "Phil was all over Shaq, all the time. But Shaq could take it. It worked for him."

Opponents around the league began noticing that O'Neal was more focused, more effective with Jackson's coaching. "He's handing out a lot of punishment, too," Phoenix coach Danny Ainge said, after the Suns lost to the Lakers on November 15. "He's like the neighborhood bully. He's like a sixth-grader playing with second-graders."

O'Neal had 34 points, 18 rebounds, and 8 blocks against Phoenix. "I'll tell you what," Lakers forward Glen Rice said. "He could do that every game."

November had brought immediate trends, for O'Neal and the team. They opened the season with a big road win over Utah, only to be followed by a loss to Portland in which Pippen's fierceness clearly intimidated the Lakers. He seemed to know where the Lakers offense was taking them before the Lakers knew, a development the team first saw in a preseason game.

DEREK FISHER: "They knew the plays we were going to run before we did. They had this new attitude."

"The presence of Pippen on the court was really felt," Jackson said. "The effect that Scottie had when we played against Portland because of his ability to read the triangle, how to disrupt our offense, how to play Glen Rice, some of the things that he did are obvious."

Jackson's answer had been to sign free agent and former Bull Ron Harper, who would provide leadership throughout the season, especially later with Bryant's return. Harper would be a steadying, calming influence whenever the young guard's competitiveness raged to the point that it pushed him out of control.

The Lakers recovered from that November setback in Portland to cruise through the month with an 11–4 record, which helped O'Neal earn Player of the Month honors.

Bryant returned December 1, when he came off the bench to score 19 in a win over Golden State.

"It was nice to have Kobe's energy," Jackson said afterward. "He's just a wild, impulsive kid right now. He's still feeling his way."

"God, I had a headache I was so excited," Bryant told reporters. "My head was literally throbbing. The first half, I felt like I was on speed or something. I couldn't calm down."

Immediately the media began asking about the prospects of Bryant and O'Neal getting along with Bryant's energy changing the Lakers' attack. "I don't foresee any problems," Jackson said. "If there is, we'll rein him in."

The Lakers used the young guard's presence to secure a much-needed win over the Trail Blazers the very next game. Bryant settled the issue by blocking a late Pippen shot and corralling Portland's Damon Stoudamire on defense. All the veterans on the team had been eager to see Jackson immediately begin disciplining Bryant. But that didn't happen.

DEREK FISHER: "I think Phil wanted to see firsthand how things were, how Kobe participated in the games and practice, how we felt about him, how he felt about us. Phil waited to see all that before he made any judgments about whether there needed to be adjustments. He didn't just come right in telling Kobe he needed to curtail his game or his creativity. He really allowed things to develop, then here or there when it was pertinent, he would say something."

The season would also bring a quick answer to Jackson's own ability to get along with West. "I was worried when I first came out here," Winter admitted. There was the public perception that West and Jackson might have differing opinions on personnel issues, egged on by Jackson's penchant for offering his opinion to the media.

But Winter suspected that Jackson's presence had helped take the pressure off of West, who had been faced with trying to sort out the team's gnarly chemistry problems.

"I think Phil helps get the monkey off Jerry's back a little bit," Winter said. "I think they're gonna be all right. At least I think so."

With the addition of Bryant, they would instead soar off to a winning streak. They would continue to show surprising poise over the coming weeks, losing a game to Sacramento before ripping off 16 straight wins that would carry them well into January. Finally they lost a January 14th game at Indiana's Conseco Fieldhouse, and like that the Lakers came unglued. Suddenly they found themselves in a 3–7 free fall, and all the old panic resurfaced. O'Neal's feelings against Bryant gained strength. Soon the players were again pointing fingers and blaming Bryant's desire for stardom as their problem. "We can't win with Kobe" was O'Neal's insistent message.

Winter, though, saw the problem as nothing more than bad defense and maybe a touch of self-satisfaction in O'Neal. "We're getting broken down," the assistant coach said. "We've been vulnerable to penetration all year long, the high screen and roll. Kobe has a real tough time with it. So does Derek Fisher. And the side screen and rolls. That's most everybody's offense this day and age, especially against us."

As for the chemistry issue, Winter said the coaches were treading softly. "Most coaches, Phil included, have always sort of had a whipping boy," Winter explained. "And I think he's very careful not to have that become Kobe, because he realizes that he's got a great young player here and he doesn't want to squelch him too much. And yet he wants to control him."

As for O'Neal, Winter said, "He's not easy to coach. He has kind of a resentment for anybody to tell him anything that he's doing wrong.

"I think Phil treads very softly on Shaq," Winter said. "I think he still is trying to read the situation as to what is the best way to motivate Shaq. I don't think he knows yet. And I certainly don't know."

Mainly, Jackson focused on encouraging O'Neal to put away his anger. The harsh feelings against Bryant could surge through the entire roster. It helped that Bryant seemed to come out of All-Star Weekend a changed man, as a player focused on team play, Fisher said. A big factor had been Jackson's quiet encouragement of Bryant not to participate in the Slam Dunk contest. Bryant was defending champion, and Vince Carter was drawing raves. Fisher said the Lakers knew Bryant wanted to have a go at Carter, but he set that aside so that it wouldn't bring a focus on individual accomplishments over team things. It proved to be a crucial factor in the team's growth, although O'Neal was clearly mimicking Bryant's crossover dribble during All-Star warm-ups, then tossing the ball up into the stands to emphasize the guard's turnovers. Such open hostility had to cease, Magic Johnson confided, concluding that Jackson would soon get it under control.

But another factor at All-Star Weekend was Seattle's Gary Payton helping Bryant to understand screen-and-roll defense.

KOBE BRYANT: "I don't think Gary knows how much he helped me. I wasn't scared to ask. If I don't know something, I'm gonna ask. I'm willing to learn, and Gary's one of the best defensive guards in the league. For him to actually open himself up and share some of that knowledge was fantastic. Just in those brief moments he helped me out tremendously."

How important was the lesson? Right after the All-Star Game, Bryant began shutting down guards on other teams, beginning with a nationally televised game in which he held Philadelphia's Allen Iverson scoreless in the second half.

MAGIC JOHNSON: "That's what it's all about. To have a guy like Gary, who could have a chip on his shoulder, some people know him like that, to talk to Kobe. That went a long way."

Bryant demonstrated such dramatic defensive improvement afterward that he would wind up being named to the league's All-Defense first team.

Ultimately, it was the winning that helped the Lakers put away the hard feelings. A late February victory over Portland sent them on another victory binge, this time 19 straight games of surging confidence, which ended finally in a mid-March loss in Washington. Afterward, new Wizards executive Michael Jordan enjoyed a cigar at his former coach's expense. "Phil has always been the master of mind games," Jordan said of his old coach's new success. "He still is."

RICK FOX: "We had won 19 games in a row. Honestly, this was sad to say, but the game had gotten to where there was no real challenge. We were playing our best ball during that stretch. We were hitting on all cylinders. It was clicking, it was routine. Each night, we stepped out and it was rhythmic. Everything seemed to play out just as it did the game before. And so, you look at that and you realize, we started creating the challenges ourselves. We started to test the system, we started to become lax on defense. We wanted to see how big a hole we could dig ourselves before we came out. It was like we were testing how good we really were."

The highlight of the win streak was the 61 points O'Neal scored on his birthday in a win over the lowly Clippers. Immediately after losing to the Wizards, the Lakers ran off another 11 wins, with the grins growing taller at every stop on the schedule. All the trouble, however, had not been vanquished. April brought a pair of disappointing losses to San Antonio, including one to end the season in which Spurs power forward Tim Duncan sat out with an injury.

RICK FOX: "It wasn't the most confident way to finish a 67-win season, losing two games, including one on the road. Tim Duncan was not in the game and we still lost. I wouldn't say your confidence wavers, but it's obvious there was a tension."

The Surprise

For so many years the Lakers had been screwing up in the playoffs. Swept by Utah. Dismissed by Utah. Swept by San Antonio. It became a part of their personality. But Jackson had helped them to a 67-win regular season. Suddenly hopes surged that their playoff troubles were behind them. The Lakers coaches, though, weren't so sure. They were uneasy about how this fragile team would perform in the playoffs.

Sure enough, they struggled to put away Sacramento and Phoenix and Portland. A key win came in Game 2 of their second-round series with Phoenix. Bryant hit a last-second shot to seal the victory. Nothing had to be said; the message had been clearly sent that this team could win a title with Bryant.

It was the battle against the Blazers in the Western Conference Finals that provided the kind of challenge that forces a team to grow up. As the series opened, Jackson figured to distract Pippen, the Blazers leader, with a run of trademark mind games. Behind the scenes, the Lakers coaching staff plotted a strategy designed to put even more pressure on Pippen, often criticized over the years as being mentally fragile, by making him do more and more over the course of each game. They wanted to force him into running the Blazer show and initiating the offense. "Ultimately," Jackson told reporters, "he's the one."

Asked if he was feeling the pressure that Jackson was trying to put on him, Pippen replied, "He's already tried to do that, saying our team has no leader and that we're overpaid."

In Game 1, the Lakers survived a desperate fouling tactic by Portland coach Mike Dunleavy aimed at sending O'Neal to the line. Such efforts had long been dubbed "Hack-a-Shaq." Repeatedly squeezing, holding, and wrapping him up, the Blazers forced O'Neal to shoot 25 free throws in the fourth quarter. It did little more than delay the game to the point of irritation. The Lakers used the stopped play to set up their defense for each possession and won handily.

Jackson used Game 1 to probe Pippen's psyche. In the first half when Pippen was working furiously on defense, the Lakers coach called Pippen over. "I told him he can't guard everyone on the whole team," Jackson said. "He said, 'I'm gonna try.'"

Told that Jackson had revealed their conversation, Pippen frowned and said, "We'll leave it at that. I'm not even thinking about my relationship with Phil Jackson."

The Blazers then changed the tenor of the series by claiming Game 2 in a massive 106–77 win in the Staples Center. Needing to make a show of their determination, the Lakers had strangely played without emotion and energy. The coaching staff left the building dumfounded.

"What we remember is the attitude Portland carried off the floor," Jackson said. "[The Blazers] were kind of jackals down there on the bench."

The Blazers contained Bryant for most of the second half in the third game in Portland, but he produced some big plays in the game's final moments to give the Lakers a 93–91 victory and a 2–1 series lead. Bryant blocked a last-ditch shot by Portland center Arvydas Sabonis to preserve the victory. Bryant also had a big steal on the Blazers' previous possession.

With the Blazers fuming and seemingly divided, the Lakers then got another win in Game 4, with both contests marked by the Blazers' high energy to open the games and with the Lakers' late surge to win.

Down 3–1, the Blazers returned to L.A. and found a way to win in a game that reflected Pippen's great competitive nature. Jackson had pointed out that Pippen threw an elbow in John Salley's head late in Game 4, an act that should have brought Pippen's suspension.

Pippen responded with fire in Game 5, using the occasion to break Jordan's all-time record for playoff steals. "We know in our hearts we can outplay this team," said Pippen, who scored 22 points, grabbed six rebounds, had six steals, blocked four shots, and got the entire Lakers backcourt into foul trouble.

After Game 5, Jackson told Pippen he shouldn't have been allowed to play.

"Phil is not my coach," Pippen said when asked about the exchange. "I'm not listening to Phil. I'm not listening to nothing you tell me about Phil."

His play helped the Blazers to produce a convincing win in Game 6 back in Portland. Only six other times had an NBA team come back from a 3–1 deficit to win a series, but the Blazers seemed capable of pulling it off.

The Lakers were strangely passive again in Game 6, obviously intimidated by Pippen's mental toughness. Only Rick Fox off the bench attempted to stand up to Pippen's aggressiveness, which brought a heated exchange in the fourth period. To the fans, it perhaps seemed like a silly incident, but to the Lakers coaches the gesture was significant. Jackson knew that someone had to stand up to Pippen's intimidation.

RICK FOX: "That was our downfall the previous years. We never really went out in the playoffs and set a tone and sent a message that we were fighting for this game and that we were about doing whatever it took to win. I told myself I was just not gonna let a series go by where we went down as cowards basically."

Mainly, the Lakers lost because they were no-shows on defense, which forced them into a seventh game back in the Staples Center. "Now we have to bite, scratch, kick, and claw," Brian Shaw said.

But the Blazers outplayed the Lakers in Game 7 and took a 16-point lead that seemed sure to end the Lakers' championship hopes. Faced with elimination, Jackson's team miraculously produced the biggest Game 7 fourth-quarter comeback in NBA history.

Portland led 75–60 with 10:28 to play, but the Lakers stopped Portland 10 consecutive times. It was Bryant's block of Bonzi Wells's shot that led to a Shaw trey that cut the lead to 10 with 9:38 remaining. Afterward, the Blazers could only look on in glum, stunned silence as Los Angeles celebrated its first trip to the NBA Finals in nearly a decade.

The Blazers had controlled the early periods by again gumming up the lane and not allowing O'Neal to do his heavy lifting. But then the Lakers did a little gumming of their own, getting stop after stop after stop in the fourth period as the Blazers settled into a mask of horror.

"You lose yourself in it," Glen Rice said of the comeback, a 25–4 run. "We were thinking keep going, keep applying the pressure, continue to keep going down on the offensive end and keep getting good shots and hopefully this team will fall in the end. And they did."

Once the Lakers got going, the Staples crowd fed their energy, which was highlighted by Bryant's alley-oop to O'Neal for a thunder-happy slam and an 85–79 lead. O'Neal offered up his approval afterward: "Kobe's a great player. When he went to the hole, we caught eye contact and he just threw it up."

Kobe Bryant: "I thought I threw the ball too high. Shaq went up and got it, I was like, 'Damn!'"

Jackson, the coach known for being so reluctant to use time-outs, used two key ones to tighten the Lakers' concentration and to shift their intentions away from simply throwing the ball down to O'Neal in the post, a move that the Blazers had shut down time and again.

Through the third period, O'Neal had but two field goals for the game and would not score from the field during the disastrous third period. "What we basically told the team is that every time we forced the ball into him, we were creating turnovers either for Shaq or for us," Jackson said.

BRIAN SHAW: "Phil told us not to worry about getting the ball to Shaq. He said to play, to take what the defense was giving us."

Just as impressive, the leadership that Jackson had encouraged in O'Neal all season finally showed up in grand fashion. It was O'Neal's dealings with his mental approach that struck the coaches and his teammates. Instead of sinking into frustration in those difficult moments, he showed his teammates that he could stay focused and positive.

BRIAN SHAW: "When you have a leader like that, everybody's watching him, to see his body language. And, despite the fact that things weren't maybe going the way he wanted them to, he still kept his wits about him."

The other keen development in the win over Portland had been the signs of a bonding between O'Neal and Bryant. It was as if Bryant refused to get discouraged. "I think they came to respect each other," Winter said, although the coaches could never be sure what the players were merely doing as a public gesture and what they truly felt.

KOBE BRYANT: "We just did it our separate ways. That's all we did all season long. It just depended on what we needed in certain situations. So even though we went our separate ways, it all linked up in the end."

O'Neal's words had much more weight than outside observers could have ever imagined. They emphasized an emerging yet still tentative bond between the two, and they rewarded one of the finest, most intensely psychological coaching efforts of Jackson's distinguished career.

SCOTTIE PIPPEN: "I cherish the memory of playing against Phil's team in that series. If we had come out on top, I could have said that I defeated the triangle. But I didn't. I knew Tex's system well. It's hard to defeat it. I may have shown them my best hand early when we beat them early in the year. They were prepared for me in the playoffs. Phil knew I knew that offense. He knew I'd eat that offense up."

Together

Many observers thought that after their win over Portland the NBA Finals against the Indiana Pacers would be anticlimactic for the Lakers, but Jackson and his staff were concerned because the Pacers were such a fine shooting team. They didn't look that way in Game 1. Reggie Miller made just one of 16 shots, and the Lakers won in a breeze, mainly by getting the ball to O'Neal and watching him work against an Indiana defense that for some strange reason failed to double-team. His 43 points and 19 rebounds produced a 104–87 victory in Game 1.

"This offense is designed to go away from pressure," Derek Fisher said. "We tried to attack the pressure against Portland. Indiana tried to single-cover Shaq. I'd be surprised if they don't play the next game differently."

Certainly Pacers coach Larry Bird and his assistants quickly tired of answering questions about their strategy. So the Pacers offered quicker, stronger double-teams in the second contest, and the Lakers answered by shooting out to a 33–18 lead after the first quarter. Bryant suffered an ankle injury early in the contest.

KOBE BRYANT: "I thought I broke something. I heard a pop. I was laying on the floor and thinking this couldn't happen."

Eventually, the Pacers' double-teams had some effect, and they cut the lead to two points in the third period. But the late stretches of the game became Shaw's hour to shine, just as he had down the stretch in Game 7 against the Blazers. His shooting and O'Neal's overpowering presence were enough for Jackson's group to take a 2–0 series lead, 111–104.

Hobbled and on crutches, Bryant was unable to play in Game 3. Presented that edge, Indiana finally got a win, to pull within 2–1.

Game 4 will be remembered as Bryant's moment. He returned from injury and joined O'Neal in matching the Pacers bucket for bucket down the stretch. The battle went to overtime, O'Neal fouled out, and Bryant was faced with leading the Lakers by himself in a key moment. In a gesture brimming with more meaning than fans could understand, Bryant went over to the center who had questioned him so long.

KOBE BRYANT: "I told him, 'I've got you, big fella.' And he said okay. We went out there and just played. I felt that I was in the backyard again. I was a kid. We weren't on NBC. This wasn't the NBA Finals, it wasn't a thousand fans in the crowd and people watching on TV. It was a game about putting the ball in the basket. That's all it was about for me."

In the past in Chicago, Jackson and Winter had spread the floor in such moments and allowed Jordan to go to work. But with the Lakers, spreading the floor had never worked, Winter explained, because opposing teams would never leave O'Neal and kept the defense packed in. The spread floor might have worked if O'Neal had been willing to develop a 10- to 15-foot shot allowing him to move away from the basket. But he had resisted that at every turn.

Now, though, he was off the floor, and Jackson ordered the Lakers to spread the formation wide to spread the defense. This allowed Bryant the room to work, and it was further aided by his sore ankle, which meant that he pulled up for midrange jumpers rather than trying to drive all the way to the hole.

Observers would later describe the performance as Jordanesque. In overtime, Bryant delivered the Lakers and offered irrefutable evidence that O'Neal had been wrong. The victory gave them a 3–1 lead in the series.

KOBE BRYANT: "We were able to spread the floor, and I hit a couple of jump shots for us and took us to the brink. During the season, I wanted to use the spread floor. I told him, 'Phil, man, why don't you open the court?' He said, 'We're not ready for that. We'll get to that.' I said open it up. That's when I can go to work. But I'm glad that we waited till the playoffs to use it."

TEX WINTER: "It was the moment that opened the door for all of his performances beyond that point. He felt that way in his heart, and he went out there and did it."

DEREK FISHER: "To knock down the shots that he knocked down in that game, it was only something that great players have the ability to do. At such a young age he put a notch on his belt for taking his place as one of the greatest players to ever play the game."

Before the Lakers could be crowned, though, they suffered a terrible defeat in Game 5, which sent the contest back to the Staples Center in Los Angeles.

KOBE BRYANT: "I was sitting on the bench during the blowout, I looked over at Shaquille. I told him it would be much better to win it at home anyway. And he said you're probably right."

Closing out at home proved fitting, because the city hadn't celebrated an NBA title since Magic Johnson and Kareem Abdul-Jabbar led the Lakers to a win over the Detroit Pistons in the 1988 NBA championship series.

This time, the honor was O'Neal's. Bryant scored 26 points (on 8-for-27 shooting), grabbed 10 rebounds, and had four assists, two of them to O'Neal as the Lakers charged back to take the lead for the first time since the first period. With Fox and Horry hitting key shots, the Lakers moved to a 101–94, despite a stretch of O'Neal missing free throw after free throw. The Pacers, meanwhile, used free throws themselves and a Rose trey to tie it, 103–103, with 5:08 left.

The Lakers surged again to 110–103, with 3:02 left, but the Pacers pulled within one with 1:32 left, at 110–109. This time the Lakers coaches went to screen-and-roll action out of their offense, a surprise for the Pacers in that the Lakers rarely used it. That was enough, with O'Neal setting high screens for Bryant, to get enough late free throws from Bryant for a 116–111 victory and the franchise's first championship in a dozen seasons. The big center, so loathe to set picks and do non-scoring chores on offense in seasons past, was executing Jackson's disciplined vision of the game.

KOBE BRYANT: "We went back to the same thing that worked for us in Game 4, spreading the floor and penetrating, and then attacking them. I was able to get to the free throw line and knock down some free throws."

SHAQUILLE O'NEAL: "I think we needed Phil to do it. Phil and his coaching staff was a staff that was going to bring this team over the hump. We always won 50, 60 games. When we got into certain situations in the playoffs, we could never get over the hump. We had home-court advantage, but we made a lot of mistakes in the playoffs. But Phil was able to keep his poise and have us watch film. When you look at a guy like Phil, if you're a leader, he's not worried. Why should you worry? He prepared us very well."

Could another coach have done it? the *L.A. Times* asked Jerry Buss. "Great question," the owner replied. "I guess the answer's no. There's some great coaches, but I think this took a very special combination of talents. Pat Riley, a long time ago, was able to knit together a bunch of superstars and make them into a team. Phil has been able to do that with this team. And at least in my mind, I'd have to doubt that anybody else could have done it."

BRIAN SHAW: "Phil beat his drum with a persistence on the morning of our last game. Everybody on the team seemed to perk up at the sound of it. We heard it. It made a difference."

17

Lifted High, Pulled Asunder

The Lakers had long been known as an organization that generated a goodly number of rumors. This was due in no small part to Jerry West, who over the years had come to include a variety of people—mostly officials with other teams, reporters, and players—in his circle of confidants.

Thus it was of no great surprise that, as the Lakers made their way through the 2000 playoffs, a rumor began making the rounds that West was planning to leave the team after four decades as a player, coach, and executive. West had seemingly contemplated retirement, or at least contemplated leaving the organization, virtually every year for a decade, but now, according to the rumor, he had finally come to the end.

Since Jackson had taken over as coach, West had largely kept his distance from the team, and by spring seemed thoroughly detached from the proceedings. He had made appearances at a few playoff games, but for many others he stayed away, trusting one friend or another to keep him abreast of the score with a call to his cell phone. Ostensibly, the reason for his absences was that the games simply made him too nervous to watch.

J. A. ADANDE, *LOS ANGELES TIMES*: "The amazing thing is that he was so insecure and so uncertain of things. Here was this great team that he had put together, and he could barely even watch it. He'd disappear down the tunnel during games and head out on the road. This team he put together, his lasting tribute to L.A., his last couple of years he wasn't even watching it. He was driving up to Santa Barbara. That stuns me more than a bit. Obviously the guy was Mr. Clutch as a player. Here he was with the game on the line, and he was the calmest guy on the court, wanted the ball in his hands. He could control everything and always come through in the end and make the shot. Here was this guy who was so cool under pressure and yet sitting in the stands he would crumble. He was a mess."

As he had every summer for years, West began agonizing over his future with the team, only this time he stayed away from the office the entire summer of 2000 and offered little input on personnel decisions.

Word of West's plans reached the press not long after the team celebrated its championship victory with a parade through downtown L.A., but no one in the organization would confirm that West planned to retire.

Then, in July, broadcaster Larry Burnett, working as a freelancer for the CBS affiliate in Los Angeles, contacted Jackson at his summer home in Montana and received on-the-record confirmation that indeed West's 40-year tenure with the team was finished.

It would be weeks before West himself would make that declaration, after a wry aside about Jackson's sense of timing. West made his announcement in early August in a brief written statement that thanked many but made no mention of Jackson, even though the coach had just directed West's beloved Lakers to a championship.

At the time, news reports out of Los Angeles indicated West was unhappy that Jackson, after the breakup of his marriage to wife June, had taken up with Jeanie Buss.

Not long after West's announcement a new sort of rumor began making the rounds of the league's innermost circles. According to the story, Jackson had "kicked West out" of the Lakers' locker room at one point during the postseason as the team was making its run to the NBA title.

Although most were reluctant to discuss it publicly, an official with the Bulls said he had heard about the incident, as did Eddie Jones, the former Laker, who talked frequently with many of his former teammates, including Bryant and O'Neal.

"How do you like that?" the Bulls official said. "Phil kicked the logo out of his locker room. How smart is that?"

Jones, a West admirer, had spoken with West privately before the Hall of Famer announced his retirement from the team in August.

Inside some NBA coaching circles, it was said West's competitive streak, his obsessiveness about his team, made the Lakers difficult to coach. Jones, an All-Star who played four years in Los Angeles before being traded to Charlotte in the middle of the 1999 season, had witnessed the situation firsthand. Jones said he wasn't surprised that Jackson had moved to exclude West from the team.

EDDIE JONES: "I knew it was coming. As a coach, you gotta have guys' confidence, you gotta have guys who believe in what you're saying. You don't want anybody in their ear saying this and saying that."

Actually, Jackson had asked West to go out of the locker room rather than "kicked him out." Sources within Jackson's tight inner circle said it happened at the end of a game, when Jackson liked to speak privately with his players for a few moments without interruption. The moment came immediately after a game during the Lakers' playoff series with Portland.

Tex Winter confirmed that, coming into the job, Jackson had concluded he would not be able to coexist with West in Los Angeles. Jackson saw West as too weird, too unpredictable, possessing too much ego (which to some sounded much like Jackson himself). Even one very loyal longtime Lakers staff member acknowledged that West had always been "an active general manager," brilliant in his acquisition of players but sometimes too anxiety-ridden and meddlesome to allow the team to settle down and function smoothly.

Winter said Jackson had calculated that West's pride would be hurt by Jackson requesting that he step out of the Lakers' locker room so that the coach could have a word with the team. It was seemingly a subtle thing, yet its implication rang like a hammer through the organization. By doing it, Jackson had sent this message: Jerry West, who had lived and breathed the Lakers for 40 years, was not part of the team. The coach, it seemed, had found the perfect way to nudge West out of the organization. As coach of the Bulls, Jackson had used a similar technique and called it "setting boundaries." Only a few were allowed inside the team circle. In L.A., West was no longer one of them.

DEL HARRIS, FORMER LAKERS COACH: "Only someone with six rings could have done it. I don't know if it was so much Phil as it was his status. I don't know that that needed to be done. I always felt Jerry was a plus for us, not only by getting the players there. Yes, the Lakers had always been Jerry's team, but if there were other issues that came up, I could always count on Jerry to [help] good-guy, bad-guy it [with players]. It's true that Jerry's involvement was a factor, but I didn't necessarily see it as a negative thing."

Not surprisingly, West didn't show for the press conference announcing his departure. "If you knew Jerry, I think you knew he wouldn't be here," Mitch

Kupchak, his successor as Lakers vice president in charge of basketball operations, told the gathered media.

"Obviously, Jerry West is irreplaceable," Jerry Buss, who also failed to appear, said in a prepared statement. "What he has meant to the Lakers franchise over the past 40 years is immeasurable."

Jackson's dislodging of West from the organization would later prove to have far-reaching implications. It left both Buss and new team vice president Mitch Kupchak wary of Jackson.

TEX WINTER: "I think Mitch Kupchak was a little intimidated by Phil. I think Phil did it on purpose with his persona and his style. He's very strong-willed, very overpowering, very intelligent. All you have to do is look at Phil's record and look at the people he's gone over, at how Phil has just willed himself over people."

Jackson had used the force of his personality to tame the entire Chicago Bulls roster, including the substantial egos of Jordan and team general manager Jerry Krause. In Los Angeles, he had shepherded Bryant and O'Neal into championship form, then numbered West among his victims.

There was little wonder then, that three years later in 2003, when Tex Winter was contemplating his own retirement, Kupchak supposedly told Winter that the team needed him to stay on the job "because no one else in the organization can stand up to Phil." The comment implied that Buss and Kupchak both remained concerned about Jackson's power games.

There was no question that Jackson had longed for more control of the team's personnel matters. If he was going to sustain a run of championships in Los Angeles, Jackson figured he needed to bring in players that fit his sophisticated approach to the game, the triangle offense. With West's departure, Jackson had the personnel control that he had wanted since his Chicago days. But it soon became clear what a challenge the team's personnel issues would present. The Lakers needed a power forward, a backup center to give O'Neal some help, and a strong perimeter shooter. But Jackson was like Jerry Krause in that no other NBA team seemed willing to do him any favors, Winter said. Dallas Mavericks owner Mark Cuban and coach Don Nelson had even publicly congratulated themselves over breaking up a trade that would have given the Lakers forward Christian Laettner.

TEX WINTER: "People thought that Phil had gotten enough already. They didn't want to help him."

On the other hand, West was highly regarded by all around the NBA and had offered the Lakers their best hope of dealing with other teams. Under the guidelines of his departure, West agreed to at least accept the phone calls that Kupchak made to seek advice. West badly wanted release from his long-term Lakers contract, which would allow him to work for another team. But Jerry Buss wouldn't want to give West that release.

Which meant that in the wake of his departure, West was left to stew unhappily, and the Lakers front office seemed more than a bit disoriented. After all, West had been the heart and soul of the team for so long, the rock from which everyone else in the organization had gained a sense of stability.

Whereas owners in both Portland and Dallas had spent huge sums to beef up their lineups, the Lakers remained a tightfisted operation headed by Buss, who had made known his desire to cut costs in the wake of the championship.

"It will be a challenge," Winter predicted.

The situation, however, eased later in the off-season after Kupchak engineered a trade that sent disgruntled Glen Rice to New York while bringing in Horace Grant from Seattle to fill the team's need at power forward. Also added were troubled guard Isaiah Rider and rookie Mark Madsen, another power forward.

There was yet even more change in the wake of the team's NBA championship and West's departure. Bryant had moved out of his parents' home into his own place nearby in Pacific Palisades. And he had begun courting Vanessa Laine, an 18-year-old high school senior he had met on the set of a Snoop Dogg video shoot. In an amazingly quick turnaround, Bryant acknowledged that he was romantically interested, then proposed and presented Laine with a diamond worth an estimated $1,100,000. Jackson raised his eyebrows and wondered publicly if his young guard wasn't moving too fast. Winter, though, had regularly advised Bryant that he needed more in his life than just basketball.

KOBE BRYANT: "When he found out I was engaged, he said, 'Oh good for you. Now you can kinda take your mind off of basketball a little bit; now you can finally relax a little bit.' I thought, 'Yeah, Tex, maybe you're right.'"

The relationship and Bryant's eventual marriage would bring an estrangement from his parents, who disapproved. His answer to this conflict and upheaval in his personal life was to work harder on his game.

Sufficiently stocked with talent, the Lakers seemed set to defend their title. Instead, they quickly found trouble in the early moments of the 2000–2001 season. First, O'Neal had celebrated too hard during the off-season and came into training camp way out of shape, a development that deeply disappointed Jackson and his assistants, not to mention the hardworking Bryant. Of course, O'Neal hadn't been alone in his sloth. Jackson said that only forward Rick Fox and Bryant had come into camp in shape and ready to play.

For the 2000 season, the Lakers had been a 67-win juggernaut. But in 2001 they would have to close the season on a remarkable 8–0 streak just to reach 56 wins. One key factor was the loss of point guard Derek Fisher to foot surgery. He would miss three-fourths of the season before returning in March.

As assistant Bill Bertka explained, Fisher was the only Lakers guard who could provide pressure on the opponent's ball handler. Ron Harper had once provided such pressure brilliantly for the Bulls, but he was simply too old, his knees too creaky. And Bryant showed a fine ability to pressure the ball, but it also made him vulnerable to foul trouble.

Without ball pressure, the Lakers defense, so effective the previous season, now shriveled. The lack of defensive intensity only worsened the chemistry problems. O'Neal's lack of conditioning had left him vulnerable to injury and poor play. He started the season by missing shots he usually made and shot less than 50 percent during key stretches. His free throws plunged into the 20 percent range and made him a laughingstock around the league. With the center struggling, Bryant reasoned that he should take over the offense. It wasn't long before O'Neal and his teammates were grumbling that Kobe was acting selfish.

TEX WINTER: "Shaq started pouting. In effect he was saying to us, 'If I'm not the primary option on offense, don't expect me to work hard on defense.'"

Although he played well, Bryant himself struggled to find consistency. He would make just 8 of 31 shots in a home loss to Milwaukee, then hit 20 of 26 to score 45 points in a win at Houston. After the Houston win, Jackson compared him to Jordan, but O'Neal fumed that Bryant was trying to hog all the glory. It was clear that the nasty conflicts of the past had come back to life. And to some observers, the dislike seemed greater than before.

"I'm just going to play within the flow of the game," Bryant said. "If people want to criticize that, they're going to criticize that."

Jackson conceded that Bryant, who was leading the league in scoring as the new year neared, was playing the best ball of his life. Some observers began calling Bryant the game's best all-around player. "He's got a level of commitment to his game and to wanting to be the best that few guys have," Phoenix Suns Coach Scott Skiles said. "Nobody on our team has that commitment, that's for sure."

The Lakers entered the new year with a 23–11 record, but there was a sense of uneasiness about the team. Bryant confided that despite his individual success he was miserable and even had doubts about his love for the game.

TEX WINTER: "Kobe said that he'd spent a lot of time working on his game in the off-season, working on his shots, working on his moves, and improving his game so he would have a chance to be the best player that he could possibly be. Then to come back and have people fault the efforts he made through the summer to make himself what he was, that was very discouraging to him. My wife Nancy indicated to me that she thought Kobe's heart had been broken at that particular point."

His resentment would become a pattern for the Lakers. It was based on the fact that Jackson seemed willing to overlook O'Neal's laziness. Because of O'Neal's extreme sensitivity to criticism, his shortcomings brought mild rebukes. All the while Jackson maintained his aggressive criticism of Bryant. This double standard became increasingly difficult for Bryant to accept. Bryant said he finally decided such despair served no purpose and used his strong will to throw it off.

KOBE BRYANT: "I just woke up one morning and decided I wasn't going to let it affect me anymore."

January brought a cover story about Bryant in *ESPN The Magazine*, in which he revealed that Jackson had come to him in November and asked him to back off his aggressive approach. Bryant said he told Jackson that instead of backing off his game he needed to step it up more.

Bryant had warned his teammates before the article came out and even tried to back off his tough talk, but the story infuriated O'Neal. The center told reporters that Bryant's selfishness was the main reason the team wasn't playing well.

Bryant countered that O'Neal still wasn't in shape and still wasn't playing defense. Jackson likened the two of them to little children arguing in a sandbox. Not surprisingly, the Lakers dropped four of their next seven games. Their 15 losses equaled the losses for the entire previous season.

February brought injuries to O'Neal and rumors that the center was again trying to have Bryant traded. Although Bryant and an injured O'Neal appeared to be buddies at the All-Star game in Washington, that wasn't the case.

March brought more trouble, this time with a host of rumors that there was a rift between Jackson and Bryant, who was sidelined by injuries to his shoulders, ankles, and psyche. Toward the end of the month, Jackson made what he would later admit was an unbelievable blunder in an interview with Rick Telander of the *Chicago Sun-Times*. The coach revealed the contents of a private conversation with Bryant and, for some reason, decided to discuss an old rumor about Bryant "sabotaging" his team's high school games to make himself a game savior.

Winter was furious with Jackson for his comments to the newspaper. So was Bryant's old high school coach from Pennsylvania, Gregg Downer, who told reporters Jackson needed to apologize for spreading a story that had no basis in truth. Bryant was clearly wounded by the betrayal, although he made little public comment. The incident would frame Jackson's relationship with his star guard.

Bryant and his agent, Arn Tellem, turned to Jerry West for counsel about how to deal with Jackson's serious breach of trust. To make matters worse, Jackson got wind that Tellem was threatening a slander lawsuit against him for his statement.

For a time, it appeared to some Jackson observers that the coach might even have panicked as his team fell apart before his eyes. It was then that Jackson apparently leaked a story to Sam Smith of the *Chicago Tribune* that the Lakers might well trade Bryant in the off-season. Jackson apparently had his associates imply other threats to Bryant that the young guard better get in line or face the trading block. To longtime observers, the moves were trademark Jackson, a use of media messages and other pressures to influence events.

Jackson appeared on NBC's "The Tonight Show," and host Jay Leno asked the coach if he wanted to announce a trade of Kobe Bryant right on the air.

Jackson just smiled. With another organization or another owner, a coach of Jackson's power might have set enough of a public relations agenda to force the trade.

While Jerry Buss had a relationship with Bryant, Buss and O'Neal remained distant. The owner had also distanced himself from Jackson, even though the coach's relationship with Jeanie Buss had matured to the point that she suggested matrimony.

SHAQUILLE O'NEAL: "Jerry Buss has been good to me. He's given me two great deals in one lifetime, so I can't ever complain about what I've gotten. I've spoken to him a couple of times, but nothing really serious. I'm not gonna go to the man upstairs and schmooze him. It's just not my style."

TEX WINTER: "Jerry Buss stayed out of the way, at least openly. The coaching staff rarely saw hide nor hair of him. It was strange, but he was inclined to have a number of people on his payroll that he listened to."

Among those confidants minority owner Magic Johnson held definite opinions about the team's chemistry. "He's not going to get traded," Johnson told reporters. "Just point blank. Enough said. I definitely think it has put a strain on the organization. You never want an organization or a team to seem like it's divided, or guys jumping on sides and things like that.

"Our whole organization has been built on the fact that we've always taken care of our own. We've never aired our dirty laundry. We've taken care of it in-house.

"Because now it's more than Kobe and Shaq. It's much more than that. Now instead of focusing on basketball, we're focusing on issues outside of basketball. And I think that's taken a toll on the team."

Strangely, in the midst of the controversy, the Lakers set off on an extended streak, winning each of their regular season games in April, then pushing on to finish the greatest run in NBA playoff history, a 15–1 dash to their second straight league championship.

Just what was it that made the Lakers change for the good? At one point during the tumultuous spring of 2001 West had reportedly told O'Neal, "I played with two of the all-time greats, Wilt Chamberlain and Elgin Baylor. You don't think we had personal rivalries going on back then? You've got to stop being a baby. Put all this personal stuff aside and do what's important. Put the team's success first."

West's circle of confidants spread the word that he had become extremely upset with the chemistry and status of the team. He had long held Bryant's ear on a number of issues, meaning that in some ways, the tug of wills between Bryant and Jackson really reflected the coach's conflicts with West. West, though, refrained from making it personal. Some of Bryant's effort to placate O'Neal came from West. The guard respected West and heeded his opinion that the ball needed to go inside.

"In the last two or three days, I've heard Shaq say, 'I've rededicated myself.' To me, that's big," Magic Johnson told reporters as the tumult began to calm. "I've heard all the other stuff. But now, Shaq is saying, 'It's me. I'm the one who has to get into shape. I'm the one who has to be ready for the second half run. I'm the one who has to close the middle down like I did last year. I'm the one who has to do it.' You see, now he's saying what he has to do. He's not blaming everybody else."

Team psychologist George Mumford said that things weren't quite as bad as they had been perceived. Another factor was that Jackson had Mumford working quietly behind the scenes for months, patiently dealing with chemistry issues. The team's mind-set was healing even as tempers flared.

"We learned some things," Jackson said, "through some real hard lessons."

One saving grace was the March 13 return of Derek Fisher. He began making jump shots, leading the team and running the offense. More important, as assistant Bill Bertka explained, his return meant that the Lakers could again pressure the ball, a key to the rest of their defense being effective.

"Everything that we lacked the first part of the season, he's brought with him," Laker Brian Shaw said of Fisher. "His toughness, his defensive prowess, he's been knocking down the outside shot consistently, and we just feed off of his energy."

It was during the stretch, with team anxiety at its highest, that Bryant sat out 10 games with an assortment of injuries. The team went 7–3 in his absence, capped by a sweep of a four-game road trip in early April. Closing the season with an eight-game victory streak suddenly revived their confidence.

With the arrival of the playoffs, the Lakers faced Portland, Sacramento, and San Antonio in order. To get them ready for that run of teams with strong power forwards, Jackson spliced scenes of *Gladiator* in and around the scouting tapes he showed the team. As with most of his video selections for his previous teams in Chicago, Jackson was seeking to build "togetherness" for the playoffs.

"The reality is this is kind of a gladiator's life—here today, gone tomorrow," the coach explained. "And you've got to develop that teamwork and that team play, and that's really the challenge of coaches right now and of teams.

"We know what we are. We know what we're built on. We're built on the fact that Kobe and Shaq are the best one-two combination in the game, and the complementary players around them want to play as a team and want to figure in this."

In retrospect, the veteran role players—Rick Fox, Ron Harper, Derek Fisher, Brian Shaw, and Robert Horry—would weigh large as a factor in the team's ability to win three straight titles. And as they wore down, the team's effectiveness would disappear.

"One of the main reasons they won the titles was the surrounding cast," explained one of Jackson's assistants. "The team's two major talents were so eaten up with narcissism that it was the veteran leadership that made the difference at all the key moments. Harper was a leader on the floor, Horry was an intellectual leader, Fox stepped up and helped the team find its emotional level, and Shaw was a spiritual leader. Those guys should get a lot of the credit."

O'Neal had averaged 33.7 points over the final 11 games of the regular season, and when Bryant returned from injury, the guard showed that he was ready to build on the center's energy. After all, O'Neal was now in shape and playing defense as well as offense. The two stars working together was another obvious key. "It's going to make things a lot easier," Bryant predicted. "Then he and I can just run screen and roll. You're going to have to pick your poison." Portland, Sacramento, and San Antonio all found themselves facing that choice. The Lakers swept all three on the way to an 11–0 run to the NBA Finals against Philadelphia.

Along the way, Bryant worked as a playmaker, then found the right situation for exploding in big offensive games. His first big explosion was Game 3 against Sacramento, a 103–81 Lakers win that saw him score a playoff career high of 36 points. The Kings were keying on O'Neal, who had scored 87 points in the first two games.

"Shaq came up to us and said, 'Don't worry about me, you guys, just do whatever it takes,'" Bryant said.

In Game 4, the Lakers' 11th consecutive win, Bryant set another career high, 48 points. "Kobe was just fantastic," Sacramento coach Rick Adelman said. "He was possessed. Even when he missed shots he got them back."

"His enthusiasm infuses this basketball club," Jackson said of Bryant. "That's a real important factor to remember, that he's got the energy, the drive, the moxie, and also a feel, an uncanny instinctual feel for this basketball game that's really showing."

Bryant's momentum again surged in Game 1 of the Western Conference Finals, a 104–90 Lakers blowout of the Spurs in San Antonio. Hitting 19 of 35 shots, Bryant had another 45, to go with O'Neal's 28.

"You're my idol," O'Neal said afterward.

The stunned media sat waiting for some snide comment to follow, but O'Neal insisted he was serious. Indeed, the guard and center would move into a period of understanding and seemingly mutual appreciation. This would be important for the role players that stocked the Lakers roster.

With O'Neal's huge salary, Buss had been unwilling to pay for a third star, which meant that one or more role players would have to step up in key situations to perform. That task had increasingly fallen to Robert Horry over the 2001 playoffs. In the first round against the Trail Blazers, Horry hit a three-pointer with 2.1 seconds left to end the series in Portland.

And in the conference semifinals, although Bryant and O'Neal had played brilliantly, it was Horry who nailed a three-pointer with 56 seconds left to push the lead to seven points as the Lakers eliminated San Antonio.

"For the people in L.A., who have followed this for a long season, that compliment coming out of Shaq speaks volumes for where we've taken strides as a team," Lakers forward Rick Fox said. "People ask me, 'Why are you playing the way you're playing?' It's very evident now that we all have learned to respect each other as players and to enjoy each other's company and understand how much we can make each other better."

It all helped carry the Lakers into the NBA Finals against Allen Iverson and the Philadelphia 76ers. There, on the grand stage, it would again be O'Neal's time to dominate.

First, though, the Sixers erased the Lakers' perfect slate with an overtime victory in Los Angeles in Game 1. Afterward Jackson chided O'Neal for his lack of defensive intensity. The center would respond by flexing his dominance over the rest of the series as Los Angeles swept the next four, finishing off a record-setting playoff run of 15 wins against that single loss.

The series hinged on Game 3 in Philadelphia when Horry made his presence known with a three-pointer with 47 seconds left that sealed the Sixers' fate. "That puts him up there with all the clutch people you would name—Reggie Miller, Jerry West," Brian Shaw told reporters.

ROBERT HORRY: "I guess I've always been able to hit shots because I don't care if I miss or make it. A lot of guys put so much pressure on themselves to make shots in the end. But with me, I'm like, 'If I make it, I make it, if I don't, I don't.' But I don't worry about it. Because there are always more important things in life."

The Lakers simply ran through the injured Sixers in four straight games as O'Neal played brilliantly, blocking shots on defense (after Jackson prodded him to be more aggressive) and using his strength to control the tempo on offense. The ball went to the center, and he pounded the Sixers with a string of 30-point performances.

Once again, in the delight of the championship party, it seemed that all was well with the Lakers, that their turbulence and infighting had settled, that they had bonded in their success.

Yet even then there was ample evidence that the old conflicts lingered just under the surface. On the eve of the league championship series, Tim Brown of the *Los Angeles Times* wrote a story about Jerry West working behind the scenes to help Bryant deal with the ugly situation that had unfolded over the spring.

The story infuriated Jackson and some of his associates because it seemed that West was claiming credit for the turnaround. Jackson wondered if West had leaked the story to the media.

Bryant himself offered a further dig at Jackson by showing up at the team's championship celebration wearing a number 44 West jersey. "Oh man," the young guard said. "Jerry West was my mentor. And with everything that went on this season he meant so much to me."

West, though, in an interview with T. J. Simers of the *Los Angeles Times*, was only gracious in his comments, saying, "When basketball is played correctly with good players it is something great to see. It looks easy, but it's not. That's a tribute not only to the players, but to Phil Jackson and his staff, who got the players to buy into what they wanted. That's Phil's plan, having all the players touch the ball, and watching everyone contribute—that's how basketball should be played."

A Changed Man

As his teams won championships, Jackson's ego, already substantial, seemed to surge, and with this growth came a distancing from his old friends and assistants. "Phil changed once he got to L.A.," they said. As a result, Tex Winter said, the process of working with Jackson had become more frustrating. Part of Winter's role in the past had been to help keep that ego in check. But with eight championships on his résumé Jackson didn't listen like he used to, Winter confided. "It's become a question of what I'm getting across."

Coaches who knew Jackson from his early days in the CBA—when he had to rely on assistant Charley Rosen to install the simplest flex offense—were amused by the lofty perch he now held in the basketball world. When Jackson came to the Bulls as a first-time NBA assistant in 1987, he was obviously needy. Winter was assigned to be his mentor, to teach him how to coach. They'd been together ever since, except for the season that Jackson sat out after the Bulls won their sixth championship in 1998. For years, Winter had gone over the tapes of the team's previous game as well as a tape of the upcoming opponent, explaining to Jackson the various factors.

TEX WINTER: "He used that process to teach himself. As we studied tapes, I commented and he took note of it. He liked that."

Winter also had the chore over the years of planning and running much of Jackson's practices. In the wake of the 2001 title, Jackson wanted Winter to continue those parts of the relationship. But the Lakers coach decided that he no longer wanted his assistant sitting beside him on the bench, but rather behind him on a second row.

Jackson explained the move as being a consideration of Winter's age. But Winter wondered if Jackson hadn't become overly concerned with making sure he got the credit for the team's success.

Another factor may have been Winter's close relationship with Bryant. Jackson's difficulties with Bryant had only served to emphasize Winter's role as Bryant's defender on the coaching staff. "You can't quit," Bryant told Winter over the summer. "If you do, I'll go crazy."

Conversely, O'Neal disliked Winter's criticism of his game. Winter said the center never accepted his coaching, and Jackson's moving of the veteran assistant served as something of a gesture for the center. It did little, though, to

stop Winter's upbraiding of anyone, including Bryant, who violated the principles of the triangle offense, Winter's half-court system that prized ball movement and team play.

September brought the jolt of the terrorist attacks on the World Trade Center and the Pentagon. Scheduled to play a series of exhibition games in Japan,
the Lakers saw those plans altered. They still held their training camp in
Honolulu, but the trip overseas was put aside due to travel concerns.

Further clouding the situation, the team was hit by a host of troubles.
Derek Fisher again injured his foot and required another surgery and another
long recovery. And O'Neal injured a toe that required surgery, so that meant
he would miss training camp. Jackson himself missed much of training camp
due to the death of his 94-year-old mother, and Bryant retreated to Philadelphia to bury his grandfather.

The setbacks combined would only serve to pull the team closer together,
O'Neal told reporters. In the wake of the terrorist attacks, the country had
swelled with a sense of unity, and the center acknowledged that it would be
hard for basketball players to be divided by pettiness when so many other
unfortunate people had to overcome much greater problems.

If anything would prove a problem for the Lakers in 2002, it was the new
zone defenses, allowed for the first time in league history. Although he sat out
with his toe injury, O'Neal watched with anger as teams began experimenting with new defensive schemes. He knew those zones would be used to cor-
ral him as soon as he returned from injury.

In the biggest development of all, team captain Ron Harper retired. His
presence had gone a long way toward helping Bryant and O'Neal resolve their
differences. Eventually he would be sorely missed. The team replaced power
forward Horace Grant, who left for Orlando in free agency, with Samaki
Walker, a free agent from San Antonio. Also in camp as a free agent was
Dickey Simpkins, who once played for Jackson with the Bulls. Tex Winter
considered Simpkins a smart player who understood the triangle offense.

Later, the coaches would surmise that they might have been able to win a
fourth, even a fifth championship if they had been able to keep Simpkins. But
the forward had no guaranteed contract, and Buss wasn't about to cut a player
with guaranteed money to keep a second-line forward.

At guard, the Lakers brought in Lindsey Hunter from Milwaukee to help
with shooting and point guard play while Fisher recovered from yet another
foot surgery. Another key issue was the development of swing player Devean

George, long considered by the Lakers coaches to be absolutely brimming with talent. The same was true for power forward Slava Medvedenko, an intriguing offensive player limited by language barriers. O'Neal predicted that the 2002 troubles would only bring the team closer together.

And he was right. Despite the range of setbacks and the Lakers struggling through the regular season, they would manage 58 wins and a 15–4 run through the playoffs to their third and most harmonious championship.

They again swept Portland in the first round, then crushed the Spurs in the conference semifinals for the second straight season. Again, Bryant delivered the key blows just as it seemed the Spurs were about to force the issue. The Lakers took a 2–1 edge in the series, but San Antonio seized control in the second half of Game 4 in the Alamodome and had a 10-point lead with just under five minutes left.

Bryant answered by scoring 10 points in the final five minutes, his last two on a rebound and putback with 5.1 seconds left to push the Lakers to an 87–85 win and a 3–1 series lead. It was the team's 11th consecutive road win in the playoffs, dating back to their huge run in 2001.

On the day, Bryant had 16 of his first 23 shots when he launched the scoring outburst that included making two three-pointers within 43 seconds of each other. Jackson had moved him from guard to small forward, where he was able to get behind the defense and find the open looks. The final bucket came as he knifed between the Spurs' seven-footers for the putback.

"The first thing about [Bryant] is that his talent is astounding," Spurs coach Greg Popovich offered. "The second thing is his body exaggerates that talent with his height and his length. The third thing is he has the uncommon will to win. It's the same exact will to win as Michael Jordan." Bryant's heroics propelled his team into the next round, where they struggled through a classic seven-game showdown with the testy Sacramento Kings. The presence of Jackson and his team in noisy Arco Arena always seemed to goose Sacramento's fans to new levels of excess.

DEREK FISHER: "I describe it like high school basketball. Most everybody has played high school ball, and you had that one crosstown rival that when you went there, they were going to be throwing rocks at the bus and spitting on the court and doing everything to try to get you off of your game. Arco is that place. That city, that town, just loves that team, and they come out to support that team like no other place in the league."

The outcome of Game 4 in the series will gnaw at Kings fans as long as there is a Sacramento. The vision of their torment will be Robert Horry whisking away their opportunity to take a 3–1 lead in the 2002 Western Conference finals.

The Lakers had to endure the booing of Staples Center regulars after they fell behind 40–20 at the end of the first quarter. The Kings pushed that to 46–22 before the momentum began to turn. The omen for Sacramento came with Samaki Walker's three-point desperation heave that was counted although it just missed the halftime buzzer. It was the second three-pointer of Walker's career.

The Lakers tightened their defense and clamped down on the boards in the second half, and the Kings began their descent, which made for an extremely tight close. At 1:39, Horry floated in a three-pointer that cut Sacramento's lead to 96–93. Then, surprise, O'Neal canned two free throws to cut the lead to one with 26.9 seconds to play. Kings center Vlade Divac answered by making one of two free throws with 11.8 seconds to go. Their lead at two, the Kings stood for one final defensive effort.

Bryant drove the lane but missed, as did O'Neal on an offensive putback. Divac batted the rebound outside, hoping to knock it out of play. Instead, it traveled right to Horry, waiting in three-point land.

"When it came rolling out, it was like, 'Oh, look what I got,'" he said afterward.

He floated in the winner as time expired.

"It was a great day, it was a blessed day for us, thank God for Robert," O'Neal told the media afterward. "I knew the shot was going down the second it left his hand."

ROBERT HORRY: "The funniest thing that happened, I have some friends who are club promoters. After the game, they were calling me up, trying to get me to come out. I was like, 'No, I'm not coming out.' They were like, 'We'll do anything. We'll send a limo for you, we'll send everything for you.' But I just wanted to go home and calm down and get ready for the next one. I've seen that replay about 15 to 20 times. It always gives you goose bumps to see that, not the fact that I made it, but to see the reaction of the fans and stuff. I don't even like watching the shot. I like to see that overhead view, where you see the crowd jump up, and you can see one of our ball boys run from that end of the basket down to the other end. It's so funny to see that. It's a fantastic feeling, especially in a game as important as that. The funniest thing, every-body in my family knows I don't keep memorabilia. But I have that shot blown up in my house."

Horry finished with 18 points and 14 rebounds, and the Kings were left grumbling. The strange turn of events was just the edge the Lakers needed. Instead of being down 3–1, they pulled even at 2–2.

ROBERT HORRY: "The Kings are so cocky, they didn't really pay attention. They were like, 'We still got home-court advantage so we can still win this thing.'"

Instead, Sacramento closed out the series with poor rebounding and a collapse at the free throw line that saw them fall at home in the seventh game. The Kings safely in their wake, the Lakers returned to the NBA Finals to find the revamped New Jersey Nets, led by Jason Kidd and coached by former Laker Byron Scott. They had no answer for O'Neal, who won his third straight Finals MVP award as the Lakers gained the first championship sweep in their history.

They also joined the Minneapolis Lakers, Bill Russell's Celtics, and Jackson's Chicago Bulls as the only teams to win three straight titles. Still, Magic Johnson told the Associated Press that Jackson's club wasn't as good as his Showtime teams, or Jordan's Chicago Bulls, or Larry Bird's Boston Celtics, for that matter. Johnson explained that the other teams featured stronger, deeper rosters, while Jackson's Lakers consisted of two stars and a host of role players.

In fact, Bryant and O'Neal scored 71 of their team's 106 in the pivotal Game 3. The dramatic sequence came down to Bryant again living on the edge, losing his dribble under pressure by the Nets' Kidd and Kerry Kittles, then resecuring the ball and hitting a spinning jumper near the foul line to push the lead to 104–100 with 19 seconds left.

"Big players make big plays," Kidd told reporters afterward.

That, of course, could serve as the Hollywood-style premise for the entire history of the team. The championship was Jackson's ninth title as a head coach, tying him with Red Auerbach for the most championships won by an NBA coach. The outcome was also playoff victory number 156 for Jackson, pushing him past Pat Riley for the most coaching postseason victories.

Although Jackson was registering his third three-peat, the Lakers finally had one of their own to celebrate. "The first one, it's a novelty and it feels real good," Bryant told the media. "The first one will always be the best one. The second one, the adversity that we went through throughout the course of the year made that one special. We proved that we belonged. And this one, it's kind of making us step up as one of the great teams. It feels great."

Facing more Hack-A-Shaq, O'Neal had set a four-game Finals record for points scored (145) and free throws made (45) and attempted (68).

"I'd like to congratulate Phil Jackson for bringing out the best in us," the center said. "He gave us a plan when we first met him. He gave me a plan when we first met him. He promised us if we stuck to the plan that everything would work out. I'm just glad that Jerry West was able to get him to sign up, because it was something I needed in my life. I was sort of a great player that didn't have any championships. Ever since I met Phil, now I have three."

Three, of course, would prove to be the limit. Jackson and his assistant coaches had come to that conclusion during their years in Chicago. It seemed the most they could squeeze out of any situation was three straight titles. Success had its boundaries, and that certainly seemed to be the maximum for the human element in the modern championship equation. The Lakers found themselves making strange, frustrating attempts to stretch that envelope over the next two campaigns. In the process, they would find out more about themselves than perhaps they wanted to know.

Persona

It had once seemed that the Lakers icons would roll on forever. Time, though, eventually revealed that the maximum tenure runs about 40 years in the Lakers pantheon. Jerry West left the Lakers after the 2000 championship season and wound up taking on the task of building the Memphis Grizzlies into a contender. And Chick Hearn, who seemed intent on broadcasting every game the Lakers ever played, died in August 2002, four decades after he first broadcast a Lakers game in 1961.

Los Angeles Times writer Mark Heisler quipped that Hearn would operate from "that great press box in the sky," but the broadcaster and West would always be the ultimate figures in the team's lore. For years they were the very public faces of the team's success. Hearn broadcast better than 3,300 games over the years, enduring a zillion road trips, bumpy flights, bad meals, and noisy hotels. He was pushing 90 at the time of his death, but you'd never have known it, and it had nothing to do with the hair color. His crisp delivery and imagination snared Lakers fans from the very start. He once pointed out that the Lakers' great games provided him with ample drama over the years. But he took that drama and blew it up in the minds of his audience. Almost overnight, he made the Lakers seem like the most important event in Southern California.

J. A. ADANDE, *LOS ANGELES TIMES* **COLUMNIST:** "I grew up in Santa Monica and I listened to Chick. Prime Ticket came around in like 1985, and for the home games it was Chick. That was it. Even when the Finals would come around you'd still listen to Chick on the radio. I think that was a very common experience for everyone. You'd turn on 570 AM KLAC. When you'd turn on the TV it'd interfere with the radio a little bit. You'd have a little bit of a buzz, but it was still better than listening to Tommy Heinsohn on CBS. There was definitely this shared experience, and you see it and hear it in this generation of broadcasters who have come up in Los Angeles. Everyone incorporates some Chick Hearn phrases. Any time you watch a game, no matter who's doing it, you can hear Chick Hearn sayings, even in the first season after his death. You know, the ball hits the rim and goes up over the backboard, you can still hear Chick saying, 'Up and over and out.'"

MARK HEISLER, *LOS ANGELES TIMES* **COLUMNIST:** "Chick of course was an incredible hot dog, but with this perseverance. One of his nicknames that nobody paid attention to was The Iron Mic. But he really was. This guy was a locomotive. I took a look at this guy relatively early in our experience together and I said, 'I'm not gonna mess with this guy.'"

RON CARTER, FORMER LAKER: "Chick was a power player because he had that bully pulpit. He could kill you on radio or television by putting out the bad vibes. We were playing the Celtics, and they took a shot. I'll never forget this. I went up and I caught a shot before it touched the glass. I caught it with two hands. I tapped it off the glass. I had a ghetto flashback moment and turned to go on the fast break. They called goaltending on what was a great defensive play. Later when we got back to L.A., Norman [Nixon] and I sat over at his house watching the films. We were listening to Chick, and Chick lambasted me, just raked my ass over the coals. 'That's the kind of hot-dogging you don't do in a Lakers uniform.' That was the setup language for me to leave. That told me I wasn't long to be a Laker."

J. A. ADANDE: "I've never seen any single thing like it when he died, especially in L.A. It's a good sports town, but it doesn't have the passion that some other cities have. It's a very knowledgeable sports fan base, but you rarely see people deeply moved by sports. But when Chick Hearn passed away, I mean 20,000 people came down to Staples Center just to walk by a little tribute set up at his old broadcast booth, where they had his old microphone and his game notes and some of the other things he utilized during his broadcasts. He meant so much to these people, and he was just a guy who broadcast these games. Because the team won so much as well, he was associated with this winning. The common thing was, since he had been there from the beginning, you had three generations that associated him with their youth, from the '60s, '70s, '80s, even a touch of the '90s. People thought back to their younger days when they first fell in love with sports, and they could hear Chick Hearn's voice. Chick held that for millions of Southern Californians. He was a common bond. I think that's why it struck so deep when he passed away. He was the voice of the Lakers."

Hearn first came to Los Angeles in 1956 to broadcast Southern Cal football games. Since Lakers owner Bob Short talked him into broadcasting that first game in 1961, Hearn went decades only missing two Lakers games, both in 1965. On the first, he was on assignment covering a golf tournament for NBC. The second time he was grounded by a snowstorm in Nebraska covering a Southern Cal football game. Otherwise, he shook off innumerable colds and illnesses to call the Lakers action.

First it was the trials and tribulations of Elgin and Mr. Clutch that Hearn brought to life for radio listeners. Then, in 1965, Lakers owner Jack Kent Cooke added a television package to the format. The owner wanted to move Hearn into that, but he was afraid of losing the radio audience. So he created the simulcast, with Hearn broadcasting the team's games simultaneously on radio and television.

CHICK HEARN: "At first, I didn't think it could be done. But I learned to trim the verbiage. It made the radio leaner and the television beefier."

His sense of humor and imagination made it work. He gave a special name to everything. When he tabbed Cooke's new building "the Fabulous Forum," the owner promised a little something extra in Hearn's next pay envelope. Sure enough, there on payday was a picture of Cooke himself. As might be expected, many of Hearn's best adventures over the years have happened off the air.

CHICK HEARN: "One time we were forced to change and dress in a railway baggage car. There was a coffin with a body in it in the baggage room, and there we were getting dressed. We had been forced to travel by train because of a snowstorm. That was in Pennsylvania back in the '60s. The storm hit, and we had a forced march from our hotel to the railroad station. Then we got dressed with the coffin."

Over their umpteen years working together, Stu Lantz came to enjoy a good relationship with Hearn as his broadcast partner. But life in the booth with Chick wasn't always easy street. During the 1960s, he was determined to work alone.

CHICK HEARN: "ARCO, the company broadcasting Lakers games, had provided a salary for a color analyst in its 1967–68 contract with the team. Jack Kent Cooke decided if the money was there, they should use it, and I couldn't talk him out of it."

Al Michaels, then in his twenties, was hired because his father was a close friend of Cooke's.

MERV HARRIS, LAKERS REPORTER FOR THE LOS ANGELES HERALD EXAM-INER: "Chick would open the broadcasts by saying, 'This is Chick Hearn with Al Michaels.' Then you wouldn't hear from Michaels until halftime, when Chick would say, 'And now here's the first half scoring with Al Michaels.' Then Chick would do the second half and at the end say, 'Here's the game scoring with Al Michaels.' After about three games, Hearn went to Cooke and said Michaels was taking too long reading the scores."

The Lakers released Michaels, a future national sportscaster of the year, after he worked six exhibition and four regular-season games.

CHICK HEARN: "Al had a lot of talent, but I'd never worked with anyone before. I'd always worked alone. I didn't believe two people could do basketball. But I would be proven wrong."

JACK KENT COOKE: "Chick didn't like Al. Chick didn't think Al had what it took. I thought the boy had a lot of promise. His father was a very dear friend of mine. But I knew it wouldn't work because Chick would dominate the broadcast and Al couldn't get a word in."

MERV HARRIS: "Michaels didn't last long, but that established the concept of Chick Hearn having a broadcast partner."

Next came Dick Shad, followed by Hot Rod Hundley. Later would come Shackelford, Pat Riley, Keith Erickson, and Lantz, all former Lakers.

HOT ROD HUNDLEY, UTAH JAZZ BROADCASTER AND FORMER LAKER: "He was tough. I said, 'Chick, I'm working with you.' But when they put me in there, he didn't like that."

Hearn would crisply deliver the play-by-play, pausing only occasionally for Hundley to jump in.

HOT ROD HUNDLEY: "You'd say, 'Yeah, great play,' and it would go right back to him. He'd just cut right in on you. He was rude. But he was a good teacher. I learned everything I know about broadcasting from Chick. After a while, he accepted the fact that I was gonna be there."

CHICK HEARN: "I didn't think it could work. But after we worked at it a while, it ran smoothly, as long as the color and play-by-play men knew when to get in and get out."

The Lakers celebrated Hearn's 2,500th consecutive broadcast at a road game in Cleveland in March 1992. Hundley, Erickson, Riley, Shackelford, and Lantz all flew in for the occasion.

JACK KENT COOKE: "Chick's the greatest basketball announcer the world has ever known, or will ever know. There will never be another one like him."

STU LANTZ: "The last few years, Chick obviously mellowed a little bit. Chick was a Laker through and through. He lived and died with the Lakers. When they played well, Chick was as happy as can be. When they didn't play well and they lost, he was almost like Jerry West in that he took it very, very hard."

The Big Irony

There were many challenges for Jackson and his Lakers over their seasons together, and just about all of them were related to this: Jackson, a man known for establishing strong relationships with his players, would fail miserably at building a relationship with Bryant.

After the team chemistry had disintegrated in 2004, one of Jackson's close associates would offer that the mishandling of Bryant as a player was a primary factor in the eventual unraveling of the team. Certain things happened early in that relationship that eroded Bryant's ability to trust his coach.

KOBE BRYANT: "Phil was trying to figure me out a little bit. One of things I told him is, 'There's nothing to figure out. I'm just trying to play the game and learn the game the best I can.' Once we got that established we started moving a little bit. But I didn't get into his mind games. I had so many other things to think about with this game. I didn't really have the time even to do that. I did notice Phil when he was trying to play mind games. It was funny. I found it funny."

Bryant's conflict with Jackson flared throughout the time they worked together.

TEX WINTER: "Very early in our time in Los Angeles, Phil made the decision to go with Shaq, and he made it clear to Kobe and the press and everyone else that it was Shaq's team. He made it clear he was far more interested in accommodating Shaq than he was Kobe. Kobe seemed to accept this."

Yet accommodating O'Neal seemed to necessitate that Jackson take an aggressive posture with Bryant, to the point that Winter expressed concern that Jackson making Bryant a "whipping boy" might hurt the young guard's development. A "whipping boy" in basketball is a player singled out for discipline because his psyche and status allow the coach to discipline him rather than the star atop the team's hierarchy. However, Bryant's own strong nature prevented the coach from taking the concept too far. In the process, their relationship suffered extensive damage.

"I was very much on Kobe, riding him and working with him very hard earlier in his career, and had to back off, basically, to a point where he felt better about our relationship—where I wasn't as restrictive with him," Jackson admitted to the *Los Angeles Times*. "He felt I was always on him, always on him. He did too much, he tried to do too many things. The more I let him have [some freedom], the better he got as a basketball player. The more I restricted or got restrictive with him, the more adamantly he would go about doing the things I didn't want him to do."

At the same time, the coach took a hands-off approach with the immensely gifted O'Neal, who did not favor working hard. The discrepancy sometimes ate at Bryant as did Jackson's penchant for attacking him in the press.

One of the worst examples came early in the 2002–2003 campaign when Jackson's former assistant coach and coauthor of two Jackson books, Charley Rosen, wrote a story for ESPN.com blistering Bryant for selfishness. Rosen witnessed a heated exchange between Winter and Bryant on the bench. Then the writer quoted portions of private conversations with Winter that left the assistant coach taken aback. It seemed obvious to observers that the story was yet another effort by Jackson to shape Bryant's public image, and worse yet, to damage the relationship between Winter and Bryant.

TEX WINTER: "Phil was dealing with two mighty big egos. But in my mind I blamed Shaq more than Kobe. Kobe tried to sacrifice. Kobe tried to please Shaq, because Kobe realized the team's effectiveness began with Shaq. But if you look at Shaq's quotes in the paper, it was always me, me, me. Give me the ball. It's my team, my city. Shaq is a wonderful person in a lot of ways. He's very compassionate, very generous. He has a great sense of humor. But he's moody; he's unpredictable. And he's very self-centered."

The fundamentals of the personalities always lay just underneath the surface of the Lakers' chemistry. After three championships, the personalities took a break in 2003. Yet the team struggled throughout its most harmonious season, plagued by injuries to O'Neal and caught in a battle to make the playoffs.

Such a situation meant that there were few highlights, except perhaps for Bryant's amazing streak of nine straight games scoring better than 40 points. In previous seasons such an outburst might have ruptured the peace, but it survived tenuously over the early weeks of 2003. Then again, Jackson had ordered his guard to be more aggressive. The streak allowed Bryant to tie Jordan's streak, but it fell short of the 14 straight games racked up by Wilt

Chamberlain. Bryant also scored 35 or better in 13 straight games, still short of the prodigious Chamberlain. It began in Phoenix on January 29, when Bryant rang up 40 points on the Suns. From there, the Lakers won 12 of 14 games, including 5 in a row.

"He's on a great run," Michael Jordan, playing for the Washington Wizards, offered during the streak. "He's really finding a way to do it within the structure of the offense." (Bryant would later thank him by scoring 55 against the Wizards in Jordan's last visit to Los Angeles in March.)

"The streak is a streak," Bryant said afterward. "It's not going to win us any championships."

Indeed, nothing would that spring. Jackson missed the first game of his coaching career that spring with a kidney stone. Similarly, his team showed signs of wear, managing to win just 50 games in the regular season. Finally, in the playoffs, Robert Horry's magnificent threes stopped falling. And in the conference semifinals against San Antonio, the rest of the operation came apart. In the middle of the series, Jackson missed another weekend as doctors discovered his immediate need for an angioplasty procedure, following months of unexplained fatigue.

Despite his return to the bench, the Spurs eliminated the Lakers in six games, closing out the deed at Staples Center. The loss terminated Jackson's record run of winning 25 consecutive playoff series, and it meant that he would not get past Red Auerbach for NBA titles won as a coach. The Lakers themselves had won 13 straight series, from the first round against Sacramento in 2000 to the first round against Minnesota in 2003.

"We are severely disappointed we couldn't make a run for the championship and get our opportunity to win a fourth," Jackson told reporters. "It tells us something about how difficult it is and how much dedication and discipline you have to have to win four years in a row. We had a great run."

The loss left Bryant, Fisher, the Laker girls, and numerous fans in tears. "It's a foreign feeling," Bryant, who had averaged 32.1 points during the playoffs, told reporters. "I don't like the feeling. I don't think anybody else likes the feeling. I don't ever want to feel it again."

Eagle and Beyond

At the end of June, Bryant flew on a private jet to Colorado, where he was scheduled to undergo knee surgery. That night, as he rested in a Colorado resort hotel, the Lakers guard had sexual relations with a 19-year-old resort employee. Their differing accounts of the evening would explode into one of the biggest stories in Lakers history. She said Bryant raped her; he later told police the sex was consensual.

The incident seemed in such contrast to Bryant's image that reporters, fans, teammates, and team employees expressed shock at the news that the 25-year-old guard would be charged. Soon the shock would give way to the reality of tabloid headlines, 24-hour cable news coverage, and a story that threatened to swamp the team.

The incident erupted virtually as the Lakers announced the signings of future Hall of Famers Karl Malone and Gary Payton, both of whom took millions of dollars in pay cuts to join the team as free agents. Poised to harvest the media attention and speculation over just how great their club could be, the team's management instead found itself dealing with issues of a more serious nature. The accuser believed she had been assaulted, and Bryant faced charges that under Colorado law could land him in prison for decades.

The issue sat suspended through much of July 2003 until authorities in Colorado could decide how to proceed. Bryant had apparently informed his young wife of the charges near midnight on July 3. Public records revealed that a 911 call was made from the couple's house shortly thereafter, and reporters secured a confirmation from the Newport Beach Fire Department that paramedics treated a female at the residence at 1 A.M. Soon there were press reports that he had purchased her a $4 million diamond ring later that month.

"When everything comes clean, it will all be fine, you'll see," Bryant told the *Los Angeles Times* in a phone interview. "But you guys know me, I shouldn't have to say anything. You know I would never do something like that."

On July 18, the district attorney in Eagle County, Colorado, filed a charge of felony sexual assault against Bryant. Vanessa Bryant subsequently appeared with her husband at the hastily assembled press conference discussing the case and later made other public appearances.

"I'm innocent," Bryant told reporters at the press conference. "You know, I didn't force her to do anything against her will. I'm innocent. You know, I sit here in front of you guys, furious at myself, disgusted at myself for making the mistake of adultery."

From that beginning would come a steady run of Bryant court appearances in Colorado, with hundreds of media representatives descending on the community of Eagle. With reporters came a throng of spectators, many of them wearing Lakers jerseys, sporting signs, and cheering for Bryant, who posted a $25,000 bond in regard to The People of the State of Colorado vs. Kobe Bean Bryant, Case No. 03CR204.

The guard's life became a battle fought on four fronts. There was the managing of a tense relationship at home, plus the demands of his legal defense. Beyond that, his relationship with his coaches and his teammates grew yet more strained, and he found himself scrambling to stop the disintegration of a carefully built portfolio of endorsement income. He had a lineup of contracts, with Coca-Cola, McDonalds, and Nike, that was the envy of the NBA, yet he would watch each of those relationships wither over the coming months, a development that cost him millions.

Beneath the fantastic turn of events, the Lakers themselves still harbored their strained relationships. It was true that O'Neal and Bryant had found a level of cooperation over the 2002 and 2003 campaigns. But the relationship between Bryant and Jackson still suffered, so much so that some of Jackson's assistants had urged him at the end of the 2003 season to "make peace with Kobe."

Jackson, however, declined that route and opted to take an even more aggressive strategy in dealing with the young guard. With the coach's relationship with Bryant obviously deteriorating by the day, it would not take long for O'Neal to pick up on those vibes. Not surprisingly, the tentative truce between the team's two stars quickly disappeared and another pissing match seemed ready to break out.

Jackson foresaw trouble on the horizon. Bryant had reached the point in his contract where he could opt out and entertain offers from other teams. The Lakers' protection in this situation was that the team could ultimately offer more money than other teams to induce him to re-sign.

Opting out was a relatively routine process for NBA players, and Bryant in limited interviews on the subject had indicated that he would indeed test the marketplace, if for no other reason than that it offered him the opportunity to secure a raise from the Lakers.

Jackson, though, apparently sensed a growing conflict in which Bryant would have more power than ever in dealing with his coach. Jackson himself was heading into the last year of his five-year deal with the team that paid him roughly $6 million per season.

The coach opted to move forward with an aggressive public relations strategy, a tactic that he had employed with great success against Bulls GM Jerry Krause in Chicago. Jackson called this tactic "seeding" ideas with the media.

The coach, after all, had long ago learned that reporters were hungry for his inside tips about team issues. His preseason comments as training camp and the season neared in the fall of 2003 were aimed at suggesting that Bryant was being disloyal by planning to opt out of his contract during the summer of 2004. Raising the issue was the coach's way of setting the media agenda, and it suddenly meant that Bryant had yet another issue to address in his busy young life. At the same time Jackson was expressing support publicly for the young guard, the coach was making his first moves in a months-long public relations battle.

O'Neal as well was hoping for a contract extension. While he had nearly three years remaining at a whopping $30 million, he was hoping the team would extend the deal with a pay raise. The team, on the other hand, hoped O'Neal would take less money in consideration of his age, his conditioning, and the number of injuries that had led him to miss games in recent seasons. O'Neal was not happy about the issue and openly pouted. At one point during a preseason game, he would yell at Jerry Buss, "Pay me." It was not a mature move, or a smart one, and the owner wouldn't forget it easily.

Meanwhile, Bryant had spent the weeks leading up to training camp entertaining thoughts of not playing the upcoming season while he battled the charges against him. Faced with indecision, the guard missed the start of the team's training camp in Hawaii, where a host of camera crews and reporters waited to take in the spectacle of an accused rapist attempting to play basketball. With Bryant's absence, reporters asked O'Neal what it felt like to not have the whole team in camp.

"I can't answer that," O'Neal replied, "because the full team is here."

Jackson had long used Bryant's "outsider" status as a means of motivating and controlling the Lakers roster. But the comment from the team leader set the conflict at a new level. Using Jackson's principle of boundary setting, O'Neal had in effect declared that Bryant was not part of the team.

The guard showed up in Hawaii the next day, and Winter noticed his teammates seemed eager to pull him into the group and reassure him. But O'Neal's comment had lit the old fires that burned between the two.

Bryant shook off the comment and told reporters he'd rather be back in Los Angeles with his family. "You can't imagine what it's like going through what I've gone through, what I'm still going through," he said. "But I come out here to play, this is my job. I'm going to come out here, I'm going to do it well."

The charges, Bryant admitted, had left him "terrified. Not so much for myself, but just for what my family's been going through."

Distractions

The addition of Karl Malone and Gary Payton created an instant euphoria among Lakers fans. Recruited by O'Neal, the two had turned down substantial offers from other teams to sign with Los Angeles because it seemed an excellent opportunity to win a championship. The team had been repeatedly victimized by the screen and roll against San Antonio during the 2003 playoffs, and it was projected that Payton, an excellent defender, would help fix the team's defensive woes. Malone, on the other, was just the power forward the team needed at both ends of the floor. Nearing 40, Malone remained the best-conditioned athlete in the league.

Neither man, however, had any experience with Winter's complex triangle offense. As a rule of thumb, it took a player two years of work to become comfortable with the on-court reads and decisions the offense required. Payton and Malone were both known for their great skill in the running game, and both said they planned to run as much as possible to avoid the need for setting up in the offense. For years, the Lakers had been slowed by O'Neal's disdain for the running game. Now, though, Malone warned his friend the center that he "better be ready to get out and run."

And that's exactly what the team did in its amazing jaunt through the first two months of the schedule. The Lakers zipped along on Malone and Payton's energy, and in the process they managed to throw off much of the cloud of Bryant's status. As they pushed their record to 21–3, the Lakers invited accolades as perhaps the NBA's greatest team ever.

SHAQUILLE O'NEAL: "We had everybody for our first few games, and we looked pretty good. We got off to a great start."

The fairy tale ended quickly, however, when Malone sustained a knee injury, the first major injury of his long career. It would keep him sidelined for most of three months, and as the team's performance sank, the tensions between O'Neal and Bryant and Jackson rose.

Particularly curious were Bryant's numerous trips to Colorado for the various pretrial hearings he faced. These trips interrupted the schedule of team practices and games. A week before Christmas Bryant flew at dawn to Colorado for a hearing, then managed to make it back to Staples Center just before the second quarter of a game in which he would be accused of taking too many shots. Still, he settled the outcome with a last-second jumper that would begin a pattern of unique performances on court days.

Staples Center was scheduled to host the All-Star Weekend in February with the idea that it would be an opportunity to celebrate the great history of basketball in Los Angeles. A statue of Magic Johnson outside Staples Center was to be unveiled during the week before the game itself, and an array of old Lakers agreed to help host the weekend events.

It just so happened that the days leading into the occasion also brought yet another round of public squabbles within the team. Sadly, questions about the team's chemistry dominated the All-Star event and overshadowed any planned celebration.

The big news came from Jerry Buss with the announcement that the team was suspending its ongoing contract extension talks with Jackson. The announcement led to immediate speculation that Bryant, who had become vocal in his criticism of his coach, had managed to undermine Jackson's position with the team.

"Team insiders believe owner Jerry Buss suspended contract negotiations for O'Neal and Jackson as protection against future ultimatums brought by Bryant, who called out O'Neal, accusing him of being out of shape and lacking leadership skills, and revealed he held little respect for Jackson off the court," the *Los Angeles Times* told its readers. Winter, however, revealed that it was Jackson who had precipitated the halt in negotiations.

TEX WINTER: "The thing that happened before the All-Star break is that Phil came into a meeting with us and made the comment that he couldn't coach Kobe anymore and he wouldn't come back next year if Kobe came back. He apparently then told Mitch Kupchak the same thing. Mitch, being the general manager, relayed that information to Jerry Buss. It was really at that time that Jerry Buss made up his mind that he was going with Kobe and not Phil."

It didn't help that Jackson had asked for a doubling of his salary, from $6 million per season to $12 million. Jackson had had both a contract offer from the Lakers and a marriage offer from Jeanie Buss sitting on the table since the end of the 2003 season but had acted on neither proposal.

TEX WINTER: "It came out in the papers like the team was breaking off contract talks with Phil because of Kobe. That was not Kobe's demands; it was Phil's. He didn't feel he could coach Kobe. And apparently word got back to Kobe. He got very belligerent at that point, but he got over it."

Not surprisingly, Jackson spoke openly with reporters about Bryant's belligerence and cited it as another example of the guard's disrespect for him, but the coach never explained to the media that he had precipitated the breaking off of negotiations himself. Jackson obviously enjoyed the idea of the public interpreting the split as Bryant's effort and ploy.

Said another of Jackson's close associates, "It had crossed the line to where Phil just decided he couldn't work with the guy. That happens in relationships."

Buss, meanwhile, remained circumspect about his plans. He had said earlier in the season that he thought of Bryant as family. "I felt a lot of pain for him, [the way] a father experiences tremendous pain for the problems his son is having," Buss had said in November.

Jackson appeared to have employed a high-stakes strategy to win control of the team from Bryant and lost. Once the owner broke off negotiations, Jackson began treating Bryant better.

TEX WINTER: "Phil started giving Kobe much more attention. He started meeting with him individually. And Kobe's attitude toward Phil really changed. Their relationship got better, but it was too late. Buss had already made up his mind at that point. By that time, he had already told Phil he was not coming back. He had told Mitch Kupchak, too. Mitch seemed relieved that Buss had made a determination."

Despite the team turmoil and the rape charge, fans made Bryant the top vote-getter among Western Conference players for the All-Star game. If there remained any doubt in Jackson's mind that Bryant's popularity remained strong, he heard solid proof most game nights in Staples Center when the team's fans chanted, "MVP! MVP!"

Even so, the media descended upon the All-Star proceedings with questions about the breaking off of Jackson's negotiations and the team's drama.

"I think we would be a funny-looking organization if we didn't have drama," O'Neal said. "I've been here eight years, and we've had drama every year. I wouldn't want to come play for a bland organization in a bland city."

The turn of events had left both Malone and Payton dumfounded. They had turned down big contracts thinking they would find a championship chemistry in Los Angeles. The situation left some Lakers regulars trying to help their new teammates cope.

DEREK FISHER: "I thought it was important, especially for the guys who hadn't been here before, that they see us stay steadfast and stay strong in our basic foundation, in our beliefs. When guys like Bryan Russell or Luke Walton or even Karl and Gary, guys who were in their first year on our team, it was important for them to see guys who have been here before really be able to keep a stern face and to keep focused and to continue to have a positive attitude and to have a certain work ethic when you come to practice because they're watching us. We were able to avoid the crisis mode. We'd been at the brink several times, but I think what Phil and his entire coaching staff brought was the ability to float around the brink of danger, to float around the brink of really maybe falling apart, and to still be able to figure out ways to stay composed and stay poised."

SHAQUILLE O'NEAL: "Most of the time we found a way to get it together. When it's all said and done, we knew how to get it done."

They somehow managed to do that after the All-Star break. It would help that Malone returned from his knee injury in March and they regained a trace of their early chemistry.

Bryant's role, though, remained problematic, especially his shot selection. He averaged 27 points after the All-Star break. In March, after some internal criticism, he took three shots at home against Orlando and scored just one point in the first half, which left the Lakers trailing by 11. He went for 37 in the second half and tied a franchise record with 24 in the fourth period as Los Angeles won in overtime.

In April, against Sacramento, Bryant again turned in a strange first half, taking just one shot against stiff defense. The second half was little better, and he finished with eight, leading to speculation that he had tanked the game in response to criticism over his shots. One anonymous teammate told the *Los Angeles Times*, "I don't know how we can forgive him."

Furious over the comment, Bryant declined to speak with reporters for a week and a half, although he did go on an L.A. radio station to defend himself against the charge. "I play hard, play my heart out, play hurt, and then they want to accuse me of tanking a game," he said.

The issue quieted after Jackson began urging him to be more aggressive offensively. In Portland on the last day of the regular season, he scored 37, including two spectacular late three-pointers, one to force overtime and another to win it in the second overtime. His performance made the Lakers the surprise champions of the Pacific Division.

Their ongoing drama had continued to spike their TV ratings. Earlier in the season, Mavericks owner Mark Cuban had predicted that Bryant's charges would draw more interest in the league, a comment that was quickly discounted. Yet network executives weren't alone in seeing them as the main story line. League commissioner David Stern himself had made the mistake of quipping that the NBA's best option for the championship series would be "the Lakers against the Lakers." Sadly, despite their projections as a great team, the Lakers never lived up to it, mainly because they had never jelled defensively.

TEX WINTER: "There were times when we played pretty good defense. Defense in pro ball is predicated on the support around the basket, the big man. Even though Shaq was a big presence, he was not a great shot blocker. And he didn't like to play the screen and roll, so he put his teammates in jeopardy. He didn't like to help. He liked to lay back off his man."

That situation would leave Payton open to criticism in the playoffs. The 36-year-old guard fumed as he sat on the bench for lengthy stretches against Houston in the first round as Jackson played Fisher. And against San Antonio in the second round, the Spurs attacked Payton again and again with the screen and roll. Offensively, Malone and Payton never found a comfort level in the triangle offense.

TEX WINTER: "It was late in both their careers. I think Karl could have learned the triangle in time. It was a struggle. That's not to say he didn't try. He was great to coach. It was just hard for him to find a comfort zone after spending so many years in that Utah offense. The really big thing is that he got hurt and missed so much of the season. That really killed us. And Payton had gotten older. He could have run the offense, but he wanted the ball. He was never a good shooter. He felt he worked better in another kind of offense."

The Lakers quickly fell behind the Spurs 2–0 in the conference semifinals. It seemed the series would end quickly with the Spurs' Tony Parker and Tim Duncan running screen and roll after screen and roll. But back in Los Angeles the Lakers righted themselves and began one of the most improbable comebacks in league history.

Game 4 offered the chance for the big failure with Bryant again arriving by jet after a hearing in Colorado. The Lakers trailed by 10 late until Bryant drove them to the win.

"I think everybody is impressed with the way Kobe is able to compartmentalize," Spurs Coach Gregg Popovich said afterward. "He's going through a tough time. You feel badly for him, for the young lady, for their families. The whole situation, it's just awful for everybody. You wish people didn't have to go through that, but that's the reality of the thing. . . . He made some unbelievable shots, but he's an unbelievable player."

Popovich said the Lakers had suddenly begun to play as they did earlier in the year, when they launched their 16–3 run. Indeed, Malone struggled with his shot through much of the series, but his energy, his steadiness, his presence on defense had again become a major factor.

Then came the improbable Game 5 in San Antonio, when the Lakers were clubbing the Spurs well into the second half until they began blowing their 16-point lead. The Lakers crumbled, lost the lead, regained it with a Bryant jumper with 11 seconds to go, then saw Tim Duncan launch an 18-foot prayer from the top of the key with O'Neal squarely in his face. The shot fell with 0:00.4 left, and Spurs fans erupted in delirium. This was clearly the swing game and clearly the edge that San Antonio needed to once again overcome the Lakers.

Duncan's shot only served to set up the unbelievable. Payton, struggling to execute on the inbounds play, found Derek Fisher circling to the left of the lane. Fisher, a left-hander, had just enough time to catch and toss. Swish. Now it was the Lakers' turn to explode in delirium as the crowd sat stunned.

"That's the cruelest loss I've ever been involved with," Popovich said.

The ball had fallen as the horn sounded, leaving the Spurs to say they would protest the ruling that the shot was good. But it was good.

Spurs guard Manu Ginobili was all over Fisher on the shot, Duncan said. "He did as good a job as he could have. But the ball went into him [Fisher], he turned and shot it and Manu's chest was on him and his hands were straight up in the air. Perfect defensive position, nothing else you could have done."

Now leading the series 3–2, the Lakers headed back home where they finished off San Antonio, leading media and fans alike to figure the Lakers had just won their fifteenth title. That sense only deepened with their performance against the Minnesota Timberwolves and league MVP Kevin Garnett in the conference finals. The Wolves were much stronger with the addition of Latrell Sprewell and Sam Cassell, but none of that mattered against O'Neal and Bryant. If Malone hadn't reinjured his knee, the Lakers might well have claimed Jackson's tenth title, but without Malone they had no answer at power forward against Ben Wallace and the Detroit Pistons in the league championship series. After losing the first game at home, the Lakers managed an overtime win in Game 2 on yet more late-game heroics and a deep three from Bryant.

They were, however, strangely out of synch in Detroit, and their woes on the defensive boards deepened as they allowed the Pistons second shot opportunities time and again.

TEX WINTER: "Shaq defeated himself against Detroit. He played way too passively. He had one big game. Outside of that he didn't do much. His boxing out and rebounding in the championship series was awful. He had one assist in one of the Finals games. He's always been interested in being a scorer, but he hasn't had nearly enough concentration on defense and rebounding."

The undermanned Lakers lost all three games in Detroit and fell 4–1. Buss left the building early during the second half of Game 5, a blowout. As early as February, the owner was confiding to associates that he had grown tired of Jackson's set offense. Buss longed for the running game, for the days of Showtime. Winter, who had developed the triangle over years of coaching, said afterward he didn't blame Buss for wanting to change. "The way we ran the offense was terrible," he said.

In the wake of the Finals debacle, the owner confirmed that Jackson would not be asked back as coach. In the days following, it became clear that the owner had no desire to meet O'Neal's contract extension demands and began making plans to trade the center.

The turn of events sparked speculation that Bryant, himself a free agent, was now running the team, that he had demanded the trading of O'Neal and the firing of Jackson. Buss, Bryant, and even Lakers general manager Mitch Kupchak all said the dismissal of Jackson and trading of O'Neal was not done to placate Bryant. Suspicions only increased, however, after Buss, who had talked to reporters just once during the season, arranged a conference call in July while on vacation in Italy to explain the changes to reporters.

"The decision with Phil, the decision with Shaq was made totally independent of Kobe," Buss said. "As a matter of fact, I thought maybe even Kobe would think that. So I went to Kobe and I said, 'Kobe, I just want you to know, what I'm about to do has zero to do with you or your free agency.'"

Jackson himself took his own turn at influencing reporters as he drove from Los Angeles to his summer home in Montana. He dialed up columnists and radio talk shows to offer his version of events. And Jeanie Buss herself would weigh in later with a *Los Angeles Times* interview in which she explained that neither she nor the team could pin Jackson down on a commitment.

TEX WINTER: "It all really came down to the fact that Phil didn't want to make the commitment. And I don't blame him because of his concerns about his health and the angioplasty. They wanted him to do it. It came down to Kobe or Phil, and Jerry Buss went with Kobe. Word got to Buss that Phil didn't want to coach Kobe. The irony is, by the end, they had worked things out to where they were working pretty good together by the end of the season. At least I felt like they did."

With Jackson gone, the team moved quickly to trade O'Neal to Miami for forwards Lamar Odom, Brian Grant, and Caron Butler and a future first round draft pick. Later the team signed former Laker Vlade Divac, and Kupchak traded Payton to Boston for Chucky Atkins and backup center Chris Mihm.

After considering offers, Bryant accepted a seven-year, $136 million contract with the Lakers. The guard showed up at his news conference at the team's training facility with his wife, Vanessa, by his side and his daughter, Natalia, in his arms.

Bryant said he was bothered by speculation "that I had something to do with Phil and Shaquille leaving. That's something I didn't laugh at. That upsets me, it angers me, and it hurts me. They did what they had to do. They did what was best for them and their families. I enjoyed playing with them. I even said at the end of the season that I wouldn't mind playing with them for the rest of my career. But they each did what was best for their family. I let it be known that I'm comfortable playing with Shaq. We have our disagreements. We have our arguments. I said I'm comfortable playing with him and playing for Phil for the rest of my career. I told Phil that specifically. He asked me if him coming back made any impact on my decision coming back whatsoever. I said, 'No. I love playing for you.' We never really got along much as people. But as a coach, I thought he was absolutely excellent and I learned so much from him."

He told reporters he had little to do with Jackson's decision and the trading of O'Neal, but none of them seemed to believe him. The next day's papers were filled with columns lambasting his manipulation of the team. In Montana, Phil Jackson must have been smiling.

Beyond the trading of O'Neal and the firing of Jackson, the worst news of the summer for the Lakers was the departure of Derek Fisher to Golden State as a free agent, the trading of Rick Fox's rights to Boston, and the retirement of Horace Grant. There remained hope that Karl Malone might agree to come back with the team for one more season, but Malone wasn't sure of his knee and seemed intent on taking his time with his decision.

Buss and Magic Johnson said they were determined to build around Bryant's talents and again become a running team. To replace Jackson, they tried to lure Duke coach Mike Krzyzewski, at the request of Bryant. Krzyzewski considered their offer but ultimately decided to remain at Durham. The Lakers then hired Rudy Tomjanovich. Tomjanovich, of course, had once figured in Lakers history as the victim in Kermit Washington's ill-timed punch.

He had been the coach of the Houston Rockets for 12 seasons, taking them to two NBA championships in 1994 and '95, but had to step down in May of 2003, two months after being diagnosed with bladder cancer. By the summer of 2004 he had gotten clearance from his doctor to resume coaching, and the offer from the Lakers seemed such a blessing that he retreated to a Los Angeles beach to contemplate what it meant. "I said a prayer of thinks to God for what he has done for me in my life," Tomjanovich told the L.A. media upon his hiring. "I've had a lot of wonderful things happen. But about a year ago, I had had one of the darkest times in my life. I found out I had bladder cancer and thought it was best that I separate myself from the team that I love, from the players that I love and from the game I love. Through a positive attitude, through a lot of hard work and a trust in God, I beat cancer. And I'm so grateful to be here. It changed my life and now I have a chance to start a new family with the Los Angeles Lakers. And to me, that is a tremendous honor to name me their coach [for] one of the most successful franchises in the history of sports."

At 55, he would be taking over a team that no longer featured the game's most dominant player, but it was a team eager to move on to the next phase of its surprising evolution.

"All the great players, all the great coaches, all the championships, and I have a chance to be a part of that great tradition," Tomjanovich said. "Believe me. I am humbled, humbled to be here."

EPILOGUE

Kobe Bryant had wavered over the summer of 2004 in his decision to return to the Lakers while he listened to pitches from other teams, the best one coming from the crosstown Clippers. Coach Mike Dunleavy pointed out that if Bryant joined his club, he could leave behind the controversy and refocus his basketball life.

Bryant knew what response that would bring. On the radio talks shows and in the local papers, there were already castigations that he would be leaving the loyal Lakers in the lurch. He seemed poised to take that path, to be rid of the whole nasty debate, until Jerry West suggested that his best move was to stay a Laker.

Usually West could be trusted to provide the soundest advice available. But even West had erred on occasion. For example, when Jack Kent Cooke and his staff were deliberating in 1979 whether to draft Magic Johnson or Sidney Moncrief, the owner asked each of his five top people to vote. West once admitted to casting the only vote for Moncrief, although he later denied it.

If anything, the tale suggests that even Jerry West was prone to an occasional miscalculation. As the 2004–05 Lakers season unfolded in a series of nasty turns, some observers couldn't help but wonder if this one time Bryant hadn't been ill-served by his counsel.

Bryant would soon depart the purgatory that was the state of Colorado legal system. After prosecutors dropped charges in his rape case, his lawyers took only weeks to reach a settlement in the civil suit brought by his accuser. The conclusion allowed him to move on, but it left him with the image in many minds of a man who had used wealth and power to escape justice.

As if that weren't enough, his conflicts with the departed O'Neal only seemed to intensify. O'Neal's new team, the Miami Heat, charged out to the best record in the Eastern Conference. Jerry Buss commented to reporters that his former center had lost 60 pounds in preparing for the season. Buss implied that if the center had lost 60 pounds earlier, the Lakers might have kept him. O'Neal later would dispute those reports, saying Buss and the team had always used his weight against him.

SHAQUILLE O'NEAL: "The number thing with the weight was something they made up to make me look bad and feel bad, so that I would take less money. It didn't matter. If I was winning championships and taking them to the Finals, it didn't matter."

O'Neal would talk frequently to reporters about the issue, bringing it up even when they didn't ask about it. It seemed the better the Heat played, the more the center felt an urge to talk about the place he used to work.

SHAQUILLE O'NEAL: "Once Jerry West left the Lakers, there was no one in the front office I could trust. Jerry West always told the truth. After that, there wasn't anyone there. When it came to my leaving, [Kobe] could have spoken up. He could have said something. He didn't say anything."

TEX WINTER: "It was just the situation that developed. As much as anything else, it was Shaq that broke them up. He was the one that left. He left because he couldn't get what he wanted—a huge pay raise. There was no way ownership could give him what he wanted. Shaq's demands held the franchise hostage, and the way he went about it didn't please the owner too much."

As much as Buss had seemed eager to rid the team of O'Neal and his salary (which ran about $30 million a season), the owner also wanted to lose the triangle offense and replace it with a running game that would herald a revival of the team's Showtime appeal.

Lakers assistant GM Ronnie Lester had predicted before the season that it would take the Lakers two years to build the kind of depth needed to be a solid team. That became apparent as Rudy Tomjanovich took the team through training camp and into the early weeks of the season. Instead of a strong running team, the Lakers settled into an awkward identity as a drive and kick team that more often than not settled for the three-pointer. During the early part of the season, when the schedule was favorable, the Lakers prospered, so long as their three-point shots were falling.

However, it became increasingly clear that the team was headed for trouble when the schedule toughened dramatically over the second half of the season. They were headed into a run of road games against tougher teams. It also became apparent that the Lakers were not a good defensive team. They lacked toughness and energy and commitment.

It was hoped that Karl Malone would return from knee surgery in time to help with all those weaknesses. Malone, who had missed 39 games the previous season with a sprained right knee, had contemplated retirement. Little did the public know that behind the scenes, Malone and Bryant were feuding, which would erupt in a public spat over Malone's supposed inappropriate remarks to Vanessa Bryant. Malone apologized publicly for the misunderstanding, but it was clear his relationship with Bryant had been severed. A few days later, Malone announced his retirement from the game, ending the coaching staff's hopes for his help over the second half of the season. The real fallout from the incident was more damage to Bryant's public image. The last thing he needed, it seemed, was yet more conflict in his life. The once-popular guard saw his standing with Lakers fans take yet another plunge.

KOBE BRYANT: "I don't really think about my image. It will shake out. People who talk about me in a negative manner, they don't know me. If they had a chance to be around me, to kick it with me or whatever and get to know me, then they could judge. I think that will come out as the years go by, or whatever. People will see how I truly am, what I'm really about."

As if things weren't difficult enough, Bryant suffered a severe ankle sprain as the schedule turned toward 2005 and missed weeks of action.

KOBE BRYANT: "My ankle. Whew, that was tough. That was the worst injury I've ever had. By far."

As days grew into weeks in January, the direction of the team stalled and turned sour and the situation began to grind on Tomjanovich. Long accused of being an outsider distant from his teammates, Bryant had announced before the season that he was going to have a more pronounced leadership role, and once training camp opened had seemed to relish offering advice and guidance to his teammates. With Tomjanovich's offense often slipping toward inertia, Bryant soon began talking of the team again employing parts of the old triangle to provide better spacing and ball movement. Tomjanovich assured reporters that he was fine with these ideas from Bryant, but his demeanor suggested otherwise.

Once again it was a situation that cast Bryant in an unfavorable light. Having been accused of engineering the ouster of Jackson and O'Neal, it now appeared he was intent on running the team.

Then on February 2 came the abrupt resignation of Tomjanovich due to mental and physical exhaustion. Despite his five-year, $30 million deal, the 55-year-old Tomjanovich was stepping away from the game again. Buss, in a show of largesse that had some speculating that the coach was being paid off, announced that Tomjanovich would be paid a $10 million settlement, despite coaching just a half a season.

The situation sent the team into a tailspin. Longtime assistant Frank Hamblen took over, but the team's defense worsened.

KOBE BRYANT: "It was tough to gauge where we were as a team, because of the things we had to go through with Rudy T stepping down. But it was obvious that we had problems with consistency. That was really true on defense."

Tomjanovich's resignation started immediate speculation about a Phil Jackson return, but the former coach made it clear he wasn't going to join the club at midseason. One of the team's few accomplishments was time spent gaining more experience with the triangle offense.

KOBE BRYANT: "I think the triangle and its principles are extremely important. Consistency was a problem on offense, too, and the triangle helps with that. We did a good job with it when we started running it in the middle of the season, but it was tough because we were trying to learn it on the fly. You know how hard it is to learn it even when you have training camp. But we did a good job, though. And that bodes well if we run it this coming season. I got a call from Tex during the end of the season. He told me, 'You guys are doing good.' That was a real compliment. That's the biggest compliment in the world coming from Tex. He's such a great basketball mind. When he gives you a compliment that really lifts your heart."

As much as Winter thought of Bryant, the coach didn't hesitate to scald him with criticism. "There's no balance to his game right now," Winter said of

Bryant in April 2005 during an interview for this book. "He still has to learn to hit the open man, that if he does, the ball will come back to him. In some ways, he listens to me. In other ways, he's never really listened to anybody, has he?"

Bryant's trademark stubbornness combined with his elevated attempt at leadership seemed to further damage his image, if that was possible. Teammate Chucky Atkins told the L.A. writers in late March that Bryant was the team's general manager, a sarcastic confirmation of the fans' belief that Bryant had too much power with the Lakers. Atkins later complained that reporters tricked him into making the statement, but that didn't seem to be the case.

TEX WINTER: "Kobe had a tough time. I think his teammates really got down on him. He tried too hard to be a leader."

Bryant, meanwhile, shrugged off Atkins's comment and kept working to bring the team together and to make himself a better leader. The Lakers, though, were beset by injuries and fell deep into a losing streak that in turn deepened Bryant's depression.

Back when he was an assistant coach with the team, Winter used to remind Bryant of the things he needed to do to make his team better. Once Winter had retired to a consultant's status and moved to Oregon with his wife Nancy, the tables turned. It became Bryant's lot to track down the 83-year-old guru for advice on how to fix the broken Lakers and their offense. Bryant frequently asked Winter to call him to discuss team and personal issues. The star readily admitted that he depended heavily on what he heard.

KOBE BRYANT: "Tex's wife wasn't well this past season. He had to stay home and take care of her, so watching us on TV seemed to lift his spirits, even though we weren't playing well. He was very supportive. It was an opportunity for him to take his mind off that situation. We all just prayed for him and his family and wished him all the best. I called him a lot late in the season and let him know each time how we felt about him. I love Tex. If it wasn't for Tex, I wouldn't look at the game or interpret the game the way I do. The way he teaches the game is different than any other coach I've been around. He can be very critical in his comments, but that's the only way you improve. He looks at the game in a different way. He actually teaches momentums, how to build momentums and how to break momentums. He looks at the game from the total concept of the game and then plays it like chess. It's amazing to sit there and learn from him to where you can actually go out on the court and apply that knowledge. It works. I started looking at him like Yoda. You know what I'm saying. I'm telling you it's incredible."

Over their years of working together Bryant and Winter on occasion had testy exchanges over basketball issues.

KOBE BRYANT: "It's obvious that when we had those exchanges people really blew it out of proportion. Tex and I wouldn't be as close as we are today if those exchanges were anything more than debate in the heat of the moment."

TEX WINTER: "He contacted me several times late in the year. I told him he was being too aggressive, taking too many bad shots. There is no question that the team has needed him to do more and more, so it's not an easy thing to state exactly. When is he doing too much? Some nights the Lakers need him to do a lot."

Late in the season, a key injury to top rebounder Lamar Odom was followed by an injury to center Chris Mihm and finally by a leg injury to Bryant himself. But as the losses wore on a positive outlook became increasingly difficult. Even worse, attendance began to drop, which only increased the pressure on the entire franchise.

Meanwhile, O'Neal's Heat team continued to show strength in the East, despite his own nagging injuries. The time off only gave O'Neal more time to ponder what had gone wrong in his time with the Lakers.

SHAQUILLE O'NEAL: "On this team there's nobody wanting to outdo another guy on the team; there's nobody wanting to be MVP. You know what it is, when you're on a mission, everybody's on the same page. But when you accomplish a mission, there are always some people who say, 'Hey, I can do this by myself.' That's what it was all about. Before we got our first championship, we were going real good. But as we got one, two and three, people were thinking that they could do it by themselves. A lot of people tried to talk to him, but as the years went on, we weren't on the same page. I found out a long time ago that you can't do it by yourself. You have to do it with the team. Then Phil taught me the formula. The formula basically is that you have to lead the way and be consistent. Let's say that I would average 25 and he would average 20. You've got to do that every night. Now, every now and then, you can get spectacular, score 30, 40 points, but we always have to be consistent. Even if we have horrible games, they've got to be horrible 25s. And all these other guys, they just had to master their little roles. We had to master our big roles, and they had to master their little roles. When you put that together, you got something. When you look at all of our championship teams, we never had no super talent on those teams. No super talent on those teams. By the time Phil got there, a lot of our talent was gone. Most of the big stuff was done by me or Kobe, and every now and then Robert or Brian Shaw or Ron Harper. That's all you need. A lot of people want to harp on talent, talent, talent. But what's the last time a team won the championship in recent years that wasn't a true team? If you don't have a relationship with your guards or your shooters, then you won't go nowhere. Everybody has to be on the same page. But some people are very superficial and worry about individual things rather than the team."

O'Neal may have been consumed with bitterness over his departure from the Lakers and his dislike for Bryant. (But it didn't dampen his generous spirit. When former Lakers great George Mikan died of complications from diabetes in early June of 2005, he was nearly destitute. Upon hearing of his passing, O'Neal immediately offered to pay all funeral expenses, an offer the Mikan family gratefully accepted.)

Former Lakers psychologist George Mumford said the situation added up to a huge piece of humble pie for Bryant to consume. Accused of hubris, the guard accepted the forced humility as he has every other difficulty that has come his way since he entered the NBA at age 17 in 1996. He offered a stoic face and promised to keep working.

At least one of the bright spots had been small forward Caron Butler, who came to the Lakers in the Shaq trade to Miami. Butler showed a willingness to take on responsibility for scoring as the team closed out the dismal campaign with a 12–29 record down the stretch.

"I just want to help take the pressure off of Kobe," Butler explained.

"That was a nice thought," Winter said privately. "But Kobe's life with the Lakers will always be pressure-filled. It doesn't matter which way he turns."

And by the final weeks of the season, the pressure for Bryant had become overwhelming. The guard had become the youngest player in NBA history to score 14,000 points. While he had been the league's second-highest scorer in the 2004–05 season behind Allen Iverson of Philadelphia, Bryant made only 43.3 percent of his shots and failed to make the NBA all-defensive team for the first time since 1999.

"I think Kobe has hit the wall," Winter said in early April as criticism of Bryant began peaking toward a crescendo. "I'm worried about him. I don't know what it will take to get Kobe revitalized. Expectations for the team have been so high because of the way things broke up."

The guard was under tremendous pressure to play well, and the Lakers were about to do something they'd rarely done over their long history—miss the playoffs. It had been 11 years since the last time they'd missed. They would finish the 2005 season with a 34–48 record, behind the Clippers.

Now the Lakers front office faced a task it had been dreading—selling season tickets for the 2005–06 campaign and listening to the numerous complaints of the clientele. The franchise found itself right back where it was in 1999, needing to make a personnel move that inspired the faithful to renew their tickets. Since Tomjanovich's resignation in February, there had been a steady and growing buzz about the new coach. Most of that buzz concerned the high hopes that the next guy would have a penchant for burning incense.

The Phil Factor

Before he left for a late winter trip to New Zealand, Phil Jackson told Tex Winter that he felt great and wanted to coach again in the NBA. Jackson even confided that it looked good for him to wind up coaching the Denver Nuggets next season. Apparently Jackson had been talking behind the scenes with the Nuggets and thought he had the job in the bag. But, while Jackson was off vacationing in the Pacific, the Nuggets hired George Karl as their coach.

It seemed that Denver GM Kiki Vandeweghe had fancied hiring Jackson, but team owner Stan Kroeneke grew impatient and opted for Karl. Jackson, it seems, had told Denver he wanted to wait until the fall of 2005 to start to work. Denver's sudden move wasn't the first time the former Lakers coach had encountered difficulty and rejection in the job market.

When he first interviewed for an assistant coaching job in the NBA, Jackson showed up at the Chicago Bulls offices wearing sandals, beach clothes, and a straw hat with a bird feather in the brim. Stan Albeck, then the Bulls head coach, later told associates there was no way he was going to hire somebody as weird as Jackson. The next year the Bulls fired Albeck and hired Jackson as an assistant coach, and he went on to become the head coach that led that franchise to six NBA titles.

Then in 1999, as he was finishing up a year away from basketball, Jackson quietly interviewed with the New York Knicks, who then had Jeff Van Gundy as their coach. When newspapers broke the story that Jackson was talking with the Knicks, other coaches roundly criticized Jackson and suggested that he was trying to sneak in and steal Van Gundy's job. Jackson was stung by the criticism.

WALT FRAZIER, JACKSON'S OLD TEAMMATE AND ROOMMATE WITH THE KNICKS: "He wasn't trying to steal anybody's job. All these other coaches criticizing him is just them being jealous of his success."

Regardless, that criticism from 1999 had left Jackson wary about the hiring process.

"He wants to make it clear that he's not after anybody's job," Winter, who spoke with Jackson frequently, explained in April. "He's going to wait until May, see how he feels about coaching one more year, then decide from the jobs that are available and offered."

Jackson even had his agent, Todd Musburger, issue a statement in early March declaring that he would take no job during the season, that he would decide only after the season.

"Phil doesn't want any coach to feel he's breathing down his neck," Musburger said. "He doesn't want distractions to any teams and their staffs. He respects the job of every head coach. It's become uncomfortable. He wants to sit back and enjoy the season and not speculate on what's going to happen in the future. He feels uncomfortable being brought into these discussions on what he might or might not do. Phil may not return to coaching at all as he goes on to his next step in his life and career."

That didn't stop NBA teams from firing their coaches and appointing interim replacements as if they were all lining up for a Phil Jackson sweep-stakes in the off-season. Cleveland would offer the opportunity to coach LeBron James. Portland would offer lots of money in a city that Jackson liked. Orlando might try to lure him with a piece of the franchise. Ditto for Minnesota. And Milwaukee (the team that first interviewed Jackson for a head coaching job years ago). Maybe even Dallas or Seattle. Or how about him shoving Van Gundy out in Houston? All of those were mentioned.

The big speculation, however, centered on the New York Knicks, the team that Jackson once played for in the city he loved. Or the Lakers, the team that he'd already coached to three NBA titles. In late March and early April, Jackson began showing up at Lakers offices and even attended a game with Jerry Buss.

Winter figured the Lakers were the favorite because of Jackson's affection for Jeanie Buss and the fact that he already had a home in Los Angeles. It didn't hurt either that the Lakers were a team with some experience in the triangle offense, meaning the learning curve there might be shorter. In fact, it could be argued that Bryant knew the triangle better than any other player in the league.

"Several of the Lakers players know the triangle well, so that may be a factor," Winter said. "But Phil also looks for the best players, so it's not certain that he'll wind up in Los Angeles."

Jeanie Buss told the *New York Post* she had no idea what Jackson would do, even though she remained his girlfriend. "It was such a great time of his life," Buss told the *Post* of Jackson's New York playing days. "I totally see him back in New York."

Buss admitted holding out hope that Jackson will return to her Lakers. "Kobe is not the reason Phil is not the Lakers coach," she said. "The reason he's not the Lakers coach is he had the opportunity to sign the extension and he waited. My father was coming to the conclusion he was going to trade Shaq. Kobe was a free agent and he had a coach who was noncommittal. He had to make a decision. Phil has always said Kobe is one of the best players, and any team with him can compete for a championship. I don't see it being a problem."

"I don't know where he's going," Tex Winter said. "I'm not a betting man, but I do know this. Wherever Phil goes, he's gonna want to coach good players, players who know how to play, players who can adapt to the triangle. Los Angeles has some of those players. Does Phil think they're good enough players in Los Angeles to win another title? We'll have to see. That's what he wants. He wants a tenth title, which would make him the winningest coach in NBA history. That would be more titles than Red Auerbach won with the Boston Celtics. That would be his reason for coming back."

Some observers wondered if Bryant could get along with Jackson, especially after Jackson criticized the guard and wrote in his bestselling book *The Last Season* that Bryant was "uncoachable." Bryant obviously needed help in turning the Lakers around. And Jackson, for all the coaching offers he had, needed a team receptive to the unique offense.

Winter, a mentor and confidant to both Jackson and Bryant, chuckled at the idea of Bryant and Jackson needing each other. It was the perfect irony to the high drama that had unfolded during Jackson's tenure in Los Angeles.

In a further note of irony, as Jackson pondered renewing his relationship with the Lakers, he sought a meeting with Bryant. The guard declined, saying he didn't want to be blamed if Jackson decided not to take the job.

Winter pointed out that during their five seasons together Jackson had declined to so much as meet with Bryant yet regularly criticized him to the media. Winter said Bryant didn't become belligerent toward Jackson until their final season together, and that was because Jackson treated Bryant with disdain and detachment. Now it was Bryant's turn to decline to meet.

"In the final analysis, it's the coach's responsibility to manage the team in the proper manner and not have those things happen," Winter said.

Winter noted there were more serious complications than the meeting trivia. Even if Jackson did return, it wouldn't be easy for the Lakers in 2006. The team was already $20 million over the salary cap, and that didn't include the option for backup center Vlade Divac, another $5 million.

Jackson's other considerations went to his health. How would he react to a team that lost a lot of games? Would the stress send him into a tailspin as it had Rudy Tomjanovich? Jackson had never been a good loser. He once threw two chairs on the floor during a Continental Basketball Association game in Albany. Could he handle the stress this time around?

As May became June, Jackson turned sour on the idea, phoned his agent and told him he didn't want to coach again. Then he changed his mind again. Ultimately, Jackson announced his decision to accept a three-year deal at a record $10 million per season on June 14, calling the decision at his Staples Center press conference a story of "reconciliation, redemption, and resiliency."

"It wasn't about the money, but the intrigue of this situation," Jackson said. "It's a tremendous story and a tremendous opportunity. It's a story of reconciliation, redemption, of reuniting—a lot of things in this make for a wonderful opportunity for the team, the Lakers and myself."

Thought to have mixed feelings on Jackson taking over again, Buss was vacationing in Europe and said in a statement that he was "pleased to have Phil return to the Lakers. His record speaks for itself, and his success in this sport is unparalleled. Quite simply, Phil is the best coach in the business and probably the greatest coach of all time. We feel that he is the best person to lead this team and hope that he will be able to lead us back to the point of being a championship-caliber team."

Jackson wore a suit and sandals to the press conference and talked of the lessons he had learned. "More than anything, the lessons were about stress," he said, "in particular the stress that you get and how the release from that changes personalities. My kids, who have all weighed in on this, all wanted to talk about why I wanted to come back to this stressful job."

Only after he assured his family that he could manage the stress had Jackson proceeded.

"I hope in the month of March you don't see me at a different level," he joked during the announcement, "with the kinds of bags under my eyes I was carrying around while I was in Australia."

Still, his return certainly meant that he was shouldering some of the burden that so weighed on Bryant.

"I'm not the panacea for this basketball club," Jackson told the hastily assembled press conference. "It's not going to happen overnight. It's going to take some time. But we do think there is some hope, and we can make some changes that will really benefit this team and we can get back into the playoffs again."

For his part, Bryant, who was nearing his 27th birthday, had seemed less than enthusiastic when reporters asked in May what he thought of Jackson's candidacy to return. The guard, however, issued a prepared statement saying, "When the Lakers began the search for a new head coach, I put my complete trust in Dr. Buss and Mitch Kupchak to select the person they thought was best for the Lakers organization. In Phil Jackson, they chose a proven winner. His hiring is something I support."

Jackson made a point of telling reporters that Bryant had phoned his congratulations that morning. "You know, I think after we play a few games and get kind of a feel of working together, we'll really feel like we're ready to go," Jackson said. "I really encourage him to find a way to get his zest back for the game . . . He wants to come back and make some people eat some words."

An ESPN reporter tracked down O'Neal for his take on the news. It seemed obvious that the center was deeply troubled to see his old coach back with his declared enemy. O'Neal's Heat had just lost in Game 7 of the Eastern Conference Finals to the Detroit Pistons. One of Jackson's staff commented privately that as much as the center disliked Bryant, he would have to admit that the Laker guard could have helped him win that seventh game. "Kobe is the only player we ever saw who had the same level of competitiveness as Michael," the Jackson staffer said. "No one else is even close."

The other side of that, the staffer added, is that Bryant likewise needed O'Neal to lead the team into contention. It was a tragedy of postmodern basketball that the two never fully realized their value to each other.

O'Neal, who was expected to exercise the final year option on his contract for $30 million, said he was "absolutely happy" for Jackson. The center said that he wished Jackson luck, then smiled slyly and said he was going to need it.

BIBLIOGRAPHY

A number of excellent books and periodicals provided me with background for this project.

Magazines and Newspapers

Extensive use was made of a variety of publications, including *AirCal, Basketball Times, Boston Globe, Boston Herald, BusinessWeek, The Charlotte Observer, Chicago Sun-Times, Chicago Tribune, The Detroit Free Press, The Detroit News, ESPN The Magazine, Esquire, Flint Journal, Forbes, GQ, Hartford Courant, Hoop Magazine, Houston Post, Let's Talk!, Lindy's Pro Basketball Annual, Los Angeles Business Journal, Los Angeles Daily News, Los Angeles Herald Examiner, Los Angeles Lakers Illustrated, Los Angeles Sentinel, Los Angeles Times, The National, New York Daily News, The New York Times, New York Post, New West, The Oakland Press, The Orange County Register, Philadelphia Inquirer, The Roanoke Times and World-News, San Diego Tribune, Sport, The Sporting News, Sports Illustrated, Street and Smith's Pro Basketball Yearbook, USA Today, Vanity Fair,* and *The Washington Post.*

The Writers

Without the frontline work of a variety of reporters and writers over the years, the compilation of this book would not have been possible. That group includes the following: J. A. Adande, Mitch Albom, David Aldridge, Jim Alexander, Elliott Almond, Neil Amdur, Dave Anderson, Howard Beck, Ira Berkow, Steve Bisheff, Greg Boeck, Mike Bresnahan, Cliff Brown, Tim Brown, Ric Bucher, Bryan Burwell, Kelly Carter, E. Jean Carroll, Mitch Chortkoff, Marlene Cimons, Doug Cress, Karen Crouse, Tim Deady, Frank DeFord, Kevin Ding, David Dupree, Larry Donald, Mike Downey, Ron Dungee, Melvin Durslag, David Ferrell, Joe Fitzgerald, Mal Florence, John Freeman, Tom Friend, Bud Furillo, Frank Girardot, Sam Goldaper, Brian

447

Golden, Alan Goldstein, Ted Green, Allen Greenberg, Don Greenberg, Milton Gross, Donald Hall, Merv Harris, Randy Harvey, Mark Heisler, Steve Henson, Randy Hill, Bruce Horovitz, Scott Howard-Cooper, Mary Ann Hudson, Bob Hunter, Michael Hurd, Doug Ives, Bruce Jenkins, Roy S. Johnson, William Oscar Johnson, Tim Kawakami, Dave Kindred, Leonard Koppett, Tony Kornheiser, Doug Krikorian, Rich Levin, Leonard Lewin, Bill Libby, Mike Littwin, Jackie MacMullen, Jack Madden, Allan Malamud, Jack McCallum, Sam McManis, John L. Mitchell, Kevin Modesti, David Leon Moore, Morton Moss, Bruce Newman, Scott Ostler, Sandy Padwe, Chris Palmer, John Papanek, Charles Pierce, Bill Plaschke, Diane Pucin, Pat Putnam, Brad Pye, Jr., Ron Rapoport, Bob Ryan, Steve Springer, Bill Steigerwald, Marc Stein, Larry Stewart, Eric Tracy, Brad Turner, George Vecsey, Peter Vecsey, Michael Ventre, Lesley Visser, Mike Waldner, Peter Warner, Mark Whicker, and Alex Wolff.

Books

Abdul-Jabbar, Kareem, and Peter Knobler. *Giant Steps*. New York: Bantam, 1983.

Abdul-Jabbar, Kareem, and Mignon McCarthy. *Kareem*. New York: Random House, 1990.

Anderson, Dave. *The Story of Basketball*. New York: William Morrow & Co., 1988.

Barry, Rick, and Jordan E. Cohn. *Rick Barry's Pro Basketball Scouting Report*. Chicago: Bonus Books, 1989.

Bell, Marty. *The Legend of Dr. J*. New York: New American Library, 1981.

Berger, Phil. *Miracle on 33rd Street: The New York Knickerbockers' Championship Season*. New York: Simon and Schuster, 1970.

Caughey, John, and LaRee Caughey, eds. *Los Angeles: Biography of a City*. Berkeley: University of California Press, 1977.

Chamberlain, Wilt. *A View from Above*. New York: Signet Books, 1992.

Chamberlain, Wilt, and David Shaw. *Wilt*. New York: Macmillan, 1986.

Chansky, Art, and Eddie Fogler. *March to the Top*. Chapel Hill: Four Corners Press, 1982.

Clary, Jack. *The Lakers*. Greenwich, CT: Brompton Books, 1992.

Dickey, Glenn. *The History of Professional Basketball Since 1896*. New York: Stein and Day, 1982.

Frazier, Walt, and Neil Offen. *Walt Frazier.* New York: Times Books, 1988.

Goodrich, Gail, and Rich Levin. *Gail Goodrich's Winning Basketball.* Chicago: Contemporary, 1976.

Green, Lee. *Sportswit.* New York: Fawcett, 1986.

Halberstam, David. *The Breaks of the Game.* New York: Knopf, 1981.

Heisler, Mark. *The Lives of Riley.* New York: MacMillan, 1994.

Heisler, Mark, and Roland Lazenby. *Giants.* Chicago: Triumph Books, 2003.

Hession, Joseph. *Lakers.* Petaluma, CA: Foghorn Press, 1994.

Hollander, Zander, ed. *Basketball's Greatest Games.* Englewood Cliffs: Prentice Hall, 1971.

Hollander, Zander. *The Modern Basketball Encyclopedia.* Garden City, N.Y.: Dolphin, 1979.

Hollander, Zander, and Alex Sachare, eds. *The Official NBA Basketball Encyclopedia.* New York: Villard, 1989.

Holtzman, Red, and Harvey Frommer. *Holtzman on Hoops.* Dallas: Taylor, 1991.

Hundley, Jessica, and Jon Alain Guzik, eds. *Horny Los Angeles.* Los Angeles: Really Great Books, 2001.

Johnson, Earvin, and Rich Levine. *Magic.* New York: Viking, 1983.

Johnson, Earvin, and William Novak. *My Life.* New York: Random House, 1992.

Johnson, Magic, and Roy S. Johnson. *Magic's Touch.* Boston: Addison Wesley, 1989.

Koppett, Leonard. *Championship NBA.* New York: Dial Press, 1970.

Koppett, Leonard. *24 Seconds to Shoot.* New York: Macmillan, 1980.

Lazenby, Roland. *The Lakers: A Basketball Journey.* New York: St. Martins Press, 1993.

Lazenby, Roland. *The NBA Finals.* Dallas: Taylor Publishing, 1990.

Levine, Lee Daniel. *Bird: The Making of an American Sports Legend.* New York: McGraw-Hill, 1989.

Libby, Bill. *Clown.* New York: Cowles Book Co., 1970.

Manchester, William. *The Glory and the Dream.* Boston: Little Brown, 1974.

Meyer, Ray, and Ray Sons. *Coach.* Chicago: Contemporary, 1987.

Murray, Jim. *The Jim Murray Collection.* Dallas: Taylor Publishing, 1989.

Nadel, Eric. *The Night Wilt Scored 100.* Dallas: Taylor Publishing, 1990.

Neft, David S., and Richard M. Cohen. *The Sports Encyclopedia, Pro Basketball.* New York: St. Martin's Press, 1992.

Ostler, Scott, and Steve Springer. *Winnin' Times.* New York: Macmillan, 1986.

Packer, Billy, and Roland Lazenby. *College Basketball's 25 Greatest Teams.* St. Louis: The Sporting News, 1989.

Packer, Billy, and Roland Lazenby. *50 Years of the Final Four.* Dallas: Taylor Publishing, 1987.

Padwe, Sandy. *Basketball's Hall of Fame.* New York: Grossett and Dunlap, 1973.

Patterson, Wayne, and Lisa Fisher. *100 Greatest Basketball Players.* Greenwich, Conn.: Bison Books, 1988.

Peterson, Robert. *Cages to Jump Shots: Pro Basketball's Early Years.* New York: Oxford University Press, 1990.

Pluto, Terry. *Tall Tales.* New York: Simon and Schuster, 1992.

Reisner, Marc. *A Dangerous Place.* New York: Pantheon Books, 2003.

Riley, Pat. *Showtime: Inside the Lakers' Breakthrough Season.* New York: Warner Books, 1988.

Russell, Bill, and Taylor Branch. *Second Wind: The Memoirs of an Opinionated Man.* New York: Random House, 1979.

Salzberg, Charles. *From Set Shot to Slam Dunk.* New York: Dutton, 1987.

Schron, Bob, and Kevin Stevens. *The Bird Era.* Boston: Quinland Press, 1988.

Springer, Steve. *The Los Angeles Times Encyclopedia of the Lakers.* Los Angeles: The Los Angeles Times, 1998.

Stauth, Cameron. *The Golden Boys.* New York: Pocket Books, 1992.

Thomas, Isiah, and Matt Dobek. *Bad Boys.* Grand Rapids: Masters Press, 1989.

Vecsey, George. *Pro Basketball Champions.* New York: Scholastic, 1970.

West, Jerry, and Bill Libby. *Mr. Clutch.* New York: Grosset & Dunlap, 1969.

Wolff, Alexander. *100 Years of Hoops.* Birmingham: Oxmoor House, 1992.

Wooden, John, and Jack Tobin. *They Call Me Coach.* Waco, Texas: Word, 1972.

INDEX